Praise for *Small Schools, Big Ideas: The Essential Guide to Successful School Transformation*

"In *Small Schools, Big Ideas*, authors Benitez, Davidson, and Flaxman help us understand the structural complexities of creating nurturing environments in which all students can use their minds well. They also courageously guide the reader into examining the explosive cultural issues, like systemic racism, and offer an authentic path forward for educators in the trenches to instigate school-wide transformation."

—Glenn E. Singleton, president and founder, Pacific Educational Group, Inc., and author, *Courageous Conversations About Race*

"*Small Schools, Big Ideas* shares the Coalition of Essential Schools' long track record of redesigning schools so that they are successful and learner-centered. The knowledge that these authors and their colleagues across the country have accumulated over many years and many successful schools inspires us to reconsider what young people, and the schools that serve them, can do with the right conditions and support."

—Linda Darling-Hammond, Charles E. Ducommun Professor of Education and faculty sponsor, School Redesign Network at Stanford University

"This guide will help those who believe *all* students need to be prepared for post-secondary education to re-imagine high schools and confront all forms of inequity that have existed for far too long."

—John P. Welch, superintendent, Highline Public Schools District Washington

"*Small Schools, Big Ideas* reminds us that *small school* is neither an adjective nor a noun; it's an aspiration, a desire. Like democracy, Small Schools embody a vision of what must be: messy work, undertaken through collective participation, spiked with vibrant questions, in a deep and restless community, with strong commitments, fueled by raw vulnerabilities and generations of wisdom. *Small Schools, Big Ideas* interrupts the white noise of privatization, charters, testing, centralization and Racing to the Top, delicately reminding us of the graceful work and sensual practice of making successful public schools grounded in justice, relationships, and democracy."

—Michelle Fine, Distinguished Professor of Psychology and Urban Education, The Graduate Center at the City University of New York

"The authors of *Small Schools, Big Ideas* do a wonderful job of providing a useful road map for how administrators, practitioners, families, and communities can dream big and work together to improve education through a democratic process. Especially notable is that it presents relationships and student-centered policies and practices as the core elements that hold promise in restoring the public's faith in public education. This book is a must read for anyone who is committed to a progressive social agenda on how public schools can better serve children and youth who deserve no less. This is an outstanding scholarly achievement."

—Angela Valenzuela, University of Texas professor in the College of Education and author of *Subtractive Schooling: U.S.-Mexican Youth and the Politics of Caring*

SMALL SCHOOLS, BIG IDEAS

SMALL SCHOOLS, BIG IDEAS

The Essential Guide to Successful School Transformation

Mara Benitez
Jill Davidson
Laura Flaxman

JOSSEY-BASS
A Wiley Imprint
www.josseybass.com

Published by Jossey-Bass
A Wiley Imprint
989 Market Street, San Francisco, CA 94103—1741—www.josseybass.com

Readers should be aware that Internet Web sites offered as citations and/or sources for further information may have changed or disappeared between the time this was written and when it is read.

Jossey-Bass books and products are available through most bookstores. To contact Jossey-Bass directly call our Customer Care Department within the U.S. at 800-956-7739, outside the U.S. at 317-572-3986, or fax 317-572-4002.

Jossey-Bass also publishes its books in a variety of electronic formats. Some content that appears in print may not be available in electronic books.

Library of Congress Cataloging-in-Publication Data

Benitez, Mara, 1965–
    Small schools, big ideas: the essential guide to successful school transformation/Mara Benitez, Jill S. Davidson, Laura Flaxman; foreword by Theodore R. Sizer and Nancy Faust Sizer.
        p. cm.
    Includes bibliographical references and index.
    Summary: "Developed by The Coalition of Essential Schools, one of the nation's leading school reform networks, The Essential Guide to Successful School Transformation provides a comprehensive, principle-based approach for redesigning public schools and creating new schools that enable all students to achieve at high standards. Featuring stories and examples from schools that have successfully implemented the CES model, this powerful blueprint for district and school-level administrators, teachers, reform activists, educational policy makers, and professors distills insights and wisdom gleaned from over 20 years of work restructuring public schools"—Provided by publisher.
    ISBN 978-0-470-25907-8
1. School improvement programs—United States. 2. Coalition of Essential Schools. I. Davidson, Jill S., 1968—II. Flaxman, Laura, 1967—III. Title.
    LB2822.82.B445 2009
    371.2'070973—dc22   2009026351

Printed in the United States of America
FIRST EDITION
PB Printing   10 9 8 7 6 5 4 3 2 1

CONTENTS

FOREWORD

The best communities are built around words—not any old words, but ones that can inspire and galvanize. We say *best* because these are the communities that last. They did not rise from a temporary problem or a pragmatic accommodation; instead, they came together because people saw in each other a similarity of outlook and a way in which they could help and be helped by each other to accomplish important things.

There are many such communities, but the best-known examples of the words that bind long-standing communities together are the sacred writings of the world's religions and the Constitution of the United States. More than battles won or an economy shared, the major ideas in the Declaration of Independence and the 1787 Constitution are what have seen a large and diverse nation through tough times. These words remain inspiring to the vast majority of Americans to this day in no small part because of the struggles of many to broaden these ideals in ways more inclusive than the founders could conceive. One of the best ideas in the Constitution, however, was expressed in the carefully constructed amendment process. It said, in essence, "This is what we think and could agree on today, but tomorrow may be different. Don't change these ideas lightly, but let them evolve slowly, and when most of you are sure that the words in this statement no longer express your highest ideals, then change them to do so."

It seems immodest, but we in the Coalition of Essential Schools (CES) would like to count ourselves among the many communities that have used words and convictions to express their connection. The words in the CES Common Principles were heard first in a variety of schools all over the country as leaders, teachers, and students described what they were doing to make their schools better. From these educators came the conviction that each child will learn more readily if he or she feels comfortable and known well. Also from them came the idea that a student's progress in mastering a topic should be measured not by how many weeks were devoted to teaching it but by what actual and important work was done over those weeks. Because each student learns differently and at a different rate, classrooms should be set up to facilitate a variety of learning styles, with respect for all. Our mutual agreement that these CES Common Principles made sense became the core of our colleagueship.

Like the 1787 Constitution's framers, we have understood that the CES Common Principles would need amendment, reinterpretation, and evolution. Sure enough, after a few years, it seemed wise to make the priority of democracy in school design and equity among students—implied by the original language—more explicit. The principles reflected our actual assumption and work already, but the words could help in furthering it. In addition, over the years, many new practices developed, and more and more, the CES Common Principles came to characterize what we were doing and why we valued our community.

Years ago, we were on a call-in radio program and we got a call from a person who described himself as a "Coalition teacher." Before he had a chance to ask his question, the moderator asked, "Well, what is a Coalition teacher?" A bit taken aback, the teacher hesitated; we held our breath. Finally, he said, "A Coalition teacher does a lot of professional development."

The fact is that professional development is not expressly called for in the CES Common Principles. However, the way we teach is unusual; starting with a student's needs before the state's rubrics or even the teacher's lesson plans requires a good deal of thought, conversation, and new ideas. There is no model that is ready to plug in. Though our words guide us, much observation will be needed in order to know what actions are appropriate to take and much more evolving will need to occur before we are content with the kind of learning that we are facilitating in our schools.

Every dynamic institution will grow and change, often in response to demands for social justice. Our schools are such institutions, and so are individuals in the Coalition itself. Teachers and principals will learn from their own analyses of what has worked and what still needs work, but they will also learn from other like-minded people in the Coalition and beyond. The CES Small Schools Project was founded on this idea. Mara Benitez and Laura Flaxman brought wisdom and experience as CES school leaders to bear as the Small Schools Project emerged as the next chapter of CES's history. As leaders of the CES Small Schools Project, Benitez and Flaxman established the framework and conditions for the emergence of a network of fifty small schools, some veteran and some new, based on the conviction that a commitment to equity joined with the wisdom accrued from exemplary Coalition schools can result in powerful new examples of schools that have the power to change lives. Thus, the original CES Common Principles have been joined by a goodly number of new principles and practices, just as the small number of original colleagues has grown and spread during the past twenty-five years.

Over the years, the publication *Horace* (which since 2001 has been the responsibility of *Small Schools, Big Ideas* author Jill Davidson) has helped to document these changes in our practices and our beliefs. Our tone has always been realistic but hopeful, depending largely on examples. Our message is more inspirational than scholarly, but that's the way we like it. Now, this book draws from that work and from a number of current educators in the field to describe further how some of the old principles have changed, how some new principles have emerged, and how our work inside schools has grown and been improved in response to the challenges that our students currently face.

The best communities are built on words. These are our words at this point in time, and they are carefully chosen by our fascinating, vibrant, hopeful people.

Harvard, Massachusetts   Theodore R. Sizer
February 2, 2009   Nancy Faust Sizer

ACKNOWLEDGMENTS

Mara Benitez: I am grateful to my baby girl Lulah Divina for inspiring me to do the work of transforming schools. She keeps me focused on changing public education, knowing that one day soon she'll be attending public schools just like her mommy. I'd like to acknowledge my partner Tahajiye Edwards for being a great parent, cooking great meals, and generally catering to all of my needs during the process of researching and writing this book. Special thanks to my mother-in-law Catherine for taking such good care of my baby. I wouldn't have had the time or energy to write without her help. Thanks to the *mujeres* in my circle, who believe in me and the cause. Thanks to the CES staff, especially Brett Bradshaw and Jay Feldman, for their thoughtful and constructive feedback and to Kyle Meador for the excellent job in identifying and organizing the tools, references, and resources in the book. Special gratitude goes out to our executive director Lewis Cohen for holding the vision for this book to happen, believing in us as writers, supporting our crazy schedules, and most important, being an excellent sounding board and editor. I am honored to have had an opportunity to collaborate with my two amazing co-authors. Many thanks to you for your support and wisdom.

Laura Flaxman: I would like to acknowledge my wonderful partners-in-crime on this endeavor, Mara and Jill, for the journey that has led to this book. I definitely would never have been able to do this without you. Lewis Cohen, you made this book possible from start to finish, from creating the space for us to work on it to your eleventh-hour editing. Thank you also to all of the many educators, colleagues, students, and friends who continue to inspire me as an educator and as a human being, many of whom grace the pages of this book. Thanks in particular to my colleagues, my students, and the families at ARISE, and to my co-founders Romeo Garcia and Emma Paulino. Your goodness, passion, and commitment to the community we serve continue to inspire me and your support keeps me going even on the toughest days. Finally, thank you to my daughters, Ava and Aziza Purser, and my husband, Kenny Purser, for supporting me as I juggled the balls of principal, writer, mother, and partner. And thank you to the rest of my family, both immediate and extended—Andrew, Ruth, Caroline, Gary, Nancy, Connie, Asti—and the many other family members and friends in my life who have had such an influence on who I am and the work I have chosen to do. I love you all.

Jill Davidson: I am deeply grateful for the inspiration of the founders of the Coalition of Essential Schools, especially Ted Sizer, without whom none of what we describe in these pages would have happened. Ted holds a vision of what is possible, and he has created the circumstances for many of us to work toward his vision. My voice joins thousands of others in gratitude. Thanks, too, to Nancy Sizer, for unflagging support, wisdom, encouragement, and great cheer. Deborah Meier has been a source of powerful insight; her public work and private words have deeply shaped my thinking about the purposes of schools and the limitless capabilities of students and educators. Thanks to all of my colleagues at the Coalition of Essential Schools, past and present. Ramon Calhoun deserves kudos for his fantastic, speedy attention to detail. The energy and vision of CES's executive director, Lewis Cohen, made it possible for us to get this project started, supported us along the way, and helped us move this project the final mile. I am grateful for all that I have learned from my partners in this journey, Mara Benitez and Laura Flaxman; thanks to both of you for your vision, commitment, and persistence. Many thanks to my parents, Marge and Bill Davidson, and my sister, Jennifer Davidson, who contributed her excellent editing skills. My husband, Kevin Eberman, and my sons, Elias Abraham, Leo Maurice, and Henry Theodore, believe in our vision and weathered with grace the many long hours required to articulate it. Thanks, guys!

All of the authors acknowledge the many early CES pioneers: without your contributions, we could and would not be doing this work. Your efforts have improved and transformed many thousands of lives in communities across this country. As well, we acknowledge the current CES network educators who contributed to material in this book. In addition to the dozens quoted in the text and the hundreds, perhaps thousands more upon whose work the accomplishments documented in these pages have been built, we want to extend special thanks to the following people, who reviewed sections of the text and helped to improve it: Vince Brevetti, Pam Espinosa, Romeo Garcia, David Greenberg, Lisa Hirsch, Misha Lesley, Lisa Karlich, Lawrence Kohn, Ann Mantil, Adelrich McCain, Emma Paulino, Gregory Peters, Beth Silbergeld, Al Solis, and Laura Thomas. We also are grateful for the financial support of the CES Small Schools Project that has been provided by the Bill & Melinda Gates Foundation.

The Coalition of Essential Schools

The Coalition of Essential Schools was founded at Brown University on the Common Principles articulated by Theodore Sizer (1984) in *Horace's Compromise: The Dilemma of the American High School* in order to re-imagine and reorganize high schools. This set of beliefs, considered radical twenty years ago, is now widely accepted by educational scholars as the key to promoting high achievement for students. (See Appendix A for the CES Common Principles.)

Essential schools work to create academic success for every student by sharing decision making with all those affected by the schools and deliberately confronting all forms of inequity. Essential schools focus on helping all students use their mind well through standards-aligned interdisciplinary studies, community-based real-world learning and performance-based assessment. CES schools are places of powerful student learning where all students have the chance to reach their fullest potential. (See Appendix B for an overview of the benefits of the CES approach to education.)

The Coalition sees school transformation as a local phenomenon made real by groups of people working together, building a shared vision, and drawing on the community's strengths, history, and values. While no two Essential schools are alike, all Essential schools share a commitment to a set of beliefs about the purpose and practice of schooling. As they develop their own programs, schools take guidance from the CES Common Principles to examine their priorities and design structures and instructional practices that support

- Personalized instruction to address individual needs and interests in which the teachers' role is to guide students through inquiry
- Small schools and classrooms in which teachers and students know each other well and work in an atmosphere of trust and high expectations
- Multiple assessments based on performance of authentic tasks in an atmosphere of independent learning and intellectual rigor and richness
- Democratic and equitable school policies and practice
- Close community partnerships

Currently, there are hundreds of schools that are affiliated with CES and twenty-six affiliate centers across the country. CES affiliate centers are independent organizations guided by the CES Common Principles that provide long-term coaching, professional development, and technical assistance to schools. CES affiliate centers work with schools and school districts to develop plans for change based on the CES Common Principles. The guidelines for membership vary from center to center and are responsive to the needs of local schools.

CES has documented the accomplishments and challenges of Essential schools through its journal *Horace,* the three-part CES EssentialVisions DVD series, research reports, and other material. For more information about the Coalition of Essential Schools, CES member schools, CES centers, or CES affiliation, please visit http://www.essentialschools.org. For more on the benefits of the CES approach, see Appendix D, "The Benefits of the CES Model."

The Small Schools Project and Network

Small Schools, Big Ideas: The Essential Guide to Successful School Transformation focuses on the work of the CES Small Schools Project, funded by the Bill & Melinda Gates Foundation. Founded in 2003, the CES Small Schools Project is dedicated to creating and supporting small schools throughout the country that are instructionally powerful and sustainable and that offer challenging curricula to students who have been denied a meaningful education. The CES Small Schools Project is committed to effecting broader change within the public education system and meeting the needs of young people and communities who traditionally and systemically have been underserved—students of color and students from low-income backgrounds. Most of the schools are located in urban areas; however, as a whole, the body of schools is diverse, representing various geographic regions and demographics across the United States. The project has also launched CES ChangeLab (http://www.ceschangelab.org), a Web site with behind-the-scenes access to the effective tools and strategies used by CES Mentor Schools.

Through this initiative, CES has built a robust network of over fifty schools that use the CES Common Principles to set priorities and design practices to meet the needs of their students, families, and communities. CES's national organization has developed a system of CES Mentor Schools, a peer-to-peer model that builds on and codifies the process that successful CES small school have developed over the Coalition's history. The CES Mentor Schools partner with new small schools that have been created as a result of large high school conversions into autonomous small schools or design teams preparing to open the doors of new schools. Some of these new small schools are charter schools; others are in-district public schools that have been or are being created through explicit agreements with a variety of school districts.

The CES Small Schools Network (CES SSN) is the professional learning community that includes these exemplary CES small schools in various stages of development. Through quarterly meetings (including an intensive weeklong Summer Institute), visits to each other's schools, and various forms of ongoing informal contact, the CES SSN brings together the best thinkers, practitioners, and innovators in education today to learn from the lessons, challenges, and best practices of their peers. This attention, grooming, and constant inspiration have created an environment that stimulates rapid growth, instills best practices, and supplies the endurance needed to transform our schools and the systems on which they depend. The CES SSN's process of incubation and support has helped to fortify the new schools, providing their school leaders with a network of experienced leaders who are engaged in a similar mission of starting and transforming schools. The CES SSN not only provides conditions for growth for the design teams and new schools but also provides a lush learning environment for the Mentor Schools that have made a commitment to continuous improvement.

The History of the Coalition of Essential Schools

1984: Theodore R. Sizer, professor of education at Brown University, and several colleagues publish their findings from "A Study of High Schools," a five-year investigation of teaching, learning, and school history that found that American high schools generally were remarkably similar and simply inadequate. *Horace's Compromise* describes how the typical structures of schools helped to make these inadequacies all but inevitable. Sizer considers how schools might be designed more wisely and chooses to approach reform not with a new and improved model to be imposed but with a set of ideas, the Common Principles.

1984: Twelve schools in seven states agree to redesign themselves on the basis of Sizer's ideas and to form the Coalition of Essential Schools (CES), based at Brown University.

1993: CES and Brown University receive a generous gift from Ambassador Walter H. Annenberg, part of the Annenberg Challenge, a $500 million gift to support school reform nationwide. The Annenberg Institute for School Reform is founded at Brown University.

1994: With hundreds of affiliated schools around the country, the national office of CES helps to arrange the founding of CES affiliate centers, geographically diverse school restructuring support organizations that provide technical support and coaching to schools in order to develop their capacity to demonstrate the CES Common Principles in every aspect of school life.

1997: "Commitment to democracy and equity," the tenth Common Principle, is added through democratic action at Fall Forum.

1998: Ted Sizer retires as executive director of CES; he has remained involved as chair emeritus of the CES National Executive Board. The CES national organization relocates from Providence, Rhode Island, to Oakland, California.

2003: CES receives a grant from the Bill & Melinda Gates Foundation to form the Small Schools Project, a network of over fifty Mentor Schools and newly formed small schools dedicated to creating and supporting small schools throughout the country that are instructionally powerful and sustainable and that offer challenging curricula to students who have been denied a meaningful education.

2003: With support from the Annenberg Foundation, CES launches the EssentialVisions DVD project to demonstrate CES principles and practices in action.

2004: Debut of CES ChangeLab, an online resource that provides behind-the-scenes access to the best practices of the CES Mentor Schools (http://www.ceschangelab.org).

2005: The EssentialBlog launches (http://www.essentialblog.org).

2006: National Exhibition Month, a nationwide campaign that occurs every May to promote and celebrate exhibitions as a preferred form of student assessment, is founded.

2006: *Choosing Small: The Essential Guide to Successful High School Conversion* is published by Jossey-Bass.

2006: Theodore R. Sizer Dissertation Scholars Grant Program is begun.

2007: Essential Analysis, a resource for supporting data-based inquiry that supports Essential Schools, is opened to the CES network.

2008: CES updates the CES Benchmarks, a tool for teachers, schools, and centers that is designed to address the challenge of helping schools translate the CES Common Principles into practice by describing what the work of the Coalition looks like as they plan their programs and develop ways of assessing their reform efforts. (See Appendix B for the CES Benchmarks.)

2009: CES celebrates its twenty-fifth anniversary as a national leader in the reform and restructuring of schools and school systems to make equitable, personalized, and academically challenging schools the norm of American public education. The sixth annual Summer Institute takes place in Providence, Rhode Island. *Small Schools, Big Ideas: The Essential Guide to School Transformation* is published. In New Orleans, Louisiana, CES hosts "Changing Schools, Changing Lives," its annual Fall Forum, and builds on its strengths to sustain and create programs and services that change our schools and change our world.

THE AUTHORS

Mara Benitez brings twenty years of experience in urban education to her role as senior director of school development for the Coalition of Essential Schools (CES). She leads the program design of all CES professional development opportunities and, since 2003, has led the CES Small Schools Project, an initiative funded by the Bill & Melinda Gates Foundation that started twenty new CES small schools across the country. She leads the CES Small Schools Network, a national professional learning community of over fifty exemplary small schools. Before joining CES, Benitez served as executive director of alternative education for the Oakland Unified School District. As part of her charge, she helped to launch new small schools and programs that serve vulnerable youth. For ten years, Benitez taught humanities at several small schools in New York City and was director of Arturo Schomburg Satellite Academy, a small alternative high school in the South Bronx community where she was raised. She holds a master's degree in education from Bank Street College of Education and is a graduate of their Principals Institute. She lives with her family in Oakland, California.

Since 2001, **Jill Davidson** has been the editor of *Horace*, the quarterly journal of CES's national organization. As CES's director of publications, Davidson directs all CES publications and editorial projects and has published work in national journals and publications. Previously, Davidson was an online community producer at various Web sites, directed the Learning Center at the University of San Francisco, and taught high school English and social studies. Davidson is on her second tour of duty with CES; she worked as a CES research assistant after graduating from Brown University. Davidson holds an M.Ed. from the Harvard Graduate School of Education. She lives with her family in Providence, Rhode

Island, where she is a local community leader and activist for excellent public schools.

Laura Flaxman is co-founder and co-principal of ARISE High School, a new small charter school in Oakland, California. Laura brings twenty years of experience in urban education to her current role. Prior to joining ARISE, Flaxman served as co-director of the Small Schools Project for CES. Flaxman came to Oakland in 2000 to start Life Academy, a new small autonomous public high school, where she served as principal. Flaxman founded and served on the board of the Oakland Small Schools Foundation, a nonprofit organization dedicated to supporting and strengthening small public schools in Oakland. Prior to her work in Oakland, Flaxman worked for Expeditionary Learning Outward Bound in New York City, helping to create several new middle schools and to support existing high schools. She completed an internship at Boston Arts Academy, taught at Thomas Jefferson High School in Brooklyn, a residential treatment center in Manhattan, and South Bronx High School. Flaxman holds two master's degrees: one in educational leadership from Harvard University and the other in English from the Bread Loaf School of English. She earned her B.A. at Wesleyan University.

INTRODUCTION: AN ACADEMICALLY CHALLENGING EDUCATION FOR ALL

Small Schools, Big Ideas: The Essential Guide to Successful School Transformation tells the stories and shares the evidence and lessons of the powerful collective experience of the Coalition of Essential Schools Small Schools Network (CES SSN) as it creates the next generation of Essential schools. In an educational climate dominated by national policy that demands recall and memorization, diminishes critical thinking and problem solving, rewards standardization to the detriment of high academic standards, and sorts schools and students into categories of winners and losers, our first successful generation of CES schools—represented by CES Mentor Schools—has defended against these assaults on personalized, equitable, and academically rich and rigorous education. In these pages, CES Mentor Schools and the new small schools of the CES SSN share the ways they use their challenges and accomplishments to create growth, sustain the strength and number of Essential schools, and create a critical mass.

Far too often, school restructuring initiatives lack vision. Daunted by the enormity of the task, school reformers who want to create better educational options for all children suggest tinkering with nineteenth-century schools instead of creating twenty-first century systems of schools for the post-industrial era. Despite increased high-profile attention at the national and state levels to the quality of American education, many schools and school systems are not able to transform the educational experiences and lives of most young people. Trends that characterize our current school reform era such as the standards movement, No Child Left Behind legislation, and the movement toward privatizing public schools have exacerbated inequities and the achievement gap between white students and students of color. Incidents of school violence abound, and many students, particularly students of color from low-income backgrounds who are living in urban areas, attend schools at which they continue to be educationally neglected, underserved, and often unsafe. Many researchers have documented and described these conditions, but few solutions create effective change to transform those conditions. We propose and demonstrate that as a product of our twenty-five years of experience in creating student-centered, innovative, high-achieving schools; with an increased capacity to address equity in our work; and with the results of the CES Small Schools Project, CES provides a powerful blueprint for creating the equitable conditions in which a new type of schools designed to produce learners, workers, and citizens ready for the twenty-first century can thrive.

Today's students must learn how to use their minds well. They must become resilient and persistent, able to complete tasks and work in groups, in order to become citizens who effect change in their communities. With numerous examples of school creation and transformation work in action, successful experiences in a variety of settings, and explanations of effective school practices, *Small Schools, Big Ideas* contains the largest collection of practical and effective applications of the CES Common Principles (see Appendix A) and related practices that have yet been gathered. For district-level administrators interested in systemic reform, individual educators interested in initiating change, and parents and family and community members seeking guidance on participating in the process of school creation or transformation, this book provides a useful road map. We use data and examples from schools committed to the principles and practices of the Coalition of Essential Schools to demonstrate how locating students firmly at the center of school planning and operations while engaging all education stakeholders in a democratic process can lead to nurturing, effective learning communities capable of producing powerful student achievement results.

Before we discuss the contents of *Small Schools, Big Ideas,* we offer three notes about what could not be included. First, although small schools are, as the title suggests, a big idea, this book does not comprehensively document the complex terrain of the small schools movement of which CES has been among the leaders. We focus on the schools in the CES Small Schools Network (CES SSN) in these pages, and even with that tight focus, we have not been able to describe and discuss the achievements and challenges of them all. (For a list of the schools and organizations that are referred to in these pages, see Appendix C.) We are painfully aware that we have had to omit powerful lessons from many of the CES

SSN schools, some that are successful and hugely influential and others that are new and growing strong. Second, due to its focus on the CES SSN, this book does not discuss the significant achievements and wisdom of the hundreds of CES affiliate schools or the important coaching, research, and support work of many of the CES affiliate centers. While many of these schools—transformative in their communities and powerful arguments for CES principles and practices—do not grace these pages, we recognize and are grateful for their work. Third, this book focuses primarily on high schools and schools that combine the middle school and high school grades. The CES network is rich with many powerful, exemplary elementary schools, and within our movement, we are inspired by their success and learn vastly from them. However, because the focus of the CES Small Schools Project is the development of new small secondary schools, those schools are the focus of this text and its accompanying Web site (see Additional Resources for School Transformation).

Additional Resources for School Transformation

For extensive additional resources on the school transformation practices featured in this book, please visit the *Small Schools, Big Ideas* Web site, which provides extensive tools, resources, curriculum, examples, links to related sources of information and support, and much more that will inspire, inform, and guide school designers as they create personalized, equitable, academically challenging schools and the systems that support and sustain them.

This site also provides wide-ranging links to information about the Coalition of Essential Schools, CES's network of schools, and the CES affiliate centers—independent organizations guided by the CES Common Principles that provide long-term coaching, professional development, and technical assistance to schools.

Web site for *Small Schools, Big Ideas: The Essential Guide to Successful School Transformation:*

http://www.ceschangelab.org

Small Schools, Big Ideas contains four sections. Part One describes the distance our school systems need to travel to serve all students well. The first chapter establishes the terms of our argument: changing schools is about changing the lives of individual students, their families, and their communities, as well as the direction of our country. The key elements of transformation are a relentless focus on equity, an understanding of the capacities and qualities that schools designed to effectively educate students for the twenty-first century must possess, small school size, and the power of professional learning communities.

Chapter Two documents the barriers that keep children from an equitable, personalized, and academically vibrant and rigorous education: schools do not adequately prepare all students for the future; an alarming number of students drop out or are pushed out of school; demographics have a devastatingly accurate predictive power over student success; our current national and local policy climates reinforce the status quo in education instead of creating the conditions for success for all; and most school reform proposals address the symptoms of the systemic equity problems that confront us rather than the root causes.

Chapter Three presents the change options for new schools—the ways that new schools can come into existence—and the strategies for creating new schools that will establish them as fundamentally different from the persistent status quo: working within a network dedicated to the principles of equity, utilizing school-to-school learning, employing disruptive innovation, and working with the school district to develop the essential conditions for thriving schools designed to work for all students. This chapter also examines some of the key elements that need to be in place at the district and system level: a balance of autonomy and accountability, control of resources at the school level, policies that promote transformation, leadership that initiates and sustains change, the creation of mass demand for educational equity, and the need to work both from the bottom up and the top down to change schools and school systems.

Part Two shifts to action, laying out the steps that are necessary to create and staff transformed schools. Chapter Four covers the school design process, which requires that school planners start with the school's mission, vision, and desired outcomes and plan backward from there; plan strategically and divide the work among different groups and individuals; create inclusive design teams; communicate new school development plans to the larger community; develop partnerships; and find a place in a supportive network of schools. As well, Chapter Four maintains that the process should model the outcome: a democratic and equitable process should fully engage all design team members and include democratic and participatory structures that establish the foundation for a democratic and equitable school.

Chapter Five focuses on the development of transformational leadership and the creation of a shared vision and leadership across a school community. The chapter details the roles and responsibilities of leaders who are dedicated to creating equitable schools that transform the conditions of teaching and learning and open up opportunities for students. This chapter describes key practices for transformational leadership: leading a discourse of transformation; being a different kind of principal; committing to a shared mission and vision; engaging in equity-focused inquiry; nurturing a culture of shared ownership, accountability, and leadership; cultivating teacher leaders; developing youth leadership; and bringing families to the decision-making table.

Chapter Six discusses how to nurture professional support and growth among a school's educators. This chapter covers the need to know what adult learners need, cultivate a mission-driven schoolwide learning community, develop a culture of accountability and trust, establish effective facilitation structures for equity-focused learning communities, implement effective professional development, make time for the work of professional learning communities, and participate in learning communities beyond the school.

Part Three delves into the inner workings of Essential schools. Chapter Seven concentrates on the key CES Common Principles that describe educational experiences that are designed to support all students' growth (the principles of learning to use one's mind well; personalization; student as worker, teacher as coach; and less is more, depth over coverage), offering detailed descriptions of aligned practices in action.

Chapter Eight maps the assessment terrain that accompanies student-centered teaching and learning. This chapter discusses strategies for providing structured time and support for performance-based assessment; the qualities of a coherent instructional program that aligns instruction and assessment; how performance-based assessment promotes community-wide accountability for equitable student outcomes; the need for professional development that supports performance-based assessment; and the ways that performance-based assessment can meet and influence state accountability requirements.

The specific practices that schools use to prepare students for success after graduation from high school are the subject of Chapter Nine. These practices include reworking their curricula to align with higher education expectations; building partnerships between high schools and higher education institutions; creating personalization through advisories and other structures to support higher education and career success; engaging families as partners; introducing students to the world of work and active citizenship through internships and other real-world educational opportunities; and providing proactive support, training, and counseling to prepare students for the inevitable challenges of the postsecondary world.

Part Four of *Small Schools, Big Ideas* gathers the practices that Essential schools use to establish and maintain a positive school culture and environment, as well as the strategies employed to sustain the work. Chapter Ten explores the ways in which educators can build a school culture that supports equitable teaching and learning, professional learning communities, and manifestation of the CES Common Principles. These approaches include building strong relationships through advisories and other structures, establishing staffing patterns in which school staff members take on multiple roles, promoting a clear statement of values for which the school stands, creating rituals and celebrations, involving the entire school community in positive discipline and restorative justice practices, building strong and positive connections with families, bringing the school together for community meetings, and creating school schedules that make these priorities possible.

The final chapter of this book examines the practices common to Essential schools that have experienced long-term durability and success. Chapter Eleven looks at the ways that schools handle the career development and eventual transitions of school leaders and school staff members, and it establishes the importance of stakeholder commitments; partnerships; supportive district and policy conditions; negotiating funding and resource challenges; creating a power base through outreach, branding, and advocacy; and the role of networks that support schools as they pursue their mission.

School transformation for all students and communities is urgent, and we aim to meet readers in various stages of implementation. We believe that systemic change is necessary, that creating small schools is a critical component of personalization, that the focus of schools and the systems that contain them needs to be on teaching and learning, and that schools require a high level of autonomy to be able to achieve the results we write about. Nevertheless, for individual teachers in large high schools that do not have these attributes, there are specific tools and strategies in *Small Schools, Big Ideas* for creating change. The road we describe to better schools and school systems for all children may seem long and daunting, but as poet Audre Lorde wrote, "When I dare to be powerful—to use my strength in the service of my vision, then it becomes less and less important whether I am afraid." Use the lessons in these pages to plan the journey. Dare to be powerful.

SMALL SCHOOLS, BIG IDEAS

PART ONE Setting the Stage for Transformation

A Commitment to Equity

The work of creating equitable schools has been the
heart and soul of the work of the Coalition of
Essential Schools. In an equitable society, test
scores and graduation rates are not predetermined
by incomes, race, or gender. Today's schools mirror
the imbalances that exist in our society and are used
to reproduce a culture of inequality. If we do not
intentionally and meaningfully interrupt these
inequitable practices and restructure public
education, we will continue to deny a great majority
of students their right to a quality education.

—Excerpt from a letter to participants of a coaches' training for an
equity-based Critical Friends Group facilitated by the Coalition of
Essential Schools

Small Schools, Big Ideas is about changing schools in order to change lives.
This book is intended for practitioners, policymakers, family members, teachers
of educators, and students of education committed to transforming schools
into personalized, academically challenging, and equitable places of learning.
Schools dramatically affect the lives of children. Schools can capture children's

imagination and ensure the promise of a fulfilling life, or schools can severely diminish children's self-worth and their access to skills and knowledge, making it impossible for them to reach their full potential. Quite often, our schools do both: they improve the lives of children coming from our country's cultural and racial majority groups and from wealthier communities, and they create even greater challenges and disruptions in the lives of children of color who are raised in often poor, often urban communities.

The ways that we educate our children through the institution of schools can improve significantly in life-changing ways for all children, their families, their communities, and their teachers. We are not offering advice for those interested in tinkering with schools as they have been and are now. Our proposition is not to work around the dysfunctional edges of our schools. Instead, we examine what it will take to bring individual schools and systems of schools into the twenty-first century. We discuss the pathways that will create the climate and the conditions to transform education from the outdated factory-style school system already in its decline to a high-performing system of schools that creates equitable places of learning. In this book, we look at the urgency needed to move from reform to the systemic transformation of public education so that it can add value to society, find ways to close the achievement and resource gaps for all students, and prepare our youth for the demands of good citizenship, college, and career.

We use this book as an opportunity to move the discourse beyond the conventional ways that we have defined and measured achievement. The achievement gap is conventionally defined as "the troubling performance gaps between many African-American and Hispanic students, at the lower end of the performance scale, and their non-Hispanic white peers, and the similar academic disparity between students from low-income and well-off families. The achievement gap shows up in grades, standardized-test scores, course selection, dropout rates, and college-completion rates" (Editorial Projects in Education, 2004). Within the Coalition of Essential Schools (CES), we define achievement in ways that go beyond the limitations of a standardized set of compartmentalized knowledge items measured exclusively by standardized pen-and-paper tests. To us, achievement means obtaining a broader, deeper skill set that gives students the capacity to find information and to apply it meaningfully to a changing world. As we explore ways of closing the achievement gap, we include both the economic and information gaps that negatively affect poor students and students of color by limiting their opportunities and access to an education that supports the habits of using their minds well, becoming lifelong learners, and gaining the enduring and emerging skills to participate fully in this country's economic and democratic promise. This is a gap that not just poor students and students of color experience, though they may suffer its effects most acutely.

In our current antiquated model of education, schools have not fully prepared students, especially students of color and poor students, with enduring literacy and numeracy skills—those fundamentals, often described as "the basics," that high-stakes standardized tests aim to assess. Nor are our schools responding well to a new challenge to teach a set of emerging skills that includes higher-order thinking; applying what has been learned; collaborating productively; influencing and negotiating power; communication and presentation skills; and understanding mathematical, technical, and scientific issues—all necessary in today's knowledge-based economy. The evolution of our education system has been halted by the imposition of a set of content standards across the country that are designed to make sure that each student is learning the same thing. The outcome has been standardization at the risk of limiting teaching and reducing learning to a set of multiple choices. By advocating for higher standards in teaching and learning and an assessment system with multiple measures, CES has surpassed the movement that enforces a set of standards that result in graduating students neither with a sturdy set of enduring skills nor with a robust set of the emerging skills needed to participate fully in and meet the demands of the twenty-first century. In *The Global Achievement Gap*, Tony Wagner (2008, pp. 14–39) names initiative and entrepreneurialism, agility and adaptability, accessing and analyzing data, and curiosity and imagination, among other competencies, as the "survival skills" that matter most for the twenty-first century (see "Twenty-First-Century Skills" sidebar). In a climate of high-stakes standardized assessment that generally limits the scope of testing to content standards, these emerging survival skills are not measured. As a result, they hold less importance in the classroom, thereby limiting the scope of education for all of our students.

Twenty-First-Century Skills

The following list represents a core set of survival skills for today's workplace, lifelong learning, and active citizenship:

- Critical thinking and problem solving
- Collaboration across networks and leading by influence
- Agility and adaptability
- Initiative and entrepreneurialism
- Effective oral and written communication
- Accessing and analyzing information
- Curiosity and imagination

Source: Wagner, 2008, pp. 14–39.

Educational Equity

The equity we seek expands on the limited, hollow version of equity that some are using to legitimize a test-driven, top-down reform agenda. In New York City, Joel Klein referred in 2007 to the need to test students five more times per year in addition to the many mandated summative exams already at the core of his "equity" education agenda (Rose, 2007). Such equity comes in the form of opportunity and access to the malfunctioning remnants of the status quo: outdated curriculum and instruction that lack rigor and relevance and high-stakes standardized tests that lower the standards of teaching and learning. *Small Schools, Big Ideas* documents an authentic form of educational equity that spurs intellectual, social, and emotional growth among our young people and equips them with the tools they need to apply new knowledge in constructive ways in their lives and communities.

Like Ted Sizer before us, and John Dewey before him, we believe that the role of public education is to teach and prepare students to "use their minds well" so that they can participate in civic life. Nearly a century ago, Dewey wrote, "Democracy has to be born anew every generation, and education is its midwife" (Dewey, 1993). As so many others have lamented, public education is not doing its part. For the most part, in urban, suburban, and rural schools, students are not learning how to be lifelong learners, earn a living wage, or develop the agency to access and contribute to an active citizenry that works for democracy and equity. What we share in these pages is intended to raise awareness about the ways that we can remake schools to become high-performing, powerful places that prepare children and adults to be full participants in a democratic society. Through this book, we, the authors, and the Coalition of Essential Schools as an organization, network, and movement, offer ourselves as allies to families, community members, and educators interested in reinventing our school system so that it can afford all children a meaningful education that prepares them for what we know and what we can only imagine the future holds.

The historic concept of public education as a way to level the playing field has yet to be fulfilled. We hope that our descriptions of the strategies and practices used by CES practitioners across the country will move us toward fulfilling that dream, and we hope that the brave voices that speak from these pages will not be drowned out by the discontent, isolation, and frustration that many of us feel about the state of education. Take this opportunity to learn what has been accomplished, what is possible, and what we can do together to create equitable schools that will help move us toward a more equitable society.

Educational equity means that all students have access to all of the experiences, conditions, and support that they need to grow as learners and be prepared for postsecondary options. To be engaged in the pursuit of equitable education for all students means that we are "raising the achievement of all students while narrowing the gaps between the highest and lowest performing students and eliminating the racial predictability and disproportionality of which student groups occupy the highest and lowest achievement categories" (Singleton and Linton, 2006, p. 46; also shown in sidebar). As we described earlier, when we refer to the gaps that exist, we mean much more than differences on standardized tests. Because we cannot address racial achievement disparities without addressing systemic racism, this work has to involve an examination of the attitudes and practices that keep these racial disparities intact (Jones, 2000). Therefore, the ways that we interrupt these inequities in our classrooms, schools, and school districts must be bold, unforgiving, strategic, and compassionate. The practices and principles shared in *Small Schools, Big Ideas* provide a road map to achieving schools and educational systems that mitigate and challenge the effects of systemic racism and shed light on the obstacles that schools, school systems, and communities face on this journey.

Definition of Educational Equity

"Educational equity is raising the achievement of all students while narrowing the gaps between the highest and lowest performing students and eliminating the racial predictability and disproportionality of which student groups occupy the highest and lowest achievement categories."

Source: Singleton and Linton, 2006, p. 46.

Twenty-Five Years of Experience

Small Schools, Big Ideas both acknowledges the achievements of the Coalition of Essential Schools (CES) over the past twenty-five years and recognizes its challenges. We hope to explain the conditions that impeded many Essential schools from sustaining their successes and most school districts from taking the lessons of those successes to a deeper systemic level. Many of the short-lived reform efforts of the past several decades—which represent but a short segment of the continuum of continually disappointing attempts at silver-bullet educational reform (Tyack and Cuban, 1995)—have left many educators pessimistic about the possibility of real change. In this constantly varying, increasingly hostile climate, CES practitioners have focused on creating principle-based schools focused on equity, personalization, and high academic standards. In many instances, they have had much to celebrate as they pushed through seemingly insurmountable obstacles to improve their schools. Those leaders modeled (and are often still modeling) the kind of effort and persistence at all levels that this work demands. When these renegade leaders ran into systemic walls and were unable to continue to take cover "under the radar," they invented ways to keep moving the work forward, showing us what schools can look like when we are creative, caring, and thoughtful about putting students and families at the center. And from their tenacity grew the proof that it can be done; even under unpredictable and difficult circumstances, we can create amazing schools. In this book, we acknowledge the fruits of their labor and we stand on the shoulders of CES Mentor Schools such as Quest High School in Texas, Urban Academy Laboratory High School in New York City, and Fenway High School in Boston. They have dealt with changing mandates and conditions beyond their control that challenge the growth of their work and innovations, yet they still have produced positive results from students.

The work of the Coalition of Essential Schools started with courageous educators focused on the relationships between students and teachers. Over time, these educators created an ambitious yet attainable vision that drives today's most successful educational change efforts, which have created exemplary small schools, systems, and networks of schools. Big Picture Schools, The Boston Pilot Schools, High Tech High Schools, the New Small Autonomous Schools of Oakland, the New York Performance Standards Consortium, and other such efforts were founded and are driven by major players with roots in the CES tradition who use the CES Common Principles to guide their work. Deborah Meier, a longtime educator and leader of CES, reflects on the work of the early years of the Coalition: "We may not have changed the paradigm of American education back then, but we're still out there fighting. Take note that of those who participated in the original schools, they have been active, and our ideas persist. Failure is not just failure. It was sometimes a way for people whose schools didn't work in one context to take those ideas elsewhere and make them work."

Throughout *Small Schools, Big Ideas,* we will be referring to these examples and to the CES Common Principles, the set of ideas created twenty-five years ago when the Coalition first came together as a collective effort to reform education. The motivation for reforming schools was a desire to change instruction and the relationships between teachers and students in order to dramatically improve student outcomes. One of the major findings of CES founder Ted Sizer's pre-CES work (and related work by others) was that students were disengaged. Therefore, the impetus for reforming schools was to encourage them to re-engage students in active learning. The focus on engagement and student outcomes put the spotlight on the student-teacher interaction, and the earliest Coalition efforts viewed the classroom as the unit of change. That view has continued to expand due to both practical and moral considerations. The stories in this book illustrate how the CES Common Principles continued to be the backbone and philosophical underpinning of the work as we took it deeper and beyond the walls of the classroom to transform schools and the systems on which they depend. (Please see Appendix A for the CES Common Principles in full.)

The last Common Principle, referred to as "Democracy and Equity," provides the overarching motivation for this expanding view. It states: "The school should demonstrate non-discriminatory and inclusive policies, practices, and pedagogies. It should model democratic practices that involve all who are directly affected by the school. The school should honor diversity and build on the strength of its communities, deliberately and explicitly challenging all forms of inequity." Throughout our work and within these pages, we reaffirm that our charge is to model and uphold the Common Principle of Democracy and Equity by deliberately creating small, equitable schools and systems of schools that function democratically to support a culture of learning that encourages all children and adults to reach their highest potential.

In the 1980s and early 1990s, small, public Essential high schools such as New York City's Central Park East Secondary School, founded by Deborah Meier, and rural Thayer High School in Winchester, New Hampshire, founded by Dennis Littky, challenged the ways that we envision public education (see sidebar). Put into action in the classroom, the CES Common Principles—in the ways that decisions were made and in the ways the school nurtured the relationships between teachers and students—became the basis for relevant, challenging, and student-centered experiences of teaching and learning. Such schools served as role models to stimulate other educators who were unhappy with the culture and the results of traditional schooling. Examples from Essential schools propelled others to take action. Central Park East Secondary School, Thayer High School, and other early CES schools were driven by the belief that public schools are vital to a sound democracy. Public schools have an essential public purpose: to prepare all citizens to be educated and play a vital role in our democracy. These early CES schools changed outcomes and the lives of young people; for example, one of Central Park East's achievements was a stellar college-going rate among students for whom expectations of college attendance were bleak (Bensman, 1995).

Many educators, inspired by these early adopters, worked to restructure their public schools one classroom at a time, using the CES Common Principles as their guide. Through these experiences, we learned to use these pockets of excellence within schools to stimulate schoolwide change by implementing the lessons learned in model classrooms across the school community. The work quickly moved beyond the CES teacher leaders' classrooms to a "one school at a time" school improvement approach that leveraged reform trends and programs to achieve more student-centered, teacher-driven schools in which everyone was learning to use their minds well. They created new small public schools wherever the climate would allow, using small school size as the vehicle to infuse personalization, rigor, and relevance into the learning environment. While many of these first CES schools helped to leverage deeper systemic change within some districts, the work of these stand-alone "boutique" schools did not affect the learning conditions for a great number of students still stuck in failing large comprehensive schools. And in some instances, the bold yet fragile attempts were either ignored or swallowed up by the system.

Deborah Meier and Dennis Littky: Early CES School Leaders

For more about the work of Deborah Meier and her colleagues at Central Park East Secondary School, read her books, which include *The Power of Their Ideas: Lessons to America from a Small School in Harlem* (1995) and *In Schools We Trust: Creating Communities of Learning in an Era of Testing and Standardization* (2002), both published by Beacon Press. Meier is currently on the faculty of New York University's Steinhardt School of Education as senior scholar and adjunct professor. She is also active as a board member of many organizations, including Mission Hill School and the Coalition of Essential Schools, and she is a convener of the Forum for Democracy and Education.

For more about Dennis Littky's work at Thayer High School, read *Doc: The Story of Dennis Littky and His Fight for a Better School* by Susan Kammeraad-Campbell (Association for Supervision and Curriculum Development, 2005), and for more on Littky's subsequent work as co-founder of the Big Picture Company, read *The Big Picture: Education Is Everyone's Business* (Association for Supervision and Curriculum Development, 2004). Dennis Littky is the co-founder and co-director of Big Picture Learning and the Met Center in Providence, Rhode Island.

Small Schools by Design

In *Small Schools, Big Ideas,* we discuss how small school size establishes the conditions that allow the CES Common Principles to guide the practices that cultivate an engaging culture of learning, motivating even the most vulnerable students to become active learners and promoting equitable access and opportunity for all students. As well, small school size provides the opportunities for autonomy, collaboration, and relationships that are necessary to create new ways of designing and restructuring both the learning process and the organizational practices and policies. However, the notion that due to their size alone, small schools can change the deep-rooted inequities and dysfunctional practices in comprehensive secondary schools and raise achievement is flawed. To believe that smallness unto itself can tackle the important changes that need to take place at the cultural, institutional, and interpersonal levels of schools and districts is to miscalculate the deeply embedded causes that have led us to the status quo of students and communities ill served and ill prepared by most educational systems.

We do believe that if schools are not small or do not otherwise have conditions that allow relationships to flourish, inquiry to proceed in a sustained and challenging way, and communication to keep everyone focused on the school's mission, the status quo will persist indefinitely. *Small Schools, Big Ideas* provides further examples of why small size is one of the most important conditions for improving student engagement and performance (see also Coalition of Essential Schools, 2006) and why restructuring efforts centered on small school size must be accompanied by significant changes in our belief systems and the ways that those beliefs about students and their potential manifest in the daily decisions, operational systems, and instructional practices of public education as a whole.

In recent years, as the world of small schools became broader and more densely populated with well-intentioned funders, service providers, and practitioners, much of CES's contribution toward the philosophical underpinning of the small schools movement was either lost or misinterpreted. We know that many districts and some states, as well as the federal government through the Smaller Learning Communities grant program, have jumped on the small schools bandwagon in the course of the last decades, making it a notable trend in the annals of American school reform. Some did so because small size was part of their design principles. Many others moved toward small schools simply to chase the funding that was available. Unfortunately, the premature rush to "scale up" decoupled theory and practice, resulting in a diluted version of the small schools movement as we conceived it. To many, the final verdict on small schools is that they are yet another failed attempt at changing schools (Bloomfield, 2006), based on the claim that the pace of results is not quick enough and the value added not measurable by mainstream metrics such as standardized tests. Many make the claim that small schools are not a viable and sustainable model to which school districts should aspire because they cost too much when implemented in school districts that rely on economies of scale, although research has consistently refuted this idea (Lawrence and others, 2002; Lawrence and others, 2006).

In his 2009 annual letter, Bill Gates, co-chair of the Bill & Melinda Gates Foundation, reflects on the nine years of work and $2 billion in grants that the foundation has invested in creating better high schools through their U.S. program. The goal was to provide additional resources to schools over a period of time to "make changes in the way they were organized (including reducing their size), in how the teachers worked, and in the curriculum." To that end, many of the small schools that were funded had more improvement in their attendance and graduation rates compared with their peers, but the majority did not significantly improve their academic outcomes. According to Gates, these "tended to be the schools that did not take radical steps to change the culture, such as allowing principals to pick the team of teachers or change the curriculum" (Gates, 2009, p. 11).

Gates's statements demonstrate that neither giving schools more money nor reducing their size will increase student achievement. The changes in schools have to go beyond surface reforms to more significant, deeper changes that transform the relationships, the schools' ability to control and deploy resources, and the pedagogical philosophy. These changes cannot happen in a vacuum. They must be done in relationship to school districts and with the involvement of teachers, students, families, and community partners; otherwise, the system will quash the momentum and dilute the change effort, rendering it useless. The exemplary schools that are discussed in these pages combine their size with intentional practices that affect the lives of students by transforming the relationships in the building and creating more personalized learning environments in which all children are well known and challenged to use their minds well. "Small schools in drag," Michelle Fine (2005) writes, will produce the same results as failing large schools. Small schools by design, however, have the potential to significantly transform outcomes and prepare all students for college, citizenship, and work.

The CES Small Schools Project and Small Schools Network

In 2003, when the Bill & Melinda Gates Foundation granted CES the support to launch a five-year small schools project, the CES Small Schools Project became CES's flagship initiative. This project has established us as a leader of the national conversation about small schools, and it has distinguished us by focusing on equity as the goal of these schools. This focus on equity is critical to the vision, and it is what drives the work of the schools featured in this book. Held across all of the small schools involved in the project is the belief that students deserve to be engaged in their learning and leave school fully prepared for access to and success in multiple postsecondary options. This goal is particularly urgent for students whom the system has not served well in the past. We should not relegate our most needy and vulnerable students to the most dispiriting, unengaging schools. As long as our states and nation continue to heavily regulate and underfund public schools, particularly those in urban areas, and limit access to and opportunities for learning for a great majority of students across class and racial groups, we are reducing the potential contributions and livelihood of future generations. Small, personalized, and academically vibrant private schools exist in communities across America, and we cannot allow such schools to be the norm for only a small segment of our society. The goal of the CES Small Schools Project is to make them the norm for American public schools.

Today's CES approach is the result of a growing commitment to systemic trans-formation on multiple levels. With twenty-five years of experience at the forefront of school reform in the United States, the Coalition is poised to contribute a new method of school change. Partnering with our Mentor Schools across the country, CES has shaped a peer-to-peer school development approach that taps into the expertise and experience of some of the most successful small schools in the country. The twenty-four CES Mentor Schools, with their concentration of decades' worth of collaboratively constructed knowledge, have contributed valuable wisdom and experience to the landscape of small schools and the promise of equity. Using small school size as a vehicle and the CES Common Principles as their guide, these schools have given us a diverse set of models that can be used to transform our public school system. Under difficult and frequently uncertain circumstances—sometimes flying under the radar, sometimes taking on the systems to which they belong head-on—CES Mentor Schools have added value to the small schools movement by achieving high academic gains for some of the most vulnerable students in our nation. Throughout these chapters, we share the lessons they learned as they surpassed their counterparts by narrowing the achieve-ment gap in their schools, supporting more students in reaching higher education options, and preparing them for the twenty-first century (Coalition of Essential Schools, 2006). One of their most notable accomplishments has been their ability to engage stakeholders in deep and meaningful ways for the cause of transforming our schools. These schools have learned ways to build partnerships with parents and community members while continuing to empower teachers to lead.

The CES Small Schools Project and the resulting CES Small Schools Network (CES SSN) allowed CES to use its collective knowledge to broaden its reach and engage new constituencies in rethinking and redesigning large comprehensive high schools and growing new small schools. The Small Schools Project gave us the opportunity to examine and document the progress of some of the most exemplary schools in the country. Today, while we still believe that teachers are essential units of change, we have expanded this concept to include other important stakeholders who are often left out of the conversation: youth, families, and community. As the first decade of the twenty-first century has unfolded, CES's work has involved engaging these players in taking a more active role in change efforts at their schools, across districts, and across the country. Through the years, we have remained steadfast in the conviction that change in classroom instruction is the most important element that will increase student achievement. However, we have learned that in order to transform teaching and learning, one has to change the culture of schools and actively redesign entire systems to support and sustain those changes. The work described in these pages has evolved into creating learning communities that share best practices for improving their schools while positioning themselves to have greater influence beyond the walls of their school communities. We tell the stories of how fostering a sense of ownership in the process and outcomes of school transformation among parents, community members, and policymakers has become a priority for educators who once saw themselves as the sole leaders of early reforms. The growth of a critical mass of people who are committed to growing equitable small schools has made it possible for more students and families to experience the transformational results of attending a CES school. And given the pressures facing small schools across the country, it is essential that there be a critical mass of empowered stakeholders who can fight for and demand the climate and conditions to grow and sustain small schools as a way of delivering an equitable educational option to all students.

Building a Professional Learning Community

In *Small Schools, Big Ideas,* we offer the experience of the CES SSN as a professional learning community that has been codifying its work while implementing, testing, and documenting best practices in order to explore and learn about the importance of establishing learning communities that engage in ongoing inquiry aimed at creating constant improvement of student outcomes. While the SSN schools are engaged in their own continuous improvement, as a network, these schools are moving through a collective cycle of inquiry that poses questions about challenges, looks at data, creates practices based on that data to respond to those challenges, measures the impact of the changes, and then continues to raise more questions that push for new innovations. This process stimulates an engaged teaching faculty, providing professional development as part of the inquiry process, and encourages the inclusion of all stakeholders in both the creation and modeling of innovative solutions. The intentionality that drives this process creates the teaching and learning that raises the standards of our schools above and beyond state and federal mandates to ensure that our students graduate as scholars, artists, and active citizens prepared to create and participate in a democratic society.

These pages contain the voices of teachers, students, and leaders of CES schools who, as a result of being part of a larger movement of small schools, comprehend more clearly what is possible within their schools and demand more of the systems and institutions to which they belong. The exchanges that happen within these learning communities and as part of the CES SSN demonstrate that schools need to be part of interschool, systemwide professional learning communities of practitioners who are concerned about similar questions and empowered to critique and challenge each other and push for change as needed. Innovative schools need the systems of which they are a part to carve out a space for like-minded schools with more freedom and flexibility to act on behalf of their students and to use multiple approaches to achieve and demonstrate their progress.

To this end, CES has been working with a range of districts and local partners to ensure the systemic viability of our new small schools. Hard-learned lessons led us to this work; many wonderful, magical, and influential first-generation Essential schools did not maintain their programs because they were islands. Their Essential school efforts were not part of their larger districts and systems or supported by them. From experiences such as that of Denver's Manual High School, CES learned that unless the district creates the space within its system to own its reform with top-down support, change will not last. Schools will become embattled with the powers that be, dissipating their energy in the struggle. Each time such schools go under, children, their families, and the public suffer the multiple blows of unmet needs, broken promises, and lost hope in public education.

We cannot build walls around Essential schools to shield them from the influences of district, state, and federal policies. Instead, we need to use their existence as levers to create the climate and conditions for the growth and sustainability of small, equitable schools. In this book, we share our most compelling examples of success—the Boston Pilot Schools, the Belmont Zone of Choice, and the schools that are part of the New York Performance Standards Consortium—as networks of schools that have policies in place that allow the schools some genuine autonomy from the systems in which they reside. Though such arrangements are not the current norm, they urge us to create policy environments that allow more autonomy while continuing to demand accountability. Through the innovative disruption that we discuss, the architects of these networks influenced policies, developed agreements, and secured commitments that both ensure the sustainability of new and existing small schools and can serve as a catalyst for the improvement—and eventual transformation—of all schools in the district. The kind of innovative disruption that we propose can spur district leadership to rethink systems, policies, distribution of resources, and the district's relationships with schools.

Since its founding, CES has acted on the belief that practitioners—educators and school leaders closest to students and the processes of teaching and learning—are the experts and should be at the forefront of any change effort. Intentionally, they are among the loudest and most pronounced voices heard throughout this book because through their firsthand experience, we learn what works best for children and youth. Through their leadership and involvement, we are reminded to keep students at the center and make every decision with the intention of improving academic results for all students. The CES SSN has also furthered the involvement and leadership of students themselves in the work of school transformation—for, of course, no one is closer to the students than students. Their voices are well represented in *Small Schools, Big Ideas,* too. In addition, the idea that we are all learners and that in order to find the solutions that we are searching for in urban education, we need to nurture and include all voices is embedded in this book and in the overall mission of the CES Small Schools Project. Over the last five years, we have invested in nurturing and lifting the voices of teachers of color and creating a diverse new cadre of CES leaders. The CES SSN has served as a place to grow our craft as educators, and it has opened up another important opportunity: the chance to sharpen our focus on issues of educational equity and speak out loud our commitment to this work.

That is why equity, captured for us in the "Democracy and Equity" Common Principle, is the project's focal point and the underlying intentional thread that weaves together the chapters of this book.

Leading for Equity

The current thrust of federal education policy—top-down policy that does not support innovation, punishes schools, and invalidates the experience of teachers and students—cannot endure without further inflicting serious damage to the system of public education and our nation as a whole. The constant drumbeat decrying failing schools saps public confidence and undermines the willingness to provide the kind of resources that an endeavor of the magnitude and importance of reinventing public education requires and deserves. The increasing resistance to state and federal mandates such as No Child Left Behind is a good indicator that the American public, while seeking more accountability from schools, seeks change in the ways that we provide resources to our schools and evaluate their performance (Rose and Gallup, 2007). Many educators, family members, students, and community members have already come to understand why our current system is not working for the great majority of students, including poor students and students of color. What they now need are examples of what else is possible today. CES is committed to developing healthier ways of fully educating our young people by creating better schools for them, influencing the climate and conditions in which those schools exist, and advocating for performance-based assessments that can truly measure the skills that matter. Educators in thousands of schools nationwide—as evidenced by participation in the federal Smaller Learning Communities grant program and other measures—are looking for material that will help their schools immediately improve their students' academic performance. We respond to that sense of urgency by sharing the stories, data, and tools in these pages, which those seeking different ways to achieve better outcomes for students may find useful or even transformative.

We don't pretend that this work will be easy. Public education is already badly underfunded, and this situation is not likely to change anytime soon. This situation cannot be a barrier to action; rather, it should be a call to use what resources we have more wisely. It makes no sense to continue using funds in ways that we know can't achieve the desired results. In these pages are stories of schools that have used the resources they have in smarter ways—ways that truly serve all children.

The ideas and practices we share in this guide will help school communities find ways to address their sense of urgency through equitable teaching and learning and to take action at a deeper systemic level in order to sustain their achievements. With this new work, the Coalition has been able to focus with intensity on the CES Common Principles, the original ideas that drove our work toward the essential condition of smallness. And through development of new tools such as the CES Benchmarks that have come out of the CES SSN, we are contributing a new body of knowledge and practice that documents the best organizational and instructional practices of CES. (For more on the CES Benchmarks, consult Appendix B.)

Through the vehicle of education, CES has taken up the work of equity and thus the fight for social justice. We remind readers to think of the urgent charge at hand: to close the racial and economic achievement gap and create equitable learning environments for all. Equitable learning environments cannot be created while we remain silent about the institutionalized oppressive practices and attitudes that create the disparities that mar our schools and negatively affect our students. Achieving these goals involves raising the race and class consciousness of educators and moving the discourse from reform to transformation. CES practitioners attempt to move the discourse about school change beyond remedies that address the symptoms to strategic thinking, planning, and action that address what causes the United States to have a failing public school system. Without the work required to identify that failure's root causes, we will continue to use the same approaches that got us to where we are now.

As part of that charge, we will need to cultivate the voices of those who have taken up the work and prepare them to engage in authentic dialogue across differences to better understand how people experience oppression, power, privilege, and hegemony in and out of schools. This book provides a space for educators, family members, students and community members to speak their truths, push against the mainstream, and rattle the status quo. In these pages, we weave these stories, experiences, practices, and ideas together and unleash the power that educators have to tell our truth, to face what we do not know, and to learn together how to transform our schools for the sake of our children.

Small Schools, Big Ideas aims to stimulate hope and action by sharing the best of the experiences of educators, families, students, administrators, and community members who successfully started or remade their own schools. We invite our readers to join this movement for educational equity.

Facing the Challenges

If we are going to become better and different fast, I knew that we had to name the issues of racism and classism that permeate the system, from the design of the student weighted formula to our system of school choice.

—Tony Smith, deputy superintendent of instruction, innovation, and social justice, San Francisco Unified School District

We contend that the public school system is not broken, but obsolete. The public school system requires transformation, not fixing or reform. People will rarely take up such a challenge, an endeavor that involves unconventional thinking and substantial risk, absent a crisis-driven sense of urgency. The crisis exists, as endless reports and reams of data conclusively demonstrate: high school drop-out rates of 30 percent overall and nearly 50 percent for students of color (Editorial Projects in Education, 2008); overcrowded, underfunded urban schools; and a punitive, disengaging environment that breeds more despair than hope. Yet an honest accounting of the roots of this problem remains largely beyond our grasp because we lack the tools and the will to tackle these painful truths, finding solace instead in a myriad of technical fixes aimed at the symptoms rather than the causes of our collective failure. What is needed is an admission that our present system is designed to meet the needs of only some children, followed by a bold effort to create a new approach that meets the needs of all.

While the data are compelling and should demand a swift and urgent response, most service providers, intermediaries, state agencies, and other organizations that help schools and districts get better at serving children respond with an incremental approach to change. This slow-paced, piecemeal approach has gained little traction and made few gains in student success, as is evidenced by the persistent gaps between the achievement of students of color and white students and the alarming drop-out rate (Kirsch, Braun, Yamamoto, and Sum, 2007; Orfield, 2004; Greene and Winters, 2005; Swanson, 2008). This tinkering does little to reduce the large number of undereducated students, pushes disillusioned teachers out of the field of education, and continues to taint the image of public education. Despite how insurmountable the problems with our educational system seem, to continue on the present course will have a profoundly negative long-term impact on our society as a whole. The many challenges we face at the start of the twenty-first century—economic, environmental, and social—demand that we access the full potential of all of our people.

Some will argue that public education lacks the resources to undertake the fundamental changes we are calling for. While it is true that we need more funding for schools, including better pay for teachers, it is also true that the types of changes we call for can and have been accomplished within existing financial constraints. This work would be far easier with adequate resources, but it must happen regardless.

The first step in solving any problem is to name it. To make the necessary critical changes, we will need to face the truth and see the conditions as they really are for far too many of our students. Let us be honest about the reality that those in our schools are living with. Let us not sugarcoat, whitewash, or dismiss the circumstances that our children and youth live with every day in and out of our schools or pretend that who they are and the reality of their lives do not influence the ways that schools operate, the way they are funded. and the ways that our teachers interact with students and families.

Unprepared for the Future

The data show that our high schools are overwhelmingly failing our youth. Many students are not being adequately prepared for the new economic realities that we face in this country. They are not taught the skills and knowledge that they need to make a living wage and participate as active citizens in our society.

Instead, they are in antiquated, factory-style environments that fifty years ago were obsolete and now are in extreme decline. While there was a time when young people could enter the world of work right out of high school and make a living wage, the data show that those days are gone. The median income of high school dropouts aged eighteen and over was $12,184 in 2003. By comparison, the median income of those aged eighteen and over who had completed their education with a high school credential (including GEDs) was $20,431 (Laird, DeBell, and Chapman, 2006, p. 1). As the twenty-first-century United States moves toward an increasingly global economy, more individuals are discovering that higher levels of education are essential. Almost 85 percent of current jobs and 90 percent of new jobs in occupations with both high growth and high wages will require workers with at least some postsecondary education (Business–Higher Education Forum, 2003; U.S. Department of Labor, 2006).

The number of low-level jobs that once existed in the service industry are shrinking, leaving a larger demand for highly qualified employees. In the face of this increased demand, the skills and knowledge base of the potential workforce are decreasing due to the state of our educational institutions. Hence, we may have jobs, but most of our population will not be adequately prepared to hold those positions. This will result in higher unemployment rates and more individuals and families unable to enjoy the American promise of economic prosperity.

Alarming Rate of Dropouts and Push-Outs

High school graduation rates peaked at 77 percent in 1969, falling back to 70 percent in 1995 and remaining there into the current decade. Meanwhile, the graduation rate for students of color is thought to be closer to 50 percent (Kirsch, Braun, Yamamoto, and Sum, 2007, p. 2). (A number of alternative methodologies have been developed by educational researchers to estimate high school graduation rates. For a discussion and review of various approaches, see Orfield, 2004.) Among those students who do make it to the twelfth grade and graduate, a majority do so ill equipped for college-level work and the demands of the twenty-first-century workforce (Greene and Winters, 2005; Swanson, 2008). Specific schools, notably those in low-income communities, have a disproportionate percentage of dropouts, very low achievement rates, and are overwhelmingly attended by youth of color (Swanson, 2008).

Every school day, 7,000 U.S. students leave high school without graduating. In 2004, approximately 3.8 million sixteen-through-twenty-four-year-olds were not enrolled in high school and had not earned a high school diploma or alternative credential such as a GED (Laird, DeBell, and Chapman, 2006, p. 6). Given the state of many of the overcrowded schools in this country it is not hard to understand that many students feel these schools are robbing them of their humanity, leaving them with no real choice but to flee. This can be seen as failure on their part or as a sign of resistance.

To make matters worse, there is a growing trend among failing schools to push out students who not do well on standardized tests. Many schools, in response to pressures from test-based accountability regimes to boost overall test scores, may actually encourage poor students to drop out (Figlio, 2006). According to Linda Darling-Hammond (2007b), "perhaps the most adverse unintended consequence of NCLB is that it creates incentives for schools to rid themselves of students who are not doing well, producing higher scores at the expense of vulnerable students." No Child Left Behind sets sanctions for districts that do not meet the proficiency goals in English and math, but it does not set an expectation for a national graduation rate. Bob Wise, former West Virginia governor and current president of the Alliance for Excellent Education, sees this as a flaw in the federal law: "I liken N.C.L.B. to a mile race. Under N.C.L.B., students are tested rigorously every tenth of a mile. But nobody keeps track as to whether they cross the finish line" (Dillon, 2008).

The Predictive Power of Demographics

Schools are not color-blind. They reflect the social inequities that exist in our society. While schools can potentially be the vehicle for access, opportunity, and social justice, unchecked, they will maintain and perpetuate the status quo. Schools serve either to liberate or to indoctrinate. They affect how students see themselves, how they see their role in the world, and how prepared they are to participate in and contribute to society at large. They can be useful in lifting and enlightening individuals and communities to develop agency and change their circumstances, or they can suffocate communities by denying members their rightful voice and place within a democratic society.

In schools, there are overt and covert forces that play out, deciding who has the capacity to learn and who does not. These beliefs shape how we relate to students and their families, as well as how and what we teach students. These cultural forces appear in the policies and practices of institutions as well as in the hearts and minds of the individuals who run them. For example, black boys are more likely to be referred to special education and among the least likely to be identified as gifted (Jackson, 2008). In general, schools are still tracking students by ability groups, creating camps of managers and workers—haves and have-nots—and lowering some young people's chances of being exposed to high-quality instruction, learning experiences, skills, and knowledge and predetermining their social status as adults (McFeat, 2005).

Academic performance outcomes generally reflect broader patterns of inequality that are evident elsewhere in U.S. society (Tatum, 2008; Kozol, 1991; Noguera, 2003b). The social boundaries that separate our communities by race and class also shape the character of schools and neighborhoods. Recent data demonstrate that fifty-five years after the landmark Supreme Court decision to desegregate schools, *Brown* v. *Board of Education,* schools and neighborhoods in many regions across the country remain separate and unequal (Tatum, 2008). There is a demonstrated correlation between the race and class of a community and the quality of education they can expect to receive (Kozol, 1991). For example, in most regions of the country, property values determine the funding for education that is available for children and youth; property values are dramatically lower in most urban communities that serve students of color and in rural communities across the economic spectrum. Given these funding inequities, it should not come as a surprise that the recipients of an under-resourced education are not prepared to perform at the same level as others who have received an adequately funded, quality education (Noguera, 2003a).

The demographic composition of many schools predetermines the challenges faced by those schools and the ways in which policymakers respond (Noguera, 2003a, pp. 13–15). For example, unemployment rates have been in the double digits for people of color for many years and grow more rapidly during periods of economic decline. The lack of affordable housing and the violence in black, Latino, and poor neighborhoods increasingly create a culture of despair among our youth. Many poor or working-class youth of color cannot fathom a future for themselves in the mainstream economy of this country; they see high unemployment rates and the corrosion of their communities as a sign of what their future holds. They experience firsthand the disproportionate effects that drug addiction, homelessness, incarceration, and poverty have on communities of color. Without an education that provides them with the tools they need to deconstruct and critically analyze these conditions, young people are left to wonder about their self-worth and whether failure is inevitable. Most of these young people attend schools in which adults turn a blind eye to these realities, allowing children and young people to grapple with devastating social inequities alone. This disregard creates a culture of neglect that is internalized by students and creates a distance between them, the teachers, and the learning process.

National leaders such as President Obama's Secretary of Education Arne Duncan have begun to refer to education as "the civil rights issue of our generation" (Dillon, 2009). The controversial federal No Child Left Behind Act made closing the racial disparities in achievement the focus of federal education policy. For those paying attention, the existence of separate and unequal schools is hardly a revelation, but shining a spotlight on the least-served children and communities is a powerful step away from lip service to equality and toward an approach that is based on equity. Meeting the needs of these neglected communities and students will strengthen our educational system and our democracy.

The Academic Achievement Gap

At a meeting of a citywide community coalition to close the achievement gap convened in the spring of 2008 by the San Francisco Education Fund, Tony Smith, San Francisco Unified School District's deputy superintendent of instruction, innovation, and social justice, shared the district's five-year strategic plan. In his comments, he named the problem that the plan aimed to address:

> On the surface, San Francisco has one of the highest-achieving school districts in California. Once I looked at the data and saw that we also have the widest gap between the highest- and lowest-performing students, I couldn't reconcile the high degree of satisfaction with the current reality. In San Francisco, we are failing African American, Latino, and Samoan students. And if we are to become better and different fast, I knew that we had to name the issues of racism and classism that permeate the system, from the design of the student weighted formula to our system of school choice. While our goal is to be a service organization that serves every child, I know that we are not equally able nor do we adequately support everyone to fully

use the system. We need to diminish the predictive power of the demographics. It should not matter what zip code you live in or what primary language you speak. Schools matter; they influence the lives of children in and out of school. Schools need to figure out how to support all students to be high-achieving and get twenty-first-century skills. [Smith, 2008]

Smith's observations on San Francisco's challenges could apply in many urban areas nationwide. Measurements of literacy and numeracy demonstrate that the academic performance gaps that exist between white children and children of color are persistent and stable. Data from the National Assessment of Educational Progress (NAEP) reveal that between 1984 and 2004, reading scores among thirteen-year-olds and seventeen-year-olds remained flat, and the achievement gaps were large and relatively stable. For mathematics, the data paint a somewhat different picture. While the mean scores for the nation's thirteen-year-olds and seventeen-year-olds improved minimally, they did so across all groups, with the result that the average size of the black-white and Hispanic-white achievement gaps remained large and relatively stable (Kirsch, Braun, Yamamoto, and Sum, 2007, p. 3). And the picture becomes more bleak when national surveys indicate that large numbers of our nation's population sixteen years of age and older do not demonstrate sufficient literacy and numeracy skills to fully participate in an increasingly competitive work environment. Worse, the data show that these skills are not evenly distributed across groups defined by race/ethnicity, country of birth, and socioeconomic status. In fact, there are substantial differences in average proficiencies among these groups that influence their long-range social, educational, and economic opportunities (Kirsch, Braun, Yamamoto, and Sum, 2007, pp. 3–4). While transforming our educational system will not solve all the challenges associated with existing inequalities, if our society's overall levels of skills and knowledge are not increased and the existing gaps are not addressed, there is little chance that segments of our nation's population will experience economic stability. Unless we are willing to make substantial changes, the next generation of Americans, on average, will be less literate and have a harder time sustaining existing standards of living. Addressing the inequities and lifting the quality of education for the most vulnerable in our society will have the effect of raising the bar for everyone and thereby overhauling a system that presently does not serve anyone well. Working to transform our schools and focusing on closing the achievement gap will ultimately improve the overall system and bring a higher-quality education to all children, even those whose social, racial, and economic status do not place them at a disadvantage.

Unprepared to Serve All Students Well

Latinos and African Americans comprise 80 percent of the student population in schools where 90–100 percent of the population is considered poor, placing them at a educational disadvantage (Orfield and Lee, 2005). As demographic shifts occur beyond these school districts, regions across the country are experiencing dramatic changes in their school populations. The U.S. Census Bureau (2006) projects that by the year 2050, about 50 percent of the U.S. population will be African American, Hispanic, or Asian. The Alliance for Excellence in Education (2009) reports, "This demographic reality and its impact on the future economic and social well-being of the United States is one of many reasons why it is imperative to educate these students to high standards. However, current statistics demonstrate that there is a wide achievement and attainment gap that must be bridged before that goal is met."

During the past two decades, the fastest-growing population of students in public schools is Latino. The percentage of white students has declined, and that of African American students has held steady (U.S. Department of Education, National Center for Education Statistics, 2006). Districts that are already ill equipped to meet the needs of their present population are less likely to respond adequately to the needs of these new Latino communities, which include many English-language learners. English-language learner (ELL) enrollment is soaring in almost every part of the country, including states that have not been home to large ELL populations in recent decades, such as Nebraska, Tennessee, North Carolina, and Georgia. In 2004–05, America's public schools enrolled more than 5 million ELL students whose proficiency in spoken or written English was not yet strong enough to permit them to succeed in an English-language classroom without extra support (Alliance for Excellence in Education, 2009). Yet nationwide, 31 percent of ELL high school students had underqualified teachers who did not have a major, minor, or certification in the field of bilingual education, creating substandard learning circumstances that could negatively affect their achievement (U.S. Department of Education, National Center for Education Statistics, 2002).

The data demonstrate that students in the bottom quartile of achievement are twenty times more likely to drop out of school than those in the top quartile, and test scores for ELL students indicate that they consistently occupy that bottom quartile. For example, in 2005, 31 percent of all eighth graders were found to be at least proficient in reading (that is, reading at roughly an eighth-grade level or higher); for ELLs, the figure was only 4 percent (Editorial Projects in Education, 2008). It should not come as a surprise that English-language learners complete high school at very low rates. Only about 58 percent of Latino students, compared with 78 percent of white students, graduate from high school (Editorial Projects in Education, 2008).

Lack of Role Models and Culturally Relevant Teaching

Because race and class affect the likelihood that students will see their culture represented and endorsed in school, schools have become a source of self-doubt rather than self-development for communities of color (Delpit, 1995). Our public schools, particularly in urban centers across the United States, are attended by a majority of students of color, and their numbers are growing even in places where historically we have not seen communities of color. Many schools and school districts teach a majority of students of color, yet the national pool of teachers remains predominantly white, middle-class, and otherwise unlike and unreflective of the population of students being served. At the same time, the curriculum does not represent or account for the diversity of the students; this affects the connection that students have with their teachers and the relevance they experience in the curriculum. *Small Schools, Big Ideas* author Mara Benitez in discussing her return to her neighborhood in the South Bronx to teach and lead a small school, recalls how important it was for her students to see themselves reflected in her, a Puerto Rican educator working with students from her own community. Benitez recalls, "I intentionally came back to teach in the South Bronx because I thought that I could be most useful working with students whose challenges and life circumstances were very similar to my own. I related to the stories of my students from firsthand experience. I saw myself in them; our stories were intertwined. And in me, in my successes, they saw the hope they needed to keep striving for a different future."

According to Johnston and Wetherill (1998), having role models "is very important to any students who have a marginal status position in society and who are bordering on feelings of alienation and estrangement." Students who do not hold membership in the dominant culture of our society need to see examples of successful adults participating meaningfully in the life of schools and as citizens able to take on the diverse roles available in society.

One of the biggest challenges in creating culturally relevant schools is for teachers to be cognizant of the role they play either to teach students to assimilate to the dominant culture, characterized by competition, greed, and the message that there are limited roles for people of color or from poverty, or to uplift themselves to become enlightened free thinkers prepared to become productive citizens. The latter requires that we understand the political nature of schooling and the role that it has played in perpetuating the status quo and creating a stratified society (Eubanks, Parish, and Smith, 1997).

Lack of Relevance and Rigor

Young people attending schools today report feeling bored and uninterested by the curriculum, claiming that it has nothing to do with their daily existence and is far removed from how they see the world. In a national survey of nearly five hundred dropouts, 50 percent reported that they left school because they were bored and didn't see how what they were learning would get them a job (Bridgeland, DiIulio, and Burke Morison, 2006).

A study funded by the Bill & Melinda Gates Foundation found that while poor skills are among the reasons young people drop out, the lack of engaging, relevant, and challenging curriculum is what is whittling away at the motivation of most students to care about learning and is the central cause of their decision to drop out of school. (Bridgeland, DiIulio, and Burke Morison, 2006). Most schools do not create learning experiences that engage students in dealing with real-world problems. Students do not see themselves in the curriculum and are not being motivated to tap into their own interests and passions. Emphasis is placed on what they do not know instead of what they bring to the table. The focus on memorizing content and passing tests numbs the will of students, making it impossible for them to want to learn in genuine ways. The threat of failing tests and not graduating is not enough to motivate students to stay present and push through the monotony of school.

Students report not feeling challenged by the curriculum, whether it is a set of worksheets that require mere memorization and recall or an Advanced

Placement (AP) course. Whether students are doing less work or more of the same monotonous work, if the curriculum is detached from their lives, separate from real-world experiences and application, and void of intellectual interaction, students will retreat intellectually. They will do the minimum needed to get by or to pass the tests (Bridgeland, DiIulio, and Burke Morison, 2006). AP courses, which are considered college preparatory courses in many schools across the country, continue to define rigor as more of the same: more textbooks to read and more content to memorize, after which students are asked to recall static events, facts, and pieces of compartmentalized information on standardized tests. When asked how this is considered rigorous teaching and learning, instructors tell us that they are preparing students for the long lectures and textbook-driven instruction they will have to endure in most institutions of higher education.

Whether in mainstream courses or AP classes, for the most part, students are still enrolled in classes that keep their thinking at the basic level of recall and memorization, giving them very little opportunity to think critically and share their opinions (Washor and Mojkowski, 2006–2007). Teachers, for the most part, continue to be the "sage on the stage," lecturing and attempting to fill the empty vessels with which they have been entrusted, seldom stopping to ask students what they think or feel or how they see themselves in relationship to the rest of the world. The reality is that we are not preparing students for the world of work, citizenship, or higher education. Without courses that allow students to participate in research projects, write essays, analyze data, or learn the skills needed to enter and succeed in college, it is no wonder that so many youth never make it that far. Those who do often require more than four years to obtain an undergraduate degree, and according to the Alliance for Excellence in Education, because so many students are not learning the skills needed to succeed in college or work while they are in high school, they must take remedial courses once they enter postsecondary education (Amos, 2008). The lack of relevance and rigor results in students' lack of interest in learning, undermining their intellectual growth and their future ability to thrive as adults.

Harsh Disciplinary Policies and Practices

In the worst cases, our schools are more like jails than learning environments. Students are known by a number rather than their name, passed through metal detectors and patted down when they arrive at school, and policed throughout the campus. Those who still attend spend their days shuffling from one overcrowded classroom to another, lucky to find a seat and glean some attention from the teacher. In schools of 1,000, 2,000, and even 5,000 students (common in Los Angeles and Florida, among other places) it is easy to be anonymous and unaccountable. Students feel invisible, with little sense of belonging and connection. A walk through the hallways of a large diverse school demonstrates how it mirrors a segregated society; youth are separated by race and ethnicity. These divisions create an isolating and volatile environment for students from different groups, making it almost impossible to engage in a positive way that crosses the boundaries between groups. And these are the divisions that occur within diverse high schools; many other high schools, as we discussed earlier, are as segregated as they have ever been, creating physical divisions among students of varied backgrounds. Instead of interrupting the racial and class separations that exist among youth, schools pretend to be color-blind, only later addressing the conflicts that arise with punitive interventions.

In recent years, rates of suspension have increased dramatically, from 1.7 million in 1974 to 3.1 million in 2003, and these figures are most dramatic for children of color (Advancement Project, 2005, p. 15). Suspended and expelled children are often left unsupervised and without meaningful educational activities; they fall behind in their coursework, leading to a greater likelihood of disengagement and dropping out. As a result, some struggling students return to their regular schools underprepared while others are permanently locked into inferior educational settings within "alternative" schools (American Academy of Pediatrics, Committee on School Health, 2003). Overly harsh disciplinary policies push students out of mainstream schools and into a pipeline that can lead to the juvenile justice system. Students of color—who are far more likely than their white peers to be suspended, expelled, or arrested for the same kind of conduct at school—are particularly likely to travel down that pipeline from the school disciplinary process to the juvenile justice system (Wald and Losen, 2003). These students find themselves in juvenile detention facilities, many of which provide few educational services, if any. Students who enter the juvenile justice system face many barriers to their re-entry into traditional schools. Many students are propelled further down the pipeline from school to jail, making it impossible for them to catch up and join their peers. The vast majority of these students never graduate from high school (American Civil Liberties Union, 1996).

It seems only fair that, at the very least, schools should help students cope with the harm that society inflicts on them. Yet on a daily basis, the best we seem to be able to do is to control students and punish them when they fail to be controlled. The idea that students will leave who they are or what they are struggling with at the schoolhouse door is fallacy. Students bring the community with them to the classroom, and we need to take advantage of their life experiences as assets for learning about a complex world. Because most of our students learn best when given an opportunity to address problems that are meaningful to them, it makes sense to link their learning to important issues in their lives and to teach them how to address those problems by equipping them with the tools they need to face and work through those problems. Schools should teach students critical thinking and problem-solving skills in order to help them make important decisions about what success means to them, the ways in which they plan to realize their goals, and strategies for overcoming the barriers that may get in the way. Instead, many schools erect additional barriers by creating unfair and rigid structures and policies that sabotage even the most well-intentioned students who are looking for a way out of their circumstances. The fear and distrust—sometimes blatant, sometimes covert—of young people that is evident in the hallways and classrooms of many of the nation's large comprehensive schools make it hard for students to feel connected and accountable. That fear and distrust make it hard for them to learn.

The messages about how important education is and who it is for may be best evidenced in the ways that we disproportionally fund prisons over schools. According to the Forum for Education and Democracy,

> As we under-invest in children, an increasing share of our government funds is spent on incarceration rather than education—a fact highly correlated with education, as most inmates are high school dropouts, and more than half the adult prison population has literacy skills below those required by the labor market. Some states are said to predict the number of prison beds they will need in a decade based on third grade reading scores. This relationship between under-education and incarceration creates a vicious cycle, as lack of adequate investment in early education increasingly reduces the funding available for educating subsequent generations. For example,

as prison enrollments have quadrupled since 1980 state budgets for corrections have increased nearly three times as fast as budgets for education. With one of every 100 Americans now behind bars, several states are now spending as much on corrections as they spend on higher education and the nation is spending about $44 billion annually on corrections. [Forum for Education and Democracy, 2008, pp. 8–9]

It is not a huge leap for young people to wonder whether there is already in place a master plan that anticipates that they will end up in prison or whether there is a conspiracy that creates the conditions for many of them to end up there.

Pockets of Excellence Remain Isolated

Some of the reform efforts we have seen over the last few decades created much-praised pockets of excellence—the magnets, the academies, the school-within-a-school models—that became havens for educators who were craving better working conditions, closer relationships with students, and a place to sharpen their tools and fine-tune their practices. These efforts put a Band-Aid on an antiquated, ailing system, treating only the symptoms, not the causes, and thereby creating escape valves for the same systems to continue. In general, these efforts responded to the first signs of declining enrollment or white flight in urban centers across the country by providing choices for middle-class parents who felt that their children's needs were not being met in the large comprehensive schools and for communities such as Boston that saw busing and the integration of schools as a threat. Educators who left the confines of traditional schools for the flexibility of alternative schools where they could be more innovative responded with great enthusiasm. These efforts sometimes provided relief to underserved students, but in some cases, they predominantly served middle-class white students whose families could advocate for their inclusion in the special program or became dumping grounds for students who had already been written off by the system and were available for experimentation. The well-intentioned educators who led those efforts soon found out that the system gobbled up their vision, watered down their innovations, co-opted their efforts in order to satisfy its own agenda, and eventually returned to the status quo.

Current Educational Policy Climate Does Not Serve All Students

In school districts across the country, the accountability pressures of the No Child Left Behind legislation have pushed school districts to reexamine the effectiveness of the traditional large comprehensive high school model. NCLB was designed to address what the George W. Bush administration described as the "soft bigotry of low expectations" (Spellings, 2008), forcing schools to track data on low-income students and students of color, and holding school districts accountable when they did not demonstrate academic achievement. Under the legislation, schools have to show that all students are making adequate yearly progress or face tough penalties under the law. The law now holds states accountable for making sure that all students achieve academic proficiency, and at best, it brings to light the proof of educational inequity as demonstrated in the lack of proficiency of historically underserved groups of students in comparison with others. Supporters of the law would like us to believe that it is making a real difference in its attempt to narrow the achievement gap between white middle-class students and students of color, but as the NAEP scores demonstrate, not much progress has been made. Originally proclaimed as a bipartisan breakthrough and celebrated by civil rights activists for its focus on raising achievement for students of color, English-language learners, and students with disabilities, NCLB has been met with increasing skepticism and resistance.

The response to the pressure created by NCLB and similar state-based accountability systems is the promotion of standardization over innovation. In schools facing sanctions for declining test scores, making slow or no yearly progress, and receiving no recognition for student achievement, school administrators are paying closer attention to outputs (test scores) rather than the inputs that matter (teaching and curriculum that engages and advances students). If this policy climate continues, districts, afraid of facing sanctions for low-performing schools, will continue to lead by mandating curricula, pacing charts, and anything else that can be used to keep everyone in lockstep.

The policy environment emphasizes an overuse of standardized tests, diminishing the possibility of using more authentic multiple measures to determine the knowledge and skills of students. Therefore, educators, students, and their families get a limited, sometimes skewed, and one-dimensional perspective of what students know and can do. It is impossible to acquire a holistic view of a student from a standardized test. These high-stakes exams are designed to be gatekeepers instead of tools that can be used by schools to adjust their educational programs to meet the needs of students. These exams are used to determine which students are prepared to move on and graduate. In terms of instruction, little is done differently to prepare those who do not pass the exams; they just get more of the same. In some cases, failure to pass the exams allows them even less exposure to academic courses and more exposure to mind-deadening test preparation. Schools are afraid of the sanctions they will receive for low test scores. Consequently, they water down the curriculum and teach to the test, hoping to get better results.

In addition, in the name of equity, all students are tested equally, without regard for the conditions of their learning experiences. According to Linda Darling-Hammond (2003), "In states where 'high stakes testing' is the primary policy reform, disproportionate numbers of minority, low-income, and special needs students have failed tests for promotion and graduation, leading to grade retention, failure to graduate, and sanctions for schools, without efforts to ensure equal and adequate teaching, texts, curriculum, or other educational resources. A new generation of equity lawsuits has emerged where standards have been imposed without attention to educational inequalities. 'Adequacy' litigation in Alabama, California, Florida, New York, South Carolina, and elsewhere has followed recently successful equity lawsuits in Kentucky and New Jersey." Nevertheless, despite such legal action and despite some NCLB alterations designed to moderate the one-size-fits-all nature of the testing requirements, the inequity that Darling-Hammond describes continues unabated.

Historically, poor students and students of color have not done well on high-stakes exams, even in circumstances when alternative teacher-directed assessments demonstrate that they have considerable knowledge and skill levels. Focus on the test creates a situation in which the preparation such students receive to pass high-stakes standardized tests takes the place of higher-level curricula and pedagogy, placing these students at a greater disadvantage when and if they do graduate. This climate does not move us toward solutions. Instead, it threatens to move us further away from the innovations that could help to bring our schools into the twenty-first century and help our students to learn the higher-order thinking and performance skills that would give them real equity, access to postsecondary opportunities, and a real chance to achieve postsecondary success. For more on the practices that CES schools use to create meaningful postsecondary access and opportunity, see Chapter Nine.

Surface Reforms Address Symptoms, Not Causes

Even the most well-intentioned district leaders and school administrators who attempt whole-school or districtwide reforms are not getting at some of the real problems that exist below the surface. While they are motivated by the pressures of NCLB to reexamine their low-performing schools and look more closely at the student achievement data of subgroups that they have historically ignored, they are remiss in acknowledging societal and systemic failure and instead focus on the "deficiencies" of students or teachers.

Scrambling to fill the gaps between expected and actual school performance, district officials often lean on top-down mandates and prescriptive curricula that have yet to produce the results expected. Under the surface of these mandates is the system's distrust of teacher capacity. The suspected lack of teacher preparedness is exacerbated by the misalignment of district-sponsored professional development or in-service programs that fail to address the real need of teachers to grow their craft by working collaboratively on the challenges that they and their students face. Instead, they train from the user manuals of pre-packaged curricula. Most reform initiatives focus on program change rather than the systemic redesign needed to target changes in policy, budget, resource management, and governance in order to change the conditions in which schools operate (Mass Insight Education Research Institute, 2007, p. 4). Popular initiatives such as ending social promotion or doubling the amount of instructional time devoted to math and language arts are premised on the assumption that repeating or doubling up on more of the same failed approaches will somehow lead to different results. These reforms do not address the causes, and because they superficially name the problems and don't provide real solutions, they are short-sighted, short-lived, and misguided silver bullets that at best leave only surface wounds. Sometimes they give an illusion of progress, but in the end, the bad news emerges when the numbers do not rise. At that point, teachers and students are blamed, school boards eventually get frustrated, superintendents leave or are fired, and as soon as the new administration is in place, the cycle of "reform" starts over again.

As these reforms come and go, instead of shifting the power, changing the structures, and opening up new possibilities for transformational change, the culture of the institution swings back toward business as usual, in which the same players are at the table making the decisions and the same academic results emerge from the classroom. The constant churning of new reform initiatives breeds apathy, mistrust, and alienation from the ground up, among educators, school leaders, students, families, and the general public. Teachers are not trusted by systems that use them as scapegoats and blame them for low test scores. In turn, they blame the students and families whom they are entrusted with serving. These failed attempts cause parents, students, teachers, and administrators to lose hope and confidence that the system can ever deliver the goods or will ever acknowledge the profound changes it will have to undergo in order to even come close to serving all children.

Solving the problems of failing schools and districts will not happen with the same remedies that have been used over and over. It is time for creative ideas and thinking that move beyond a deficit model into real action. What we need are efforts that go deeper, to challenge the status quo by disrupting the business-as-usual mentality of systems that are used to moving on autopilot.

Declining Enrollment and the Rise of Charters

The lack of confidence in the ability of districts to spur real change is one of the key reasons for the declining enrollments of many large urban districts. Los Angeles Unified School District lost nearly 30,000 students to charter schools over a short period of time (Rubin and Mehta, 2007); Minneapolis hemorrhaged a quarter of its students over a five-year period (Relerford, 2008); and so goes the national trend. Families are voting with their feet and looking for better options for their children, finding them in private schools or in public charter schools or moving to more affluent districts when they can. But those who don't have the cultural capital or economic power to identify and gain access to better choices for their children remain in the systems that continue to fail them. We see that the impact of declining enrollment faced by many school districts across the country hits these most vulnerable populations the hardest. They have the least voice in how decisions are made and have the most to lose from ill-planned reforms that do not increase student achievement and do not stop the hemorrhaging of students and resources.

Public charter schools were thought to be a way to reform public education by stimulating innovation among educators and community partners. These innovations would somehow pique the interest of public school systems, which would use the charters as learning labs to develop best practices that could be brought back into districts. Instead, the creation and growth of the charter school movement has turned into a competition for families and students, shrinking districts and depleting them of much-needed resources. The innovations taking place in charter schools are mostly happening in isolation; the learning opportunities to exchange best practices and foment additional reform within the system are not happening. Although progressive educators are taking notice, there is no system in place to facilitate that exchange, and in most places, there is no real awareness of charters as a resource for reform.

Often, the instructional practices that charter schools use—the ways that they organize their days or staff their school—are seen as incompatible with the policies and culture of district central offices and their schools. Unfortunately, in most cases, the climate and conditions needed to apply these practices do not yet exist, so many educators do not see the value in establishing professional exchanges with charter school educators. Until these conditions are in place, a charter school movement for public school reform will not be successful in changing the climate and conditions in order to support innovation. The barriers involve restrictions due to union contracts as well as the schools' lack of autonomy in controlling their own resources, making decisions about hiring, and organizing their educational program. (For an example of the areas of autonomy developed by the founders of the Boston Pilot Schools, see the "Areas of Autonomy in Boston Pilot Schools" sidebar in Chapter Three.)

Mark Sanchez, president of San Francisco Unified School District's board of education, is among those with a growing interest in the practices that charters are using to be successful with students and, more generally, in the ways that they use their smallness and autonomy to attract students and serve them well. "We look at the charter schools that are already in our system. These are successful small schools that have a personalized pedagogical model. And we can learn from them." Unfortunately, charter management organizations and districts—organizations that could be tapped to create the structure to support learning exchanges between charters and in-district schools—do not see this as a priority.

Healthy competition between public charters and in-district schools might serve as a motivation for districts to create schools that are more like charter schools, but so far, the only significant sign of that is the creation of the Boston Pilot Schools and, most recently, the Belmont Zone of Choice in Los Angeles (see sidebar). Bob Pearlman, education strategy consultant and past coordinator of educational reform initiatives for the Boston Teachers Union, observes,

> One of the things to look at in terms of the Pilot School phenomenon is that the idea that a union and management would get together and sponsor innovative schools within districts really has not taken hold elsewhere. You don't need state charters to do this kind of innovative work. That the Pilot Schools are an anomaly so far represents the failure of superintendents that lead districts and union leadership to position that kind of reform within the system. As a result, almost everywhere, the charter phenomenon grew and grew, and occupies a substantial niche today. This is not the same as the original dream of charter school improvement, which was to influence local districts and pressure them to get their act together, rather than eroding them.

While districts get their acts together, families are voting with their feet and choosing small, more personalized schools wherever they can find them. Meanwhile, enrollments in many urban school districts continue to decline.

Boston Pilot Schools and Belmont Zone of Choice

The **Boston Pilot Schools** began in 1995 as the result of a unique collaboration between the Boston mayor, a school committee, the superintendent, and the teachers union. They were conceived as a research and development arm of the Boston Public Schools that would promote and further develop CES best practices and be a catalyst for change that could be transferred to the rest of the system. Although they are members of the Boston Public Schools, these twenty schools have freedom to make their own decisions about their budget, staffing, governance, curriculum and assessment, and school calendar. The Center for Collaborative Education, a CES affiliate center, provides technical support, coaching, and network coordination for the Pilot Schools. For more information about the Boston Pilot Schools, visit www.bostonpilotschools.org and www.ccebos.org.

Source: Center for Collaborative Education, 2009.

During the summer of 2006, the Los Angeles Unified School District (LAUSD) and union officials announced that the Pico Union area of East Los Angeles would be home to the **Belmont Zone of Choice**, the first replication of the Boston Pilot Schools model outside of Massachusetts. While many stakeholders were crucial in establishing the Belmont Zone of Choice, the initiative was originated through a partnership with the leadership of LAUSD Local District 4 and the Belmont Educational Collaborative, a powerful group of over forty local community-based organizations. The plan includes the development of up to ten Belmont pilot schools, each with a targeted enrollment of four hundred students and autonomy in regard to budget, staffing, governance, curriculum and assessment, and the school calendar, following the model of the Boston Pilot Schools.

Source: Nesoff, 2007.

Losing Good Teachers to Charter Schools

Good teaching is almost universally recognized as the most important way that schools can affect student achievement. Good teachers want to respond to the individual needs of their students. They chafe under mandated one-size-fits-all instructional approaches. Yet few districts are willing to provide "charter-like" autonomies to teachers and schools in order to facilitate innovation and implementation of research-based best practices. This unwillingness threatens not only students but also teachers. Within three to five years, 50 percent of new teachers leave the profession due to lack of control over their working conditions, lack of resources needed to do a good job with students, and lack of respect for their work (Lambert, 2006). Especially for urban schools that serve poor children of color, this attrition has translated to a dearth of experienced, savvy teachers and, in many situations, has created significant challenges for the recruitment of math and science teachers in particular. However, Dan French, executive director of the Center for Collaborative Education, a CES affiliate center, reports that not to be the case among Boston's Pilot Schools. "Boston Pilots have ample candidates applying to teaching positions," says French. "Teachers are happier when they work in environments where they have greater say about decisions for the school and time to collaborate with colleagues to build their craft." French continues, "Go and visit Pilot Schools, talk with teachers, and you will find that they say,

'Yes, we have to work some extra hours, but we make that decision and it's worth it because we work with fewer kids, work with colleagues more productively, and make decisions that matter.'" The Pilot schools' experience bears out the idea that under the right conditions, teachers will persist, mature in their profession, and bring great skill and experience to serve students with great needs.

Conclusion

Now, more than ever, we need a concerted effort to change our schools and deliver them from the grip of the status quo into a new level of transformation that will both strategically and contagiously spread beyond the "boutique schools" that we have come to admire. We need to raise the consciousness and the hope of teachers who feel stuck in large comprehensive schools where they do not see a glimmer of hope. The system is failing students, families, and teachers—the very people whom we need to draw into this mission for equity, to put grace and power back into the profession of teaching, to situate our schools as true institutions of learning, and to make the promise of leveling the playing field a reality for each student. The stakes are high, and the case in favor of urgency has been made time and time again. We have the data that we need to decide to either respond to the crisis with Band-Aid solutions or swiftly and strategically remove the barriers that get in the way of real transformational change of the kind that can bring about greater equity, the kind that will become institutionalized, grow roots, and push our schools into the twenty-first century.

Creating the Climate and Conditions for Change

chapter
THREE

School districts have exactly the kinds of schools
they're designed to have. If you want something
different to take place at the school level,
something different has to take place at the district.

—Eric Nadelstern, New York City Department of Education

A major lesson that CES has drawn from our twenty-five years of practice is that change at the school site level is not enough. We have seen that isolated schools operating at the periphery of school systems cannot make a significant impact on the status quo. Though many successful schools have been established by using the CES Common Principles, we have learned that in order to create long-term educational equity, schools engaged in change must use their success with students to spur change among other schools and leverage change within their system.

CES educators have sought out ways to take the school change work that started decades ago to a deeper level. They have ventured beyond their school sites and created networks and systems of schools that represent new approaches to organizing and transforming public education. CES has organized exemplary small schools into professional learning communities that provoke and inspire dramatic changes in schools and districts. These have helped to push down the

43

walls of traditional reform and create a road map for real transformation of schools and the systems on which they depend.

Cultivating Professional Learning Communities

One of the most powerful elements of the CES approach to transforming education is the creation of professional learning communities, which are exemplified by the CES Small Schools Network (CES SSN). The opportunity for educators to collaborate in professional learning communities and networks of schools in their districts and regions, in which practitioners can learn from each other and have the kind of ongoing conversations that can bring about transformational change is rare and desperately needed in public education. Educators see a value in being affiliated with other like-minded practitioners and schools in order to share practices, reflect, and help each other grow. Creating opportunities for educators to plan innovations together and to adopt research-based best practices that have been successful in other places has produced results. We have learned that using a discourse of transformation creates changes that produce access, opportunity, and equity for all our children. In the CES SSN, teachers and principals from district, charter, and independent schools are willing to engage each other to create ways to share practices and learn from each other's expertise and experience. Central to their learning is the conclusion that to truly engage and serve all students well, the conditions that exist in our schools as a whole have to be transformed. They have learned that in order to participate in that transformation, a sustained critical discourse among educators that addresses why the inequitable conditions persist and an examination of their own roles in promoting equity is essential. They have learned the value and power of being affiliated with a group of like-minded educators who are working toward educational equity and that a commitment to continuous improvement is required if equity is ever going to happen. These exchanges among educators ignite the need to see and do things differently and to collectively demand and work for change.

Change Options for Public Schools

Presently, there are three change options that are available to schools within the public education system if they are interested in transforming the ways that they serve students and families and moving beyond the norms of traditional public education:

1. In-district innovative schools that work "under the radar" within the system
2. Charters that work outside the system of the traditional public schools
3. In-district innovative schools that have charter-like areas of autonomy—agreements that allow them to work around the internal structures of the school system

In-District Schools Working "Under the Radar"

In reality, districts lack the capacity to monitor compliance across schools, so many schools fly under the radar by maintaining decent scores on standardized exams and keeping incidents of violence low and attendance high. Many schools are making reforms undercover, covertly steering away from district mandates and incorporating more and more innovations. Once in a while, open-minded central office administrators might even collude with these schools and keep them buffered from the mainstream. Such was the case during the career of Mara Benitez, one of *Small Schools, Big Ideas'* authors, as a teacher and administrator working in New York City. Benitez worked for two such superintendents: first, Stephen Phillips and, later, Richard Organisciak, both reformers who trusted practitioners and were interested in creating the climate and conditions for schools to enjoy some autonomy to create and implement the mission of their school as long as the schools did not call attention to themselves. As a teacher and director of a small school in the South Bronx, Benitez thought it was a reasonable request and a decent deal. While this stability was maintained, the schools were safe and their methodologies showed real results in student achievement. Yet these situations remained fragile and the lessons learned seldom became institutionalized into new practices that affected the culture of schools across the district. The changes, lessons, and good work that take place under these sometimes silent agreements cannot become permanent unless policies are created to sustain the changes and outlive the inevitable turnover in leadership at both school and district levels.

Charter Schools Working Outside the System

Charter schools, as originally conceived by Ray Budde and promoted by Albert Shanker, were intended to help reform the public school system (American Federation of Teachers, 2008). The idea was that charters would use their flexibility and freedom from the traditional public school system to create the kind of educational innovation that would invigorate and stimulate the broader system. Instead, many charter schools have played a minimal role in reforming school districts. They have limited their role to providing competition for school districts. Unless a channel for the professional exchange of policies, structures, and instructional practices between district and charter schools—and districts and charter management organizations—is created, we will not realize this objective.

We want to learn from charter schools in the CES SSN such as Parker Charter Essential School in Devens, Massachusetts; Leadership High School in San Francisco; Greenville Technical Charter High School in Greenville, South Carolina; and Amy Biehl High School in Albuquerque, New Mexico, among others, that have had excellent results with students and have intentionally built relationships and opened their doors to educators from district schools with the hope of infusing some of what has worked well in their schools into district schools. They are committed to transforming education on a larger scale in order to create more accessible, equitable, and powerful places of learning for all children. While they are interested in sharing their practices and creating opportunities to collaborate, they have not consistently been able to find such opportunities within the districts in their regions.

In-District Schools with Autonomy Similar to That of Charter Schools

In 1994, Boston established a set of in-district charter schools through collective bargaining. The Boston Pilot Schools, like charter schools, were granted a high level of freedom from district regulations and a more flexible contract with the teachers' union. The decentralization of power over curriculum, schedules, hiring, and resource management generated opportunities for these schools to attract highly qualified teachers, build a collective vision, and unleash their creativity in powerful ways that have resulted in improved academic outcomes for the students they serve (Center for Collaborative Education, 2007).

In a major reform effort of the Department of Education (DOE) in New York City, almost all 1,500 schools are divided into over seventy networks. School leaders are empowered to affiliate with schools of their choice and to select network leaders to shepherd their work as a network. Vince Brevetti, network leader for Empowerment School Organization Network Number 3, describes his role and the structure of networks within the New York City public school system: "My network of twenty-seven schools (eighteen elementary, including two charters, and nine secondary) affiliated on the basis of wanting their schools' missions actively respected, particularly in the face of increasing central mandates, and on the basis of recognizing the need to control as many curriculum and assessment decisions as possible. My role is to facilitate the process for schools to implement their missions while at the same time adhere to the demands of the system. I see myself as a buffer, an interpreter of the system and an advocate for the integrity of the schools." For example, when the DOE announced that all schools needed to administer five standardized interim assessments (IAs) per year, the schools in Brevetti's network pushed for a "design your own" option. "Administering IA was not the objection," says Brevetti. "However, we insisted that they be of our own making, aligned with our schools' curricula, and with the capacity to deliver formative assessment information." With support from within the DOE and a careful rollout, the schools in Brevetti's network created three IAs in English language arts and two in mathematics. The positive student data and survey results allowed them the space to continue into what is now the third year of implementation. Brevetti observes, "My job was to find points of alignment between what the DOE wanted and what was compatible with our schools' missions."

The Boston Pilot Schools and the New York City Empowerment Schools have created a protected space for innovation. Without those agreements, these schools would not be allowed to evolve and mature; they would spend all of their time pushing on their system and would lose their focus on instruction and their energy to persist. When practitioners become embattled with the very system that helped to create their school and allow them to exist, the school community's energy may be derailed and eventually drained from the fight.

Much good work is already happening in districts across the country. The question is whether school systems are permeable enough so that the good practices that are growing in schools will seep into the central offices of school districts and spread systemwide. The missing ingredient in most cases is a clear purpose and deliberate actions to make substantive changes that will transform culture, practices, policies, and relationships across the board.

Intentionally leveraging the pockets of excellence created by networks of exemplary small schools by establishing professional learning communities within and across these schools helps to shift the instructional culture of a district and build the capacity of its educators. Creating clusters of schools that are invested in being engaged in a mission to equitably serve all students well and giving them the space and support to improve can help set the stage for change within a district. To operate within this space, schools will need to be held accountable to a set of clear expectations. They will need a broader set of indicators and multiple measures that look at successful inputs and outputs. Districts will need to rethink the latitude that they give school leaders in regard to the allocation and distribution of resources within their school.

Disruptive Innovations

June Jordan School for Equity, a small public school in San Francisco, represents a form of disruptive innovation. The existence of such schools within districts requires a certain level of persistence and endurance as they push for change from the inside. These schools experience the rough edges of a system that wants to accommodate change without really changing its form, the rules, or the players. Shane Safir, founder and former co-principal of June Jordan, and now a coach at the Bay Area Coalition for Equitable Schools, describes the school's relationship with the district:

> The fact that June Jordan grew out of a community-based movement that presented a strong vision of redesigned schools created a tension with the district. There were philosophical differences about how to best approach student learning, particularly around assessment. We just had a different vision than the district leadership. While we had allies in the district and on the school board, it was still very challenging to run the school before the board passed the Small Schools by Design policy that allows for more flexibility. The tension was fundamental to our identity as a school that pioneered a new way

for other schools, but it drained attention and resources from the internal development that needed to happen. We spent a lot of time negotiating autonomies, time spent not in classrooms or dealing with instruction.

If we transfer aspects of the notion that Professor Clayton Christensen of the Harvard Business School calls "disruptive innovation" (Christensen, Raynor, and Anthony, 2003, pp. 1–4) from a business scenario (Putz and Raynor, 2005), four potential strategies for seeding and incubating change within school districts emerge:

1. Create a parallel process for developing and shaping disruptive ideas, one that acknowledges their distinctive features.

2. Do not evaluate with the same screens and lenses the company already uses.

3. To address challenges facing managers, disruption theory prescribes using a separate organization to incubate the work.

4. Create a separate business plan for this work that is navigated by managers who understand how to use it.

Translating the experiences of the corporate world, we can adapt these strategies and use them for our own purposes to create a space with the climate and conditions needed for schools to develop innovative ideas and practices within the boundaries of public school districts. When a mechanism is established for learning from the incubated work, that space can help stimulate further growth in the system. The idea is not to create a set of elite schools nor an impenetrable bubble; these schools need to be in the best position to share their practices and ideas. The intention is to create peer-to-peer and school-to-school opportunities for learning, so that the innovations can spread beyond the walls of the schools that have taken the initial lead. The idea is to carve out a space so that the ideas, the practices, and the new attitudes about how to equitably educate students, engage families, and use resources can permeate a system that inevitably may experience these as foreign and even threatening. A deliberate use of the space would create a parallel structure that would afford the larger system an opportunity to experiment with the changes the organization wants to embrace in order to become healthier, more effective, and more productive for the children and families it serves. The space could help the district architects fashion a redesign that could later be brought to scale.

Modeling Change from Within

Communities and districts across the country are fostering the growth of a critical mass of practitioners, families, policymakers, and community members who can see for themselves in their own contexts how their schools have become increasingly personalized, intellectually vibrant, high-performing places of learning for students and adults. More and more small schools are becoming lab schools that are embedded in school districts and used to demonstrate best practices in action. Through their exemplary work, other schools and educators see what is possible. Their presence in a district demystifies the change process and encourages others to pursue new, more effective ways of organizing their schools and more powerful instructional approaches. These small schools encourage a shift in attitudes about how to engage parents and community in the business of educating their children. When district leaders see the work of these schools as an opportunity for the entire district to learn and transform itself, reform has a stronger potential to take hold and grow across the district. The momentum also makes it possible for these sometimes fragile schools to get protection so that they can continue to improve their work and share it with others.

The story of Quest High School in Humble, Texas, is an example of how an innovative small school can help to influence the district to create the conditions for change to happen throughout the district. Kim Klepcyk, principal of Quest, a public CES Mentor School, talks about the role that the district's superintendent, Guy Sconzo, sees for Quest in their system. "Our superintendent calls us his research and development school all the time," says Klepcyk. "At our graduation, he spoke at length about the role of Quest in our district and thanked all of our staff, our facilitators, and our parents for what we do, not just for our school but for our entire district in terms of leading them down a path of making things better for all kids. He gets it that our mission is not just being a great small school but also being an impetus for reform for the larger system." Quest, like many other small schools in the country, has positioned itself to serve as a laboratory of learning. With a commitment to continuous improvement, the school models a culture of learning that extends from students to every adult in the building—a culture of sharing knowledge and making meaning together.

Pushing Change Beyond the Walls of the School

In the preceding example, the support that Quest receives in order to do its transformational work comes from the top. Because the practices and policies that Quest uses at the site level have not become institutionalized across the district, its existence remains vulnerable and dependent on the fate of district and school leadership.

The three new small schools that have come out of Tyee High School's conversion from a large school to three small schools in SeaTac, Washington, near Seattle, share a similar circumstance of real change at the school level that is supported by the top but is not necessarily in alignment with the district as a whole. Tyee High School's conversion started a new chapter of reform within the Highline School District. Joan Ferrigno, principal of Odyssey, one of the three Essential small schools born out of the Tyee conversion, carried the charge of equity from the inception of the conversion into the mission of her school. She believes that the district's attempt to support the new small schools would be best served by working on becoming a more equitable organization:

> For me, equity means figuring out a way to serve all students. An example is that we are really committed to inclusion at Odyssey because we believe that every student here deserves an equitable educational experience. We don't track students by their perceived abilities; instead, our courses are designed to teach each student how to use their mind well. Based on that principle, we are raising the intellectual bar for all students and leveling the playing field by making sure that students have access to the learning opportunities and experiences they need. When it comes to the district, equity would mean that we'd have to straighten out the imbalances. Funding-wise, there are imbalances; staffing-wise, there are imbalances; and so, in my role as a school principal, I am really pushing [the district administration] to use an equity lens to look at their practices systemwide. The district's equity agenda would be best served by mirroring our efforts at the site level.

In order for the changes in schools to last, grow roots, and spread, the system has to catch up by absorbing some of the lessons learned at the sites and redesigning itself to better support and sustain the changes on the ground.

Role of Districts in Facilitating Change

The skill and the will must be present at the district level to create the climate and conditions needed to facilitate the growth and sustainability of change. According to Steve Jubb, former executive director of the Bay Area Coalition for Equitable Schools, one of the architects of a major district reform effort in Oakland, California, the district can be a facilitator of change: "The role that the district office can play is to ensure the equitable distribution of resources by ensuring that a maximum amount of money flows to schools to do the work that schools need to do, and to facilitate the learning among schools by creating a professional learning community within schools and across districts to get teachers what they need to continue to grow their craft."

Mapleton Public Schools (MPS), a district outside Denver, Colorado, has concluded that schools cannot change unless districts change the ways that they do business with schools. Using the CES Common Principles as its guide, Mapleton sought to transform its entire system of schools. In 2001, the urgent need for better academic results motivated the wholesale restructuring of all Mapleton high schools. This wall-to-wall redesign of the high schools ignited the need for substantive changes at all levels of the system. Reflecting on the district's CES legacy, Mapleton superintendent Charlotte Ciancio notes,

> The principles of the Coalition provide a proven path for getting to student achievement. They match our beliefs about how kids learn, about choice options, and about what we're trying to become as a community. The complexity of the principles causes a school district to change; you have to be willing to have difficult conversations and change practices. You can't do high school reform without reforming a school district. You can't go down the path successfully without adjusting the way you do your work. Most importantly, you can no longer only lead from the top. It becomes the district's responsibility and superintendent's role to engage everyone. You have to adopt the belief of 'student as worker, teacher as coach' in a district context. My job as superintendent is to facilitate the system, not direct the system. [Davidson, 2005]

In the case of the Mapleton schools, purposeful school transformation has led to the creation of a "road map to reinvent the district," as Ciancio put it. Mapleton continues to sustain its drive to work through the hard questions at all levels of the organization and is making great strides.

Superficial changes can occur in schools while keeping other pieces of the system intact, but the transformation of schools cannot be sustained without transforming the systems on which they depend. The power dynamics that keep schools under tight centralized control by districts must change in order to unleash the power of principals and teachers to take responsibility for the teaching and learning that takes place in their building. As well, districts must better define the goals to which they are holding schools accountable and more effectively provide the support and resources that schools need to meet those goals (see "Districts as Facilitators of Change" sidebar). According to Ted Sizer, "The purpose of the district is to channel the resources available, recruit the best people we can find to be school leaders, hold them accountable for results, support them, incent them, and protect them. District leaders should demand of each school clear goals, these within a broad district (and state) framework, and a sensible means to assure these goals. And districts (and state authorities) should sensitively inspect these schools on the basis of these goals" (Coalition of Essential Schools, 2005b).

Districts as Facilitators of Change: Redesign Elements

These strategic elements would bring districts closer to becoming facilitators of change:

- Create a different and more efficient use of the resources they control.
- Shift the paradigm of the relationships between the central office and schools to position the central office in service of school sites.
- Update operations systems and practices at the district level to meet twenty-first-century standards.
- Establish a broader set of indicators and multiple measures that examine successful inputs and outputs.
- Reduce the bureaucracy at the central office by decentralizing operations systems—for example, hiring, purchasing, and budgeting can be done at the site level.
- Populate the district office with leaders and administrators who are trained in collaborative leadership approaches.
- Make decision-making processes more transparent.

Autonomy and Accountability

Principals and teachers should be held accountable for increasing learning outcomes for all students. However, to achieve those goals and best serve the needs of their students, they need more autonomy and flexibility. Eric Nadelstern, currently chief schools officer at the New York City Department of Education, shares his perspective on autonomy as a prerequisite:

> I believe that the people closest to kids and the classroom—principals, teachers in consultation with parents, and, at high school level, the kids themselves—are the people who are best positioned to determine what kids need to learn, how they can best learn it, and how to assess that learning. This needs to be scalable to the entire school system. There is no school that would not benefit from this relationship, even if it means that as a result of this construct, it was determined within a few years that a school doesn't deserve to exist and should be closed down to give other people an opportunity to do a good job. Even that is a valuable contribution. [Coalition of Essential Schools, 2005a]

To foster and accommodate school transformation, districts need to make numerous changes in the ways that they operate in relationship to schools, and perhaps none is more important than creating more autonomy at the site level. Giving schools autonomy over their hiring, budgets, facilities, governance, and curriculum similar to that enjoyed by charter schools has the potential to unleash creativity and innovation and thereby increase student achievement. Dan French, executive director of the Center for Collaborative Education, a CES affiliate center located in Boston, makes the case for autonomy at the school level as a prerequisite for success, commenting, "All of the autonomies are indispensable and interdependent, and the autonomies help you think more expansively about how schools can be shaped. If you want scheduling autonomy but don't have staffing autonomy—that is, if you don't have the right staffing pattern and job descriptions—you will be limited in what you can do. If you want to shift all staffing into the core academic curriculum that all kids take, with streamlined electives and teachers in dual role as advisors, but don't have budget autonomy, you have limits." (See the "Areas of Autonomy in Boston Pilot Schools" sidebar for descriptions of the areas of autonomy in which the Boston Pilot Schools operate.)

Areas of Autonomy in Boston Pilot Schools

The following five points constitute the "autonomies" that members of the Boston Pilot School network are granted in exchange for strong performance on a wide variety of measures. These autonomies have served as a model for other districts' efforts to create a separate zone of innovation and improvement.

Staffing: Pilot Schools have the freedom to hire and excess their staff in order to create a unified school community. Teachers should play a significant role in staff hiring. Pilot Schools:

- Decide on the staffing patterns and work assignments that create the optimal learning environment for students.

- Hire staff who best fit the needs of the school, regardless of his/her current union status (member of the district or not, although every teacher hired becomes a member of the Boston Teachers Union bargaining unit).

Budget: Pilot Schools have a lump sum per-pupil budget that allows the school to decide on spending that best provides programs and services to students and their families. Pilot Schools:

- Have a lump sum per-pupil budget, the sum of which is equivalent to other district schools within that grade span and includes salaries, instructional materials, consultants, and more.

- Choose either to purchase identified discretionary district services or to not purchase them and include the per-pupil cost in the school's lump sum per-pupil budget.

Curriculum and Assessment: Pilot Schools have freedom to structure their curriculum and assessment practices to meet students' learning needs. While all Pilot Schools are held accountable to federal- and state-required tests, including the Massachusetts Comprehensive Assessment System (MCAS), these schools are given the flexibility to determine the school-based curriculum and assessment practices that best prepare students for federal and state assessments. Pilot Schools:

- Are freed from local district curriculum requirements—they can choose what content to cover and how to cover it.

- Set their own promotion and graduation requirements, although they must be comparable in rigor to the district requirements. Pilot Schools have an emphasis on competency-based, performance-based assessments.

- Decide on professional development in which faculty engage.

Governance: Pilot Schools have the freedom to create their own governance structure that has increased decision-making powers over budget approval, principal selection and evaluation, and programs and policies, while being mindful of state requirements, including MCAS and school councils. Pilot Schools have governing boards that assume increased governing responsibilities, while being mindful of state mandates, including the following:

- Set and maintain the school vision.

- Select, supervise, and annually evaluate the principal, with final approval by the superintendent in all cases.

- Approve the annual budget.

- Set their own policies that the school community feels will help students to be successful.

Schedule: Pilot Schools have the freedom to set longer school days and calendar years for both students and faculty in accordance with their principles or school reform models. In particular, research supports a correlation between increased faculty planning time spent on teaching and learning and increased student achievement. Scheduling that allows for summer and school-year faculty planning time contributes to a more unified school community and education program. Pilot Schools:

- Increase planning and professional development time for faculty.

- Organize the school schedule in ways that maximize learning time for students.

Source: Center for Collaborative Education, 2006a, pp. 7–8.

We believe that as schools increase their ability to meet the needs of their students, they should gain the flexibility needed to accomplish those results in ways they deem appropriate and effective. With demonstrated capacity, schools should assume more direct programmatic, professional, and financial responsibility for management of their instructional program. Ultimately, schools are responsible and should be accountable for achieving results with their students. Schools should then be supported in developing and implementing plans for improving student learning. In CES schools that participate in the SSN, principals work in collaboration with staff, family members, and students to prepare plans that outline their goals, objectives, and activities. For example, Boston Pilot Schools are the only schools in the district that go through a five-year quality review process. The Pilot Schools share a common set of benchmarks that are criteria for high-performing schools. The Pilot Schools create a portfolio of evidence based on those benchmarks and bring in an external team of reviewers who spend three days in the schools, shadowing and interviewing students and teachers, sitting in on classes and meetings, and reviewing the portfolio. These visitors evaluate the school in benchmark areas and present their findings and recommendations to a joint district-union steering committee. The school is then required to develop a plan of action based on the report (Center for Collaborative Education, 2007).

Many CES schools struggle with districts over flexibility in curriculum, instruction, and assessment. In order to create a more personalized learning environment for students, schools need the freedom to propose alternate forms of curriculum and assessment that are aligned with the needs of the particular students they serve. In CES small schools, using common standards and working backward from desired student outcomes, teachers create their own curriculum and use various kinds of formative performance-based assessments that are aligned with that curriculum to provide more authentic insight into what students know and can do. If schools do not have autonomy over curriculum and assessment, they are unable to structure educational programs that fulfill the mission of their school.

Richard Alonso, superintendent of Los Angeles Unified School District 4, reflects on his work with the Belmont Educational Collaborative, a grassroots ad hoc group that drove the creation of the Belmont Zone of Choice, a small schools initiative in the Pico Union neighborhood that is fashioned after Boston Pilot

Schools. Alonso shares the reasons that motivated him and others to seek ways to create autonomous small schools within his district:

> I knew we needed the ability to create small, autonomous schools within my local district to become part of the portfolio of options. Our area is so densely populated that I have seventeen charters in my area alone. Of course, they're going to take the kids and the parents who are most eager to get a personalized education. So I said, "Why do people have to leave the district to do something different? If my schools are the lowest-performing in the Belmont area, I need to do something drastically different. So that concept and that plan got me in trouble because that is not what the superintendent wanted to hear. But it was what the board members wanted. So I kept my job, but I had to go underground in terms of letting the Belmont Educational Collaborative push the effort. I don't know of any other major reform in L.A. Unified that had the UTLA [United Teachers of Los Angeles] teachers behind it, the administrator's union behind it, parents behind it, elected offices behind it, and community-based organizations behind it. Everyone felt that we couldn't continue to put Band-Aids on the situation. We really need to look at new thinking that is based on research and has proven results.

In the case of District 4 in Los Angeles, the changes that were implemented helped to facilitate academic growth across all groups of students, especially among the most vulnerable students, and would help the district reinvent the role of the central office and the systems and operations that get in the way of schools making progress with students.

In order for districts to free up schools to have greater control over teaching and learning, real dialogue has to take place with unions to get them on board with new policies that would grant schools more discretion over staffing patterns and hiring. The greatest changes take place in the working conditions of teachers, and this fact could ultimately affect the collective bargaining unit. A key to the Boston Pilot Schools' successful start was that union and management collaborated to sponsor innovative schools within their own district. Dan French describes the relationship between the district and the teachers union that made the Boston Pilot Schools agreement a reality: "It's important for unions to know that the pilot model is a creation of district-union partnership. It's a teacher empowerment model more than anything else that shifts the locus of decision making to the local school level, putting decisions about students in the laps of administrators, teachers, and parents."

We need districts to collaborate with unions to create teacher contracts that support professional working conditions that achieve greater student performance in ways similar to what took place in Boston and what is happening within the Belmont Zone of Choice in Los Angeles (Nesoff, 2007). These contracts should require teacher involvement in developing school improvement plans as well as budget, personnel, and professional development plans. The contracts should give principals and schools the ability to hire teachers who fit the goals and mission of their school without regard to seniority and permit teachers to be evaluated based on their students' academic performance. These agreements should embody a framework for collaboration between the teachers union, the schools, and the district that is driven by student achievement.

Whoever Controls the Money Controls the Decisions

Two important conditions for school transformation are schools' ability to receive adequate resources to serve the needs of the children in their charge and schools' ability to have the autonomy to manage and allocate resources—both monetary and personnel—to help them achieve the mission of their school. To different degrees, various districts across the country have experimented with more equitable practices of channeling the distribution of resources from the central office to the school site. Others have even taken larger steps to decentralize control over those resources and place more authority and accountability over their allocation and management in the hands of certain schools and school leaders.

The strategy that has been most effective and that we feel is best suited for schools and districts interested in creating educational equity is the weighted student formula (WSF). The premise behind the WSF is simple: in order for schools to best serve the diverse set of students in their charge, they need to have adequate and appropriate resources. Districts already design school budgets based on per-pupil amounts that are determined by the state and based on the number of students enrolled at the school. Students' daily attendance forms the basis of a school's budget.

With a WSF, school budgets would reflect not only per-pupil funds but the allocation of additional funds determined by individual student needs. For example, in the late 1990s, Seattle's school board implemented a weighted student-focused funding system that allocates resources based on each student's educational needs. Certain students receive a higher per-student spending allotment due to a variety of factors (for example, low income, low achievement, learning disabilities, or limited English-speaking abilities), and resources follow the student (Education Commission of the States, 1999, p. 34). The idea that resources would follow students to whatever school they attend is quite revolutionary, going beyond an "all parts are equal" norm to a stance that recognizes that those who need more should get more—the essence of the difference between equality and equity. This concept is an important step in school transformation that takes the original mandate of public education—equal opportunity and access—to a level that begins to respond to the diverse needs of the majority of students being served in public schools today. The WSF is a way for the system to grant the resources needed to give and receive a quality education to everyone.

Unfortunately, the dominant discourse in school communities has prevented many from understanding and embracing the ideals behind this strategy. For instance, tensions arise when middle-class families question whether their children are being put at a disadvantage with the new formula and so in some districts, the political controversies about the weights, who decides their values, and how the pie of resources is divided has stalemated the process and the potential of this measure.

In addition to the per-pupil monies that each school receives, there are categorical funds, funds that are earmarked by the state or the federal government for specific populations. In some ways, state legislatures already use a weighted formula to distribute these funds, and these formulas are similar in some cases to those that have been used by districts to devise the weighted student formulas (Ouchi, 2003, p. 90). The categorical monies are controlled by the district and used to hire personnel who deliver services to school sites. In most cases, schools do not see this money directly, nor do they see the significance of the services, given that the services are often disjointed, spread thinly across the district, and, in most cases, not aligned with the programmatic or instructional needs of the school.

The Edmonton school district in Alberta, Canada, is a classic example of a district that used the WSF as a reform mechanism. During the 1976–77 school year, Edmonton was the first large North American urban district to introduce the WSF (Ouchi, 2003, p. 88). The Edmonton Public Schools' restructuring effort illustrates much of what we propose in order to put schools on a faster path toward real transformation. While there have been other attempts at implementing a WSF in cities like Seattle, San Francisco, Oakland, and Houston (Ouchi, 2003, p. 88), none has established the kind of bold changes that Edmonton continues to exemplify. As described in the November 1999 Education Commission of the States report *Governing America's Schools: Changing the Rules,* some of the major changes the Edmonton school administration made in its governance roles in relationship to schools and the management of their resources include the following:

> The Edmonton school district establishes goals for education and guiding principles for management processes. It defines results, indicators and improvement targets, gathers data and uses this information to make decisions. Results focus on customer satisfaction and student performance. Together with the teachers' organization, the district has drawn up a simple yet powerful contract. The central office focuses on holding schools accountable for achieving student results. It also provides customer-driven service to schools in quasi-open market conditions. The central office also identifies, develops and retains good principals and replaces ineffective ones. Authority for program design and resource allocation at the school level rests with the principals, who use a variety of means to engage colleagues and the community in decision making related to district-defined results. Principals have the resources and authority to provide overall direction for instruction, and they are accountable for achieving improvement targets. Teachers have many opportunities for professional development and leadership. [Education Commission of the States, 1999, p. 19]

Edmonton exemplifies the kind of transformation for which we are calling—transformation that demands modifications in the way that districts govern their schools, including the amount and extent of authority given to principals over decisions that involve the use of funds and the deployment of staff members. American public school systems should strive for the balance that Edmonton has created between accountability and autonomy. A decade ago, the Education Commission of the States used this example to illustrate the kind of governance systems and policies that would help to put American schools on a trajectory toward raising the quality of the education we deliver in this country. The Education Commission of the States stated, and we agree, that

> in a system of public education certain decisions most appropriately belong with schools and parents. Within this system, schools have the authority to develop a culture focused on student learning and achievement. The individual school:
>
> • Develops, implements and continuously fine-tunes plans for improving student learning
>
> • Hires, evaluates and fires teachers and other school personnel
>
> • Writes its own budget and receives funding on a weighted per-pupil basis
>
> • Raises private revenue (up to a limit)
>
> • Allocates resources as it sees fit
>
> • Determines staffing patterns and class sizes
>
> • Determines employees' salaries
>
> • Purchases services from the district or from outside providers [Education Commission of the States, 1999, p.19]

In this schema, the district creates an environment that allows schools to focus on teaching and learning and individual schools are held accountable for results. Schools with the capacity to achieve district standards continue to "gain freedom to accomplish results in ways their staffs deem professionally responsible and demonstrably effective" (Education Commission of the States, 1999, p. 19).

Redesign efforts need to reconsider their district's budgeting models, which frequently are inflexibly designed for the operation of large schools. Los Angeles's Richard Alonso highlights this change in budgeting authority as one of the initial changes a district committed to transformation needs to make:

> The first change has to be budgeting, because the whole concept of budgeting large, comprehensive schools is based on formulas, and so if you have X amount of kids, the formula says you get one of these

and one of those, and that's not going to work. We're proposing that schools get to treat their monies almost like a block grant, so we let the school make decisions about how to use the money. The funding model for comprehensive high schools will not allow us to successfully fund small schools because we're used to funding schools with 5,000 students. When you look at huge numbers in comparison with small schools, if they are funded through the same funding chart, small schools wouldn't be getting any resources, because they aren't even on the chart.

How does this play out? The principal of a school with four hundred students that is designed to create a more personalized, academically focused school that will support all its students in gaining entrance to and succeeding in four-year colleges, particularly historically underserved students such as those in Los Angeles's Pico Union neighborhood, runs into big problems. For example, if the formula requires five hundred students for every one counselor, this school is not getting a counselor. Any reform effort that doesn't address this resource gap will not be sustainable.

Policies That Promote Transformation

An important condition for change involves establishing a policy climate that will provide clear direction for district leadership. The role of policymakers at all levels, especially the district level, is essential. Policymakers' role requires organizing to engage elected officials in creating the right policy climate for innovation to serve an equity agenda on behalf of all students. Creating policies that promote and support the transformation of schools for the purpose of eliminating the achievement gap can have huge implications for the culture of a district as a whole and lasting effects on student outcomes. Policy makes it possible to secure a mandate that has a greater probability of becoming institutionalized.

In 2007, the board of education of the San Francisco Unified School District (SFUSD) passed the Small Schools by Design policy. This community-motivated policy was coupled with a board's willingness to use its power to hire Carlos Garcia, a forward-thinking superintendent, to create traction on soil seeded for change. The change process in San Francisco demanded effort at both grassroots and policy levels. The story exemplifies the need for skilled leaders who have the will to implement reform policies that address the achievement and resource gaps faced by urban school districts. While a pro-reform policy climate can set the stage, district leadership has to be willing to take it all the way.

"When we passed the Small Schools by Design policy, people saw a glimmer of hope. We had passed a similar policy seven years ago, but we didn't have the central office support in place to make sure that reform policies were implemented. Small schools are not something that the district is pulling out of left field and shoving down people's throats," says Mark Sanchez, president of the SFUSD board of education. Sanchez comments that unlike some district initiatives,

> this is something that people want. The San Francisco Organizing Project, which is a group of forty congregations in the city, they've been pushing for it. There's been a lot of research. We had an inclination to do something different for the populations of kids that have not been served. The only way you can have this kind of policy be really successful is if you have the top and the bottom moving in the same direction. Because when you just have energy from the bottom up and total resistance from the top, you can't get the change you want. I think we have the best-case scenario right now. We did the biggest thing we could do as a board by hiring a superintendent who's willing to implement the Small Schools by Design policy and has attracted good people who want to work with him, and now we really feel like it's going to happen because the team has been assembled. I think we're in a really good position to make long-term changes that will bear fruit and lead to higher academic achievement for kids that have historically not gotten their fair share.

The decision to motivate a district to put a premium on finding ways to increase access and equity with the intention of increasing student engagement and achievement has to be owned by everyone from the classroom to the boardroom and in between. By itself, no policy in the world is going to help a district change its course and a policy is no guarantee of being able to create small, personalized, academically challenging, and equitable schools, as the sidebar "The Small School That Wasn't" reveals. Well-intentioned boards can make good policy, but their most powerful acts are in hiring the kind of superintendent who will drive the work and build the capacity of his or her administration to implement good policies.

The Small School That Wasn't: The Story of Bayview Essential School for Music, Art and Social Justice

Not every planned small school opens successfully. As an example, we offer a cautionary tale that hits painfully close to home. In 2006, CES joined a community task force led by the San Francisco Unified School District (SFUSD) charged with crafting a Small Schools by Design policy that would grant autonomy and accountability to existing and new small schools. We hoped that the policy would create better conditions for CES-affiliated small schools in the district and would help to create the circumstances to incubate and grow more small schools. Our theory of action has always been that high-performing, small, and innovative schools inside the system can be the disruptive innovation that pushes the broader system to change.

We were excited to be well positioned to open one of the first small schools under the policy, the Bayview Essential School for Music, Art and Social Justice (BES). BES was a CES lab school designed to meet the needs of the Bayview–Hunters Point community, a historically African American neighborhood in need of high-quality educational options. San Francisco had a budding parent-led small schools movement, a progressive school board with many members who had run on a platform that promised small schools, and a mayor who had several times publicly endorsed small schools as a way to address the widening achievement gap. We envisioned a cluster of schools, of which BES would be a part, serving as research and development lab schools that could play a critical role in district reform efforts by tuning and then disseminating innovative instructional and organizational practices into the rest of the system.

In early 2007, backed almost unanimously by the SFUSD school board, the Small Schools by Design policy passed. The policy exemplified the partnership between SFUSD, the community, and school reform advocates and helped to usher in a new wave of reform driven by bottom-up demand to which a new administration could offer top-down support. Everything was falling into place for the cause to create small, personalized, autonomous schools that would serve vulnerable students, close the achievement gap, and push the district to rethink and redesign some of its antiquated systems and policies. However, the lack of knowledgeable mid-level leadership and a process for incubating new schools presented persistent challenges. Within a climate of declining enrollment and school closures, putting the small schools policy into operation became less and less of a priority for district leaders unwilling to take risks. The clock ran out, and the new school did not open in 2007.

When it appeared that the door was closing, the announcement of SFUSD's new superintendent, Carlos Garcia, gave us great hope. We went back to our community advisory board to re-energize them with a new date for the BES opening: fall 2008. Garcia and his new deputy superintendent, Tony Smith, were enthusiastic supporters. In the winter of 2007, we went back to the school board with yet another resolution declaring the partnership between CES and SFUSD to open BES. The State of California required this resolution so we could obtain an official school code for a new school.

We thought we were on our way to achieving our goal. There was a small gathering of community and CES folks in the audience, and we all got up and cheered with excitement. Unfortunately, after that great moment, the process took another bad turn and we embarked on an uphill battle to get the pieces in place for the smooth opening of the school. Soon, it became apparent that the district hadn't adjusted key practices, policies, and procedures to accommodate a school designed to educate a historically underserved population. Space, staffing, curriculum, assessment, budgeting, and the student recruitment process needed to establish that this new small school differed from the district's norms and required up-front agreements. Despite the fact that BES had the seal of approval from the new administration and was operating under the cover of the Small Schools by Design policy, we hit systemic roadblocks within the district that damaged our access, communication, and ultimately the partnership. Some of the biggest obstacles resulted from the fact that BES was never introduced as a new school to SFUSD district administrators and site administrators. We did not participate in the enrollment fair, nor were we included in information sent to middle schools and families. To most of the district employees, from the facilities staffers to the student services department, we didn't exist as a school that was endorsed and due to be opened by the SFUSD. We were never fully allowed inside. BES was seen by other high school personnel as an outsider trying to take their enrollment and by feeder middle schools as a school for "bad" students. These factors made it almost impossible to meet our required enrollment numbers. We missed our enrollment target by fewer than a dozen students and were told we would have to wait yet another year to open.

At the beginning of the 2008–09 school year, district leadership appeared to reaffirm its commitment, calling the school "our baby." By December of 2008, however, the district issued an ultimatum: if we wanted to open in 2009, we had to serve truant and over-age students from across the city, rather than focusing on Bayview–Hunters Point. This communication reinforced our belief that SFUSD still did not comprehend our mission. It had always been our intention to serve vulnerable students, but not in this scattershot way. We had designed BES with neighborhood partners and were committed to our vision. As a starting point to understanding the district's position, we sought clarity on several questions: How would the school fit into a larger district strategy to address the needs of these specific students? What services and resources were already in place for this population? What was the current process for identifying and enrolling these students in district programs and schools geared to meeting their needs?

We never got any responses to these and many other questions. BES had the blessing of the administration, yet trying to get the district to recognize its responsibilities within the agreed partnership was like walking through molasses. Once again, our energy was spent trying to gain traction from the outside. Our lack of access to district administrators to clarify agreements and make decisions to accommodate the opening of a new school—critical decisions, such as settling on a school site—damaged our ability to attract staff members and students. Ultimately, we were unable to open BES for the third year running; currently, we do not plan to try again.

What happens when a district seems to want to do the right thing, but the timing is off? What happens when the right people are not in place at the middle management level in a district? What happens when a district says it wants to serve its most vulnerable populations but lacks a comprehensive plan to do so, and no leader steps up to make it happen? From our experience, what happens is business as usual. The needs of vulnerable students go unmet, and this puts them at great risk of dropping out of high school and into a life of poverty and hopelessness.

The biggest lesson we learned is not to get too cozy with the powers that be and drop your guard. We should have organized parents and other community members as we had initially to get the board to make a decision about opening our school. Once the resolution passed, we thought we were ready to go. We thought that we had the district's word and that all we had to do was be good partners. Our biggest mistake was not to involve the press and the community in a public discourse about the reasons the district was dragging its feet. We placed our bets and went for the less radical, more diplomatic approach. After we had the Small Schools by Design policy in hand and what appeared to be the right administration, we stopped fighting and started collaborating. Ultimately, our only source of strength was not CES's twenty-five years of experience, a well-designed school, the right policy climate, or urgency and a moral imperative to serve the Bayview–Hunters Point community. Our biggest source of strength would have been to rally the community to be vigilant, and we dropped the ball. Districts will not always do what needs to be done without bottom-up pressure from parents and community to back the small school at every step. The art is in figuring out how to operate at various levels: how to have a movement on the ground pushing the district and making them feel uncomfortable, how to negotiate on another policy level to create the climate, and how to work on the inside to find champions and allies.

This story is not entirely bleak, however. Aspects of the Small Schools by Design policy have stimulated discussions and influenced the district's practices and policies as they affect small schools. We have seen added flexibility in the areas of instruction and budgeting. We are pleased to have been a part of the leadership, energy, and vision that generated a degree of internal reflection and movement, even though these changes did not result in the climate and conditions needed to successfully launch the Bayview Essential School for Music, Art and Social Justice.

Leadership for Implementing and Sustaining Change

One of the most significant criticisms from principals about their district is that those who work for the district lack understanding of the work that takes place in their school. From the personnel who supervise principals, human resources employees who handle recruitment and hiring of teachers, staff members who direct the district's curriculum and assessment, all the way to the superintendent, all are perceived as part of a disconnect between central administration and what is happening at schools and in classrooms. Of course, when the sites are attempting to make profound changes that threaten the control of the district or deviate from expected norms, this disconnect can damage any progress that they might make. Whether or not it is true, educators at school sites have the impression that people at the central office are not qualified to influence what takes place in the schools or to hold them accountable. There is a widespread belief among many who work in schools that more and more, many central office administrators charged with holding schools accountable have never or only briefly been teachers or principals themselves. The cultural and professional divide between central office personnel and school personnel exacerbates the mistrust that already exists between them. The gap continues to widen when central offices impose mandates and tighter controls that limit site-based decision making about teaching, learning, staffing, and resources. Schools have compliance-based relationships with their districts and use those relationships to get the minimum done to please their supervisors and avoid scrutiny, choosing to do what they can to create better conditions for teaching and learning in covert, under-the-radar sorts of ways that have little potential to affect the larger system.

The drivers of change are going to have to make sure that everyone is on board, able and willing to make substantive change in schools and the system. Often, the decision makers and the policymakers change course, and not everyone is aware of or signed on to the new direction. Mark Sanchez reflects on the challenge of getting central office leadership to own, support, and lead change:

> The question in my mind has always been, at the midlevel, the kind of bureaucratic level, essentially, do we have the capacity? It's painful, because there are people in the middle at the central office that haven't made the mind shift. We don't want people to feel like they are forced to do something they don't want to do, but at the same time, if it's been demonstrated that the public wants it, and the people that the public elected want it, the superintendent wants it, then we're just going to need movement, because we have a sense of urgency and we need to be driven by that sense of urgency.

The reality remains that even while changes that benefit the organization as a whole are desperately needed, there are members of the system who are thriving under the current status quo and who may fight tooth and nail to avoid change. They may have philosophical or ideological reasons for not supporting the proposed transformations. They may be dissatisfied with the pace or the new responsibilities that they will have to take on. Because what we propose moves beyond timid attempts at reforming schools, the backlash from certain groups is inevitable and there will be casualties, as Ronald A. Heifetz and Marty Linsky note:

> If you signal your unwillingness to sustain casualties, you invite people to ignore your goals. Without the pinch of reality, why should they make sacrifices and change their ways of doing business? Your ability to accept the harsh reality of losses sends a clear message about your courage and commitment to seeing through the challenge. You must choose between keeping these people and making progress. Understanding that successful change will likely cause casualties will enable you to focus on your priorities—and be more mindful about helping those people who get left behind to move on to their next position. [Heifetz and Linsky, 2004, p. 36]

Some cities, such as Boston, have benefited from stable school district leadership; coupled with the city's explicit policies and documented agreements, superintendent Thomas Payzant's tenure in Boston from 1995 to 2006 provided consistency that helped the city's Pilot School program and small school reforms to establish themselves and yield results. But Payzant is a notable exception; the norm for public education district leadership is a constant changing of the guard that creates serious challenges for the initiation and sustainability of change efforts. This high turnover rate is also a factor at the school level. District leaders and administrators are constantly on the move, producing transition delays and shifts in direction. Data reveal that on average, the tenure for superintendents in urban districts is only two and a half years (Renchler, 1992, p. 2). Turnover rates nationally for principals are also dismal; in schools at which more than 50 percent of the students are economically disadvantaged, the five-year turnover rate is 73 percent overall. The rates are even higher for middle school principals and high school principals: 79 percent and 81 percent, respectively (University Council for Educational Administration, 2008).

At schools, principals come and go more rapidly than was the case many years ago. Principals have choices, and leadership shortages in some regions exacerbate the turnover situation. Constant change at the top and at schools only serves to emphasize the importance of districts' middle management levels. Unfortunately, mid-level leadership often does not have the power or the capacity to make or sustain change and, as we discussed earlier, often has a vested interest in maintaining the status quo. These mid-level administrators frequently are seen as obstructionist, or their supportive efforts are seen by schools as inconsistent or misguided. Much of the negative reaction to change in schools comes from lack of engagement in the process and, consequently, a lack of ownership of the changes. Mid-level administrators who supervise principals who are leading change in schools and those who manage the offices and systems that work directly with schools have been left out of the conversation. They may have been at the board meeting when the decisions were made, and they may have supported the change—that is, they may have the will. But they cannot carry out the change because they lack the understanding of the new expectations for their roles and the skill required to adequately support the school site.

Pam Espinosa, former principal of Olympic High School in Charlotte, North Carolina, who led the conversion of that large high school into five small schools, foresaw the potential problems that could arise by not involving mid-level managers and chose to implement early communication strategies to bring Charlotte-Mecklenburg district administrators on board. Espinosa recalls,

> Throughout the complex change, many logistical issues arose and from the initial planning meetings to the realization of the five small schools, we received incredible support. I always began the meetings with our district support staff by selling the vision, using much the same format as when I met with parents, community members and business people. I found that when the groundwork was laid out and their input in creating the transformation was sought and valued, the district staff supported the transformation without reservation. While it takes time to involve everyone who will touch the change, it takes even more time when you don't.

The combination of old systems grappling with new expectations and administrators who may not have the capacity or the will to meet the new demands sets up tense circumstances that may hinder the work of schools. When dealing with such barriers, New York's Vince Brevetti offers the familiar Gandhi aphorism: "We need to be the change we wish to see in the world." This becomes very practical advice when dealing with educational systems at the district or state level that are resistant to initiatives that are required for school development. "Systems are formidable, but rarely monolithic," comments Brevetti. "More often than not, people, particularly in mid-level positions, may be quite sympathetic to what you are trying to accomplish. Arm yourself with data to make your case, and try to better understand what would help them support you."

Bottom-Up Change with Top-Down Support

As the CES SSN has developed during the past six years, we have seen that the process for designing, planning, and implementing the much-needed changes in schools, particularly in large failing high schools, has varied, depending on whether the push and leadership for change was coming from the bottom up, from the top down, or from the bottom up with top-down support. In most cases of successful school transformation, the changes that shift the status quo have come from comprehensive plans that are built from the ground up, with top district officials providing the leadership, resources, and access to sustain and promote the changes and bring them to a deeper systemic level.

The movement for change in SeaTac, Washington's Highline School System began at the ground level and was led by practitioners, but the role of the district was critical in getting the school through the process as well as ushering the new schools into the larger district. Max Silverman, former principal of Tyee High School, who helped to lead the conversion process at Tyee, reflects on the district's role during the inception of the project:

> Our district was very supportive from the beginning. You know, having a real equity agenda at Tyee made it a little bit easier for them to get involved. There are not many communities of privilege that attend Tyee High School, so it's an easy place for them to really be willing to be aggressive and try some new things, and I think the superintendent at that time saw the need for change. Some of his top leadership, specifically the deputy superintendent at the time, who was also deeply committed to getting better results for all kids, jumped right in. In our case, the district acted like a stakeholder and partnered with us to make the conversion happen.

Districts are uniquely positioned to hold the value of equity on behalf of the communities they serve (see sidebar "Common Characteristics of Successful School Transformation Efforts"). Oakland's Steve Jubb affirms the role of the district as a holder of the vision for equity: "[District's] greatest contribution can be to use their power to maintain an equitable stance for all of its schools and the students they serve. In a climate of limited resources and diverse interests, schools, teachers, and families should not be left to solely advocate for themselves."

Common Characteristics of Successful School Transformation Efforts

When we examine the successes of the CES Small Schools Project, such as the conversion of Tyee High School and others discussed in this chapter and throughout *Small Schools, Big Ideas,* certain qualities emerge as common factors:

- An active and engaged district that is willing to rethink its operations and policies to support changes at the site level
- A commitment to hiring principals with small schools experience who are trained in collaborative leadership or creating a professional development process to bring the principals up to speed
- A set of clear performance-based expectations embedded in an accountability model that is designed to measure the value added by the conversion
- Autonomy that gives the school control over the following:
  - A schedule that gives teachers the time to own, design, and implement the changes
  - Assessments that are aligned with the new curriculum
  - A hiring process that will staff the school with teachers whose values and educational outlook are aligned with the mission of the school
- A clear vision of equity
- A transition plan that takes leadership from one principal and deposits it with the incoming principal

District leadership and school principals must act collaboratively to define the purpose for the significant changes that need to occur within the system. Change for the sake of change has not landed public education in a better place. Reform can draw energy from trying to change a culture of unjust and ineffective policies and practices. Reform not steeped in the struggle to use education as a means to nurture a democratic society will fail. We do not need superficial change. The change that we need moves us all beyond the quick fixes and into the unimaginable. It shakes the pieces that we are familiar with and uncovers the shapes and shades of an American institution that we can rebuild together. It will require the skill and will of a great majority of people who are convinced that they have the agency to take on this enormous task. The role of district and school leaders is to build that sense of agency; to advocate for the needs of teachers, students, and families; and to hold the vision of educational equity.

Building a Critical Mass to Work for Educational Equity

True bottom-up change efforts are inclusive of the broader school community. Successfully redesigned CES schools have worked hard to reflect the needs and desires of the communities they serve and to acclimate these communities to new and unfamiliar approaches to schooling such as the move from teacher-centered to student-centered classrooms. To move beyond school change to system change, it is necessary to grow a critical mass of schools and individuals who are advocating new practices. This critical mass will raise the awareness of a broad section of our society, helping people to better understand how systems of education can change so that we can create high-performing schools that equitably serve all of our students. Achieving critical mass involves empowering all stakeholders to contribute to creating the climate and conditions for school transformation.

To rethink how we design and operate schools, we need to reevaluate the power relationships that govern the institution of education as we know it; see sidebar "Reflection Questions for School and Systems Transformation" for a guide to the process of reevaluation. In order to stop replicating what does not work, we need to examine honestly who is being served well now and who, historically, has been underserved. If we are considering changing schools to become more equitable and provide a higher-quality education that meets the needs of a changing time, we need to be thoughtful in the ways that we engage people in that change, clear about why we are making the changes, wise about which changes, and strategic about how best to make them happen.

Reflection Questions for School and Systems Transformation

School leaders, groups of educators, community activist organizations—anyone focused on transforming schools—can use these questions to envision what such change would look like and what it would require in their particular community.

- What is the big vision? What would transformation look like in your district or your school?
- How will you create the time at the school sites to do the work?
- How will you secure buy-in and build a sense of ownership among teachers and families?
- How will you engage the community?
- What is the capacity-building plan for mid-level administrators?
- What policies do you have in place that will help create the necessary climate to sustain the changes? What policies do you need to put in place?
- What are the multiple measures that will be used to evaluate success?
- Are there existing schools that are pushing the edges of district operations and showing results with students?
- How can you rethink operations at the district level to support schools' autonomy and quest for improvement? How difficult is it for schools to hire staff members, purchase materials, contract with consultants, and so on?
- Within school site councils or other governing boards, on the district school board, at mid-level district administration, among teachers, within youth empowerment organizations, and within the community, where is the will and skill that you can leverage to move toward change? Who are your allies among these groups?
- Do schools already have some autonomy? How will you negotiate to get it?

We must start by reprioritizing what is important, and the conversation that will determine how and what to redesign should include those who will be affected directly—young people, their families, and their communities—with particular attention to those who have traditionally been left out. Los Angeles's Richard Alonso concurs, discussing the importance of creating a sense of ownership among those affected by change:

> Many communities haven't had the opportunity to be engaged partners in creating the solutions that we need to solve the problems of high drop-out rates, lack of engagement, and low student achievement levels in areas that are mainly poor, where we have many immigrant parents, where crime rates are very high, and where teen pregnancy rates are the highest. What we're trying to do in my local district is bring back hope and engage the people that have the power to make those changes within our schools. We know that we don't make a decision about what a school is going to do without involving the people that are going to live in that school or are ultimately going to benefit from the changes. We listen to them, so it takes a little bit longer to build those relationships. It takes a little bit longer to build that trust, but I feel that our work will be sustainable, and other people will come and take my place and still think this is a good idea. And if they own it too, they will be motivated to continue to make a difference.

Organizing families and communities to take back their schools is a powerful way to create the critical mass needed to drive transformation. A school change process that is nestled in the heart of a community can help to develop a sense of hope and optimism about the future of the people who live there. Schools should become the center of their community, lifting the quality of life of people of all ages, and providing family and community members with the tools and resources to be informed and engaged players in the creation and transformation of their schools (Forum for Education and Democracy, 2008, p. ix).

Conclusion

The essential work of educational transformation is to prepare an empowered critical mass, to nurture leadership in others in order to help them to find their voice, to take action to change the way our schools function, and to find alternatives to the unfair and ineffective practices that are embedded in the culture of schools. This work will need fearless educators and other visionaries to lend their courage to communities in and out of school buildings in order to challenge mandated remedies and prescriptive solutions that fall short of addressing the imbalances. We can harness the energy from that collective will to unearth the inequities that persist within our educational system, speak against them, and take action toward transformation. We are collectively responsible for building our skill and will to take up the mission of educational equity. This work requires new strategies and policies at every level of government that will enable communities to engage with and be accountable for their local schools.

Fortunately, as demonstrated by the results of the CES Small Schools Network, successful new schools exist, created by educators and community members who together confronted the systemic inertia that has limited innovation and creativity in our schools. We have established learning communities in which teachers are building their capacity to create powerful curriculum and assessment strategies, redesigning the ways that we organize our schools, and nurturing a powerful vision for what public schools can become. However, many of these schools are constrained by top-down mandates, lack of resources, and lack of control over the important decisions that schools need to make at the source, involving those who are closest to students: educators, school leaders, families, and students themselves.

To grow and sustain successful small schools and re-energize a movement toward educational equity, we need transformational leadership at all levels to remove systemic barriers and to propel a much-needed nationwide change effort (see sidebar "Essentials of School and School System Transformation"). While many exciting initiatives have been developed, a strategic long-term policy that would create the climate and conditions to sustain the work and take it to scale has been missing. As the Forum for Education and Democracy (2008) states in its report "Democracy at Risk," "Congress and the new Administration will have an opportunity to work together to strengthen our public schools and take up the challenge of preparing all children, regardless of circumstance, for productive citizenship in the 21st century."

Essentials of School and School System Transformation

The following are elements from which a viable initiative for school and school system transformation can plan backward. If these elements are in place, transformation efforts with a commitment to success and sustainability are clearly under way.

- A strategic plan aimed at eliminating the achievement gap and raising achievement levels for all students
- An equity-driven mission for the district and schools
- Creation of policies that institutionalize this mission and the strategies identified to enact it
- Capable and willing middle managers to operationalize policies
- Highly capable school and district leadership with experience in democratic, distributed leadership
- Cultivation of a sense of ownership, will, and skill among stakeholders
- Community engagement in developing plans and making decisions
- Incubation process to create, grow, and support new or newly redesigned small schools
- Development of clusters or networks of schools that hold common principles and values
- Development of assessment systems not only for student performance but for the performance of the transformation initiative as a whole that include a cycle of inquiry that takes into account multiple measures and a wide variety of data
- Creation of performance-based behavioral expectations and measures for all participants
- Development of professional development opportunities in order to learn from new schools
- Redesigned formulas and systems for the distribution of resources

- Secure autonomies and clearly defined authority to act in the best interest of students at the school level
- A focus on hiring and building teams at both district and school site levels

For a district self-audit that school system personnel can use to assess their readiness to embark on transformation efforts, as well as other tools, please visit the *Small Schools, Big Ideas* Web site at http://www.ceschangelab.org.

PART TWO

Essential Principles
for School Design

Starting with Vision, Mission, and Goals

Once a school is rolling, once you've designed your school and things are in place, it's much more difficult to change than when you're starting from scratch. Once you have your initial design and you have an existing, living system, that's what your school is.

—Kim Klepcyk, principal, Quest High School

The challenges that a new generation of schools must address are formidable. Our experiences with the Coalition of Essential Schools Small Schools Network (CES SSN) have offered us the opportunity to participate in the journeys of thirty-three new schools as they evolved from possibilities to realities. Moreover, twenty-five years of CES history have provided us with a profusion of examples of school restructuring, reform, and transformation in nearly every sort of community across the United States. We have studied what worked, applied those lessons to the CES SSN, and offer here the experience and wisdom represented in the fundamentals of Essential school design.

How are personalized, equitable, and academically challenging schools started? And how are existing schools transformed into powerful places of meaningful learning that are capable of preparing all students for the challenges and opportunities of their lives? Bringing about transformational change requires clarity of purpose, careful planning, and attention to process. The most successful small schools are created through an inclusive process that understands and is responsive to the needs of the community it will serve. By devoting a significant amount of time to planning all aspects of the school, a school design team develops a clear mission, attainable goals, and a shared instructional philosophy.

A significant body of research shows the effectiveness of small schools across the country, particularly those in historically underserved communities. Studies in Boston and Chicago show increased student engagement and achievement (Center for Collaborative Education, 2004; Wasley and others, 2000). A six-year study of eighty-three new small high schools in New York City found a relationship between small school size and improved attendance, retention, and graduation rates (New Visions for Public Schools, 2007, pp. 13–14). According to Mary Anne Raywid and Gil Schmerler, the correlation between small school size and improved student outcomes has been demonstrated "with a clarity and at a level of confidence that are rare in the annals of educational research" (Raywid and Schmerler, 2003, p. vii).

This chapter covers the basics of planning and designing a new small school in order to increase meaningful learning, achievement, and acquisition of the fundamentals for successful lifelong learning for all current and future students. This new small school can be a start-up emerging as part of a school district, a new charter, the conversion of an existing large school into new small schools, or the result of intentional, planned transformation happening within an existing school community. (See the "Designing and Redesigning Schools" sidebar for an overview of the benefits and challenges of these options.) For all of these scenarios, we offer seven essentials of small school design:

- Begin with the end in mind: start with the school's mission, vision, and desired outcomes, and plan backward from there.

- Organize the work: plan strategically and divide the work among different groups and individuals to ensure that it gets done.

- Be inclusive: the design team should include educators, students, parents, community members, and school partners, with appropriate roles and support for all design team members.

- The process should model the outcome: how things get done is as important as what gets done, because the process will shape the results. A democratic and equitable process should fully engage all design team members and include democratic and participatory structures that establish the foundation for a democratic school.
- Communicate new school development plans to the larger community.
- Develop partnerships: find compatible organizations that can offer support, ideas, and resources for both the planning and the implementation phases.
- Find a place in a supportive network of schools: join a professional learning community that can provide the critical friends needed to support the planning, design, and implementation processes.

These essentials, covered in this chapter, describe the fundamental necessities for transforming schools into learning environments that change the lives of students for the better.

Designing and Redesigning Schools

This chart highlights both the benefits and challenges of the different kinds of small schools: newly created, redesigned, and converted from large schools. For a more detailed discussion of conversions of large schools into smaller autonomous schools, see *Choosing Small: The Essential Guide to Successful High School Conversion* by Jay Feldman, M. Lisette López, and Katherine G. Simon (2006).

Type of School	Benefits	Challenges
Newly created start-up school	• Opportunity to start from scratch and think outside the box: everything is open and waiting to be created.	• Everything—every policy, system, and document—needs to be created from scratch.

(continued)

Type of School	Benefits	Challenges
	• No need to negotiate or compromise with pre-existing stake-holders on programs and systems that they do not want to give up. • Various partners and stakeholders can be engaged by the excit-ing work of creating a school, thus creating widespread owner-ship of the school and fostering everyone's leadership. • Can hire entirely new faculty and staff and recruit entirely new students without deal-ing with a pre-existing school culture, adult or youth. • There is an excitement and a buzz about a brand-new school that is hard to create for redesigned schools.	• Inevitably, there will be more work that needs to get done than there are people to do it. • It will take years before the school feels at all settled; systems, cur-riculum, and schedules will probably change multiple times. • It can be frustrating at times when things are always in flux and there are no constants; it can feel as if the school is constantly starting and restarting. • Every administrative task—setting up sys-tems for transcripts, buying furniture, and more—needs to get done, even when these tasks are not central to the school's mis-sion and compete with more important work.

Type of School	Benefits	Challenges
Redesigned, existing school	• Opportunity to thoughtfully reexamine all existing practices and systems and build on positive ones without throwing everything out, therefore limiting somewhat the amount of work that needs to be done. • Many administrative tasks are less onerous because the school already exists. • Existing staff members and stakeholders carry with them certain knowledge and skills that can help make the transition easier, without some of the kinks of start-ups. • Opportunity to build on existing leadership among all the stakeholders because they are already members of the school community; students, in particular, may be easier to engage in leadership activities.	• People can be attached to aspects of the school's program and functions and want to retain them, even when they are not in the best interest of the school. • Because it is easier to use existing systems and programs, some aspects of the existing school that should be rethought and changed may not be. • People who might not be the best fit for the new redesigned school may stay on, potentially impeding the school's progress and new direction. • It is hard to transform an existing school culture for both youth and adults and ensure that negative attitudes, beliefs, and influences do not migrate to the newly designed school.

(continued)

Type of School	Benefits	Challenges
Redesigned, existing school		• More difficult to be innovative, creative, and think outside the box.
New schools redesigned from large school conversions	• Opportunity to share large school resources such as auditorium and library, as well as athletics, band, and other programs. • Students who know better than anyone else the problems in the large school can be easily engaged as leaders in the transformation effort and then also become advocates among their peers and incoming students. • Opportunity to build on existing leadership among all the stakeholders because they are already members of the school community. • Existing staff members and stakeholders carry with them certain knowledge and skills that can help make the transition easier.	• The process of negotiating and dividing up resources and space can be contentious. • People can be attached to aspects of the large school's program and functions and want to preserve them, even when they are not in the best interest of the new school. • Because it is easier to use existing systems and programs, some aspects of the existing school that should be rethought and changed may not be. • People who might not be the best fit for the new redesigned school may stay on, potentially impeding the school's progress and new direction.

Type of School	Benefits	Challenges
	• Many large schools are in need of change in order to better serve their students; transforming existing large schools into new small schools is more financially sustainable than creating the equivalent number of start-up schools.	• Dividing existing faculty and staff among the new schools can be tricky and fraught with conflict. • It is hard to transform an existing school culture for both youth and adults and ensure that negative attitudes, beliefs, and influences do not migrate to the newly designed school. • More difficult to be innovative and creative and think outside the box.

Start with a Mission Statement

In *Understanding by Design,* Grant Wiggins and Jay McTighe (2005) make the case for why planning backward is best: "Our lessons, units and courses should be logically inferred from the results sought, not derived from the methods, books and activities with which we are most comfortable. Curriculum should lay out the most effective ways of achieving specific results" (p. 14). While Wiggins and McTighe focus on curriculum and instruction, the application of this results-based approach to planning extends to all aspects of school design.

Beginning with a mission statement is an effective way to concisely capture desired results. A well-developed mission statement will act as a blueprint for a school community in the planning stages and should be given a sufficient investment of effort to get it right. At the beginning of the process, visioning activities such as creating illustrations and lists of elements that make an ideal school can help a team develop the school's mission and vision. Brainstorming, creating, and agreeing upon a mission statement is a critical early task of the team; the more succinct and clear the mission statement is, the better it will serve the school.

A mission statement should be bold, simple, and attainable. It should grab the attention of potential students, families, and teachers with its clarity of purpose, using powerful words and a compelling message. A mission statement, through its directness and spirit, has to speak to a wide array of people who might see themselves rallying around the school's cause, purpose, and outcomes.

Parlaying the mission statement into student outcomes is a useful way of planning backward, as ARISE High School, a new charter school in Oakland, California, discovered. ARISE High School was founded by *Small Schools, Big Ideas* co-author Laura Flaxman, Romeo Garcia of Mills College, and parent leader and Oakland Community Organizations organizer Emma Paulino. ARISE opened its doors in August 2007, serving 110 ninth and tenth graders and growing to its full capacity of 220 students in grades nine through twelve in the fall of 2009. The result of a partnership with the Mills College School of Education, the Mills College TRiO programs, Oakland Community Organizations, and the Coalition of Essential Schools, ARISE's focus is on preparing students from low-income families to be the first in their family to attend college. Garcia, Flaxman, and Paulino came together to start ARISE in 2004, joining the CES Small Schools Network. Working with Mentor School Wildwood School, an independent high school based in Los Angeles, the ARISE design team spent two years developing the school's Habits of Mind and Heart (see sidebar) from its mission statement: "The mission of ARISE High School is to empower students with the skills and knowledge to pursue higher education and become leaders in the world. ARISE High School will also provide an environment for training educators to become leaders in secondary school reform." The team then delineated where in the curriculum and school program they would ensure that students were gaining those habits.

Part of this work involved asking the question "How will we know whether we have been successful, and what will successfully achieving our mission look like?" Students who graduate from the school acting like x, being able to do y, and knowing z will mean that we have accomplished our mission. Articulating how to develop x, y, and z in the school program will create a pathway to get there. Starting with such outcomes in mind is essential, and it is possible through effective backward planning.

ARISE High School Habits of Mind and Heart

The Habit of Collaboration: Accepting and giving assistance; working with diverse groups of people

The Habit of Perseverance: Seeing things through and staying in there even in the face of adversity

The Habit of Exploration and Innovation: Seeking and being open to new experiences and ideas; taking risks and meeting challenges

The Habit of Leadership and Integrity: Taking initiative in the service of the common good; doing the right thing even when no one is looking; acting ethically, with honesty and compassion for others

The Habit of Convention: Meeting accepted standards in any academic area in order to be understood and to understand others; adhering to appropriate guidelines for the different environments one is in such as school, internship sites, etc.

The Habit of Perspective and Evidence: Addressing questions from multiple viewpoints and using a variety of ways to solve problems; bringing together relevant information, judging the credibility of sources, finding out for oneself

The Habit of Connections: Looking for patterns and for ways in which things fit together in order to bring together diverse material and form solutions

To see the connections between school values and curriculum development, visit the *Small Schools, Big Ideas* Web site at http://www.ceschangelab.org and look for the "ARISE High School Curriculum Guide to Developing Students' Habits of Mind and Heart."

Misha Lesley, the founding principal of Empowerment College Preparatory High School, a new CES small school in Houston, Texas, was working in a large Houston public school engaged in the process of forming smaller learning communities when she decided to create a small school in her community. Those smaller learning communities were not, in her view, challenging students to use their minds well. She and her colleagues knew that the students were capable of learning the skills needed to graduate, as Lesley puts it, "prepared for college, prepared to make a positive impact on their community. We wanted people to return to that community to uplift it and see the value of education as something they wanted to support." Lesley envisioned a school that would teach students to "be ready to do some good and important things. They would be prepared intellectually, prepared socially to make a difference." Along with a team of teachers and students with whom she had been working on an initiative to create small learning communities at one of Houston's large comprehensive high schools, Lesley formed the Empowerment design team. Lesley reflects on why the team started with a clear mission:

> Does a school have a mission? And is the mission focused on students? Is the mission focused on student outcomes, student results, student learning? Or is there some sort of de facto mission that many schools in the trenches have, of let's get through the day, stay out of the news, meet AYP, meet state accountability goals? Those can become the de facto missions of schools, regardless of what is on the marquee or what's published on the front of the school handbook. And so we wanted to create a school that was completely focused on a real, meaningful, and attainable mission.

Empowerment College Preparatory High School created its mission statement early in its year of planning the school and tied all of its planning to the mission: "Through a personalized environment, college prep curriculum, and social action program of study, Empowerment College Preparatory High School will equip students to become socially conscious problem-solvers who make a positive impact on the community." Empowerment's road map for planning was clearly delineated by planning backward from this ultimate outcome. Given its emphasis on helping students to become "socially conscious problem-solvers" and on the school's "social action program," the Empowerment planning team put significant resources and time into developing their service-learning curriculum. Creating a "personalized environment" and developing "college prep curriculum" were also priorities and, along with social action, the central focus of the Empowerment design team's backward mapping and planning. In the case of Empowerment, it was important not only to create a strong mission but also to engage community stakeholders in shaping the mission in order to create a sense of urgency and accountability from which the school could later draw. Lesley recalls the process by which they created the mission statement: "We developed the mission of the school in collaboration with students, with the parent who was on the design team, with the district member who was on the design team, and with the educators. We wanted it to be clear, short, and very student-focused, to give the community a clear idea of what the school would do every day for kids and what the outcomes would be."

All of the strategic planning for a new school or the restructuring of a school has to be done with the mission and the outcomes in mind. For example, on the topic of budgeting, the mission of a school should drive questions such as "How will the school deploy resources?" "What are the priorities that determine how money gets spent?" At Empowerment, everyday decisions about the budget were aimed at personalizing a learning environment to offer a college preparatory curriculum that would result in some form of social action. Everything that was spent had to support those three components. Schools need to be clear about their priorities and constantly weigh decisions, taking into consideration their ultimate learning goals and proposed outcomes.

Related to developing the mission statement is deciding on the instructional philosophy of the school. Schools sometimes articulate this philosophy in the form of a vision statement, explaining the program that is going to help them achieve their mission. At Empowerment, service learning—expressed in the mission statement as "a social action program of study"—was clearly at the core of the instructional approach and thus helped to drive the planning of the instructional program. ARISE's design team articulated its instructional philosophy as a way of fulfilling the mission statement. Described in a list of key features of the school, their vision included "experiential learning"—hands-on, project-based learning—as well as "learning by doing" in all classes and "community empowerment" in which students, families, and educators play leadership roles in the school and the school plays a role in making the broader community of Oakland stronger. At regular intervals during the year, faculty and staff members engage in reflection to see how they are living up to the mission and vision of the school. This sort of progress check is also a result of the backward planning that design teams do to articulate both the outcomes and the process as starting points from which to build their school program.

One of the great challenges in developing an instructional program is finding new ways of doing things instead of falling back on the methods and activities with which we are most comfortable. How can new school planners know what to do if they have never done it before? Visits to innovative, successful small schools can inspire the imagination. These learning opportunities allow educators to experience for the first time the kind of quality instruction and powerful learning outcomes that a school can achieve when it has control over its resources, curriculum, assessment, and staffing. They see firsthand the alternative ways that one might set up a schedule that could work better for students, create curriculum that is more relevant to the lives of the children they serve, and have the time and organizational support to personalize instruction. We offer observers one caution, however: avoid the temptation to replicate what is observed. A new design should be grounded in its own unique mission and responsive to the specific students it will serve and the context in which it will operate.

Organize the Work

Magda Leon, a parent and design team member for the Upper School of Capital City Public Charter School in Washington, D.C., a new small school participant in the CES SSN, believes that in order to get the work done and support a diverse design team, having one person to manage and organize the process works best.

> People threw ideas around about what to do, but until we had a former teacher from Capital City in the role of director of the Upper School project, we couldn't get all of the work done. Once she came into place, we had an extensive list of things to do with deadlines and timelines, and we just went for it. There were meetings every other week. There were agenda items. Some people started dividing into subgroups: facilities, student recruitment, communication, and advertisement of the school. As they got things off the ground, those

groups would dissolve and other groups would form, such as hiring committees for staff.

The sidebar "CES Strategic Planning That Keeps Students at the Center" provides a detailed list of strategic planning tasks that are important in designing a new school.

CES Strategic Planning That Keeps Students at the Center

Drawing from our extensive experience in working with school design teams, CES has created a planning tool to help organize the many tasks that are involved in starting a new school. The national office of CES and the CES Mentor Schools support new school design teams during their planning year (or years) in creating a strategic plan that will facilitate a successful school opening. While our philosophy states that no two schools look alike, research and experience have proven that there are components that every high school needs to address and have in place. What follows is a template for teams to use in setting their own outcomes, strategies, and timelines. "Product or Component" means specific deliverables and products needed for a successful school opening. "Description" is a brief overview of the process used to establish common understanding of the task or product. In this version, these columns are filled in with components of new school planning that many teams are likely to encounter. "Who's Responsible" refers to the person or people taking the lead on achieving the outcome, and "By When" is the due date for completing that component. These columns have been left blank so that the team can fill in the appropriate information. This list of strategic plan components that need to be addressed before the new school opens is not necessarily in chronological order; however, the professional development component, the design team, the mission and vision statements, and the professional development plan are listed first because they are the key components that will determine the direction of the planning, design, and implementation of the school. While this chart represents a wealth of experience from newly opened small schools, it is by no means exhaustive; please use it as inspiration, and add to or adapt it as needed.

Product or Component	Description	Who's Responsible	By When
Design team	Assemble a team that represents the major stakeholders in the new school, with an emphasis on engaging and including students and families early in the process.		
Mission and vision statements	Describe the school's overall purpose and the mechanism for achieving that purpose.		
Professional development plan	Outline the plan for professional development for the design team and then the school staff, including cycles of inquiry, looking at data, and creating mechanisms for continuous school improvement. Include the school team's professional development needs and when and how the team will access mentoring support to help in these areas.		
Instructional philosophy	Describe the school's philosophy about how students learn, then use it to create an organizing framework for how the school is going to teach students and improve the learning practice or process.		

Product or Component	Description	Who's Responsible	By When
Communications and marketing plan	Create a name, a tag line, a strategic plan for internal communications, and a strategic plan for external communications, including how to get the word out about the school and its vision and mission. The plan should include ways of informing students and parents so that they can make meaningful choices as well as ways of building relationships with the school's larger community.		
Resource and needs assessment	Determine the resources and needs of the particular community that the school will be serving through community mapping, surveys, and other techniques.		
Instructional and student achievement goals	Set goals and measurements related to the mission and vision for instruction and academic and socio-emotional student achievement.		

(continued)

Product or Component	Description	Who's Responsible	By When
Instructional program	Drawing on the school's mission and instructional philosophy, answer these questions: How will the school facilitate the development of each child with personalization and academic rigor? What approach will the school take to choosing or designing curriculum in math and other subjects? What will the school's advising program look like?		
Literacy plan	Define the school's approach to literacy development across the curriculum.		
Student assessment plan	Explain the ways in which students will be assessed and promoted from one level to the next, including the expectations that students will need to meet in order to graduate.		
Academic intervention and student support plan	Provide a strategy for assisting students who need extra support academically, socially, and emotionally.		
Program for ELL students and students with special needs	Decide how the school will serve students with special needs and how it will support English language learners.		

Product or Component	Description	Who's Responsible	By When
College and career preparation strategy	Detail the plan for providing students with access to college and career options after graduation. How will the school prepare all students for college and beyond? How will the school help students access resources and information in these areas?		
School schedule and calendar	Create a calendar and daily schedule for students and staff members that facilitate achievement of the school's mission, instructional goals, and the professional development time needed for educators.		
Leadership and governance structure	Describe the leadership structure and governance model for the new school, including the roles of students and parents.		
Identifying the new school leader	Create a plan for identification, needs assessment, and professional development of new school leader (or leaders).		
Hiring plan	Describe the process for hiring staff members.		

(continued)

Product or Component	Description	Who's Responsible	By When
Student recruitment plan	Determine how students will be recruited and a process for student enroll-ment that is equitable and draws a heterogeneous population. What is the phase-in enrollment plan?		
Community engagement plan	Delineate how the school will engage the community in the design of the school, including families and community-based institutions and organizations—for example, naming a parent or community liaison and arranging for advisors to conduct home visits.		
Staff handbook: school policies, practices, and structures	Explain the policies, prac-tices, and structures of the new school, clarifying expectations for staff as members of the school community.		
Student and parent handbook: creating a positive school culture	Explain the policies, practices, and structures of the new school, clarifying expectations for students and families and including agreements related to establishing a positive school culture and mechanisms for developing student voice.		

Product or Component	Description	Who's Responsible	By When
Annual school budget	Detail the projected revenues and expenditures aligned with the strategic plan for the planning year (or years) and the first year of the school.		
Small school strategic planning timeline	What developmental process will help the school grow and demonstrate gains in student achievement? What benchmarks and outcomes will be met during the planning year, first year, and so on?		
Technology plan	Describe how the school will integrate the use of technology into the learning process as well as the management structures.		
District negotiation plan	Negotiate a compact, policy, or memorandum of understanding with the district, union, or board of education that outlines and ensures autonomy and an accountability system.		
Location and physical space plan	Locate a space for the school, and determine how you will use it.		
Development plan	How will you develop a sustainable financial plan? Describe your process for seeking out and cultivating financial partners.		

(continued)

Product or Component	Description	Who's Responsible	By When
Advisory team or board	Recruit diverse interested stakeholders, community members, and business leaders to serve on the school's advisory team or board.		
Plans for continuous improvement	What are your plans for using data to drive instruction and decision making? How will you structure and incorporate regular cycles of inquiry into your school improvement process?		
Habits of mind	Habits provide an intellectual framework that students and staff members use in every classroom and throughout the fabric of school life. How are they communicated?		
Student, staff, and parent agreements	How will the school reflect a tone of respect and collaboration among students, staff, and parents or family members?		

To download a template for this school planning document, visit the *Small Schools, Big Ideas* Web site at http://www.ceschangelab.org. The planning documents and timelines for the rollout of Capital City Public Charter School's Upper School, which opened in the fall of 2008, are also available as examples and inspiration.

The timelines for this necessary strategic planning work vary greatly from school to school. The majority of new schools in the CES SSN had one year for planning, although ARISE had three and Capital City had two. There are benefits and disadvantages of both a shortened timeline and an extended timeline. With additional time, it might be easier to assemble more details and accomplish more of the planning before the school's opening, but there is also the risk of losing the sense of urgency and momentum that can push the process forward. Furthermore, as time passes, many of the participants might move on. For example, when ARISE changed its opening date from the fall of 2006 to the fall of 2007, the change meant that many of the students and families who had been on the design team would no longer be able to attend the school.

Create an Inclusive Design Team

Designing a new school is a demanding process that requires dedication and commitment. The process is best served when it is undertaken by a group or design team with a wide variety of expertise and resources at their disposal. Members of design teams participate in everything: they develop the school's mission, create job descriptions, draft a charter or other documents, present information at school board meetings, lead student recruitment presentations, select teachers, and do much more that leads to the opening day of the new school. The ARISE High School founders put together a design team that included educators, parents, students, and community members, and navigated a three-year process toward the school's opening day in September 2007. Co-founder and co-principal Romeo Garcia describes the birth of the idea that led to the school.

> It all started with a conversation. Laura Flaxman, whom I worked with when she was the principal of Oakland's Life Academy, asked me if I had ever thought about starting my own school. At the time, I worked at Mills College, where I ran the Upward Bound and Educational Talent Search programs, which I had firsthand experience with as a high school student myself. At Upward Bound, we believed that regardless of where the students came from, and they came from all over Oakland, they wanted to be successful. What they lacked was the access to resources and the support from adults who really believed in them and wanted to help them to move forward. That's the gap. Kids want to do it, but they don't have the information on how

to get it done. Their parents hadn't gone to college, and the school system was not effectively serving kids. At Upward Bound, working with kids part-time, we helped 90 percent of our students to go on to four-year colleges. "If we can do this part-time with a group of kids, well, imagine what we can do full-time," I thought, and I was ready to take what I had been doing through Upward Bound to develop a school in Oakland. As part of the process to create the design team for the school, we brought in Emma Paulino as our third founder, both because of her incredible track record as a leader and parent organizer in Oakland and because of her motivation: she had founded and sent her own children to ASCEND, a K–8 school that did an amazing job of preparing students, who were then presented with a variety of unsatisfactory high school options. We then continued to assemble a team, bringing on various parents, students, educators, and partners. Looking back, all of the design work, I believe that such a varied and collaborative group of people definitely contributed to the success of our first year, and I think that everyone who participated in the development of ARISE will always remember the experience and feel a certain amount of ownership and pride in our creation.

Ideally, design teams are composed of all of the various stakeholders of a school community: students, parents, educators, community members, and school partners. This group is responsible for much of the initial planning, whether that planning is for a large school's conversion or the start-up of a new school. The design team sets the vision, establishes guidelines, sets the tone, and creates the fundamentals of school culture and traditions of inclusivity. The design team also makes a commitment to having courageous conversations in which it is okay to disagree—in fact, the team is encouraged to respectfully argue about vision and hopes for the school, thus establishing trust and challenging assumptions.

A group of parents initiated the design team for Washington, D.C.'s Capital City Public Charter School (CCPCS), a school for students from pre-kindergarten through eighth grade that opened in 2000. CCPCS eventually created the Capital City Upper School, which was described earlier in this chapter. CCPCS founding principal Karen Dresden explains: "Capital City was the first parent-founded charter school in the District of Columbia, visualized and brought into existence by parents from a local district school who wanted a small school for their children. Family members created the design team and recruited educators. From this beginning, parents have continued to be intimately involved in the life of the school, with parents playing major roles on the school's governing board."

In 2004, parents' involvement intensified as Capital City began to plan a school for grades six through twelve. Motivation for starting Capital City's Upper School was high after seeing students graduate from the eighth grade without many attractive options for high school. Magda Leon was already an involved parent at CCPCS, serving on the school's board of trustees, when she heard about plans for extending the school through twelfth grade. She explains why she became involved in planning the new school: "I'm a believer in Capital City. It matches the philosophy I have about teaching students to become learners as opposed to teaching content and facts. I want other kids in the city to have that option in the higher grades. We are doing a great job in the lower school; our kids have a great track record, so why not do it for upper-school kids?" The frustration that Leon's family experienced in finding a suitable high school when her daughter graduated from Capital City intensified her drive to open the Upper School. Karen Dresden affirms that parents' commitment propelled forward the difficult process of opening the Upper School. "They're involved in creating something that's really important to them and that they don't see existing currently in our community," she observes.

While the lower school definitely evolved out of a grassroots process, it has been even easier to involve more stakeholders with an existing school already in place. Dresden also emphasizes that the process of opening a high school involved students in planning the secondary school in ways that the design team was not familiar with:

> When we were planning a lower school, it just was not appropriate for elementary school–age kids to be involved. But it's been really exciting to see the potential for involving older students. We've had students participate in several retreats. Students created and ran a survey. Students helped with interviewing. The insights that they're able to offer are just tremendous, because they ask questions that adults don't always ask. And they're provided with this wonderful opportunity to provide this leadership and participate in this experience. What's been apparent to me is just how much they understand and get the school and can really contribute to articulating the vision for the upper school.

Nnamdi Nwaezeapu, one of the students from the elementary school who helped to plan the high school, notes, "[Capital City] has embraced me and instilled its powerful message within me and that is why I make sure that I dedicate a good percent of my time toward making Capital City an even better place." Nnamdi spoke at a meeting of the Washington, D.C., board of education as part of the process for getting the charter for the high school. He reflects, "Not only did I talk about the upper school, I helped plan it. I was one of the students that assisted in the process of choosing the principal for the upper school. I also took a trip to a CES meeting in Washington state to gather ideas. I also went to a retreat to get a clearer understanding of how the upper school was going to look (might I mention that it was on a Saturday at 8:00 in the morning). Those experiences further connected me to Capital City" (Nwaezeapu, 2006).

The planning process offers opportunities for parents and other noneducators to offer their expertise. Magda Leon comments,

> You need to get people on board who know about finances, facilities, and programs. For the most part, at Capital City, we have been very lucky that there are parents that know a lot about those things. I am not a school manager, but I have been working at schools for twenty-three years. We had a lot of people that know about finance and facilities. You can have a great idea, build an excellent program, sell a good package, and recruit students, but if you don't have a building, the program is not going anywhere. All components have to be in sync.

When parents and community members are the driving force behind the school, they sometimes struggle with finding the right educators to participate. In the case of Capital City, the parent-led initiative moved pretty quickly to include educators who were a good match for the school, but in the case of ARISE, several challenges emerged. Many teachers, particularly on the high school level, do not have a lot of experience collaborating closely with parents. Doing so can be a potentially intimidating prospect, and there can be some cultural disconnects in terms of role, socioeconomics, and race. Emma Paulino recalls that when she was on the hiring committee for ARISE, a teacher candidate whom she interviewed would only make eye contact with the other educators on the team but not with the students or her: "The teacher thought that I couldn't possibly be a decision maker, but of course I was, and this was one of the reasons we didn't hire her."

If a teacher does not demonstrate comfort with relating to parents as powerful stakeholders, that person would clearly be a wrong fit for a school that is based on creating space for this kind of collaboration among families, students, and educators.

The process of moving from design team member to staff member also can present challenges. Ideally, the more the team includes the students, family members, and teachers who will ultimately be a part of the school, the better. However, it should not be assumed that design team participation means "you're hired!" Teachers on a new school design team should participate in the hiring process that the team develops to determine the best teachers for the school.

Design teams look different, understandably, in a large school conversion; however, many elements are the same. A conversion is a two-step process. The same emphasis on including the voices of different stakeholders is critical. After studying small learning communities and deciding to go further and create a campus of small schools, Olympic High School in Charlotte, North Carolina, started to plan its conversion. Their first step was to develop a conversion design team to plan and guide the school's division into five small, autonomous schools. The conversion team was made up of administrators, teachers, parents, business leaders, and, eventually, students. The second step was to create the five individual design teams for the new schools. The conversion team created the overall project plan that spelled out what needed to be done, when, and by whom, which was then passed along to the individual teams.

This two-step process ensured that portions of the plan were in place in order to establish the conditions required to help the actual conversion occur. Their conversion team required the individual design teams to produce certain non-negotiables; for example, each team had to develop structures to help personalize the educational experience for the students. The conversion team also researched different examples and tools to provide the design teams with ideas from which they would then create their own plan.

Like the conversion team, the new school design teams also included students and parents. Initially, many of the parents on the teams were those who were a little skeptical of what was happening and were interested in keeping an eye on the school. These parents were often leaders who, once on board, were very effective at going out into the community to reach out and help represent the views of other parents as well as get them involved. Pam Espinosa, former principal of Olympic High School, who led the school through the conversion process, recalls, "The parents on the design teams were absolutely phenomenal, and they brought a perspective that is certainly desperately needed as you're designing a school."

Creating a design team for a new or converting school provides ways to change the culture of who has a stake in schools. Even in schools in the CES network, educators are usually accustomed to working with one another and not necessarily open to bringing other voices to the table, particularly on the secondary level. As inclusive as Olympic's teams were, Espinosa still felt that they could have done a better job of bringing students into the process: "We did not bring the kids in soon enough, either. We were so busy trying to get everything up and running that even though we brought some kids into each team, we should have found a way to be more inclusive and keep kids more in the loop of what was going on. We needed to be much more focused on that student communication, and we just did not find the time to do that, and that was a mistake." If students had been more involved from the start, the small schools that resulted from Olympic's conversion would have benefited sooner from their perspectives and commitment. Without bringing all stakeholders into the process, it is hard to foster the kind of widespread ownership that schools need to be successful and fully inclusive.

It is crucial for schools in the planning stages to be intentional about who is a part of the new school planning process and what the process entails. For schools and communities interested in real transformation, the discourse about the change process and desired outcomes needs to include all stakeholders, so that all involved are a part of leading the effort. How can design teams engage all members of the school community in the change process and as leaders in it? This is an essential question that should be continually asked and revisited.

Allow the Process to Model the Outcome

Design teams lay the foundation for inclusivity, democracy, and equity. In building a school with the CES Common Principle "Democracy and equity" in mind, the process needs to model the desired outcome, and indeed, the outcome—the school itself—will reflect the kind of process that was used to create the school. This principle applies in many circumstances of school transformation: visioning and culture-setting discussions and activities are needed in all cases, whether the goal is to become a totally transformed school, a small learning community, or simply a better place for learning. Exercises to envision, set the tone for, and build school culture can be applied to changing the culture of a classroom, academy, house, or entire school.

For schools and communities that are committed to real transformation, the discourse about the change process and desired outcomes needs to include all stakeholders, so that all involved are a part of leading the effort. (For more description and tools designed to support changing the discourse in schools to increase equity, see Chapter Five.) Creating a team is the first step toward building a school community that values the voices and contributions of all its stakeholders. A new school design team's composition determines the ways the team operates, the ways work gets done, the ways decisions get made, and what the plans for the school look like. There is a strong connection between the leadership and engagement of stakeholders on the design team and in the school. If the foundation of active and inclusive participation is laid from the initial planning stage, it creates a tremendous advantage for the school. When students create student agreements and parents create parent agreements, both groups feel much more responsibility in helping their peers live up to them. When business leaders put time and resources into planning a school, they become much more invested in the school's success. Ultimately, the leaders and stakeholders on the design team are strongly connected to the leaders and stakeholders in the school itself when it opens.

As Kristen Chase, a student member of the design team for ARISE, explains, a diverse team communicates a strong message to potential students, families, and staff members, and brings valuable perspectives to the planning of the school. Potential teachers interviewing to work at the school see that the students—the people they will be there to serve—are helping to make decisions about their employment. For students, too, seeing other students on the design team is powerful. Chase says, "As far as being a young person and being a leader, especially in the community that ARISE is serving, it just shows so much to kids. Some kids were coming from communities where people tell them they can't succeed or that they're not great. For them to be able to see me be this powerful leader—I've seen it in a few of the students that we have met; they realize, 'Oh, she's on the design team, and she's a student—this is possible.'"

It is not enough to simply include all stakeholders on the design team. Attention must be paid to ensure that all stakeholders are engaged in meaningful participation. In SeaTac, Washington, three new small schools were established through the conversion of Tyee High School. Odyssey High School student Isaura Jimenez participated in the process of creating Odyssey from the larger Tyee High School. Jimenez and other students did not always easily find a place in the redesign conversations. Jimenez recalls,

> Not every student was always given the opportunity to do meaningful work. Sometimes students were there doing nothing in particular; we were just following along as teachers discussed things that we as students knew little about or had little say over. Because of this and other factors (besides coming to school when we could have been sleeping) some students stopped attending the meetings. But there were others who stayed, so each school still had a handful of students working with it. There were days when teachers were off holding their own meetings. During these times, we as students held our own meetings as well which were facilitated by an adult who made sure to give us our own space as he made us question our school system as it is now. We were given time to consider what made the perfect school and what it was that we needed in order to succeed today. This gave us extra time to think things through and enter back into our design teams with more ideas than before. [Jimenez, 2006]

While not perfect, the process created entry for students into the birth of the new schools, and this paid rich dividends when the schools opened. "Once the school year started, one could see that the staff at Odyssey—the school I chose—was amazingly open to having students take a big role in whatever was going on," says Jimenez.

> They made an effort to invite students to staff meetings as they tried to reiterate that they wanted us to take control and make it our school, to mold it into what we saw fit. We're only in our second year as a school and yet the differences between then and now are already evident. We still struggle with attendance, but the number of fights on our campus has gone down and already students feel more comfortable approaching their teachers. Students are experiencing a new type of power that has allowed us to grow proud of our school as we are given opportunities to voice our opinions and make things happen, thus allowing us to take ownership of our school. We're moving forward to a place where we can reclaim our voices. [Jimenez, 2006]

Though the commitment to students' having a voice was clearly held as a central value by all stakeholders at the school, old habits of student passivity and educators' strongly held authority died hard. Jimenez observes,

> This is easier said than done, of course, as we can't be expected to all of a sudden take control when all along we've been told that this is the way that things were going to be because someone else said so. When presented with all of this opportunity, we didn't quite know what to do with it. At times, it feels that adults aren't as receptive as they could be about students' ideas for change. Adults have their own ideas of what needs to be done and so have that as a top priority, forgetting that this isn't simply their school, it's our school. Our priorities as a school should include concerns and plans from everyone involved. Just as we as students should have to tell the adults what we want and what we need in order to get things done, they should in turn tell us what must be done this school year and what they think they need since we are a community. [Jimenez, 2006]

The habits of collaboration among a diverse group of decision makers are hard-won, and as Jimenez notes, the challenging situation of whole-school collaboration is eased somewhat by students' participation in the initial design and planning stages of the project. "The ability to invest and trust in their students to know what they need and want out of school as they engage us in this necessary work is what I believe has made the conversion process at Tyee different. This is what will ultimately lead to the success of Tyee's three small schools," Jimenez asserts. She shares thoughts with school planners about building a diverse design team that includes students:

> Make sure that if you do decide to open up and allow students to take part in the creation of your school, invite them for meaningful work that they will be able to influence. There's no need for a token student, just so that you'll be able to say that your school had student input. It'll show if your new small school does or doesn't include student voices. And make sure that you reach out to parents to keep them fully updated on what's going on. If you're a conversion school, make sure that you get that out there, that you tell families what's going on regularly through letters at the very least. And at least make

an attempt to write those letters in more languages than just English and Spanish. In its last year, Tyee held multiple meetings to inform the community of the coming changes. In an area so diverse, it's important to keep everyone informed so they feel like a part of the community instead of excluded by default. [Jimenez, 2006]

It is important to identify ways to involve the various players fully and equitably, using rituals, protocols, and hands-on activities to help bring out everyone's voices and foster collaborative decision making. For example, when fifteen members of the ARISE team, including parents, students, and staff members, attended the CES Summer Institute prior to the school's opening, they brainstormed ideas for both student leadership and student discipline through a restorative justice approach, with students taking the lead. At the end of the week, after someone proposed that the five students present serve as the interim student leadership team, everyone rated the proposal using "Fist to Five." Every person raised a hand, displaying a fist or one, two, three, four, or five fingers. A fist expressed adamant opposition to the idea, a five signified full support, and varying degrees of enthusiasm ranged between. People were asked to state the thoughts behind their vote, and had there been any fists (which there were not, in this case) a decision would not have been reached unless those people were heard out and could be convinced to increase their vote to at least a one, meaning that they could live with the decision. A couple of the students rated it with one finger at first, expressing concerns about their own leadership abilities, but were convinced by the group that they could do it. The desired outcomes, having effective and inclusive structures for student leadership and using a process that included all voices and fostered leadership in the decision making, were both achieved.

Another challenge in creating an inclusive design team is the format and discourse of the meetings and the way that the work gets done. On the positive side, creating an environment that engages students, family members, and educators equally in the process will provide a significant boost to creating a school culture that does the same. However, these three groups often speak completely different languages. Educators have their own intellectual discourse, filled with acronyms and profession-specific jargon; even parents who share the same native language as the educators speak as lay people when it comes to schools. This is complicated when there are actual language differences and when parents do not have a long or positive history of formal education themselves. Students are conversant in the language of youth culture and their own experiences, which is far less abstract than "eduspeak." Moreover, if meetings are purely discussion-based and remain in a whole-group format, educators can easily dominate at the expense of the other groups. Employing strategies such as dividing into smaller subgroups, using discussion protocols to regulate the conversation, and having clearly delineated roles and responsibilities can help foster full participation.

Connections Public Charter School in Hilo, Hawai'i, provides some interesting and successful examples of engaging all their stakeholders. Similar to Capital City, Connections was a charter school serving kindergarten through eighth-grade students in a community that did not have enough positive high school options for its students. Students and their families provided some of the initial impetus for adding a high school, and the process of the design team reflected this initiative. Principal John Thatcher describes the format:

> A typical design team meeting would start at 6:00 in the evening, late enough so parents could get off work and have dinner. At the high end, we had maybe fifty people. We had a lot of parents and community people on the team for information. Right from the beginning, we really did not have the stage model for presentations. The norm for the meetings was a discussion, and the discussion was often facilitated by kids. We really encouraged the kids right from the beginning that this was their school, that they had to help define what it was going to look like.

Thatcher realized that putting students at the center of the design process felt disconcerting to some parents. "The parents, at first, wondered, 'Why are the kids taking the lead? Why aren't the principal and the teachers facilitating this meeting?' But I think people got used to the reality pretty fast that the kids were going to have a strong voice, were going to be at every meeting, and could speak openly."

Communicate with the Community

The public has very set expectations about what schools look like: students sitting quietly in rows listening attentively to the teacher. These conceptions are grounded in personal experience and popular iconography. Transformed schools may look very different: classrooms buzzing with students actively learning and teachers coaching from the sidelines. Achieving these new designs requires school-based autonomy in curriculum and instruction, budgeting, hiring, and more. (See Chapter Three for a fuller discussion of school autonomy.) For these reasons, it is important to make school board members, opinion makers, and the community aware of the reasons driving the change and the rationale for the solutions being employed. Max Silverman, former principal of Tyee High School and current Highline School District administrator, says the design planners organized many professionally facilitated parent forums as part of the process of converting their large traditional high school into three new small schools: "The parents who were concerned that things were going to be different—band parents and all those parents—it was easy to involve them, but other parents in the community were harder. We [would] sometimes go out to public housing. We spent time going up to people's apartments, to every elementary school, and still, at some meetings, only one or two people would show up."

It is not easy to develop an effective communication strategy. At times, it may feel like it is a diversion from the more central task of designing the school. However, a successful communication strategy can help to create clear expectations of what the school will look like, build community support, and eliminate future conflict. (For more on developing an effective communication strategy, see Chapter Eleven, which has a section on creating a power base through outreach, messaging, and advocacy.)

Engage Partners and Join a Network

External partners are also a key part of the design process. Connections Public Charter School had several school partners involved in designing the school, including faculty from the University of Hawai'i's marine science, astronomy, and agriculture programs, who talked to the team about how students could get involved in their programs and how the university faculty could get involved in teaching and learning at Connections. Once the school opened, these partners continued to play a role in the school. ARISE High School's design team included a number of outside partners as well, such as the Mills College TRiO programs and Oakland Community Organizations. Having these partners working together from the beginning to plan the school added to their sense of ownership and engagement, as well as to the integration of their programs into the life of the schools once they launched. A participant in the first ARISE design team meeting several years before the school opened, who then was unable to attend another meeting, ended up yielding one of the most significant partnerships the school has, even though it was not a part of the founding charter. Michael Torres was the chair of the theater department at Laney College, a local community college in Oakland, and in the first year of the school, he pioneered a three-week intersession course for which students received college credit. This initial connection and class led to an additional Laney intersession course in ARISE's second year and then three more Laney courses during the second semester. ARISE and Laney are now pursuing ways to deepen the partnership even further and offer more courses and perhaps even associate degrees. Torres's involvement in the early days of the school's planning, however limited, got him excited about the school and led to his involvement once the school opened and to the blossoming of this partnership.

Metro High School, located in Columbus, Ohio, is another new school in the CES SSN. Metro was created with the help of a number of partnerships that were central to its mission and vision, including CES, Battelle Memorial Institute, The Ohio State University, and the Educational Council, a nonprofit organization that works with sixteen different school districts in Ohio. Founding principal Marcy Raymond reflects: "We were seeking a partnership-based school. And as a partnership-based school, we were looking at how to create a regional draw that would assist the entire school community through the education of youth, the training of the teachers, and the best practices that could be shared in the learning community. We wanted to look at ourselves as a part of the bigger community, and how we could create a school that is best able to help facilitate partnerships throughout Franklin County" (Coalition of Essential Schools, 2008b). Metro's partnerships helped the school in its design process and then continued to sustain its instructional vision and program once it opened.

Joining a network of schools with a similar mission or vision is also incredibly helpful to the design process, as well as to the growth and sustenance of a school. For schools within the CES SSN, relationships with other schools have been invaluable; each school benefits as schools in all stages of design and implementation see themselves anew through others and imagine and re-imagine what they can be. The CES SSN is an example of a national network that provides the advantage of a large national learning community that has been able to collaborate for a number of years. By bringing CES Mentor Schools together with new small schools, the CES SSN helps school communities to learn from others who have walked a similar road and provides opportunities for reflection, analysis, and growth for the more established CES Mentor Schools. Skyview Academy's John McKay, principal of a new small school, describes the meaning that participating in the CES SSN has had for the Skyview school community: "When we talk about the network, the real unique and beautiful thing about CES is that there are so many different schools that offer unique qualities and an abundance of resources. We don't have to reinvent the wheel; we can learn from experiences of others."

Conclusion

New small schools are most effective when they are designed to respond to the needs of the individual students they are intended to serve. These new schools have the greatest chance of success when they are planned backward from the end goals, when the work is well organized, when the design team is inclusive, when plans are in place to communicate with and be able to listen to the larger community about the new school, and when new schools are supported by partners in the communities in which they live. These objectives are most likely to be met through a deliberate, inclusive, and democratic design process. With ownership on the part of stakeholders and supportive partners, and the support of its school district and other governing bodies, a new school will be better equipped for the challenges of this demanding endeavor.

Transformational Leadership

Leading for equity takes commitment. One has to
explore areas of our educational system that need to
be overhauled if we are ever to give our students a
fair chance at success. It will take courageous
leaders to get us to consider alternatives that will
create a shift in power, the distribution of resources,
and the ways in which we hold ourselves
responsible for educating each child."

—LaShawn Routé Chatmon, executive director of the Bay Area
Coalition for Equitable Schools, speaking at CES
Small Schools Network Meeting,
January 2008

This chapter examines the concept of leadership in equitable, student-focused, academically challenging schools. In CES small schools, the key to creating equitable learning environments for children and adults is the commitment that every educator, family member, student, and community member makes to becoming a transformational leader. Transformational leadership refers to the set of attitudes, beliefs, and practices necessary to guide individuals and school communities to examine the intellectual and social-emotional challenges of creating an equitable school system and to develop and implement a new set of policies and practices that promote equity. CES school leaders who engage in transformational leadership intentionally work on becoming aware of their own tacit assumptions and expectations, as well as those built into the institutional culture of their school and the system of schools to which they belong. These leaders operate both in the intellectual and emotional realms, and they are committed to creating the conditions for personal insight and transformation among members of their school community. These leaders nurture these conditions and experiences to encourage growth and leadership among members of the school community, partly by modeling reflective practices that enable them to assess their own personal values, beliefs, and experiences.

Transformational leaders show courage and persistence in their constant and consistent interruption of inequitable practices in their schools, and they work tirelessly at developing the skill and the will for others in the school community to examine the cultural and institutional biases that create inequitable outcomes for students. The form of leadership they use elevates the discourse about change in education from reform to transformation. Transformational leaders believe in democracy and use the vehicle of education—its process and institutions—to work on the missteps, malpractice, and oversights that have obstructed the achievement of success for all students. As members of communities of learners, these leaders are in constant exploration and discovery of ways to raise the quality of teaching and learning and serve all students well.

In this chapter, we examine the principles and practices of a number of small CES schools that have used transformational leadership to build some of the most exemplary schools in the country:

- Leading a discourse of transformation
- Being a different kind of principal
- Committing to a shared mission and vision
- Engaging in equity-focused inquiry
- Nurturing a culture of shared ownership, accountability, and leadership
- Cultivating teacher leaders
- Developing youth leadership
- Bringing families to the decision-making table

Leading a Discourse of Transformation

If we are to make systemic change that moves beyond present norms, expectations, and results in the public school system to a system that engages all learners in using their mind well, we will need to shift to a discourse of transformation. As it stands now, "schools are a major part of society's institutional processes for maintaining a relatively stable system of inequality. They contribute to these results by active acceptance and utilization of a dominant set of values, norms and beliefs, which, while appearing to offer opportunities to all, actually support the success of a privileged minority and hinder the efforts and visions of a majority" (Eubanks, Parish, and Smith, 1997, p. 151). Leaders working for equity courageously guide us into a deeper discourse on the subject of educational change in order to transform the social reproduction and hegemonic culture of inequality that is pervasive in public education and create long-term institutionalized change. As we rethink and redesign schools, keeping a keen eye on the everyday occurrences in our schools that widen the gap between communities and between the highest- and the lowest-performing students, it behooves us to move from a discourse of reform, in which we look at the symptoms of inequity and the improvements we can make to what already exists, to a transformational discourse, in which we investigate the causes of inequity and move into the uncharted waters of what could be (see "The Nature of Discourse in Education" sidebar).

The Nature of Discourse in Education: Notes on "Changing the Discourse in Schools"

Inspired by Eubanks, Parish, and Smith's "Changing the Discourse in Schools" (Eubanks, Parish, and Smith, 1997), the Bay Area Coalition for Equitable Schools uses the following table as a coaching tool to galvanize discussion about the ways that discourse in schools contributes to inequity (Discourse I) and to push educators to envision a form of discourse that moves toward educational equity and success for all (Discourse II).

Discourse I deals with . . .	Discourse II deals with . . .
Singular truths	Multiple stories
"The change process"	The desired circumstances
Improving what exists	Changing something significant
Techniques, methods, and content	Learning and school relationships
Symptoms	Causes
The way things are	What could be
Blaming others for not meeting our standards	Questioning whether our standards are hindrances
Discipline and control	Alienation and resistance
Competency	Relevance
The familiar	The uncomfortable
Answers and solutions	Dilemmas and mysteries
Information transfer	Knowledge creation
Ability and merit	Privilege and oppression
Dropouts	Push-outs
Reproduction	Transformation
The work of adults	The learning and experience of students
World-class standards	Re-creating our society
Limited time and ability	Getting started anyway

Source: Table is from the Bay Area Coalition for Equitable Schools. Copyright © 2003 Bay Area Coalition for Equitable Schools.

To tackle what we understand as the predictable outcomes of our current system (see the Definition of Educational Equity sidebar in Chapter One for a description of those outcomes), we need to strip away the elements of the system that well-intentioned educators have learned to collude with, so that we can expose the realities of an unfair system. "Leadership often involves challenging people to live up to their words, to close the gap between their espoused values and their actual behavior. It may mean pointing out the elephant sitting on the table at a meeting—the unspoken issue that everyone sees but no one wants to mention. It often requires helping groups make difficult choices and give up something they value on behalf of something they care about more" (Heifetz and Linsky, 2004, p. 33). The transformational leader facilitates a purposeful process through conversation and action, to reinvent the system of education, changing it from a system that relegates children to being treated as numbers, sorting them by their perceived abilities, to a system in which educators know their students well, personalize their learning, incorporate their stories into the curriculum, and validate the assets they bring.

In the discourse of transformation, the notion of "highly qualified" educators stretches beyond knowing well their discipline and the craft of teaching to knowing well the students, their families, and the communities in which they live. Moving to a discourse of transformation rather than reform requires that we make significant changes to the ways in which we lead and support schools, educators, and the children they serve. The shift will require that we better understand the multiple stories of our students, their needs, their strengths, and the effects that educational neglect has had on them as learners and as people.

"Any system of oppression, through its inherent divisiveness and violence, has a negative impact on all people who fall within its ambit," write Cheryl de la Rey and Norman Duncan (2004, p. 60). Those interested in creating equitable schools struggle both with the intellectual challenges that result from educational inequity and with the emotional and psychological effects we have all had to endure while living in a society of haves and have-nots. While many understand the external changes that need to occur in our schools, those who are preparing themselves to become transformational leaders ready to fully participate in a discourse of transformation must undertake an internal exploration of how social disparities have affected their identity and the way that they see the world and their place in it. David Greenberg, administrative director of El Colegio Charter School, a CES Mentor School in Minneapolis, reflects on the ways that his personal transformation has put him in a better place to hold a leadership position at his school: "I have learned that I cannot lose sight that I am a white man in a position of power at my school, not to mention in society as a whole. I have come to better understand that people of color, our students, don't have the luxury not to consider their race or ethnicity on a daily basis. As a white man, I can ignore my background and privilege if I want to. But if I do that, I don't think I can truly support our school to work towards equitable opportunities and outcomes for all students." The process of self-examination helps leaders like Greenberg undergo their own personal transformation. Then, as educators, they reflect on the ways that they have perpetuated an unjust system and learn and internalize new behaviors and values that will influence the ways that they can interrupt inequity at all levels within their school. This process helps leaders to create and put in place equitable policies and practices that will help to institutionalize educational equity for the long haul.

The transformational leader who has assumed the responsibility to push for deep systemic change works to make and hold space for unpopular perspectives that might make matters uncomfortable but will matter greatly for the greater good. Camilla Greene, a National School Reform Faculty coach, observes, "Leading for equity means that one is not satisfied with the way the world is currently operating. The work of leading for equity is emotionally charged and messy. It means you speak truth to power and call a sham a sham. If you do not make people feel uncomfortable, you are not pushing for a different reality." Shifting the discourse beyond reform means that everyone in the building is dealing with the collective and individual biases, behaviors, and ideas that are entrenched in the culture of the school.

Transformational leaders work toward creating equity within school communities and understand that conversations across differences are essential to deconstruct the understandings and assumptions that we hold about our colleagues and students. These leaders nurture a climate of trust and respect as key elements in sustaining these conversations. To support this ongoing dialogue, CES leaders employ the Critical Friends Group (CFG), a cornerstone practice of professional learning communities, to create and sustain a space that builds everyone's emotional and intellectual capacity to remain in the conversation. Using conversational protocols, trained CFG coaches maintain a tone of decency and trust and facilitate courageous conversations that help members stay engaged and centered on issues of equity. As Glenn Singleton and Curtis Linton (2006) write in *Courageous Conversations About Race: A Field Guide for Achieving Equity in Schools,* "The challenge is to resist the natural inclination to move away from the conversation. School leaders need to be aware of this as an initial step in creating the necessary safe space for staff to stay engaged. If this safety is not created, those at the table will stand up and walk away, whether literally or figuratively" (p. 60). These honest conversations create allies within and across racial, gender, and class boundaries. (For more on the use of Critical Friends Groups, see Chapter Six.)

At Young Women's Leadership Charter School, a Chicago CES Mentor school that primarily serves African American students, the faculty engages in tough conversations. Teacher leader Adelric McCain shares his experience:

> We have started a practice of incorporating as many voices as possible into the dialogue about race and the impact that it has on the culture of our school and student outcomes. Through our participation in the CES Small Schools Network, I've seen a lot of teacher-led groups, and they have a voice in their schools. To support our work with CES around equity, we created a teacher-led CFG. The whole purpose of that group is to share dilemmas. One of the most powerful conversations we had was to name the demographics of our teaching community and how the majority of the faculty looks different from our students. Naming this reality was an important step in these conversations.

Over the last three years, McCain and other educators of color who are members of the CES Small Schools Network have formed the CES People of Color Affinity Group, coming together three to four times a year to discuss the leadership role that teachers of color can play in transforming public education. On numerous occasions, the group has identified the inability of many educators to see that persistent inequity in our nation is one of the biggest obstacles to addressing inequity in education. These educators do not believe that all teachers of color see inequity with a sharper and clearer lens, but they assert that given their firsthand life experience with racism, they are more likely to detect and name that inequity and, given who they are, be motivated to do something about it. On the other hand, they contend that their white colleagues are more likely to make excuses for why things are the way they are or to look the other way. The majority of these educators know from personal experience what it feels like to be stuck in "color-blind" schools that downplay difference as a way to make things "equal," denying differences and the effect they have on outcomes. Educators participating in the CES People of Color Affinity Group do not buy into that mentality. They have been outspoken leaders in their school communities and have risked their careers and relationships with their colleagues by speaking up and debunking these myths.

There is a dearth of people of color in the teaching profession, and in and of itself, that is a reflection of inequity in our society. *Small Schools, Big Ideas* is not going to examine why people of color generally do not become teachers—leaving the teaching profession predominantly white, middle-class, and female—but we see value in stating that schools that serve students of color need to have adults of color present and engaged in the education of those young people. Such adults do not automatically fix deep-rooted historical wrongs, but their presence, at minimum, reflects the diversity of our country and the students that we serve. More important, students of color and white students need to see their teachers engaged in productive conversations across difference about the very issues that are preventing everyone from getting a quality education. The modeling of these interactions helps to prepare students to participate in a diverse democratic society.

As part of the mission to increase equity in our schools, a deliberate attempt must be made by every individual, school district, and school to bring educators of color into the profession and thereby into the conversation, by attracting students of color into the teaching profession and recruiting teachers of color into school faculties. Making this happen will require leadership from many quarters. Our students need to see teachers of color as role models for the teaching profession. If we want to effect a change in the number of students of color who aspire to become teachers, they need to see themselves in the people who are educating them. The very acts of fostering a discourse of transformation and creating a culture that is willing to take on these hard questions in order to build the skill and will among all teachers to create equitable circumstances for learning will help to draw the interest of more teachers of color. Teachers of color who are critical of culturally biased learning environments, biased assessment methods, and the generally low quality of education that children of color experience will be attracted to schools that are willing to expose the ugly realities of the present system and are working collectively across difference to do something different for all children.

While we work on diversifying the teaching population, we can simultaneously prepare the white, middle-class teachers who constitute the majority of teachers in our urban schools to facilitate and engage in conversations about equity among themselves and across difference between themselves and students of color, their families, and the communities they serve. Kyle Meador, a program associate at CES, states, "It is the role, responsibility, and moral imperative of white, anti-racist transformational leaders who are committed to achieving educational equity to, first, take a critical look at their own privilege; second, to recognize and discuss this privilege as it relates to the tacit assumptions they and their colleagues may hold that are often unknowingly getting in the way of their ability to serve each student well; and, third, develop the courage to use their privilege to challenge racism in institutional settings." To participate in this long-range dialogue, everyone must commit to engaging in courageous conversation across schools and districts. "By collectively making this commitment they can fully embrace the conversation and ensure that it deepens their focus on eliminating racial achievement disparity and propels their efforts to do so" (Singleton and Linton, 2006, p. 60). Being fully engaged by participating and leading this discourse of transformation can take blinders off and create the internal space needed to ignite the passion and hope of those who desperately want to do better for our children.

A Different Kind of Principal

Leading a CES small school requires a broader vision, scope of leadership, and administration than most conventional schools can imagine. Small school leaders have to navigate two very different worlds inside and outside of their school community. Inside the small school, the CES transformational leader facilitates a governance process that is collaborative and inclusive; she is working to bring out the leadership of others and buffering teachers from the world of administrative minutiae and top-down mandates so they can focus their time and energy in the classroom, on the students, and on teaching and learning. In the world outside the school, hierarchy reigns and imposing regulations create an artificial barrier between administrators and educators.

Small school leaders also have to balance the role of instructional leader with the role of school administrator. In many traditional schools, principals are not focused on the classroom. The policy climate overemphasizes compliance, seldom allowing principals of large comprehensive schools to become instructional leaders. These principals rely on the administrative support of assistant and vice principals, coaches, and department heads to monitor what is taking place in the classroom and to support teachers who may need help. Principals' participation in classroom observations is infrequent and, in most cases, tends to be evaluative, given the time limitations. Small school leaders share their leadership and distribute their power in ways that maintain their primary involvement in instruction while enlisting the leadership and ownership of teachers, family members, and student leaders in the school in order to accomplish tasks such as managing budgets or crafting professional development plans. The goal is to ensure that the principal of a small school does not replicate the dysfunctional role that large school principals are forced to play. Because the culture is collaborative and inspires everyone to take risks and learn, the roles and responsibilities can be distributed and shared differently than in more traditional schools. The hope is that the school leaders free themselves enough to participate in the intellectual life of the school. In the best-case scenario, they play the role of lead teacher, and at a minimum, they are able to go beyond their management duties to participate in the shaping of the educational program. Catherine DeLaura, former principal of School of the Future, a CES Mentor School in New York City, explains how she felt supported by the other adults in her building: "I had a lot of administrative responsibilities, and with the support of a small staff and the willingness of teachers to take on some of those tasks, we managed. I am appreciative of the shared leadership model we had because it allowed me the time to also be an instructional leader in my building. Without that structure and those expectations, I don't think I would have been able to get into the classroom and support the growth of a strong instructional culture."

Fundamentally, the work of a transformational leader is aimed at transforming the teaching and learning that takes place in the classroom as well as nurturing the relationships between students, staff members, teachers, and family members in order to create a powerful instructional program. These relationships are key pieces in maintaining a tone of decency and trust and a commitment to equity and democracy in the school. Making sure that everyone is working together, creating spaces for everyone to have a say, ensuring that everyone feels that they own the school's challenges and successes, and helping to remove the barriers that stand in the way of good teaching and learning is the job of the principal or school leader—the person who holds the positional power in the school community.

David Greenberg, administrative director of El Colegio, describes his work with teachers and how he uses the structures and culture of shared leadership to remove obstacles and free up teachers to engage in powerful teaching and learning:

> Historically, at El Colegio, we've had a sense [that] ... teacher ownership is institutionalized at our school at the highest level of governance. We also have a site management team that reports to the board [and] whose membership includes the administrative director, education director, and a teacher/advisor who is selected by the other teacher/advisors. My job is to use these structures to empower teachers to help develop school policies and practices that support equitable teaching and learning. And one of my biggest roles is to make sure that teachers are not overwhelmed with other tasks or derailed by issues that get in the way of their teaching. I buffer the teachers from the burdensome administrative responsibilities so that they can focus more closely on the students.

In the same way that the principal supports individual teachers, she is also responsible for creating and protecting the space for the professional learning community. (For more on professional learning communities, see Chapter Six.) According to Lawrence Kohn, former principal and co-founder of Quest High School, a CES Mentor School in Humble, Texas, fostering a collaborative culture in which a professional learning community can thrive is one of the most important roles of a principal. It is the principal as instructional leader who helps the faculty members take a critical look at themselves and their practice, facilitates the gathering and analysis of data, guides the staff through processes of inquiry and decision making, and supports teacher leadership in the professional learning community. Figure 5.1 illustrates the school leader's role in fostering professional learning communities.

CES small schools grapple with what it takes for teacher leaders to maintain a delicate balance between what goes on in the classroom and what goes on in the school. Because teachers' preparation time is intensive, finding the time to build their practice as educators or take on other leadership roles and responsibilities in the school can be challenging. Principals and other school administrators work hard to support teachers' involvement in the leadership and governance of the school while also protecting their time with students.

Figure 5.1
Systemic View of the Integrated Themes That Positively and Negatively Influence the Professional Community

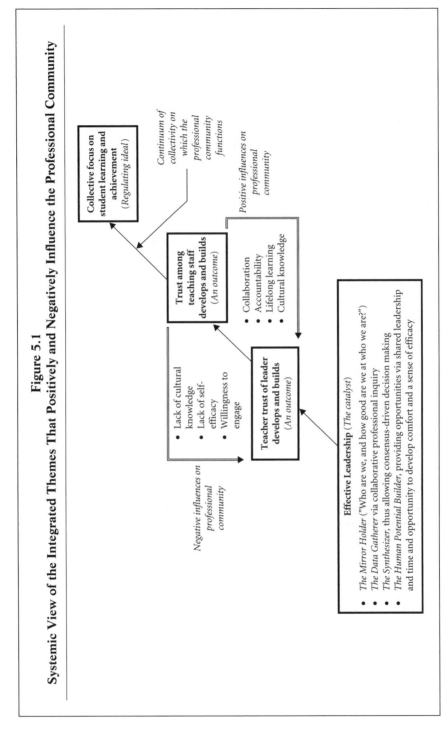

Source: Used by permission of Lawrence Kohn.

Principals and other administrators in CES schools help to facilitate the work of the whole school and, using an equity lens, provide a moral imperative and the leverage needed to keep the vision and collective energy on improving student outcomes. While small school principals wear multiple hats and manage diverse administrative responsibilities, the power embedded in their formal role puts them in the best position to help the school hold its collective vision and chart a course toward actualizing an equity-focused mission.

Committing to a Shared Mission and Vision

According to Terrence Deal and Kent D. Peterson (1999) in *Shaping School Culture,* a school's mission and purpose embody the vision of the school and give guidance about what people need to focus on in the daily operations of a school in order to ultimately manifest the concrete attributes of the mission. To work for equity, transformational leaders require a school mission and purpose that is focused on creating an equitable learning environment that results in equitable academic outcomes. The vision and mission are translated into everyday practice by formal and frequent opportunities for staff to collaborate on analyzing successes, challenges, and results. Schools that sustain this work periodically revisit and edit vision and mission statements so they remain living, meaningful documents.

CES school leaders model equitable practices and principles through words and actions to make evident what they believe in and are willing to stand for. Transformational leaders channel the norms, beliefs, and values of their community. Greg Peters, former principal of Leadership High School, a CES Mentor School in San Francisco, observes,

> Perhaps the most important role of a visionary leader is to serve as an ally to and for the diverse voices across her community while staying true to the promise of the school's mission—the promise to the community whose children the school is serving. That said, the vision of a leader must be embedded in values, not only what the leader believes to be true in order to equitably and excellently educate all children but also the values heard, held, and honored in the very community to whom these children belong. This vision of combined values—this equity stance—should be the lens through

which we hold any and all of our conversations to make decisions about teaching and learning, discipline and support, hiring and evaluation, and expenditures of money and time.

A school's mission is the locomotive that drives decisions about the ways adults and students in a school community use energy and time. A school's mission indicates what is valued and what actions and attitudes reflect those values. A school's mission, which can also be thought of as its purpose, is the basis for guidelines on making decisions about the management and allocation of resources, on developing professional learning plans, and on shaping the instructional program of a school (Deal and Peterson, 1999, p. 26). A school's mission is also used to measure its effectiveness; a mission-driven school uses every opportunity to clarify its vision to its community members and to outsiders. Paula Anderson, education director for the High School for Recording Arts, a CES Mentor School in St. Paul, Minnesota, talks about her experience with visitors and the need for them to clearly understand what the school is about and for:

> I have often been a part of school visits and quality review teams, and I have seen how, without a context for school transformation as a guiding principle of the visit or evaluation, visitors often use a rather traditional yardstick with which to measure experimental and innovative programs. This has gone unchallenged for years; the mission of the school being examined is virtually ignored while a group of evaluators, who often have the potential to greatly impact the future of the school, use their own interior agendas to make their assessments. We wanted to define the parameters of our school visits and evaluations to be more in line with our mission, so we prepared visitor folders with more than just schedules, maps, and staff biographies. We now ask visitors to read "Changing the Discourse in Schools" [Eubanks, Parish, and Smith 1997] or at least study the Discourse I and II chart ["The Nature of Discourse in Education" sidebar], as well as reading several articles about the plight of African American teenage boys in the traditional education and incarceration systems, to provide a context for our work. We have been doing this for several years, both for the erudition of our visitors and to help the team understand the rationale for our mission and methods. We feel

that taking this stance with the many visitors we receive has helped to spread a philosophy of school transformation and has helped our community appreciate our school.

Because of the historical oppression that permeates our schools, our ability to imagine new possibilities may be restricted; therefore, it is the responsibility of a transformational leader to hold and communicate a vision for what may be possible that amends the present reality. Whether a leader has come into an already existing school or is creating a new small school, it is critical that she facilitate a process for developing a shared vision for the school that can help to motivate staff members, students, and community alike to work toward equity (Deal and Peterson, 1999). In optimal conditions, leaders work collaboratively with a group of capable educators who share a vision and employ a common set of norms, goals, and values. Whether they are positional leaders or organic leaders who emerge from the community and are empowered to lead, school leaders are guided by the mission of the school, which is the road map that transformational leaders use to support the growth of the community in order to make educational equity a reality.

Once a school has decided on its purpose, its leadership and governance structures drive the work in that direction. Getting closer to the mission's explicit goals and objectives requires that leaders work toward securing and allocating resources that meet the challenges. Both monetary and human resources need to be captured and harnessed in order to accomplish the mission. The leadership charts the direction of the journey for the whole group, while consistently checking back to make sure that everyone is on board and that everyone is moving in the same direction.

Engaging in Equity-Focused Inquiry

Leaders engage the school community in investigations and discussions in order to facilitate personal and professional transformation, openly engaging in inquiries about race, equity, and achievement. Transformative leaders and the schools that they lead are committed to learning from diverse forms of knowledge and experience. Transformational leaders create professional learning communities that commit time and energy to increasing their skill and will to better serve all students well. These leaders develop a culture of learning in the school community that is driven by inquiry and use professional development as an opportunity to build a framework for action and a common language in regard to issues of educational equity. Within a community of learners, adults have opportunities to model inquiry and learning for students. It is important that young people see adults engaged in intellectual queries with each other. The learning standards of a school are lifted in a culture of learning that creates time and space for everyone to ask questions, explore knowledge, and make meaning with one another.

The cycle of inquiry (see Figure 5.2) guides educators through an examination of data that helps them reflect on the effectiveness of their present practice and grapple with the controversial unresolved questions they face about student achievement. Practitioners use a data-based inquiry process as a way to examine and identify the gaps and snags in the educational process that limit access and opportunity for students. One of five axioms of courageous leadership, according to Alan Blankstein (2004), involves confronting the data and your fears. "Facing the brutal facts is often difficult and can be unflattering," Blankstein writes, "yet naming and facing fears constructively (e.g., using a data-based approach) can be the first step to overcoming fear and expanding the range of possible actions" (Blankstein, 2007, p. 17).

The cycle of inquiry process encourages collaboration between practitioners and other stakeholders with various perspectives and levels of experience to create new practices that increase equitable academic achievement. The process involves naming assumptions, posing essential questions, examining data, proposing new practices and policies, testing new practices and policies, measuring their effectiveness, and building the cultural competence to apply learning. These cycles repeat and expand as the inquiry surfaces new questions and unearths other unjust practices and policies that need to be addressed.

At the Academy of Citizenship and Empowerment (ACE), a new small CES school that resulted from the conversion of SeaTac, Washington's Tyee High School, principal Stacy Spector convened a meeting of staff and students to explain how looking at data would help them shape the educational program of the school. "This is an opportunity to identify some of the strengths and needs of our students by looking at data from grades and attendance so that we can make very informed decisions about what courses we offer, how we schedule those offerings, and how we staff the school to meet the needs of every single student prepared for college, career, and citizenship," said Spector. In a joint effort to interrupt negative predictable outcomes, ACE students and faculty get together regularly at staff meetings to examine data and influence the policies and curriculum of the school.

Figure 5.2
Equity-Based Cycle of Inquiry

1. Assess the current reality.

- What is your interest in this topic? How does this theme apply in your school? How does it affect your practice? What data can you look at or analyze to inform your thinking about a possible problem statement? Data items could include disaggregated student achievement data, graduation rates, college entrance rates, attrition rates, teacher assignments, or student work.
- Define a problem statement that identifies patterns in student achievement or skill gaps and links them to related gaps in teacher practice or school practices.

2. Name an essential question to be explored.

- What are your assumptions about this topic?
- How will looking at this question help you look at issues of equity in relationship to teaching practice and school policy?
- How will this question help you understand the impact of teacher practices or policies on the achievement of all students?
- Who is your target of inquiry? Which group (or groups) of students do you want to affect?

3. Identify causes and potential solutions.

- What are likely causes of this problem?
- What cause of this problem, if addressed, would be most likely to create equitable outcomes for your students?
- What do evidence-based strategies and outside expertise say about this problem or cause?
- What specific practice or strategy will you change and analyze?
- Why do you think changing this practice or strategy will affect student outcomes?

Access, Opportunity, and Postsecondary Preparation

Schools need to diminish the historically predictive power of demographic data on high and equitable student achievement by increasing the achievement of all groups of students and dramatically accelerating the achievement of targeted groups of students.

4. Set goals, define measurable outcomes, and create an action plan.

- How will you know that you have been successful?
- What indicators will you use to measure progress toward meeting your goals?
- Identify the data collection tools that you will use to answer your essential questions.
- Develop a timeline and set specific dates for reaching goals.
- Establish your data collection plan.
- How might you connect your inquiry work to schoolwide, grade-level, or department work plans or to partner schools or your district?

7. Share and document your inquiry.

- Based on your data analysis, what decisions about next steps will you make?
- How will you document and share your work with members of the CES SSN network?
- How will you continue to build capacity (and the capacity of others) to implement what you have learned through your inquiry?
- How will you document and share your work and results with community stakeholders in order to obtain feedback to inform your next steps?

6. Analyze data to answer your essential question.

- Identify which students made how much improvement.
- Identify which practices affected student achievement.
- Analyze your success in reaching your goals.
- Make decisions about next steps based on data analysis.

5. Implement your action plan.

- Implement research and evidence-based strategies.
- Collect quantitative or qualitative benchmark data to inform your progress during the year.

Source: Adapted from Davidson, 2009a.

In many cases, one of the most important findings that come out of inquiry cycles is the urgent need for teachers to learn how to differentiate instruction—that is, teach and support learning within a heterogeneous group of students in ways that personalize instruction for each student and support each student in achieving success. Cycles of inquiry directed at teaching and learning outcomes are particularly important, so that those who need more will get more and those who need to be pushed harder will be pushed harder. Teachers learn ways to move beyond the traditional methods of delivering knowledge and assessing student learning. Holding low expectations for a certain groups of students or high expectations for those whom society deems smart enough to go on to college based on the color of their skin, their primary language, their family name, their gender, their economic status, or where they reside will be challenged and replaced with a new set of beliefs and practices that support everyone in using their mind well and demonstrating what they know and can do. (For more on differentiated instruction, see Chapter Seven.)

Nurturing a Culture of Shared Ownership, Accountability, and Leadership

When a school's leadership is clear about the vision and knows how to articulate it compellingly, interest and hope grow like wildfire among the school community, and additional leaders emerge. In Essential schools, it is the responsibility of the positional leadership—the principal or other named leader—to create and institutionalize democratic structures that support the work of teaching, learning, and governance and, in turn, build the voice, ownership, and leadership of members of the school community. While some believe that leadership can only come from the top, that without authority you have no possibility of leading, opportunities for exercising leadership do not depend on position. Leadership can come from any place within an organization (Heifetz and Linsky, 2004). In CES small schools, leadership emerges and is nurtured at every level of the school community. Leaders in positional or formal leadership roles, such as school principals or school directors, can use the clarity of a well-stated mission to instill a sense of ownership in others and use their power to empower others to find solutions to the issues they face within themselves. Eric Nadelstern reflects on his role as principal at International High School at LaGuardia Community College: "As a principal, I learned that people will bring their problems to you and you can spend your day solving their problems and that is very seductive and powerful, but in the final analysis, it's not the job of an educator. The job of an effective educator is to provide people with the encouragement, opportunity, and moral support needed to understand that they and their colleagues hold the solution to most of their problems" (Coalition of Essential Schools, 2005a). As the holders of the big picture, positional leaders find ways to share significant pieces of the organizational vision with other stakeholders in order to more effectively and efficiently move the whole closer to achieving the school's mission.

In CES schools, leadership is distributed widely, so that it is not all on one person's plate and so that the school can effectively utilize all of the strengths, skills, and talents of its community members. Beth Silbergeld describes her experience as a teacher at Leadership High School: "Right away in my first year at Leadership, I knew that I was empowered to propose ideas for change at staff meetings. That might look like proposing a policy change that might go up for decision by the staff, or it might look like an RSP [special education] teacher saying, 'I actually need to do some direct instruction with the entire staff around modifications.' I don't think it is the norm in most traditional schools to have structures in place where a teacher's ideas are solicited and respected." This distribution of leadership engenders a greater sense of interdependence and mutual responsibility. One of the most powerful and critical roles that transformational leaders can play in schools is to use the expansion of access to power and decision making as a means to charge everyone with the responsibility for achieving more equitable outcomes for students. (See the sidebar "The Ways That Transformational Leaders Use Their Power" for additional examples of such leadership.)

The Ways That Transformational Leaders Use Their Power

Transformational leaders

- Create structures and model practices of shared leadership
- Distribute their power in a way that maintains their oversight yet fosters a sense of ownership of the policies and practices of the school among its stakeholders

- Lead courageous discussions across differences that raise the consciousness of educators about issues of equity, diversity, and democracy
- Shift to a discourse of transformation when looking to restructure or reinvent old practices or solve problems
- Chart the course toward greater equity
- Hold the vision and the values that will nurture a social justice stance for the school aligned with the governance and instructional practices
- Get people on the bus and build their capacity to stay on the journey of building an equitable school
- Work to develop the leadership of others and apply it within the school
- Interrupt inequitable practices and use these as moments to engage the community in learning
- Build the will and the skill of all members of the school community to create and promote equity
- Work collaboratively with educators to implement teaching and learning strategies that promote equity and academic achievement for each student
- Include family and community members as leaders
- Build a strong culture of learning for students as well as adults in the school community

Creating a culture that is built on relationships and reflects and respects multiple voices and experiences is one of the primary building blocks of transformational leadership. Staff meetings, committees, and boards provide forums for members to meet, get to know each other, engage each other in learning, and hold each other accountable. These structures serve as spaces for giving input and evaluating issues that involve policies and instructional and organizational practices that affect the school climate and conditions for learning. Essential schools strive to make decision making inclusive and democratic in order to ensure that important decisions include the voices of those most directly affected by decisions. Peggy Kemp, headmaster of Boston's Fenway High School, a CES Mentor School and member of the Boston Pilot Schools network, reflects on the factors that cause teachers at Fenway to feel a sense of control in regard to their work:

> Fenway thrives because teachers feel a great deal of ownership over the school. Their teaching load is humane, and they have control over their curriculum. There are practices in place that make sure that everyone who is affected by a decision has some input. People at Fenway feel like they have a voice. We have a lot of opportunities to be able to discuss issues with each other, with students, or with adults. Among several opportunities to meet and influence decisions, we meet as a whole staff once a week. We meet as an organizational team once a week. Content teams meet once a week. The school is subdivided into three houses—one hundred students per house—and teachers within each house meet to discuss student issues, and the leadership team meets once a week: that's the house coordinators and other administrators. We also have a governance board composed of faculty, students, parents, and community members, and critical decisions are done democratically. At every level, the community is involved and has a place to provide their input.

At Fenway, staff and community members are involved in the leadership as well as the governance of the school. Their influence over the practices and policies of the school is expected and respected. Transformational leaders who work toward achieving greater equity use their power to create structures and practices that model shared leadership and empower others to act. These structures help to maintain a balance of power in the school community, providing space for practitioners, students, and parents to collaborate, give input for decision making, and drive the school toward equitable academic achievement. (For a Fenway High School organization chart, as well as a collection of other documents describing shared leadership and governance structures, please visit the *Small Schools, Big Ideas* Web site at http://www.ceschangelab.org.)

Cultivating Teacher Leaders

Historically, CES has seen teachers as the unit of change, and many CES schools have empowered teachers to become leaders with the conviction that only when teachers drive the change will classroom and ultimately school change take place. There are many different ways that schools develop and tap into teacher leadership to foster a teacher's sense of responsibility for the academic progress of all students rather than just what goes on in his or her classroom. Teachers direct staff development, facilitate staff meetings, and lead CFGs. An important role of a transformational leader is to build leadership among the adults in the school community in order to focus on the standards of practice and performance in the classroom, pushing to ensure that the daily work of the school is at intellectually high levels for all children. Through the use of CFGs, educators ask hard questions about culture and practice and collaboratively respond to persistent inequitable practices and behaviors that raise concerns. Beth Silbergeld comments on her experience as a teacher leader in her school: "In my role as a department coach, I use a peer coaching model that helps teachers to construct their own knowledge about change they may need to make in the classroom. This year, the department coaches also lead CFGs. We make decisions about the protocols that we are going to train staff on and lead discussions. We work collaboratively with the groups and give practitioners an opportunity to practice using one protocol for the year as a way of building their professional tool kit."

ARISE High School co-principal Romeo Garcia believes that working with CFGs builds trust and leadership:

> As a CFG coach, I have been encouraged by the level of engagement of participants in the seminars. We have been able to move closer to authentic self-reflection, which is necessary in order to spur others in our schools and communities to engage in the work of personal and community growth around issues of equity. The courage to share one's personal story encourages others to engage as well. I have been moved by the commitment of CFG participants, who are doing the personal work in order to become leaders in the change that help to move society forward. Part of my role is to help create and sustain the effective spaces to do this work and support people to stay in the conversation, especially when the conversations become personally challenging. When things are uncomfortable, I see progress being made.

The work of the teacher leader is primarily focused on creating the climate and conditions in the school community that facilitate the most productive teaching environment possible. Maria Hantzopoulos, a teacher leader at New York City's

Humanities Prep, a CES Mentor School, discusses how she and her colleagues work within a shared governance structure and still find the balance to stay focused on teaching and learning:

> While the principal at Prep is empowered and has the authority to make decisions on behalf of the school community—those might involve confidential personnel issues or addressing the day-to-day running of the school—generally, the school is run by consensus. Everyone has a role and a stake in what happens here. The governance structure is embodied in the weekly faculty meeting, which moves along with both school decisions by consensus and the distribution of administrative tasks. At Prep, the staff maintains a level of power over the governance of the school. We meet and make decisions on a variety of issues that affect our school culture, policy, and hiring. The meetings and the administrative tasks are sometimes hard for teachers to balance with a full teaching load. Sometimes we come together and divide the work up because we don't want these responsibilities to get in the way of teaching. If the quality of teaching was impacted negatively, it would defeat the purpose of helping to lead the school. We do it because as teachers, we know the cultural conditions and the resources that we need to most effectively work with the students in our charge.

In new CES small schools like Odyssey: The Essential School in SeaTac, Washington, another product of Tyee High School's conversion, emerging teacher leaders struggle with what it means to be empowered to make decisions and work collaboratively with their peers and principal to create the school they have always dreamed of. Principal Joan Ferrigno explains, "The new culture is one that tackles problems as a team, with teachers really owning the decisions. That's the kind of leadership that I have always wanted to be involved in; I always wanted to work with a team. But shared decision making is pretty new to the staff as a whole and while that makes it exciting to work with this group of people, they don't always feel enough power to run the school. They still ask me for permission for a lot of things. It is odd to me to have quite as much authority as I do here." It is not easy to go from being a classroom teacher with your door closed to participating in an open and democratic school community. New teachers in CES small schools or teachers who are new to CES small schools are similar to students who come from traditional schools. When they come to Essential schools, many teachers are shocked that they are asked to give their opinions and to engage in discussions with their peers. It takes them a while to feel comfortable with using their power to influence school policies and practices. Because of this, Ferrigno understands that she must use her power to model and encourage them to expand their vision of participation in the school community. "I know that I need to help them [teachers and students] to bring out their voices. I see it as my role to encourage them and build their capacity to lead the school."

Developing Youth Leadership

In many traditional schools, students play a peripheral role in leadership and governance. Student leaders organize parties and sports events and rally other students to show their school spirit and participate in public events that give the school its identity. Usually, students are not involved in any meaningful decision making; they are not consulted or included in any policy or curriculum decisions. In fact, they are absent from the decisions that affect them the most.

CES small schools put shared governance structures in place that give students access to the decision-making process alongside adult educators. There are many ways that CES schools nurture and engage youth voices, providing youth with opportunities to experience what it feels like to grapple with real-life issues and circumstances. "If you want your students to be leaders in the world, you got to let them lead—you got to show them how. They can't wait until they go to college to start finding their voice and learning how to take action for themselves and others," says Kristen Chase, a CES youth intern and a member of the ARISE High School design team. Leadership opportunities are learning opportunities that give students insight into various points of view and teach them how to express their needs and negotiate power with others. Participating in a democratic decision-making process prepares young people to participate in a democratic society by showing them how they can affect and influence their circumstances.

At Fenway High School in Boston, various formal structures allow students to participate in shaping the policies and practices of their school community. Headmaster Peggy Kemp comments,

> Students play a role. There are students on our governance board, representatives of student government. We do a report from students

to the board on student issues at every meeting. Students bring issues to leadership meeting time. As well, as we have different student groups—for example, the Voices of Liberation group, which has taken on the responsibility of the political and social education of the school. I ask them to bring their issues and ideas to me, and then we speak to [the] leadership team. They need to put it in writing—that's the primary way that we negotiate decisions with students.

(For an additional example of student leadership in school governance, see the sidebar "Recommendations for Sustainability from Lehman Alternative Community School" in Chapter Eleven.)

Out of respect for the community and every community member's humanity, CES schools aim to remain violence-free and take many proactive measures to ensure that everyone feels safe and secure. Responding to violations of school values with immediate and comprehensive measures sets the standard and puts out the message that the community will not tolerate negative behavior. The ways in which schools respond will determine whether the violators will repeat the offenses or whether others will follow the bad example with more negative behavior. The key is for students to take the lead to set behavior standards and to collaborate with educators to establish a set of values that the community can fulfill. These values become the backbone of school policies; they exist to define the ways in which the community wants to look and feel at its best. At El Colegio, student leaders collaborate with adults to create policies that make sense to students and solve potential dilemmas pertaining to school climate. Students tend to listen more attentively to their peers than to adults, and they hold each other to high standards. Having students guide and influence policy reflects the democratic ideals of the school and provides a sure way to create user-friendly policies that hold students to high standards while considering their needs. David Greenberg, administrative director of El Colegio, describes one instance:

We had a cell phone problem at the school, and the easy answer would have been to say, "Absolutely no cell phones here. If we see them, we're going to take them away." That is one kind of tack, where the adults make the big decisions. And the other tack is to state what is happening and how it is taking away from the learning, and call on the community of students to come up with a solution. Essentially, the students came up with a compromise. They recognized that it's not helping their learning if they're text messaging during class. The policy they came up with makes sense and since they own it, they feel fit to hold other students accountable for following it.

Our schools create opportunities for youth to lead in ways that contribute to their individual growth as well as the growth of their school and community. At Life Learning Academy, a CES Mentor School in San Francisco, student leaders learn to provide peer support and guidance to each other, helping students stay connected to school and achieve success. Assistant principal Craig Miller feels strongly about getting students to care and advocate for each other: "One of the things that we teach students is how to build a positive peer group around themselves so that they are fighting to change their lives together. We teach them to look out for each other. Here, being a member of our community means taking care of the people in your lives who are trying to also change their lives. We found that students' being role models for other students is vital to the success of this school."

In CES schools, students sit in on staff meetings and hold seats on governance boards. They help to hire staff and teach classes, and these activities instill a sense of agency that will last beyond their time in our schools. Such schools invest in the lives of our students by encouraging them to take control of their own learning and actively participate in shaping the school they attend. Partnership with students in the design and redesign of their school helps them to invest in themselves while they help to create an educational institution that will be serving their community long after they have graduated.

Bringing Families to the Decision-Making Table

CES small schools create meaningful ways for parents and family members to become involved in schools and work on issues that affect schooling as a whole. In many CES small schools, family representatives are on the site management team or leadership committee. They play roles in the leadership and governance of the school that go beyond the functions they might serve in more traditional PTO or PTA groups. They may participate in the daily life of the school by supporting students in the classroom or working with teachers to get instructional resources they may need. Most recently, new parent leaders have emerged and played vital roles on small school design teams at schools such as Olympic High School in North Carolina, which converted its large comprehensive school into five small

CES schools. Parent leadership on Capital City Public Charter School's Upper School design team, discussed in detail in Chapter Four, offers another powerful example.

In general, in traditional schools, relationships between families and educators mirror all of the "divisive categories and vulnerabilities" that persist in our society (Meier, 2002, p. 46). For a variety of reasons, many schools have not easily found ways to work with family members as partners. Schools themselves are not seen as user-friendly by parents. Parents report difficulty in navigating the administrative maze of a school or district office. Families perceive schools as impersonal and bureaucratic places from which even basic communication about their own children is far from the norm. In the primary grades, parents are more visible and some participate in the life of a school through bake sales and chaperoning school trips. In middle school and high school, there begins to be more of a break between schools and parents. Savvy parents advocate for themselves and their children and find ways to break through some of the barriers that would normally keep them away.

In her book *In Schools We Trust*, longtime CES educator Deborah Meier (2002) offers some suggestions on how to create more trusting relationships between schools and families: "First, schools need to be clear about their agenda—how they define what they mean by being well educated," Meier writes. Making public the mission of the school is a good step, and involving parents in the creation or redrafting of the mission can foster a deeper sense of ownership. "Second," Meier continues, "be clear how decisions are made." Being transparent and communicative about the roles that parents can play and the ways that they can participate in decision making can help them feel empowered to act on behalf of the school, not just their child. "Third, parents must be given enough opportunities to feel comfortable that the school's and teachers' intentions are good. Fourth, all parents need ways to make informed judgments about the professional competence of the school" (p. 51–53). This means allowing family members access to teaching and learning through public exhibitions of student work and student-led conferences. Frequent teacher contact and exposure to the school's central mission and work of teaching and learning allow parents to gain a better understanding of the pedagogy and teaching and learning practices and standards of the school. Schools need to be very outspoken about the strengths and assets that children and their families bring to the table. Teachers and staff members who ask questions and in turn are open to direct questions can help parents feel more comfortable in a school environment. By providing clear lines of communication and maintaining an open-door policy, schools encourage family members to rebuild their trust and confidence in schools and teachers.

Meier reflects on her experience with parents at New York City's Central Park East Secondary School and how the heart of the school's work was the creation of a bond between the school and a family member:

> We established strong bonds with parents or with someone in the family; there's always someone in that chain of family who is available—grandmother, aunt, older brother, always somebody. We invited in as many as we could and kept close ties with the ones that were more stable. Parents are more desperate when their kids are adolescents, more over their heads and needing allies. We too felt over our heads and wanted allies. So if a parent says, "I give up on that kid," CPESS could say, "Okay, this week you can, but don't next week—we might change places." We got to build relationships with parents where it felt that we were in it together to help kids and support each other. We put a lot of thought into having consistent communication with families that was a big part of our work—family conferences, calling parents, and reaching out any way we could.

Traditional schools have successfully alienated and marginalized parents and community people; their participation has been discounted so much so that in some schools, the role is now vacant and all that is heard are the voices of educators that are dictated by their own agendas, which do not always reflect the real needs of students and families. When family members do find themselves at the decision-making table, the rules, the language, and the power dynamics of the dominant culture often marginalize them, derailing their potential participation. However, genuinely inviting the voices of parents and community and truly empowering them is work that is happening in many CES schools across the country.

One way to alter the power dynamics between family members and school personnel is to encourage the collective empowerment of parents. To better prepare parents to play meaningful roles as transformational leaders in the governance structures of our schools, we are learning strategies that invest in the social capital of parents. Parents need support from community-based organizations that organize them, build their leadership skills, and inform them of their rights so that they can act as informed decision makers. Schools can support the development of parents and family members as leaders and change agents by providing them with technical assistance, translation services, child care, and other supports they need to become full participants in the life of a school. When parents are organized, their common interest of obtaining quality education for their children positions them to take action as a group (Noguera, 2003a). Schools that are genuinely interested in authentically engaging parents as partners and building their capacity for transformational leadership organize, educate, and empower them to play significant roles in the transformational efforts of schools.

Family partnerships help schools stay connected to the communities they serve by helping to broker relationships with local religious institutions, community-based organizations, and small businesses, potentially bringing in more resources and partnerships that can help schools accomplish their mission. In the broader political arena, parents can be a strong line of defense when schools are placed in harm's way by policies and mandates that do not support their mission. In CES schools, parents and family members have served as the strongest advocates for equitable schools, holding local government accountable for providing much-needed resources and helping to raise public awareness about the need to transform schools.

Powerful examples of parent activism occur from coast to coast. In an ongoing battle described by many as a David and Goliath struggle, teachers, students, families, and community members, through organizing, continue to achieve significant victories for the schools of the New York Performance Standards Consortium (NYPSC), obtaining waivers for NYPSC schools to use performance-based assessment in place of some of the state-mandated Regents exams. Parents of consortium students have organized a statewide coalition of grassroots organizations that have embarked on a number of initiatives in support of the effort, including rallies, petition drives, letter-writing campaigns, press conferences, legislative testimony, and background briefings with legislators, policymakers, and members of editorial boards. These efforts have led to the extension of the NYPSC's waiver and permission for a small and growing group of schools to use its performance-based assessment system and to have autonomy in regard to curriculum and assessment (Cook and Tashlik, 2005).

In California, a parent- and community-driven grassroots effort, led by Oakland Community Organizations (OCO), a broad multiracial, faith-based coalition, mounted considerable pressure on the Oakland Unified School District for meaningful improvement and reform. At large public gatherings, OCO pressured public officials to pledge their support for changes in the operations and management of the schools. Their efforts led to the adoption of significant policy changes such as site-based decision making and an initiative to create new autonomous small schools in the Oakland Unified School District (Noguera, 2003a).

From that effort emerged parent leader and ARISE co-founder Emma Paulino. A community organizer with Oakland Community Organizations, she has worked tirelessly to create several small autonomous schools in her community and has organized hundreds of parents to fight for equitable schools. Her involvement with schools began with her concern for the academic success of her son. Once she became aware of the larger inequities in the Oakland school system, her interest grew. Emma's story speaks to the powerful role that parents can play in leading for equity and helps us to better understand what we need to do to increase the authentic participation of parents as transformational leaders in the small schools movement:

> My participation in my child's education and making decisions around what's best for my kid is important to me. But beyond my child—for the sake of all of the students that attend public schools—we need to figure out how we can work together and really listen to each other. I became a parent leader because of the pain and the stress I felt from the lack of understanding and support my family received from the school district. I saw how the system is set up to fail kids and teachers and school principals. When I joined OCO, they gave me a voice; they helped me to address the problems my son was having in school. I learned there were year-round schools because of overcrowded schools and that there were many failing kids, like my son. I was in shock when I saw the map the OCO provided of the flatland schools and the schools in the hills. I felt hurt and disappointed when I began to understand how the school district was dealing with the schools; it was like we were in two different school systems. The schools in the flatlands were year-round because all of the schools were failing and overcrowded, and the hills didn't have this problem, so they were getting results from the kids. At that point, I said, "Enough is enough; we have to make changes."

When I was a part of the design team with ASCEND [a small elementary school in Oakland], I knew that I wanted a better education for my child. I knew that I wanted something different, but I wasn't the expert on what kind of curriculum or instruction my child needed. My main role on the design team was to help people envision a school where parents will feel welcomed, where parents will have a voice, where parents will feel like "This is the school where my kid's going to get a good education." Another role that parents can play is to give the school a better understanding of the needs of the community—for example, the violence surrounding the school or the lack of health care services. This information is not necessarily something the school would know without the parents' input, yet it can help schools better serve students. We are not trying to say, "We, the parents, are the experts in the classroom. We just want to make sure that our participation in the education of our children is valued and respected."

Conclusion

In our work to reinvent schools and design new schools for greater equity, we have to pay close attention to the ways in which we are developing leadership, so that we do not replicate traditional practices. Transformational leaders establish a culture of learning for students and adults to learn and grow together. School leaders are responsible for creating equitable conditions and practices that hold everyone to high expectations and provide each child with the learning experiences she needs to thrive and reach her full potential. In our schools, the success or failure of students is everyone's responsibility. Classroom teachers in CES small schools do not just complain about management or send students out to be disciplined somewhere else. They create shared agreements that hold everyone accountable for fulfilling the mission of the school. These leaders create a culture that encourages everyone to work toward his own transformation. Through collaboration, each individual is better prepared for the leadership needed to transform the school as well as the relationships and the practice of teaching and learning. Teachers are not working in isolation; instead, they are part of a vibrant professional learning community.

In CES schools, transformational leaders work on building partnerships with teachers, families, and students and create spaces for them to collaborate and influence both the day-to-day governance of the school and its long-term direction. Transformational leaders work to nurture student voices and provide real opportunities for students to build and exercise their leadership. (See the sidebar "Practices and Structures That Support Transformational Leadership" for examples of specific actions and habits of mind that leaders can use to lead for equity.) Transformational leaders lead schools in which families feel welcomed and heard. Transformational leaders inspire, support, and challenge teachers to grow in their craft and in leadership. Going beyond good will and good intentions will not happen by itself. It depends on individuals' championing the work and establishing the conditions for shared leadership and for the deep transformation needed to keep an eye on equity. Transformational leaders convene, facilitate, and engage the school community in ongoing discussions and inquiry that intentionally explore the intersections of race, equity, and achievement and encourage personal and professional transformation. To create and sustain the work of schools, everyone must own the mission, build up their capacity to do the heavy lifting, and lead for equity.

Practices and Structures That Support Transformational Leadership

- Use an equity lens to create or revisit the mission and vision of the school.
- Engage in planning backward from expected student outcomes to develop curriculum and assessment.
- Clarify staff expectations.
- Create multiple tools to measure success.
- Align ongoing professional development with student needs.
- Provide time for reflection for students and teachers.
- Engage in cycles of data-based inquiry.
- Hold public exhibitions of student work.
- Ensure that family members, students, and community members are represented on the leadership team.

- Give individuals significant power and authority to make decisions about issues that affect them directly.
- Align all decisions with the mission of the school.
- Be explicit about the causes that create inequitable circumstances, and change them.
- Disaggregate student achievement data, and examine it with the school community.
- Make time for teachers to collaborate.
- Have multiple spaces and times for groups to meet and discuss issues regularly.
- Involve staff members in crafting meeting agendas and facilitating meetings.

Cultivating Professional Learning Communities

> When we began, we envisioned what the school would be like. Though it was very popular to say "student-centered," we shifted it to "learner-centered" because everyone's a learner here. If we're dealing with education, then it's not just the students as learners; it's the faculty, the administration, the facility staff, the parents, the community members who are working with students.
>
> —Jeanne Fauci, former director of communication and outreach,
> Wildwood School, Los Angeles

CES schools create a culture of learning in which everyone is a member of a community of learners and everyone models the curiosity and risk taking that deep learning requires. Schools are for learning—not just children's learning but the learning and intellectual growth of all community members. Schools are at their best when they reach this potential. In order for schools to move from the ordinary to the extraordinary, they need to create schoolwide learning communities that involve everyone—adults and youths—in working together to raise the quality of teaching and learning. Tending to the learning of each member of the school community is necessary to create a strong, successful school that continues to evolve, improve, and thrive over time.

As adaptive institutions, CES small schools use schoolwide learning communities to examine each student's strengths and challenges and continually adjust instruction, curriculum, and school culture to best achieve shared goals and serve student needs and interests. A professional learning community has been defined as "a teacher's collective engagement in sustained efforts to improve practice" (Louis, Marks, and Kruse, 1996, p. 758). Schoolwide learning communities create ways for adults to connect, exchange, reflect, and open up so that they can acquire strong pedagogical skills, develop and implement relevant curriculum and informative assessment practices, and cultivate the habits of mind required to engage with others in inquiry. In these schools, educators share practice and decision making and encourage reflection, collaborative work, and learning. Creating a supportive, honest, and collaborative environment for educators plays an essential role in improving teacher practice and, ultimately, student outcomes. Adults need what students need: support for their growth and learning. Through the transformational leadership of the principal, teacher leaders, and others, the school carves out space and time for teachers to learn from each other as well as from students and the community. These spaces include teaching teams, advisories (small groups of students that meet daily with a teacher for academic and other forms of support, discussed extensively in Chapter Ten), student-focused subgroups, department meetings, and Critical Friends Groups, which are explained later in this chapter. The deliberate creation of space and time opens up opportunities for teachers to learn from each other and from partners within the school community as well as outside; partners may include coaches, district personnel, or people who are involved in a school's community partnerships.

As a national learning community, the CES Small Schools Network is committed to expanding the focus and practice of educational equity. The toxic culture in many of our schools, inadequate classroom instruction, and tense relationships between educators and families require our immediate attention. To examine and address these and many of the other challenges facing our schools, educators require the time and space to have structured and facilitated exchanges across differences about the impact of racism on themselves and their students. Through equity-focused professional learning communities, educators examine their own often unconscious biases and engage in difficult conversations, with the goal of improving practice and transforming student outcomes. In these learning communities, difficult conversations are fostered through structures that facilitate a sense of trust and safety. According to Greg Peters, executive director of the San Francisco Coalition of Essential Small Schools, "Our professional learning communities now must be places where adults can go to have the hard conversation ... do the hard work. To interrupt the systemic inequities of our schools, we must transform our own beliefs and values of what is possible (often formed by the very same system) before we will be able to see the transformed practices and results our students need." This kind of dialogue is not only an effective approach to professional development but also a powerful strategy for school change and improvement. This chapter addresses what schools can do to establish and sustain an effective and reflective learning community in order to ensure schools' commitment to equity. We will cover the essential components of cultivating an equity-focused learning community:

- Knowing what adult learners need
- Cultivating a mission-driven schoolwide learning community
- Developing a culture of accountability and trust
- Establishing effective facilitation structures for equity-focused learning communities
- Implementing effective professional development
- Making time for professional learning community work
- Participating in learning communities beyond the school

Knowing What Adult Learners Need

We take it for granted that teachers are engaged in learning. Schools and school districts devote significant resources to professional development, and state certifications often require continuing education credits in order for teachers to maintain a valid credential. However, instruction for educators—professional development—is often not responsive to how adults learn best. Usually, professional development consists of the presentation of some new program, prescribed by the district as part of what Shirley Hord (1997) describes as the quick-fix mentality toward school improvement: "This approach might be called the 'microwave oven' theory of school improvement: Pop a new program in for four minutes with a hero principal to manage it and improvement is done."

Most professional development for teachers is based on an information delivery model rather than a constructivist, learner-centered model. Research shows that adult learners are largely self-directed and bring "a broad, rich experience base to which to relate new learning" (Cave, LaMaster, and White, 2006). Professional learning communities assume that knowledge is derived from shared reflection on common day-to-day experiences in the classroom and school. Grounding improvement efforts in the actual experiences of students and teachers elicits a more effective and focused response. CES schools allot time and develop structures that facilitate this kind of constructivist, learner-centered adult learning.

In CES schools, staff members are asked to play multiple roles that can challenge even the most veteran educators. Teachers are asked to be advisors, leaders, and decision makers as well as compassionate, engaging, and intelligent instructors. They are asked to be generalists, teaching the content of the discipline for which they are trained as well as interdisciplinary subject matter and content with which they might be less familiar. They are asked to build relationships with families and often need to serve as counselors. Each of these responsibilities requires a different set of skills, making the support structures, the professional development, and the adult learning community within the school critically important. Creating a culture and environment to support the faculty in developing this myriad of essential skills is the requisite first step toward facilitating adult learning.

Cultivating a Mission-Driven Schoolwide Learning Community

Lawrence Kohn, one of the founders and former principal of Quest High School, a CES Mentor School in Humble, Texas, has spent much of his career studying and creating professional learning communities. He has found that effective professional learning communities for educators are based on the following six components: shared norms and values; collective focus on student learning; reflective dialogue; deprivatization of practice; collaboration; and effective leadership. According to Rick DuFour (2004), professional learning communities for educators are results-oriented, collaborative, and focused on student learning. To achieve these conditions requires a culture that is anchored in a common vision, promotes openness and sharing, and engenders trust. Working collaboratively requires a common purpose. Members of a learning community may disagree on how to get there, but they are all trying to get to the same place.

Effective learning communities are organized around a common philosophy—a set of principles, values, practices, and goals. School staff all should be able to clearly articulate and identify why they are engaged together in their work, and the clear starting points for these shared values are the school's mission and vision.

For April Rasmus, a founding teacher at Empowerment College Preparatory High School in Houston, Texas, one of the new schools born of the CES Small Schools Network, working with a common philosophy means making sure that all faculty meetings and discussions remain centered on their core mission and vision. As Rasmus explains, being mission-focused means keeping discussions from digressing, reminding staff not to take too much time on getting results that don't match the desired outcomes, and helping them to remain keenly focused on what matters most and has the highest impact on student achievement. "In our school," Rasmus continues, "everything has to do with three things: a personalized environment, college-prep curriculum, and social action program of study." Fully unpacking, engaging, and holding each teacher to the school's mission and vision is a key task of the professional learning community. Shared goals form the basis for genuine accountability in which colleagues hold each other accountable for accomplishing the common mission. According to DuFour (2004), "The professional learning community model flows from the assumption that the core mission of formal education is not simply to ensure that students are taught but to ensure that they learn. This simple shift—from a focus on teaching to a focus on learning—has profound implications for schools." When the focus is shifted to learning, the nature of the teaching enterprise becomes a collective endeavor. Though we teach different subjects, we are all responsible for whether each individual student learns.

Developing a Culture of Accountability and Trust

In traditionally organized schools, teaching is an isolating profession. Most teachers are on their own in their classrooms and are not collaborating or connecting in meaningful ways with other adults in the building. According to Michael Fullan (2007), "Deprivatizing teaching changes culture and practice so that teachers observe other teachers, are observed by others, and participate in informed and telling debate on the quality and effectiveness of their instruction." In CES schools, the culture is such that teachers open their doors and are often engaged in dialogue about teaching and learning. They feel responsible for each other's learning, and they work to create structures through which they can observe each other in action and look at student work as the data that helps them to identify areas that need support. "Holding each other accountable," writes CES co-founder Deborah Meier in *In Schools We Trust,* "starts with a shared and reliable knowledge base: good data—in the broadest sense of that word. The accumulation of formal and informal observations of student work, as well as of student-teacher interactions, is our primary base" (Meier, 2002, p. 64).

Empowerment's founding principal, Misha Lesley, finds that knowledge base more valuable than the council of outside experts. "We use the knowledge that is in the building. People have great experiences as teachers, and it's important that they come together with a group of colleagues to be transparent with their practice and get critical feedback. We don't disregard research, but we get more out of using and analyzing our practices in ways that are authentic." Looking at student work is a powerful way for educators to assess the learning of students as well as the effectiveness of their teaching. For example, if a school's mission is to ensure that all of its students are ready for college when they graduate, a group of teachers might look at the work of a struggling student to figure out what each must do to help her meet that standard. Linda Nathan, principal of Boston Arts Academy (BAA), a CES Mentor School, shares how looking at student work helped to create an awareness of what it means to teach in a heterogeneous environment:

> As we scored student work together, and team-taught in writing seminar, we also identified skills that we needed to further develop as teachers. BAA students' arts auditions for admission are academically blind, and as a result, we have a very broad range of students in our classrooms. Many have learning disabilities and receive special education services. Others, even though they don't have a diagnosed disability, also struggle to complete assignments and come to us reading two to four grades below average. Still others are reading at the college level. Early on, we recognized that we needed to improve our teachers' skills to teach effectively in heterogeneous classrooms without either boring our highly skilled students or frustrating students challenged by learning issues. [Nathan, 2008]

Another way of capturing the learning of teachers and of modeling good practice is through classroom observations. While classroom observation is traditionally seen as synonymous with formal evaluation, in CES schools, it has broader applications for professional improvement. Not simply a tool for supervision, classroom observation is also a peer-to-peer strategy for professional growth. To create a culture of openness in which teachers can make their practice public requires the establishment of trust. Empowerment's April Rasmus recalls that she had a breakthrough during a series of observations by her principal:

> For five years, I taught in a traditional school. I went into the classroom, wrote stuff on the board, and expected the students to respond. I had an idea that something was wrong, since I wasn't reaching all of the students, but nobody observed me and told me what it was. It wasn't until Misha Lesley, my principal and colleague, came into my classroom and modeled how to relate to students. She let me have it. She said, "April, if 50 percent of the kids fail the class, it's your fault."
>
> "How could you say that?" I cried." I teach all day long."
>
> And Misha said, "That's the problem. You're up teaching in front of the board all day long. What are they doing?" And she had these really hard conversations with me. It was hard to swallow, but because we had built a trusting relationship prior to those conversations, I was able to hear her.

A professional learning community creates a safe space for risk taking, vulnerability, and having difficult conversations about instruction, student learning, and the values and assumptions held by individuals and how they play out in the school. Time needs to be devoted to building relationships and trust and to many of the social and emotional aspects of the community in order to create the safety and trust needed to go beyond surface issues and explore the causes of challenges and dilemmas. Without trust, how will teachers be able to give each other critical feedback on their teaching, let alone engage in difficult, sometimes disruptive conversations about the ways that issues of race, class, social background, language, and other aspects of identity affect their conscious and unconscious perceptions of students' abilities and capacities? Such belief-challenging conversations are fundamental in order to drive instructional change in equity-centered schools.

According to educator David Christman, trust is the first requirement for staff-guided, student-centered professional development. Christman speaks about helping to create this process at Harmony School, a CES Mentor School and CES affiliate center in Bloomington, Indiana, and at Harmony's mentee, Connections Public Charter School in Hilo, Hawaii, where Christman now teaches. "We have to create a foundation of authentic dialogue with each other, because that's the only way we're going to build trust. And trust, I think, in all my work, is at the foundation of a strong community. I may not always agree with you. We may have different perspectives on things. But if I'm on the battle line with you, I'm going to trust that you're going to be in there with me, that you're going to be doing the good work that you believe in, that we have some common ground."

Schools build trust among their professionals by creating guiding norms for the work of the adults that mirrors what they expect from their students. Jeanne Fauci, former director of communication and outreach at Wildwood School and executive director of the Los Angeles Small Schools Center, describes the process of creating a rubric that guided faculty in assessing their fidelity to Wildwood's habits of mind and heart: "We realized that if we were asking students to do this, then we had to look at our own work and reflect on how we were doing as professionals with the habits." Co-creating such norms helps to build the foundation of trust that is critical for a learning community. Fauci comments on the sustaining powers of a learning community that is public with its process: "As you're learning and sharing your learning, then others are growing with you. It's the most powerful thing I think human beings can do. And that's why I think so many people are drawn to the profession, but because the work is so difficult, we just need to go back to that well and drink from that water of our own hopes and dreams and ambitions, where our best selves live."

Establishing Effective Facilitation Structures for Equity-Focused Learning Communities

Creating and sustaining effective learning communities requires careful planning and expert facilitation. Particularly when dealing with difficult topics, as effective learning communities regularly do, the structures, process, and expertise of a facilitator create the kind of safe space required for deep reflection and introspection. Greg Peters, executive director of the San Francisco Coalition of Essential Small Schools and former principal of Leadership High School, a CES Mentor School, says all of Leadership's professional development meetings were designed with a specific flow that modeled what is expected of teachers in their classroom. There was an opening activity that helped participants to make the transition into their work together, a time for business items, direct instruction on the main topic, hands-on time for participants to engage with the topic, and then a time for coming back together to close and make a transition to the next piece of work.

As Peters's example illustrates, effective facilitation of professional learning communities follows the guidelines of the CES Common Principle referred to as "student-as-worker, teacher-as-coach." Professional development in CES schools is not about having didactic presentations from the principal or any experts but rather is designed to allow hands-on participation and discussion. In addition, facilitation is shared among the participants in various ways. The best professional development practices model what should be happening in classrooms. Peters explains that the greatest testament to the success of professional development has been "when I walk into a classroom and I see the Socratic seminar we did two weeks ago happening. When we walk into classrooms and I see that the classes have the roles of facilitator, timekeeper, et cetera, that are shared amongst the students. When I walk into classrooms and they're using constructive listening; that's a way of entering into some difficult work. When I walk into classrooms and I'm seeing chalk talk happening because we had just done it a few weeks ago, but it's happening from a teacher who said they never did a chalk talk before." To Peters, these are examples of how there can be a direct transfer from the pedagogy of professional development to the instructional tools that teachers use in their classrooms.

Critical Friends Groups

Professional learning communities may make intuitive sense, but they do not come naturally. Teachers and school leaders need to learn—and teach—the tools and the skills that are necessary to engage actively in the peer-to-peer learning experiences that grow and sustain a professional learning community at a small school. Through participating in Critical Friends Groups (CFGs), and CFG training, practitioners learn how to facilitate ongoing discussions and learn ways to improve their practice by reflecting on student work. A CFG, according to the National School Reform Faculty (NSRF), is "a professional learning community consisting of approximately eight to 12 educators who come together voluntarily at least once a month for about two hours. Group members are committed to improving their practice through collaborative learning" (National School Reform Faculty, 2003). Critical Friends Groups work on curriculum development, instruction, and classroom management, and provide new and seasoned teachers with a space to receive support as well as valuable feedback.

CFGs also provide the tools and space for teachers to address hard questions and dilemmas about school practices and school culture. Misha Lesley, founding principal of Empowerment, used CFGs and the protocols that structure them to deal with many of the ongoing challenges her new school faced. Lesley and her teachers identified how beliefs about students' capabilities were limiting their success in mathematics. "Instilling the belief among teachers and kids that all children can learn to use their minds well is key to getting students to believe in themselves as capable learners," Lesley says. "CFGs at our campus often use consultancy protocols for questions that have to do with the affective domain, such as 'How do I get my kids to believe in themselves as learners?' For the cognitive domain, we look at student work, using the tuning protocol, which is most effective for building on expertise among staff" (see "Consultancy Protocols and Tuning Protocols" sidebar).

Consultancy Protocols and Tuning Protocols

A **consultancy protocol** is a structured process that helps an individual or team think through or consult each other about a particular, concrete dilemma. For more on consultancy protocols, see http://www.nsrfharmony.org/protocol/doc/consultancy.pdf.

A **tuning protocol** is a facilitated process that supports educators in sharing their students' work with colleagues and reflecting on the lessons that emerge, in order to design and refine their assessment systems and support higher-quality student performance; this protocol is about refining, or tuning, existing pedagogy. For more on tuning protocols, see http://www.nsrfharmony.org/protocol/doc/tuning.pdf.

Consultancy protocols ands tuning protocols were developed within CES and further adapted as part of work of the National School Reform Faculty. The protocols are most powerful and effective when used within an ongoing professional learning community such as a Critical Friends Group and facilitated by a skilled coach. To learn more about professional learning communities and seminars for new or experienced coaches, please visit the NSRF Web site at http://www.nsrfharmony.org.

CFGs help to equip educators to tackle issues of equity and democracy within their school, providing them with a framework for unpacking and exploring what is occurring within their school community. In many ways, CFGs are like advisories for adults, providing a safe space for them to get to know one another, honestly support one another, and help one another grow and develop as educators and, particularly in the equity-focused CFG work, as people.

CFG Trainings with an Equity Lens

Finding that traditional CFGs needed to have a clear focus on equity, CES developed an equity-based CFG training. Camilla Greene, longtime CES educator and pioneer of these trainings, believed that teachers were spending time doing protocols and looking at student work without seeing deep transformations in belief systems, practice, or student outcomes. Collaborating with the national CES office and two CES centers, the Bay Area Coalition for Equitable Schools and the San Francisco Coalition of Essential Small Schools, Greene has facilitated trainings that help educators confront personal issues of race, bias, and oppression as a foundation for working toward equity. Greene discusses how equity-focused CFG training moves the work to another level:

> In equity-based CFGs, everyone thinks about who they are, how they stand in the world in terms of age, ethnic identity, and gender. The main difference is that it's not protocol-driven. The work is driven by each individual having the will and courage to build the skills needed to interrupt inequity. A protocol in a more traditional CFG might use a probing question like "How do I get the boys in my classroom to pay attention to math?" versus "How do I as a white educator engage the five African American and Latino boys in my class?" Inquiry becomes more personalized and more challenging, and the feedback you get is about what you may not know and the personal transformation you may need to undergo before you can do things differently.

Implementing Effective Professional Development

School of the Future (SOF), a CES Mentor School in New York City, uses three professional development strategies that nurture a culture of sharing and collaboration among old and new staff. First, using CFG protocols, teachers at SOF commit to an ongoing practice of looking at student work as a way to open dialogue about skill development and teaching strategies. Former principal Catherine DeLaura explains how teachers established a CFG in order to look at their teaching practices by using protocols that allow them to unpack their dilemmas about their teaching, their assignments, and the best ways to prepare students for exhibitions:

> On one occasion, an eighth-grade humanities teacher wanted some guidance and affirmation from other teachers that she was on track with what the students needed. She said, "I've had these kids for over a year now, and I'll have them for another year. I know they're going to have exhibitions next year. I want to know if I'm on the right track and if what they're writing right now is going to lead them to exhibitions in a year and a half." So we read some ninth-grade exhibitions that had received mastery distinction from the previous spring. We read them as a group and defined the characteristics that really make strong writing. Then we looked at her kids' writing now. We looked at the strong kids. We looked at average kids. We looked at strugglers, and we really looked to see what she needed to work on so the kids would be ready for exhibitions next year.

Second, in order to improve their practice, the teachers at School of the Future commit to observing each other's classes, which they call "inter-visits." This professional development strategy provides teachers with opportunities to see each other model differentiated instruction and other instructional methods that personalize the learning process for students. The observations give teachers new instructional strategies that can help to engage students and foster their active participation in their own learning.

Third, because preparing new teachers is so important to maintaining the school's culture of learning and its commitment to authentic assessment, "veteran staff act as in-house professional development leaders, facilitating workshops in the Habits of Mind, coaching new teachers on how to utilize critical thinking skills in everyday lessons so that students have constant exposure to and experience with the skills that the exhibition rubrics make explicit," explains Lisa Karlich, science teacher at SOF. All of these professional growth opportunities for the teaching team help them continue to fine-tune their rubric system, refine their teaching and learning, and calibrate student work across grades and disciplines, making their school stronger overall.

Cycles of Inquiry and Reflection

Building in regular times during the week, month, semester, and year to look back and think critically about strengths and challenges is an essential component of any change effort, leading to important mid-course corrections and a culture of continuous improvement. These periodic reflections can be as informal as journal writing or brainstorming a list of what's working and what isn't, or they can be based on a more formal look at statistical data. A reflection process can be high-stakes—for instance, a school quality review in which external evaluators are brought into a school as part of accreditation or charter renewal processes. Regardless of the number of people from outside of a school who may be brought in to help the school reflect, building in regular times and structures for those inside the school to reflect and assess how they are doing is vital to the strength of its learning community.

In functional learning communities, adults and young people participate in cycles of inquiry that evolve their work, allowing them to take ownership of challenges, capitalize on what is working, and sustain successes. Many SSN schools use a cycle of inquiry that includes identifying a question that needs exploring, conducting a needs assessment, looking at data, creating an action plan to address the needs that are identified, implementing the plan, monitoring the results, and then circling back to assessing the results and starting the cycle again. Again, this cycle can be performed in a formal or extensive way—for example, as part of an annual school review—or it can happen more frequently—for example, in examining a particular instructional practice that an individual teacher or group of teachers want to try out or refine. (Please refer to Figure 5.2 for a detailed diagram of a cycle of inquiry.)

Data-Based Inquiry

Greg Peters provides insight into why engaging teachers in a cycle of inquiry increases their sense of accountability and shifts how they perceive both their roles and the ways in which they learn and engage each other in learning. Peters works with teachers to hone in on data of many kinds as the basis for inquiry. For example, when the educators at Leadership noticed that they were having an issue with students not being present in class, they looked at the issue more closely and discovered that many of their black male students were the ones in the hallways. From there, they gathered more information and structured some difficult conversations around race, pedagogy, and classroom practices. Peters explains: "By just being responsive and creating that time, we had more authentic professional development where we talked about race. We talked about classroom expectations—not expectations of the students but of the teachers. A big question that we had to pose in an appropriate way was 'What's happening the first minute of your class?' When we have a whole-staff conversation about what's happening in the first minute of your class under the umbrella of why a kid is late, it changes how we look at the problem." By examining what was happening at the start of class—what might be keeping certain students away and what those students were missing—Leadership teachers were able to restructure their practice for better results.

While the preceding anecdote is an example of how the professional learning community at Leadership was able to address an unexpected issue, the school also structures regular times during the year to more formally undertake data-based inquiry (see "Data-Based Inquiry" sidebar). Educators at Leadership have four formal days throughout the year that they call *data days*—one in each quarter. During two of these days, Leadership staff members look at achievement data, and during the other two, they look at experience data such as patterns of attendance or behavior. They then do short cycles of inquiry that are based on these data points. These cycles are conducted by the leadership team at the school, which includes the administrators and the department coaches—teacher leaders who work with the other teachers in their departments.

Data-Based Inquiry

At its heart, inquiry is not a technical process. Rather, its purpose is to create space for critical reflection, questions, dialogue, meaning making, and action. Embracing this purpose is called *taking an inquiry stance:* being open to what one does not (yet) know, experimenting intentionally, and reflecting on what happens. Inquiry also helps focus a school's work and builds authentic accountability into a school community. Eventually, inquiry becomes a habit, so that all members of the school community are

- Asking probing questions about student learning, teacher practice, and school policy
- Using various kinds of data to check assumptions, generate dialogue, and gauge progress

- Taking new actions with an intentional purpose and reflecting on results

CES has developed a detailed tool, "A Guide to Data-Based Inquiry: Using the Cycle of Inquiry to Drive Learning and Change," which is available on the *Small Schools, Big Ideas* Web site at http://www.ceschangelab.org.

Making Time for Professional Learning Community Work

As Ted and Nancy Sizer point out in the Foreword of this book, in Essential schools, all students are known well. Key to that knowing well is taking the time to understand. CES teachers take that time in their relationships with students, and they also take that time with their colleagues, with whom they collaboratively think about student work, look at data, support each other toward mastery, and challenge each other's barriers, which may be creating dilemmas or roadblocks. Making the time for reflection and developing the skills for ongoing assessment of progress is key to creating a learning community.

The learning that takes place within a professional learning community doesn't happen through a series of one-shot deals. Unlike the situation of an in-service experience provided by a district or an outside entity, in a CES school, teachers make decisions about what they need to learn, what they want to learn, and how they will do it. The key is that this learning is directly connected to the students' needs and is an ongoing exploration. The students are at the center of every professional development plan that is crafted, and the community works together to put the resources in place to support each other's learning, with the end goal of meeting students' changing needs as they emerge.

This kind of work cannot happen without a significant investment of time. Time is hard to come by during an educator's school day, which can easily be consumed by numerous small emergencies. Commitments to schedules and intentional planning time are essential to the development of habits of daily engagement that help a school community manage day-to-day activities while keeping an eye on continuous improvement. CES schools take time at the beginning and end of the year to reflect on school culture and assess the academic progress made during the school year. They proactively create regular, frequent opportunities for reflection and assessment. This reflection happens when it is appropriate: at a faculty meeting at the start of a school year, in student and teacher conversations on receipt of high-stakes test results, or among all members of a school community in response to a tragedy in the school community. Most CES small schools have several hours a week set aside for professional development in various configurations—with the whole staff, in small groups, in departments, and so on. They also have days built into the calendar for retreats and workshops. How this time is allotted throughout the year is important. When will the staff need a professional development day that is free of students? What big events will need planning in advance and reflection at the end?

Numerous occasions to take stock of progress in an assessment context are described as formative; the more that reflection and assessment are made a part of the learning process, the stronger the learning will be. These responsive habits of reflection are analogous to formative assessment measures of learning that occur at the end of a unit of study. Creating a daily community meeting, for example, with specific norms and expectations that adults and young people will build the habit of reflection exemplifies the formative assessment of a school's climate and conditions that is so critical in a learning community. When possible, habits of daily engagement need to be balanced with extended periods of time for retreats for deeper reflection and collaboration.

Participating in Learning Communities Beyond One's Own School

Many educators find that their participation in learning communities beyond their individual school has provided new challenges and extended their teaching career. Even in schools that are constantly evolving and growing, educators may feel stagnant and teachers, in particular, may become bored with the flatness of the profession. Working with other educators across schools, exchanging ideas, or being recognized for contributions by others who are outside of one's own school may provide another level of challenge, opportunity, sustenance, and growth. Leadership High School teacher leader Beth Silbergeld describes her interschool networking both with the CES Small Schools Network and the National Science Teachers Association: "If it wasn't for the extra stuff and for the other opportunities and venues for growth and for networking, I don't know that I'd be as excited about teaching, which is why I encourage other people to get involved."

CES's Peer-to-Peer Mentoring Approach

CES has pioneered a school-to-school approach to learning that mirrors what happens in CES classrooms and in CES school-based professional development. CES has paired its most successful small schools with new small schools in a mentoring relationship. Learning is driven by the participants and grounded in the actual needs and experiences of their schools. Teachers work with each other; new teachers get what they need to improve their teaching, and more experienced teachers get the opportunity to be reflective and grow.

This school-to-school mentoring takes many forms. An educator from a mentor school might spend time working with the new school. Mentoring might occur during one of the CES Small Schools Network's four annual meetings through one-on-one conversations or within specialized groups just for principals or just for math teachers, for example. Mentoring might take the form of a carefully structured visit to a mentor school that centers on questions or goals that the visitors have. At times, mentoring manifests in formal workshops hosted by mentor schools. In some cases, a teacher from a mentor school has even transferred to or served as a teacher-in-residence at the new or transforming school. This work has helped mentor schools build their capacity to work with and influence other schools in their region and across the country so that others can benefit from the important work they have done and the valuable experience they have had.

CES's peer-to-peer mentoring approach is designed to benefit mentor schools as much as new small schools. The mentor schools further their own professional learning and growth by addressing challenges and examining their practices as they collaborate with their mentee partners. Staff members from the CES Mentor Schools have found that the experience of sharing their beliefs and practices allows them to connect their learning community with the wider world. Such expansion of a school's learning community serves to strengthen it. Schools gain a great deal by combating isolation and joining networks with other like-minded schools in various stages of development. Kim Klepcyk, principal of Quest High School, a Mentor School in Humble, Texas, says that mentoring Houston's Empowerment College Preparatory High School was a transformative experience for Quest itself. "Working with Empowerment when they were designing things, it was almost like we were back in the design phase again," recalls Klepcyk. "We were able to say, 'Man, if we could go back and change things, we wouldn't have done this or that.' Now, we look at certain things that Empowerment has done that have been successful and there's a little bit of envy in that. We find ourselves thinking, 'Wow, I wish we could do it that way.' And then it pushes you a little bit to make change at home."

It can be tempting for some of the most successful schools in the country to rest on their laurels. With the kind of exchange offered by the schools and practitioners who participate in the network, the learning is constant and it is impossible for all who participate not to be inspired to try something different, to grow in some new ways, and to learn.

Critical Friends Visits

An essential practice of the CES Small Schools Network is the Critical Friends Visit (CFV). CFVs illustrate the power of being part of a larger learning community that shares similar values. During CFVs, staff and sometimes students from a Mentor School and other schools in the network spend several days at new and transforming schools to reflect what they see and hear, in order to help the school identify what it needs to improve.

Eagle Rock School and Professional Development Center has mentored two schools: Odyssey: The Essential School, one of three new small schools formed from the conversion of Tyee High School in SeaTac, Washington, and Skyview Academy, a newly formed small high school in Thornton, Colorado. Eagle Rock Professional Development Center's associate director, Dan Condon, says,

> What really excites Eagle Rock about those relationships is a partner-ship we have where we not only offer some of our experience in our reform and renewal efforts, but we learn a whole lot from both of those schools. One of the many activities that we have taken part in with both Odyssey and Skyview are a series of visits—not only those schools' visiting Eagle Rock and making connections with staff and students here but us visiting those schools and conducting Critical Friends Visits. And we are able, for a couple of days, to bring several staff and students of our learning community to immerse ourselves in the learning communities of these mentee schools. Each school, prior to the visit, works with Eagle Rock staff to devise a guiding question based on one of the CES Common Principles that we use as a lens for the visit. A question that Skyview's learning community posed during our last visit there was "How is a tone of decency and

trust being established in the Skyview community?" When we visited Odyssey, they were interested in having us use the lens of evidence we were finding that showed how students at Odyssey are learning to use their minds well. This involved shadowing students and observing every aspect inside and outside of the classroom, including passing time, meal time, prior to first period, and some after-school activities. We were able to use the guiding questions to provide some really powerful feedback and have some discussion with a sample of staff and students at the end of the final day of the Critical Friends Visits.

Joan Ferrigno, principal of Odyssey, believes that Eagle Rock's ongoing engagement with Odyssey as part of a school-to-school learning community was of tremendous benefit, without which Odyssey might not be on solid footing. "It was really beautiful that [Eagle Rock] took so much initiative in helping me and the staff think through questions that we would like answered," remembers Ferrigno.

> They asked for the master schedule, and they planned the whole thing out, which was just so helpful. That is what a mentor should do. They should say, "You are the new school, you don't have time for this, and you don't know how to do it as well, so let us do this for you." And they did. The staff remembers that those visitors asked us about our expectations for kids because through their eyes, we didn't seem to have the highest expectations when it came to student behavior. Now, we keep that in mind when we are talking about attendance or when we are talking about discipline. I just feel really supported by Eagle Rock. Even their students took it seriously. They take that work very seriously.

Professional development exchanges develop reflective leaders and practitioners who can quickly assess their instructional and organizational practices and policies, look at what they are missing, and determine what they can take back and put into place right away to improve the teaching and learning conditions in their school. They see the alternative ways that they might set up a schedule that could work better for students, create curriculum that is more relevant to the lives of the children they serve, and have the time and organizational support to personalize instruction.

Conclusion

CES schools are committed to continuous improvement, constantly revisiting their mission and vision and figuring out new ways to get the best student outcomes. With inquiry as their main driver, Essential school leaders work collaboratively with teachers to create professional learning communities that model the same pedagogical attributes, values, and standards that need to be employed in the classroom; see the "Learning Community Essentials" sidebar for the key practices of professional learning communities. To instill teacher collaboration in the culture of the school and build an effective learning community, an intentional decision has been made to create and preserve the space and time for teachers to meet, reflect, and fine-tune their practice. The school must also employ a clear set of structures and practices to help teachers stay focused on their continual professional growth. Using student achievement data to plan backward and guide staff development activities, teachers in these settings are engaged in their own learning process, which is anchored in the real experience of students. Collaboratively, these teachers participate in a continual dialogue, exploring how to improve their teaching and learning to better serve their students and increase their students' academic results. The concept and activities of professional learning communities require a major cultural shift in how professional development for educators is perceived. In the same way that schools must focus on creating the climate and practices to help students learn, the commitment to adult learning must be nurtured and supported throughout the life of the school.

Learning Community Essentials

- View and nurture everyone in the school as a learner.
- Do the work and invest the time to create a collaborative professional culture.
- Establish, clarify, and constantly work toward common goals.
- Create the space—and a safe environment—for difficult conversations, using equity-based Critical Friends Groups protocols such as the consultancy and tuning protocols.
- Dedicate significant time weekly and throughout the year for ongoing professional growth.

- Implement effective professional development by building staff members' facilitation skills, conducting cycles of inquiry, and using data.
- Create a culture of openness through classroom visits and observations.
- Connect staff members to learning communities and networks beyond the school.

Adult learning in a school is enhanced by interacting with other like-minded educators. The value of participating in networks with other schools is not limited to CES's network. Wherever a school can serve as a critical friend to another, and wherever cross-fertilization, inspiration, mentoring, and an exchange of practices and ideas are happening, these networks are of critical importance. Many CES schools are also in other networks that help sustain them and further their growth. Unfortunately, however, it is still too much the norm for schools and educators to remain isolated, without an opportunity to emerge from their school's own bubble to learn and grow within a network of fellow schools. As this chapter demonstrates, this kind of exchange is also critical for the professional growth and sustenance of individual teachers and school leaders alike.

PART THREE

Essential Principles for Learning

Student-Centered Teaching and Learning

> I discovered what it means to really know
> something, to know it so well that it consumes me.
>
> —Reflection of a student from Quest High School,
> a CES Mentor School

A fundamental concept of CES schools, first introduced by Ted Sizer (1984) in *Horace's Compromise,* is that teaching and learning should be personalized to the maximum feasible extent. In CES schools, teaching and learning are student-centered. Teaching and learning are relevant and culturally responsive, focusing on and building from the needs, abilities, interests, cultural background, and learning style of each student. This focus has many implications for curriculum design, course structure, pedagogy, content, professional development, and the overall cohesiveness of the educational program at a school.

This chapter describes

- High-leverage teaching strategies for helping students learn to use their minds well

- Several of the most effective pedagogies that differentiate instruction to provide access and opportunity for all students

- Ways to develop a student-centered educational program that teaches twenty-first-century skills and is relevant and culturally responsive to the needs of diverse groups of students

- The different roles that teachers and students play in a project-based learning environment

- Meaningful projects that take student learning beyond the limitations of the "inch deep and mile wide" scope of conventional teaching and learning

Many of the CES Common Principles focus on instruction, as one might expect, given the centrality of teaching and learning in school transformation. In order to address the low achievement and graduation rates that plague our school systems—and that are integrally connected to the disengagement many students feel—what takes place in the classroom has to change drastically. To raise the quality of instruction and thereby affect student outcomes, the practice of teaching and the roles that teachers play need rethinking and redesigning. While we are unable to give as much detail as such a central subject as "teaching and learning" warrants, this chapter, framed by four of the CES Common Principles, addresses the following essential questions:

- **Learning to use one's mind well:** What pedagogical approaches and curriculum do educators use to engage students in increasingly sophisticated critical thinking?

- **Personalization:** How do educators tailor instruction to meet the needs of individual students and take them to the next level?

- **Student as worker, teacher as coach:** How do students take ownership of their learning while teachers act as a "guide on the side" rather than a "sage on the stage"?

- **Less is more, depth over coverage:** How can educators spend quality time and instruction on a limited number of topics, allowing students to develop understanding and knowledge in a meaningful way?

Teaching for the Twenty-First Century

Given our modern environment of rapid change, students need new skills and habits of mind in order to meet the expectations and demands they will face in the twenty-first century. (See the first sidebar in Chapter One for a definition of twenty-first-century skills.) "Teachers need to work with students on critical skills that will allow them to transfer and apply their knowledge to new situations, and enable them to learn how to learn," writes Linda Darling-Hammond (2007a). "The transmission curriculum that dominated schools for the last 100 years—which assumed a stable body of knowledge could be codified in textbooks and passed onto students who could 'learn' it by remembering all the facts—is counterproductive today." The kind of instruction that takes place in CES small schools is interactive, hands-on, and relevant, requiring students to learn higher-order thinking and problem-solving skills. Teachers who were trained traditionally may see students as passive learners, and many may think that only certain students are capable of more rigorous and intellectually demanding learning. Teachers need to shift their mind-set and reflect on the impact that the quality of their teaching and their belief system has on students. The critical friendship of colleagues (see Chapter Six) can help teachers explore the ways in which they may be limiting certain students and learn new practices that promote equity for all students. All students, after all, need to be prepared for the challenges that our future will pose.

While *Small Schools, Big Ideas* focuses on the conditions necessary for entire schools and school systems to truly transform and improve student outcomes, at the most fundamental pedagogical level, any teacher in any school can make the CES Common Principles the heart of her or his teaching and yield better results for all of her or his students. This kind of teaching may not come easily, of course, particularly in isolation. Veteran teachers as well as new teachers who feel that they are not doing everything possible to reach all students may need collegial support in order to transform their practices and their beliefs about students' potential. (For a landmark analysis of such a teacher, see Sizer's *Horace's Compromise* [Sizer, 1984], the book responsible, in large part, for spreading the ideas from which CES was born.) Incorporating the principles and practices described in the sidebar "CES Benchmark for Student-Centered Teaching and Learning" and outlined in more detail in this chapter can lead to a new kind of teaching that equips students with high-level skills and habits and prepares them for success in college and beyond.

CES Benchmark for Student-Centered Teaching and Learning

- Students take leadership in the classroom, present their work, and facilitate groups. Students take ownership of their reading, writing, and learning to develop, test, and refine their thinking. Students engage in talk that is accountable to the text or task, the learning community, and standards of reasoning. Learning is negotiated and directed by students.

- The content and delivery of instruction is culturally responsive and respects and builds on the diverse resources and experiences of learners in the classroom. The school community uses best practices in language acquisition to support academic development and support in both English and native languages.

- Students work in flexible, cooperative groupings to solve problems and analyze texts to demonstrate understanding of a task or concept through multiple perspectives.

- The school supports the inclusion of all students, including English-language learners and special needs students, in regular academic classrooms through the use of best practices, such as dual-certified teachers, differentiated instruction, qualified aides, and individualized learning plans.

- Students consistently develop their own reasoning around concepts and ideas and can articulate the processes and thinking they engaged in while grappling with a task or idea. Students listen to one another as well as to their teachers, and they exchange different ideas to build upon and apply new learning and approaches to their own understanding of a concept or idea that increases in complexity.

- Students apply the habits of mind for reading, writing, and thinking in various genres and disciplines. Students make connections, pose questions, and explore solutions as a means to engage in real-world scenarios and application transfer. They apply knowledge to different contexts and scenarios.

- Talk and focus in all groupings use multiple strategies. Students use the physical environment and discussions about group roles to explore various concepts and apply them to different scenarios or problems.

- Teachers plan the types of questions and prompts at multiple entry points throughout a lesson, which build students' understanding of, and engagement toward, concepts and ideas and their application to real-world scenarios. Each teacher has clear and measurable objectives for what students will know and be able to do as a result of a lesson.

- The arts and vocational interests are included in academic curriculum, increasing students' engagement, motivating students with a variety of learning styles to succeed in high school and pursue higher education, and developing students' academic and intellectual growth.

- Schools value the health of all students, teaching them positive ways to bring balance to life's challenges and a proactive, positive approach to wellness.

- Student work is collected in a portfolio representing a selection of performance. A portfolio may include a student's best pieces and the student's evaluation of the strengths and weaknesses of the pieces. It may also contain one or more works-in-progress that illustrate the creation of a product such as an essay evolving through various stages of conception, drafting, and revision.

- Students are assessed for process, group work, and product.

- Student voices are connected with adult allies (teachers, families, communities) toward the goal of improving student life, school culture, student communities, and students' overall development.

- Examples of student-centered teaching and learning practices include advisory, service learning, and project-based learning.

These practices represent the Student-Centered Teaching and Learning Benchmark at the "transforming" level. The CES Benchmarks in full, including "early" and "developing" levels, as well as related resources, can be found on the *Small Schools, Big Ideas* Web site at http://www.ceschangelab.org/.

Source: Coalition of Essential Schools, 2008a.

Learning to Use One's Mind Well

The CES Common Principle "Learning to use one's mind well" states, "The school should focus on helping young people learn to use their minds well. Schools should not be 'comprehensive' if such a claim is made at the expense of the school's central intellectual purpose." CES schools make it their mission to support their students in learning how to think for themselves in deep and meaningful ways. In CES schools, the goal is to enable students to use their mind well rather than to absorb a set of facts or discrete knowledge sets. A serious commitment to equity in our schools demands that we teach students to think and solve problems in ways that facilitate their success in higher education, as workers, as community leaders, as friends and family members, and as active participants in our democracy. All students deserve what many white and affluent students have long received: the opportunity to leave school prepared for a fulfilling emotional, social, and intellectual life.

Each CES school demonstrates different ways of helping students learn to use their mind well. Many CES schools employ common CES practices as described in the CES Benchmarks. (See the sidebar for the "CES Benchmark for Student-Centered Teaching and Learning"; descriptions of all of the CES Benchmarks are in Appendix B.) Different schools have different areas of focus: some may concentrate on service learning; others, on internships; and yet others, on student questions and dialogue. All these approaches, done well, as they are in many of the CES SSN schools, teach students how to use their mind well. This section focuses on the following high-leverage strategies for helping students learn to use their mind well:

- Inquiry
- Making real-world connections through internships, service learning, and project-based learning
- Building literacy and numeracy instruction

Inquiry

Using an inquiry approach is one teaching strategy that CES educators use to teach students to use their mind well. Inquiry pedagogy is a constructivist approach that borrows from the Socratic tradition of teaching through questioning and helping students to develop their own questions—and then their own answers. While there are a number of CES schools that have developed their instructional program around an inquiry pedagogy, Urban Academy Laboratory High School, a CES Mentor School in New York City, has been developing its program for over twenty years and has served as a model for schools across the nation. At Urban, inquiry is the defining element in all classrooms. In a humanities class, inquiry might manifest as a heated discussion of a controversial question about the fairness of the death penalty, while in a science class it might be as simple as a question about the relationship between foot size and height with prompts for students to create a hypothesis, develop an experiment to test the hypothesis, and write up their conclusions.

Urban's Looking for an Argument course, which is designed to explore inquiry itself, has been replicated in other schools across the country from California to Colorado. Looking for an Argument, an inquiry-based course open to all students in grades nine through twelve, meets for three one-hour classes per week. Looking for an Argument teaches the habit and skills of deep, persistent inquiry, providing a setting in which students can learn and improve their abilities to debate, take notes, read and highlight, write essays, consider multiple perspectives, and engage in critique. Two teachers debate controversial issues in the news, "tackling questions such as, 'Should our society jail athletes for violent acts committed during an athletic contest? Should there be laws about who can be a parent? Should we provide help to foreign countries when they experience natural disasters?'" (Urban Academy, 2001). Students join the debates and take comprehensive notes, which they use, along with related readings, to inform weekly in-class essays that are designed to prepare students for the timed writing experiences that they can expect to face in college.

Carolyn Egazarian, who graduated from and later taught at Urban Academy, defines inquiry as "introducing information to students and letting them develop their own opinions about whether it's important or whether it's even true." She tells the story of a student who was always on the computer, looking up conspiracy theories. In his Looking for an Argument class, regardless of whether the class was discussing China or any other subject, he would always bring the discussion back to the conspiracy of September 11, 2001. At some point, another teacher took him to a mosque, where he was able to ask any questions that he liked of the imam. At no point did anyone tell him that he was wrong. Rather, Urban Academy's educators left him to his own conclusions, which eventually, through this approach, changed.

Nalo Lewis, who used to teach math at Urban Academy before taking a position at Brooklyn's Gotham Professional Arts Academy, Urban's mentee school and a CES new school, adds,

> I think the basis of inquiry is that you teach [students] how to use the knowledge that they already have to understand the things that they don't. In literature, in math, in any of the humanities courses, it's not just reading a book and believing everything but questioning the things that come up and using your knowledge to make sense of the things that you're faced with. They feel like they're in control of their learning, and they're not being told this is what it is and this is what you have to remember, but more so, this is what's out there. You have to make the decision whether or not the information you're dealing with is useful and makes sense and then formulate your opinion.

One example of an Urban Academy tool that encourages inquiry is a *sort,* an introductory activity that can be tailored to any class or topic. Students are given a pile of up to one hundred slips of paper with different names or words on them that they first individually prioritize, then prioritize in a small group using consensus, and finally prioritize as a whole class. For example, in one class, students are asked who they think are the most influential figures in American history. The teacher gives each student a stack of one hundred slips of paper, each with the name of a different historical figure, and students rank their top ten and bottom five. With the individual sorts done, they then join with others in small groups to decide on a common top and bottom list through discussion, debate, and explaining and defending their individual decisions. This process is repeated on a larger scale with the whole class. At the heart of this activity and, indeed, at the heart of inquiry pedagogy is the idea of starting with a meaningful question and asking students to "use their mind well" as they try to come up with answers.

A powerful example of the kind of student work that results from the inquiry approach at Urban Academy is the film *A Girl Like Me,* created by Kiri Davis. This award-winning film fulfilled one of the six graduation requirements in which students must show proficiency at Urban. In the film, Davis explores questions about race and identity and, in particular, identity issues for young black women in this country. She recreates the famous experiment by Kenneth Clark that was at the heart of the *Brown* v. *Board of Education* school desegregation case by asking young black children different questions about two different dolls—one black and one white. As a young African American woman herself, she was able to explore questions that had particular meaning for her, interview others, and develop new conclusions about, as she puts it, "how society affects black children today and how little has actually changed" (Davis, 2005). Of course, in this case, Davis's own learning also became a tool for building the awareness of people all over the world who have since viewed her film. *A Girl Like Me* can be viewed at http://www.mediathatmattersfest.org/6/index.php?id=2.

Making Real-World Connections: Internships, Service Learning, and Project-Based Learning

When students learn to use their mind well instead of merely memorizing facts and completing multiple-choice tests, they gain crucial skills that will help them be successful in the real world beyond high school. There is no better way to prepare students for putting their mind to future challenges than to help them make similar connections while they are still in school. This idea is the fundamental premise of the Metropolitan Career and Technical Center in Providence, Rhode Island, known as the Met. A state-funded public school district with six small schools in Rhode Island, the Met belongs to a number of school networks, including the Big Picture Company—a consortium of Met schools—and CES's Small Schools Network, in which the Met's Peace Street campus participates as a Mentor School. The Met's academic program centers on two full days per week of student internships in local businesses and community organizations coupled with time spent learning in advisory and small-group settings on the school campus. Students focus their projects on learning gleaned from their internships, creating an experience that integrates academics and real-world learning.

When a student has to write a grant proposal for her internship at a nonprofit organization, she is being asked to produce work that has real meaning—and real consequences—which requires her to use her mind in complex ways. Likewise, a student who is interning at a veterinary hospital uses science or math that has a tangible impact on the animals in his care on a daily basis. Kim Barsamian, an advisor at the Met, reflects: "Growth came when [students] did something they were passionate about, not something I gave to them and had them do. The research papers were not what they were passionate about. But if they could do the research papers on something that they were working on at their internship, those were the best papers." For the Met, it's the focus on passion—helping students follow their interests and engage with the things that they are most excited about—that forms the basis for their internships and, indeed, the whole school. Having this focus on passion is also how the Met differs so markedly from traditional schools at which all the decisions about learning come from the top rather than from the students themselves.

The same idea can be applied without such an extensive internship by asking students to do projects that have real applications and consequences in the world beyond the classroom. While every school might not be able to fully embrace the Met's internship model, many Essential schools and other schools offer internships through service-learning curricula and related programs so that their students can gain benefits from real-world connections. Quest High School, a CES Mentor School, requires students to complete a social action project, which is the culmination of a four-year service-learning curriculum that asks students to identify a need in their community and create a project to meet that need. Service learning is a form of experiential education that combines an academic classroom curriculum with meaningful service. This form of teaching enriches the learning experience by providing opportunities for creation and reflection. The process of participating in community projects that serve the common good fosters a sense of civic responsibility and engagement in students. Quest educators Kim Huseman and Lawrence Kohn (who is also Quest's former principal) explain:

> These social action projects encourage deep analytical thinking, meaningful collaboration, skill development, and authentic application of knowledge. For example, two senior groups (nine students) paired with Lowe's Home Improvement, Wal-Mart, Administaff, and Humble Area Assisted Ministries and chose five home sites of elderly and impoverished people. Together, they generated over $50,000 in materials and money and brought together over 150 people to refurbish these homes. Students and adults from the community came together, and the results were phenomenal. Three other schools in the community became involved, and some incredible transformations of homes occurred. One trailer home was in such disarray that one of the volunteers actually purchased a new trailer for the elderly owners, who are both in very poor health and were living in deplorable conditions. Other sites had wheelchair ramps built, were re-floored, repainted, and re-landscaped, and had new hot water heaters installed; literally

hundreds of improvements were made. The recipients had their lives changed, as did the lives of the students and volunteers. [Huseman and Kohn, 2006]

When students are engaged in work that has true value in the world and when the social-emotional realm is brought into education as well, students are able to gain so much more intellectually. The motivation for learning is clarified when the outcome is of use to someone else.

Other CES students have done similar real-world work, including creating *The Two Sides of the Boat Channel,* a field guide to the local bay (at San Diego's High Tech High) (by the students of The Gary and Jerri-Ann Jacobs High Tech High, 2004) and writing *Talking Back: What Students Know About Teaching,* a book that provides teachers with advice from students about how best to teach them (at San Francisco's Leadership High School) (Students of Leadership High School, 2003). At High School for the Recording Arts, a CES Mentor School in St. Paul, Minnesota, students created a project on teen driver safety, producing a CD, doing performances, and hosting summits and educational campaigns at many local schools and political venues, where they have even influenced the positions of their politicians. (For a description of this project, visit http://www.click4life.org.) In all of these examples, students were engaged in projects and activities that helped them to become lifelong learners, fully capable of using their mind well and contributing ideas and thinking that matter.

Building Literacy and Numeracy Instruction

Literacy and numeracy are paramount at all of the CES SSN schools, which have organized themselves to teach students to be fluent readers, writers, mathematicians, and thinkers through the processes of determining powerful and ambitious outcomes, planning backward from these outcomes, and then supporting students as they do the work to achieve them. High standards for reading, writing, mathematical, and thinking skills required to complete meaningful work are at the heart of all of the examples that we describe in this chapter. Many CES schools have implemented strategies for focusing on literacy "across the curriculum," meaning that teachers incorporate reading, writing, and other fundamental literacy skills in every subject. When the faculty at Federal Hocking High School, a CES Mentor School in Stewart, Ohio, identified concerns about their students' reading skills, they decided to engage in a schoolwide literacy campaign and learn as much as they could about developing strategies across the curriculum. Federal Hocking staff members brought in Harvey Daniels and Steve Zemelman (2004), authors of *Subjects Matter: Every Teacher's Guide to Content-Area Reading,* to help. After a few years of this work, according to teachers Ben Warner and Sue Collins, "The changes that we have noted are more qualitative in nature. Teachers have reported that students do not complain as much when given a reading assignment. In independent reading situations, students are reading for longer periods of time and are displaying a deeper grasp of the information during discussion. In addition, there has been a significant increase in the Ohio Graduation Test (OGT) scores across the curriculum. These improvements may indicate that our students are having greater success in understanding how the questions are stated" (Warner and Collins, 2006).

From studying the etymology of words used in science class to focusing on vocabulary in math class, Federal Hocking teachers increased their students' literacy skills in every classroom. Based on her experience and the strategies she learned from Daniels and Zemelman's work, math teacher Sue Collins created a list of suggestions for building literacy in any classroom, which are presented in the sidebar "Strategies for Literacy Improvement in Mathematics and Other Classes."

Strategies for Literacy Improvement in Mathematics and Other Classes

- **Probable passage:** Students categorize 8 to 15 key words from a passage to be read and write a gist statement.

- **Vocabulary tree:** A graphic tool focusing on linking groups of words or ideas.

- **List/group/label:** A vocabulary strategy used to cluster words based on things that the words have in common.

- **KWL:** Students list what they know (K), what they want to know (W), and what they have learned (L).

- **Exit and admit slips:** At the beginning or end of a class, students write note cards indicating an important idea they have learned, questions they have, etc.

- **Anticipation guides:** A brief set of questions prior to reading.

- **Written conversations:** After reading, pairs of students write short notes back and forth to each other concerning the content of the text.

- **Sketching the text:** Students draw simple pictures to help them understand their reading.

- **Tableaux:** Dramatic role plays in which students prepare a brief description of a reading, then role play the event.

- **TAG (text activity guide):** Students work in pairs to respond to questions about material they are reading.

Source: Warner and Collins, 2006.

Federal Hocking also implemented a Silent Sustained Reading program: a time set aside for silent independent reading schoolwide. Many CES schools include variations of this practice in their schedule. Gotham Professional Arts Academy turned students who had never read before into avid readers by bringing in highly engaging young adult titles that students loved. However, their program, called "Gotham Reads" was a failure in the first semester. Founding principal Alex White describes it:

> Our students spent ten minutes reading their horoscope and chatting, and then it was chaos. In our second semester, we started our school day every day with forty-five minutes of reading, and we had some teachers really engaged in the challenge of getting texts that students will grab, and in just a couple of weeks, we started to see this transformation. Kids that had never passed their English classes, self-professed nonreaders, were walking down the halls reading their books, looking up, saying, "Oh, this is a good book, yo," and then back to the book. It was really profound that something that was a little idea really took root very meaningfully at our school, and I think by the end of the year, we definitely saw gains in schoolwide cultural literacy and just in facility, willingness, and desire to talk about books.

For more on literacy, we recommend *The Right to Literacy in Secondary Schools: Creating a Culture of Thinking*, edited by Suzanne Plaut (2008).

CES schools approach numeracy with an interdisciplinary approach as well, contextualizing teaching for mathematics skills and competencies in projects that encourage multiple approaches to a topic. Francis W. Parker Charter Essential School's mathematics curriculum features, for example, an annual geodesic dome building project, which, according to teachers Diane Kruse and Roser Giné, captivates students as they learn trigonometry: "The challenge of building a dome is deceptively simple, which allows students to really dig in as problem solvers who need to communicate clearly. As teachers, we can then observe in depth our students' ability to respond effectively to a complex, multifaceted task. We have found that this project appeals to students on different levels. Some students are drawn to the problem solving, while others appreciate having physical models in front of them and are motivated to create something interesting or beautiful" (Giné and Kruse, 2006).

Giné and Kruse sacrifice speed to focus on this project, allowing time for students' self-directed inquiry and demonstrating that for lasting, meaningful learning, depth matters more than broad coverage. They write, "The basic new content of the unit, the Law of Sines and the Law of Cosines, can be derived and demonstrated in a few brief lessons, and with some practice and application problems, students could be finished and on to new content within a week. However, Parker students spend four weeks designing and constructing geodesic domes, working with the essential question: How can we use right triangle and non-right triangle trigonometric techniques to design and construct a geodesic dome?"(Giné and Kruse, 2006). These four weeks allow students to develop lasting numeracy skills as well as provide opportunities for teachers to differentiate their instruction in order to challenge advanced math students while supporting learners with developing skills and understanding.

Personalization

The CES Common Principle often referred to as "Personalization" states, "Teaching and learning should be personalized to the maximum feasible extent. Efforts should be directed toward a goal that no teacher have direct responsibility for more than 80 students in the high school and middle school and no more than 20 in the elementary school. To capitalize on this personalization, decisions about the details of the course of study, the use of students' and teachers' time and the choice of teaching materials and specific pedagogies must be unreservedly placed in the hands of the principal and staff." There are several high-impact strategies for personalizing teaching:

- Getting to know your students and building strong relationships
- Incorporating relevant and culturally responsive teaching and learning
- Differentiating instruction to meet the diverse academic needs of students
- Creating effective inclusion models
- Providing individualization to English-language learners

Getting to Know Your Students and Building Strong Relationships

Knowing students well is the best way to build strong relationships with them, and creating respectful, caring relationships goes far in terms of furthering their academic and personal growth. While all teachers can work to know their students better, doing so successfully is far easier when teaching fewer students. For this reason, most CES schools limit the number of students that teachers instruct. Often, CES teachers *loop,* meaning that they stay with their students for more than one year. CES schools have long used advisories as a primary strategy for getting to know students well and supporting them academically. (For more on advisories, see Chapter Ten.) Most advisory programs are designed to keep a teacher together with a group of students over a long period of time, often for the entire course of their middle or secondary school career. *Small Schools, Big Ideas* author Mara Benitez has written about her experience as an advisor at Satellite Academy, a small alternative school in the Bronx, New York:

> The bonding experience that took place in advisory created ties between students and adults that were not easily severed. For some students, it was the first time they trusted an adult outside of their family long enough to build a relationship. The role of advisor offered teachers and their students a new way to interact and relate to one another, providing them with the liberty to get to know each other without the constraints of the academic curriculum. In advisory, the students were the content to be studied and explored. Students sat in a circle and talked about life and school. They shared themselves and

revealed their flaws, analyzing what it meant to be this or that kind of student. It was there that they first established their commitment to themselves as learners and to the school as a place where they chose to learn. [Benitez, 2004]

Advisories are a powerful way to let students know they are in the company of caring adults. These relationships help the school become a safe place where students can admit what they do not know and take risks in pursuit of new knowledge, two key prerequisites to deep learning.

In any context, you can do many things that will help you discover more about who your students are and therefore how best to teach them. This discovery process is also an important aspect of developing cultural competence, particularly when you do not share the same cultural background as some or all of your students. A white teacher going to teach in a predominantly Latino school in East Harlem, for example, must work to bridge that inherent gap before even getting to know individual students. Learning about the community, perhaps by doing neighborhood mapping (an exercise in which teachers walk through the neighborhood, mapping resources and assets); making the effort to learn (or learn more) Spanish; or reading literature by Puerto Rican, Dominican, or Harlem authors will all help to create some background knowledge about your students and school, as well as provide resources and tools for becoming a more effective teacher. Kim Barsamian describes her first year at the Met: "As a ninth-grade advisor, I realized I did not know the community as well as I should have. I should have begun to know this area better. I should have known more about Dominican kids because more than half of my class is from the Dominican Republic." When she did learn more about where her students were coming from, she realized that their middle school experience hadn't been positive; many students had had teachers who didn't care about them. "They didn't trust me at all. . . . I was a white woman coming into their neighborhood, and so I had to build that trust." Eventually, Barsamian created trusting relationships with her students by taking the time to get to know who they were and where they were coming from, which helped her to teach them effectively over the four years that she was their advisor.

To get to know students better, teachers can implement activities and lessons that both relate to the particular subject matter and provide windows into students' lives, such as "I am from . . . " poems. Some teachers perform outreach activities such as visiting individual students' homes. CES has created a tool, "Putting Students at the Center," based on a document from California Tomorrow, to help teachers assess how well they know their students. This survey can help teachers think about previously unconsidered aspects of their students' identities that point toward ways to learn more about them. (To view "Putting Students at the Center," as well as other tools to support student-centered teaching and learning, visit http://www.ceschangelab.org.)

Incorporating Relevant and Culturally Responsive Teaching

For students who belong to groups that have been poorly served by schools, personally and culturally relevant curriculum that engages them is an effective way to boost their academic achievement, as Gloria Ladson-Billings has documented in much of her work. The movement to create culturally relevant schools is aimed at redefining the role of education; instead of replicating the dominant culture, education should move learners into higher-order thinking, train them as critical problem solvers, and prepare them to work in diverse environments. In culturally relevant schools and classrooms, all students are treated as capable, and they are held to high expectations. When students are treated as competent, they are likely to demonstrate competence.

The role of teachers in culturally relevant learning environments is different from their role in a traditional classroom. In culturally relevant classrooms, teachers differentiate their teaching to address the diverse needs of learners, creating access points for all students that match their varied learning styles. Teachers develop knowledge scaffolds, moving from what students know to what they need to know. In schools and classrooms that value cultural relevance, effective teaching involves in-depth knowledge of both the students and the subject matter. Teachers use the context of the community as an extension of the classroom and use the lives and circumstances of their students as central and relevant subject matter. Bringing in the issues that communities are facing serves two purposes: it teaches students about citizenship and democratic practice, and it is a way to teach respect for differences and the development of empathy and compassion as important values that uphold a democratic society. Culturally relevant schools honor and respect students' home cultures and value the diverse ways that students communicate and express themselves. They help students to deconstruct the social forces that affect their daily lives and to better understand their place in a changing world. Ladson-Billings (1994) emphasizes that culturally relevant schools and classrooms create better public schools for all children. They use the curriculum to expose students to the multiple perspectives and stories that formed and influenced our history and help to build their agency to contribute to social and economic changes in their community and their country.

Differentiating Instruction

Knowing students well, as discussed earlier, can help teachers design curriculum and lessons that respect who the students are and where they are coming from, build on their existing knowledge base and experience, and engage them in learning experiences that they find meaningful and relevant to their lives. As Carol Ann Tomlinson (1999) describes in *The Differentiated Classroom: Responding to the Needs of All Learners*: "In differentiated classrooms, students are studied as a basis for planning." Building on this foundation, it is important to meet the challenge that any collection of unique individuals brings, which is that they come with different learning styles, aptitudes, and needs.

In CES schools, grouping students heterogeneously is a matter of principle and a prerequisite for creating equitable schools. If there are different tracks for different students, if students are grouped by abilities, if adults are dictating which students are being prepared for college and which students aren't, we are replicating the inequities of our current system, in which students' race and family income predetermine their success in life. Like small school size, heterogeneous classrooms are a precondition for creating equitable schools, yet they do not ensure equity by themselves. Most untracked schools, as all true CES schools are, struggle with teaching heterogeneous groups of students effectively. And if teachers in heterogeneous classrooms are not genuinely focused on individual learners, they can perpetuate the inequities of tracked classes. Learning how to differentiate enables teachers to teach toward equitable outcomes for all students. As Tomlinson (1999) describes, there are two aspects of differentiation, each with three elements. Teachers are able to differentiate content, process, and product (aspect one) according to students' readiness, interests, and learning profile (aspect two).

School of the Future (SOF) senior Tiffany Bender describes some of the specific approaches that various SOF teachers take in order to implement differentiation, developing a culture of sharing knowledge, accountable talk, and other learning norms that helps engage students in an interdependent culture of learning, making meaning together, and seeing each other as resources and supports in the learning process:

> If I'm struggling in math, which is not my favorite subject, it's easier for me to ask for help, whereas if I were in a tracked class, I would feel like there is competition. It's easier for me to ask another student for help in math because I know that the same person I might be asking for help in math or science will be asking me for help in history or English. So it's created that balance of not being afraid to ask for help and at the same time knowing that you can help someone else. At the same time, we also learn from each kind of medium. Some people are auditory learners, some people are visual learners, and some people work best on their own, so we explore each kind of outlet to learning something. And while each time you learn the same thing through a different medium, you learn which way is best for you as well as picking up the actual subject. In physics, we often have to open up a unit with experiments. Before our teachers told us Newton's three laws, we created the laws ourselves and then went back to the textbook and we read Newton's three laws. The first medium was visual, actually acting out the experiment. The second medium was writing down what we learned and gathering our observations, creating inferences, and turning that into a thesis, and the last medium was reading the actual law.

Creating an Effective Inclusion Model

School of the Future has worked for many years to serve all of its students by using an inclusion model in which students with special needs are fully included within extremely diverse classrooms. Inclusion means that students who have different abilities learn in the same classroom and are held to the same standards. A broad mix of ethnic groups, socioeconomic backgrounds, and learning abilities is a hallmark of the school. Students with learning disabilities sit at the same tables with students who might have been in gifted and talented programs in elementary school and with wheelchair-bound students with cerebral palsy. Catherine DeLaura, School of the Future's former principal, explains that every classroom is heterogeneous. There is a minimum of one special education teacher for every grade, and these teachers "push in" to the classrooms, working with students in those classes. The special educators also lead advisories at those same grade levels and attend grade-level team meetings. DeLaura explains, "Our ninth-grade special education teacher pushes into three of the four sections, and then she meets with the math teacher, the science teacher, and the two humanities teachers . . . so they can look at the upcoming projects to modify them, anticipate issues that are going to come up with all strugglers and particularly kids who have IEPs [individualized education plans], and they can, of course, talk about individual kids who aren't producing the kind of work that they need to on this level." School of the Future has created this structure of careful collaboration among special education and "regular" classroom teachers in order to support its inclusion model and the kind of instructional differentiation that teachers do there.

The benefits of such differentiation are more than strictly academic. According to Tiffany Bender, it fundamentally changes the ways that School of the Future students view their fellow human beings: "I feel like it helps with your sensitivity as you go into adulthood, not just learning that some people are faster learners than others, but you learn that some people really do have disabilities that aren't that much different than yours. We have two students from our school who have cerebral palsy, and I just really find it amazing that they're learning the same things that we are, like on the same level that we are; they're just learning it a completely different way. That was kind of like an eye-opener."

Providing Individualization to English-Language Learners

Students who are English-language learners (ELLs) bring their own set of needs to a heterogeneous classroom. Many schools and teachers struggle to teach ELLs effectively. Even when they participate in professional development particular to teaching ELL students, it is not integrated into overall curriculum and lesson development. Practitioners in CES schools fuse research on language development and language acquisition with the vision and goals of their schools to develop programs that best meet the needs of their students. While the size and culture of CES small schools allow for educators to know students well and therefore create the more personalized learning experiences that are needed by English-language learners, size can present a challenge in terms of forming a critical mass of students who share the need for targeted services. CES schools have responded to this challenge by moving the entire school toward full integration of ELL students rather than segregating, tracking, or isolating students. This goal is supported by research demonstrating that students build language proficiency through interaction with both teachers and peers who are fluent in English (Olsen and Romero, 2007).

Several schools in the CES Small Schools Network are achieving success in teaching English-language learners. One approach is to personalize the learning experience within a heterogeneous classroom while providing students with strong support both in and out of the classroom. Moving students from "English proficient" to fluent in English requires a comprehensive approach that employs interdisciplinary teaching teams and student-led cooperative groups. Larry Simonson, lead teacher at Civitas Leadership School, a new small CES school in Los Angeles, believes that group work supports students' language development: "In our school, students of mixed English-language . . . proficiency participate in cooperative groups that allow bilingual students with developing English skills to interact with those who are more proficient." Civitas principal Rosamaria Figueroa explains that "by setting learning objectives in an audiovisually rich context and creating projects through which students will be more likely to find handles that allow them to really grasp the content in a more authentic way," teachers at Civitas differentiate instruction to engage students of diverse learning styles and English-language abilities.

CES Mentor School El Colegio has also demonstrated success working with ELLs by effectively employing the strategy of designing interdisciplinary classes that are team-taught by both ELL and content-area teachers. In these classes, language instruction is integrated with content instruction in courses that include a combination of history, art, science, and math. To scaffold the learning, teachers use modified speech, contextual clues, and multisensory learning, following the principles of specially designed academic instruction in English (Armani, 2008).

Creating such rich learning experiences for heterogeneous classrooms requires a strong professional development plan and time for educators to collaborate and build a professional learning community, in order to utilize available research. Sandra Suarez, director of education at El Colegio, says, "Every staff member participates in professional development that teaches the strategies for teaching ELL students within heterogeneous classrooms, including the use of visual aids, adapting language for different levels of English-language acquisition, and utilizing group work."

At South Valley Academy, a CES Mentor School in Albuquerque, New Mexico, support for ELLs is built into the design of the entire school. South Valley Academy was created to help students who traditionally drop out of school at a rate of 70 percent to become successful students, graduate from high school, and move on to various postsecondary options. Former principal and South Valley co-founder Alan Marks explains how South Valley's advisory program, the centerpiece of the school, serves as a major support component for their ELL population:

> Our advisory program meets every day in groups no bigger than eight to eleven students. The advisor is the direct liaison to the home. We meet with parents and students no less than five times a year for narrative conferences. We deal with daily, personal, and academic problems. The advisory is the *familia*. We celebrate birthdays and play together, go on field trips together, and take care of each other. The advisor is the enforcer of discipline; advisors play the role of counselor and problem solver. We provide advisors with structured supports that help promote student success: a strong effort is made to match Spanish-speaking students with Spanish-speaking advisors in order to support the student's native language as well as to establish a meaningful connection with parents (who may not be English speakers). We have three social workers on staff. All our staff speak or are learning Spanish, and any member of our school can bring a student that is of concern to what we call *Ed-Team*, a place to discuss and craft a plan for keeping students on track.

CES schools are effectively serving their ELLs by employing a high level of personalization, intense academic support structures, a focus on skills-based projects (including service learning), and culturally competent staff members. Along with these strategies, the cultures of our schools make the biggest difference. According to Kata Sandoval-Tonini, principal of South Valley, "Our school honors the Spanish language and the students' culture, and treats them as an asset, not a liability." In several CES schools, ELLs have opportunities to build on their native language; this forms the foundation for their acquisition of English. Because students learn through making connections between what they already know and what they are learning, making real connections to language, culture, identity, and history throughout the curriculum is fundamental and an important aspect of equity-driven teaching and learning.

Student as Worker, Teacher as Coach

Visitors at High Tech High, a CES Mentor School in San Diego, immediately get a feel for the school's hands-on, project-based approach to instruction. In the windows that line the hallways are various senior projects, all of which are interactive, mechanical displays that illustrate a concept from physics in an aesthetically pleasing way. Students worked in teams of two to create pieces like "Good Vibrations": a series of tuning forks connected to an electric tuner. A mallet is attached to the display; striking one of the tuning forks prompts the tuner to show the note just made. These window boxes demonstrate that students are clearly the owners of their work and learning. This project is just one of many examples at High Tech High of the CES Common Principle "Student-as-worker, teacher-as-coach."

The projects that line High Tech High's interior windows demanded a significant amount of time and energy to create; students' real work, many hours of it, is clearly in evidence. Students were self-directed and given a great deal of latitude for their own decision making and creativity. The end products, which are demonstrations of mastery, are evidence of universal understanding of clear and high standards. These three elements—meaningful student work, students' demonstration of mastery, and a project-based approach that uses clearly communicated and understood standards—are the hallmarks of the CES Common Principle "Student-as-worker, teacher-as-coach," which states, "The governing practical metaphor of the school should be student-as-worker, rather than the more familiar metaphor of teacher-as-deliverer-of-instructional-services. Accordingly, a prominent pedagogy will be coaching, to provoke students to learn how to learn and thus to teach themselves."

When students engage in projects that are relevant and interesting to them, they are doing meaningful work. The projects at High Tech High clearly demonstrate academic standards and alignment with the state curriculum, but for former principal Ben Daley, the most important aspect of the projects is that they are of high interest to students. High Tech High starts with the idea that high schools are typically not very interesting places for students; the school's goal is to change that, so that their students are highly engaged in their learning. This commitment to engagement and relevance demands very flexible teacher planning. "The project dictates the curriculum, and not the other way around," says Daley. Teachers develop interesting project ideas and then refer to the standards and curriculum framework and decide which elements they will include. (To view High Tech High's project planning tool, see the *Small Schools, Big Ideas* Web site at http://www.ceschangelab.org/.)

Thinking of oneself as a coach to students can help a teacher avoid the common problem of doing more of the work in the classroom than the students. If a teacher feels as if he is doing most of the work, chances are pretty good that his classroom is teacher-centered and that students are not sufficiently owning the learning. Front-loading their instructional work by planning, clarifying outcomes and structures, and developing detailed instructions for students is a fundamental shift in practice that happens for CES teachers. Giving students space to work and explore ideas within these structures allows them some freedom and choice, which in turn leads to student-driven learning and more student-centered classrooms.

Moving toward the "student as worker, teacher as coach" approach often requires a paradigm shift for the teacher, as well as a certain amount of letting go. As educators, we are usually not taught how to be facilitators of learning. Teachers can use a number of tools and structures—for example, Socratic seminars and structured roles for cooperative learning groups—to help them become better facilitators by building on shared understanding with students about the teacher's role in the learning process (see "Ten Facilitation Tips for Teachers as Coaches" sidebar).

Ten Facilitation Tips for Teachers as Coaches

1. Provide clear written and verbal instructions for tasks and activities.

2. Limit teacher talking time to less than ten minutes.

3. Create different small-group roles, and communicate directly with those in charge (facilitator, recorder, resource manager, timekeeper, and so on).

4. Spend the majority of class time rotating and checking in with individual students and groups.

5. Share backward planning with students so that they also know the big picture and the end goal and can be constantly working toward it.

6. Teach students how to critique their own and others' work, and then have them give feedback and do peer edits.

7. Use protocols that have specific time limits for speaking and that foster full participation, such as whip-arounds (rounds in which everyone has the opportunity to speak) or Socratic seminars.

8. Create regular opportunities for students to present their work to other students, including opportunities to lead lessons.

9. Begin by immersing students in an experience or activity, then follow with questions about what they learned.

10. Have students regularly reflect on their learning through writing, speaking, and self-assessments.

Some of the same protocols that are used with teachers in Critical Friends Groups can be used with students—for example, Chalk Talk, a silent way to check for understanding and generate ideas among the members of a learning group, and protocols for interpreting and discussing texts such as Save the Last Word for ME, a small-group exercise designed to clarify thinking about a text (see "Using Critical Friends Group Protocols with Students" sidebar). Creating tight structures (such as the protocols that were just mentioned) and clarifying expectations are critical to enabling the teacher to put more control of learning into the hands of the students in constructive and powerful ways.

Using Critical Friends Group Protocols with Students

As discussed in Chapter Six, we value the work that grew out of CES and has been done over nearly twenty years by the National School Reform Faculty (NSRF) to develop structured conversations and interactions, which NSRF describes as protocols, to facilitate adult learning within the framework of a Critical Friends Group (CFG). We strongly recommend that educators take part in an NSRF CFG training in order to implement these frameworks within professional learning communities and with student learners. Please visit the NSRF Web site at http://www.nsrfharmony.org/ for descriptions of the Save the Last Word for ME and Chalk Talk protocols, information about CFG training, and much more.

Less Is More, Depth over Coverage

"The school's goals should be simple: that each student master a limited number of essential skills and areas of knowledge. While these skills and areas will, to varying degrees, reflect the traditional academic disciplines, the program's design should be shaped by the intellectual and imaginative powers and competencies that the students need, rather than by 'subjects' as conventionally defined. The aphorism 'less is more' should dominate: curricular decisions should be guided by the aim of thorough student mastery and achievement rather than by an effort to merely cover content." The CES Common Principle "Less is more, depth over coverage" is closely related to "student as worker, teacher as coach." Allowing students to own more of the learning in the classroom and asking students to undergo performance-based assessment requires an investment of time. If the teacher's focus is on covering as much content as possible, it is impossible to find that kind of time and it is also impossible to go deep into the material. In the current climate of high-stakes standardized testing, the national emphasis is on coverage over depth; however, the standards that students are meeting through the sort of in-depth studies and performance tasks discussed in this chapter far exceed what is called for in multiple-choice tests.

Three high-impact strategies bring "less is more, depth over coverage" into practice:

- Essential questions
- In-depth investigations
- Curriculum development and backward planning

Essential Questions

Almost all CES schools use essential questions (EQs) as a way of organizing their classes to address the "Less is more, depth over coverage" Common Principle. EQs ask students to think deeply about an issue in ways that lead to further questions and exploration. They are usually connected to big ideas or concepts that are important in the context of the larger world. Sometimes these questions are classroom-specific, and sometimes they are schoolwide, unifying the disciplines and the grades. For example, the question "How do we create movement and change?" can work in studying history, literature, and physics. Several of the schools in the CES Small Schools Network, such as Mentor Schools Urban Academy Laboratory High School and Humanities Preparatory Academy, organize all of their courses around themes and essential questions rather than by discipline alone, allowing students to focus on less content and go deeper (see sidebar "Course Descriptions from Urban Academy Laboratory High School and Humanities Preparatory Academy").

Course Descriptions from Urban Academy Laboratory High School and Humanities Preparatory Academy

These course descriptions from CES Mentor Schools Urban Academy and Humanities Prep represent courses that are organized around essential questions.

Urban Academy Laboratory High School

Heat and Energy: Everyone knows what hot and cold feel like, but do you know what heat actually is? What is it that makes the mercury rise? And what is energy, really? Can you collect it in a jar? Oddly enough, the study of heat and energy has revealed surprising and counterintuitive concepts about subjects as fantastic as the possibility of life, the history of the universe, and even the nature of time itself. While we consider such grand topics, we will also dig into the experimental work of investigating heat and energy phenomena for ourselves. Expect to read, write, draw, calculate, do interpretive dance, and shake your head in disbelief. Chances are, this topic is not what you think.

Hip Hop Stories: First came the rappers, break-dancers and graffiti artists. Then along came everything else. To some, Hip Hop has transformed the world and its influence can be seen all over. Yet, how does one define Hip Hop? What is it really? In this class we will look specifically at a body of written work, which is being called Hip Hop fiction. What makes this genre unique? What are the stories being told? Are these stories any different from stories which have come before? In this class students will be expected to keep up with reading and writing assignments. Several papers will be assigned so there will be ample opportunity to work towards completing pre-requisite papers. It goes without saying that involvement in class discussions will be an essential ingredient to help us clarify ideas raised.

Humanities Preparatory Academy

Protest in America: How do "ordinary" people create change in American society? This class will trace efforts to create a more inclusive democracy from Reconstruction to the present day. We will focus on three contested areas—race, labor and war—and look in depth at the failure of Reconstruction and the Civil Rights movement, the strikes for worker's justice and the protests against the Vietnam War.

Great Ideas in Math and Science: Can You Dig 'Em? What are the great ideas that have changed the world? Are they relevant today? How do people invent them? What are some of the ideas that people believed once but have now rejected? Why do humans decide to reject some ideas and not others? We will examine math and science ideas of both the past and present, from the Ancient Greeks to the most modern ideas of scientists.

Francis W. Parker Charter Essential School, a CES Mentor School in Devens, Massachusetts, uses EQs schoolwide, not necessarily as the focus of a specific class or unit of study but as an overarching framework for the school's annual focus (see "Francis W. Parker Charter Essential School's Schoolwide Essential Questions" sidebar). Students select a year's EQ democratically, through voting in advisories on questions suggested by eleventh graders at the end of the school year. The school's choice becomes the next year's EQ. Parker's principal, Teri Schrader, advocates using EQs in subtle ways, tying them to the curriculum when possible but not "hitting kids over the heads with it." Schrader comments, "If you use an EQ too overtly, kids get sickened by it. If the EQ is a subtle strand, the kids find themselves incorporating insights into their work. The best EQs resonate with kids but not overtly. They become meaningful through discovery. EQs are more of a guiding influence in arts and humanities; they become one of a few stakes to put in the ground that really frame the discussion of three to four major units of study."

Francis W. Parker Charter Essential School's Schoolwide Essential Questions

What is community? (1995–96)

What is change? (1996–97)

What is balance? (1997–98)

Where are the patterns? (1998–99)

What's the limit? (1999–2000)

What really matters? (2000–01)

Where's the truth? (2001–02)

What are the possibilities? (2002–03)

What's next? (2003–04)

What is unique? What is universal? (2004–05)

What is overlooked? (2005–06)

How is it relevant? (2006–07)

What are the causes? What are the effects? (2007–08)

How do we adapt? (2008–09)

Source: Francis W. Parker Charter Essential School, 2008b.

In-Depth Investigations

Back to the High Tech High example again: the window installation project, as well as most of the school's other projects, required two to three months to complete. In some states, history standards alone might ask teachers to speed through hundreds of years in far fewer than a hundred days. In such cases, choosing several critical topics to build curriculum around—and letting go of others—is the only way to dedicate the amount of time and study necessary to engage students and help them to understand the content in meaningful ways. If we want students to develop the higher-order skills that are required for lifelong learning and success in the twenty-first century, these are the types of decisions that schools need to make. Organizing curriculum around themes and several key standards is the best way to begin.

Amelia Pluto, a recent graduate of High Tech High, describes how the "less is more, depth over coverage" principle factored into her experience:

> As juniors, our main project for the whole year was creating a San Diego Bay Field Guide, and so we were broken up into smaller groups. I was in the white sea bass group. And I spent, basically, the whole spring semester and part of the fall semester just researching white sea bass, and finding out about them and their lives in the bay. I came to see the connection between the bay in San Diego and, in general, things from around the world. I made all these bigger connections as I learned more about one specific topic. So we interviewed people who work at the San Diego Oceans Foundation and who work at the hatchery, and we even had an interview with this old-time sea bass fisherman who talked about the glory days of sea bass fishing. So it was definitely one of those projects that include all the different subjects, which was the goal because we had the humanities aspect and the science aspect. We didn't really get into the math of tracking the sea bass, but it's definitely there.

The yearlong San Diego Bay Field Guide project culminated in a published book of original research. Amelia Pluto says, "The whole book is focused on how the bay has been utilized and how resources have been depleted and how they're coming back. It's really exciting to see, like, the work that we've done become finished and go so far. And it's definitely one of those projects that has applications in the bigger community, which is really cool."

Having these kinds of in-depth learning experiences is tremendously powerful for students. Going deep and producing work that has relevance to the world beyond the classroom, as the field guide did, helps make the learning meaningful and memorable for students.

Curriculum Development and Backward Planning

Creating the kinds of learning experiences we describe in this chapter requires a different way of planning curriculum and developing lessons. The CES Common Principles that we have focused on in this chapter (learning to use one's mind well; personalization; student as worker, teacher as coach; and less is more, depth over coverage) are best used within a project-based learning framework, which produces products, artifacts, and tangible examples of what the students know and can do that are best assessed with authentic performance-based assessments. And so we plan this type of curriculum with the end in mind, starting from what we want the outcomes to be and working back from there to build learning experiences that incorporate differentiated instruction, to offer relevant and engaging courses and projects, and to provide learning experiences that will help all students get what they need to be ready to demonstrate their learning.

To create schools that embody the student-centered teaching and learning described in this chapter and in the CES Benchmarks, CES educators rely on "habits of mind" as a way of framing student learning around a set of qualitative thinking outcomes. Schools develop a list of qualities or attributes that they would like their students to acquire and plan the learning experiences that would lead students to develop these habits. "Think of a habit of mind as the self-discipline to overcome natural inhibitions to deep thought: a disposition to be open-minded, to suspend disbelief, to persevere in the face of ambiguity and complexity," writes Grant Wiggins (2008). These habits help students to think and reflect carefully about the process and experience of learning and to understand themselves as learners. Educators develop curriculum and lessons that create a learning journey that helps students learn these habits, and assessment frameworks are often designed to assess students' mastery of the habits in conjunction with specific knowledge and skills.

At Wildwood School in Los Angeles, the Habits of Mind and Heart (see sidebar) are fully integrated into their entire program. One Wildwood student remarked that he even found himself using the habits at home with his family. Wildwood's secondary program is built around developing habits of mind and heart that will serve students in their lifelong pursuit of learning. Jeanne Fauci, former director of Wildwood's Outreach Center, explained, "Our curriculum, assignments, assessments, and all else we do at Wildwood are based on these habits."

In Chapter Eight, in which formative and summative assessments are explored more deeply, habits of mind are discussed as a starting point from which to align instruction and clarify expectations for students. In Wildwood's case, students' knowledge of the habits helps them think deeply and critically about their own learning. Teachers plan backward from the desired student outcomes, creating curriculum, lesson plans, and pedagogical approaches that help students develop and internalize these new ways of thinking and behaving. For example, to focus on the Habit of Evidence, teachers create opportunities through their lessons and projects for students to do research and find evidence that backs up their theses. When the Habit of Perspective is a goal, teachers ensure that students are investigating issues from all points of view, relying on the voices of many different groups and individuals.

Wildwood Secondary School's Habits of Mind and Heart

The Habit of Perspective: The ability to address questions from multiple viewpoints and to use a variety of ways to solve problems

The Habit of Evidence: The ability to bring together relevant information, to judge the credibility of sources, to find out for oneself

The Habit of Connection: The ability to look for patterns and ways that things fit together in order to utilize diverse material to form new solutions

The Habit of Convention: The ability to acknowledge accepted standards in any area in order to be understood and to understand others

The Habit of Service to the Common Good: The ability to recognize the effects of one's actions upon others, coupled with the desire to make the community a better place for all

The Habit of Collaboration: The ability to work effectively with others, accepting and giving appropriate assistance

The Habit of Ethical Behavior: The ability to understand how personal values influence behavior and to live one's life according to ethical principles

In another use of backward planning at High Tech High, in the design and creation of projects, both students and staff rely heavily on both the use of models and the expectation that the work will be presented publicly. The planning for the projects—for both the workers and the coaches—begins with the end result in mind. Faculty share and present work among the staff and in their classrooms in order to establish expectations. Students are often shown a model, created by the teacher or by another student, of what the final product should look like. Expectations for the outcome, often presented in the form of a rubric, are clear, so that students can take ownership over the process and product, as long as it meets the explicit parameters outlined at the outset.

CES schools use various forms of performance-based assessment as end products of a course or unit of study, asking students to demonstrate what they have learned. One such form, exhibitions, are a culmination of a unit, project, semester, academic year, or entire academic career. While these assessment practices are covered at length in Chapter Eight, we note here that the form of the final assessment determines the instruction and informs the backward planning process. Performance-based assessment requires that the performance task drive the teaching and learning. Teaching in a facilitative, coaching style asks teachers to guide students toward an end goal while students actually steer the ship to the final destination. In this way, the project that students work on for months, like a window box at High Tech High, is also their performance-based assessment.

Audience is another important component to consider when planning culminating projects and performance-based assessment. As the word *performance* implies, an audience of some sort is needed for student demonstrations. An authentic audience includes people such as professionals in a connected field who care about the work that is being presented, and students' investment in their work increases as the authenticity of the audience increases. In the case of the Quest High School students who refurbished homes for people in need, their audience—the people who would be living in the homes—was extremely authentic. At Urban Academy, when students have to exhibit their proficiency for college professors in the fields they have been studying, they also have a different kind of high-stakes, authentic audience. When classes are organized around meaningful student work—as it is in these examples from High Tech High, Urban Academy, and Quest—and when the end product is relevant to others in the world beyond the school, the students become the drivers of their learning—the workers—and the teachers become the facilitators—or coaches—who envision the results and then work backward, setting the stage so that powerful learning can occur.

Conclusion

The simplicity of the expression of these ideas about teaching and learning belies the complexity of their implementation. This personalized, student-centered, project-based, and question-driven approach to instruction is not the way most of us were acculturated into the world of schools either as students or, later, as teachers. Teachers navigate a developmental trajectory in order to become skilled in the methods we have discussed; becoming expert at effectively differentiating instruction for a wide range of learners takes time and training, as do using project-based learning as a teaching strategy and implementing the other essentials of student-centered teaching and learning as described in the sidebar "Essentials of Student-Centered Teaching and Learning." On the other hand, first steps are important, and beginning to implement any of the various ideas explored here can yield positive results immediately.

Essentials of Student-Centered Teaching and Learning

- Begin planning from the habits that you want students to develop.
- Develop essential questions that can be continually asked but never fully—or easily—answered.
- Help students to generate and investigate their own questions.
- Build in opportunities to work on extended and in-depth projects that have relevance in the world beyond the classroom.
- Create performance-based assessments and plan backward from them.
- Invest time in getting to know your students, their background, and their communities in order to build relationships with them.
- Tailor your teaching to meet individual needs and provide extra support.
- Practice facilitation more than direct teaching.
- Dedicate significant time to a few topics and themes while omitting others, and study those few topics deeply.

Obviously, all of the examples in this chapter grew out of years of hard work, significant professional development, sharing practices, solving dilemmas collaboratively within schools and across the CES network, and trial and error. While we believe that small schools create the optimal environment for the kind of learning we are discussing, there are elements in every one of these stories that can be applied to any classroom anywhere. Creating classroom environments that are personalized, in which teachers act as coaches to student workers, in which students are learning to use their mind well, and in which depth is valued over superficial content coverage helps students to learn and achieve more on a deeper level, giving them knowledge and skills that will help them for the rest of their lives.

The current educational climate of standardized testing emphasizes coverage over depth, in contrast to the CES Common Principles, which urge the opposite. Schools and teachers face significant pressure to teach to the test and conform to an outdated form of teaching that does not prepare students with the skills and knowledge that they need in this new century. However, we urge others to resist these pressures and follow the examples of the schools described in this book. These schools are demonstrating results through teaching that is personalized and that requires students to use their mind well, play the role of the worker, study less rather than more, and go deep rather than broad. Students in CES schools are meeting these heightened expectations and becoming the kinds of thinkers, learners, and citizens that they need to be—and that our country needs them to be—in order to achieve a more equitable society.

Demonstration of Mastery

> When I presented my exhibition, it was great to show what I learned and how I had contributed to my community at the same time. The experience is going to stay with me longer than any test would.
>
> —Student at Empowerment College Preparatory High School, Houston, Texas

Demonstrating mastery through performance-based assessment is perhaps the best form of accountability. It gives teachers, family and community members, and other stakeholders a way to see how well students are doing and whether a school is doing a good job. CES schools provide students with opportunities to exhibit their expertise, knowledge, and abilities in order to demonstrate that they have mastered a set of skills, to make a transition from one level of schooling to the next, and to demonstrate their readiness to graduate. These assessments give a more complete and meaningful picture of the student than standardized tests alone can provide.

Interdisciplinary projects allow CES students to take on significant questions. They dive into deep investigations, collaborate with peers, and connect with experts from various disciplines. Performance assessments engage teachers in the development of tasks that reflect a range of content and skills and in the development of learning rubrics that provide invaluable feedback for improving teaching and learning. Performance assessments promote a coherent educational program that provides scaffolding for skills and knowledge across grade levels and content areas.

The relationship between assessment and teaching and learning is critical. If we want to prepare students for a successful life in the twenty-first century, we need to have twenty-first-century assessment systems that are capable of measuring the skills and knowledge that students need for success today. The demonstration of mastery through performance-based assessment lends itself to teaching and learning at a higher level, moving beyond memorization of facts, events, and formulas to solving complex problems through the discovery and application of new knowledge. The opportunity to demonstrate mastery in front of peers, community, and family gives students a place to showcase what they know and can do and receive feedback and praise for how far they have come as learners.

After defining demonstration of mastery and performance-based assessment, this chapter will describe the process and discuss the impact that establishing a system of performance-based assessment has on every important element of a school: practices, structures, relationships, values, academic expectations, and, consequently, the transformation of the culture of learning as a whole. Incorporating a system of performance-based assessment into an educational program leads to:

- Presenting a fuller picture of what students know and can do
- Providing personalization, support, and structured time for performance-based assessment
- Aligning authentic teaching, learning, and assessment
- Professional development that supports performance-based assessment
- Community-wide accountability for equitable student outcomes
- Meeting and influencing state accountability requirements

Demonstration of Mastery Defined

In full, the CES Common Principle known as "Demonstration of mastery" states,

> Teaching and learning should be documented and assessed with tools based on student performance of real tasks. Students not yet

at appropriate levels of competence should be provided intensive support and resources to assist them quickly to meet those standards. Multiple forms of evidence, ranging from ongoing observation of the learner to completion of specific projects, should be used to better understand the learner's strengths and needs, and to plan for further assistance. Students should have opportunities to exhibit their expertise before family and community. The diploma should be awarded upon a successful final demonstration of mastery for graduation—an "Exhibition." As the diploma is awarded when earned, the school's program proceeds with no strict age grading and with no system of credits earned by "time spent" in class. The emphasis is on the students' demonstration that they can do important things.

Decisions about awarding diplomas, determining promotion, or assessing attainment of other goals should be based on students' "demonstration that they can do important things." Exhibitions and other performance-based assessments provide educators with multiple forms of evidence to measure students' strengths and needs so that educators can address students' skill limitations, support further growth in the areas in which students have demonstrated competence, and prepare for students' next level of intellectual growth. To facilitate common understanding of performance-based assessment, Appendix E contains a glossary of useful assessment terms.

Assessment by demonstration was refined and documented in the early work of the Coalition of Essential Schools. In *Horace's Compromise,* Ted Sizer (1984) describes public, high-stakes demonstrations of mastery as a high-leverage school reform strategy that allows teaching and learning in a school to be assessed authentically based on students' performance of real tasks. Sizer and others conceived of exhibitions as a paradigm shift from evaluating academic achievement strictly by Carnegie units and other measures of seat time to using measures that would ensure accountability through public demonstrations of student achievement that were engaging, relevant, challenging, and aligned with established academic standards. According to Sizer, demonstration of mastery should be a foundational piece of a school's mission and practices, allowing educators to document learning through tangible outcomes, artifacts, and products that can be shared and examined. These products provide evidence of students' learning, including what they have mastered and the areas in which they still need to grow.

Demonstrations of learning, or *exhibitions,* at Essential schools are visually vibrant and engaging; students present their research and findings via photographs, charts, graphs, and video. Students use various online and offline media to demonstrate what they know and can do, using their creativity to produce screenplays, poems, and stories; to construct models, maps, and displays; and to recreate experiments and performances. In every way possible, students are encouraged to generate, collect, and refine objects, artifacts, and visual products that show their learning process and what they have learned. At an exhibition, the best of this collection is thoroughly presented, examined, and judged by panels of outside experts, teachers, peers, or a combination of all three. In addition to presenting artifacts, these learning demonstrations involve a critical interaction between the student and evaluators in which the learner defends his or her work, answers questions, and reflects on what was learned and the significance of the learning.

Incorporating a system of authentic assessment into schools can lead to rethinking the systems of grades and seat time that traditionally have dictated the ways that students can advance within an educational program. CES schools believe that rather than measuring the academic growth of students based on the time they have spent being passively immersed in a discipline, teaching and learning are best assessed by having students perform real tasks that demonstrate what they know and can do across disciplines.

CES small schools use exhibitions to allow students to demonstrate mastery in order to enter the next grade, pass a course, or graduate from high school. For example, all students at Francis W. Parker Charter Essential School, a CES Mentor school in Devens, Massachusetts, culminate their studies with a capstone senior project in which they explore a topic of their choice, either independently or with the guidance of an outside mentor. An intellectual and personal bridge between high school and the world beyond, the senior project requires students to generate an essential question; explore that question by engaging in formal academic research and collaborating with people outside of the school (for example, through internships, interviews, job shadowing, or field research); apply skills and knowledge from several disciplines to complete the project; and present the project to a panel and an audience. Parker students lead up to their culminating senior project by completing "gateway" exhibitions every two years that permit them to advance through the school, as well as many other demonstrations of mastery within classroom settings.

At Wildwood School, a CES Mentor school in Los Angeles, learning at all grade levels is project-based and includes community service and internships. To chart their progress, students are given narrative assessments rather than grades, and the program is built around developing seven habits of heart and mind. Wildwood's graduation requirements stipulate that all seniors assemble and present a portfolio that reflects two years of academic work, incorporating essays, research papers, reading logs, graphs and statistical analyses, and multimedia projects.

Presenting a Fuller Picture of What Students Know and Can Do

Becoming an educated person in this century is significantly different than it was in the nineteenth century, when our public education system was created. Today, well-rounded individuals possess advanced intellectual skills as well as the social and emotional skills needed to thrive in a complex and changing world. Good citizenship, relationships, home life, and the world of work all require social and emotional development, the ability to communicate well with others, constructive conflict resolution, and awareness of our interdependence with others—how our behavior, decisions, and attitudes affect the lives of others on the planet. Teaching all of these skills is an educational mission that is much more sophisticated and enlightened than the focus on preparing managers and workers that dominated nineteenth- and twentieth-century educational systems. To meet this challenge, educators must transform teaching and learning and the measures used to evaluate the progress that students make toward proficiency and mastery.

CES schools use performance-based assessment systems to get a deeper and more comprehensive look at students than the glimpse provided by standardized paper-and-pencil tests. These assessments match the complexity of the skills, tasks, and products that students are asked to know and create. The twenty-first-century skills that we are teaching in CES schools cannot be fully measured or demonstrated in the present systems of standardized exams. Performance-based tools allow us to assemble the evidence to assess the progress that the school, teacher, and students are making toward mastering goals.

Performance-based assessments benefit students in ways that standardized tests do not. With performance-based assessments, a student uses higher-order thinking skills in ways that foster deeper learning and result in higher retention (Ascher, 1990). School of the Future student Tiffany Bender reflects, "I noticed in my own school experience that after I completed the test, I forgot the information I studied. It just goes away. With an exhibition, where I've had to prepare a research paper as part of a project that I have to defend, I will be able to understand that more thoroughly and remember it throughout the years. After a test, you don't really know what you know, unlike at the end of an exhibition. In that case, you show what you know and everyone knows what you really know about the subject." These assessments are active and are more effective at unveiling what students know and can do than traditional measures that rely solely on data coming from narrow standardized test responses rather than open-ended responses.

At Empowerment College Preparatory High School in Houston, Texas, exhibitions are a cornerstone of the curriculum. Empowerment combines the social action work that students perform in the community once a week with academic research and multimedia presentation skills. Samantha Brooks, a founding Empowerment teacher, explains how performance-based assessments provide opportunities to practice and master skills that will serve students well throughout their life: "The whole notion of the demonstration of mastery and holding exhibitions are vital to our school, because we know just how important these skills are in the real world. You have to know how to communicate well, how to get your ideas across, and how to work through processes that are uncomfortable. When the children are working on their projects and exhibitions, they are experiencing what professionals go through in their fields. We are getting them ready for the real world from ninth grade on up."

As well, because this type of assessment has an interactive aspect—students are asked questions and given feedback by peers, family members, and others—students have an opportunity to think about their own learning as well as hear others identify their strengths and weaknesses. This sort of interaction raises the bar for learning and creates a high level of intellectual discourse among students and between students and adults that reaches back into the classroom and beyond.

Brooks's colleague April Rasmus recounts the experience of her students as they prepare to practice presenting their exhibitions in front of peers and teachers. The students know how important the final presentations will be, and they prepare to receive the first round of feedback from their teachers and peers that will help them get on track, go deeper, be clearer, and work harder before the real opening night comes around. Meanwhile, the air is filled with nervousness, as if it were the real thing instead of a dry run. The students are dressed up, and the teams are ready to face their toughest critics: their peers. With their PowerPoint slides and handouts ready to go, they are taking it all very seriously. The students that are watching know that their turn will come, and those getting ready to perform know that the dress rehearsal, for all intents and purposes, counts. Rasmus asks, "Are they ready? Well, if you ask the kids, they pretty much all say they are not ready. This is all so new for them, so they don't have much confidence. They all wish they had more time, and that is the beauty of having them practice. Some will realize how far they've come, and they all will get the encouragement they need to make the revisions needed to meet our standards. They all know that our expectations are high, so for the most part, they act as a team to push everyone to the finish line."

Exhibitions and other performance-based assessments are frequently cited as effective forms of formative assessment because students receive frequent feedback on the quality of their work as well as multiple opportunities to revise and improve before they formally present it for summative evaluation (Nichols and Berliner, 2007; Darling-Hammond, Ancess, and Falk, 1995; Gallagher, 2007; Newmann and Associates, 1996; Stiggins, 2005; Wiggins, 2006; Davidson and Feldman, 2009). Teachers in CES schools depend on performance-based assessments to measure the skills and content knowledge that students have acquired and thus help the teachers determine whether to move on to other areas of learning, to change the pace or the teaching style to fill the gaps, or to re-engage the students in their learning. From the Met's Peace Street campus, a CES Mentor School in Providence, Rhode Island, student John Phelps speaks about the importance of getting feedback at a midyear exhibition and the ways that feedback helps students to reflect on their learning and revise their work for the year's culminating exhibition: "Exhibitions are important if the person who is presenting is willing to improve on their work. You hear critical feedback from people about your work during the exhibition, and you need the humility to listen to what they're saying and act upon it by doing the revisions. If you can do that, then you're in a good place for the final exhibition."

Assessment as a formative tool can have a real impact on how students experience school, whether they are motivated, and how they achieve and therefore should be central to the way a school is organized. The formative nature of performance-based assessment can be used to structure students' personalized learning plans and inform the overall educational program of the school. These kinds of assessments drive good instruction and measure the learning of students who are engaged in tasks with real-life relevance. These assessments promote a critical form of accountability to both internal and external stakeholders; they have the potential to be a tool for transforming the school into a learning organization that is authentically accountable to students, families, and community members.

In an assessment system that is performance-based, students are given structured opportunities to collect and refine work over a period of time for a specific discipline or an interdisciplinary project. For example, when students are called on to compile portfolios, the worker or creator of the products—the student—collects pieces of work that demonstrate growth over a period of time and that later may become artifacts that serve as examples of her best work. Often, these collections are works in progress that require further revision and fine-tuning before being selected for a final presentation or exhibition. If structured properly, the portfolio can be an excellent tool for documenting a student's progress over time, as well as a wide array of talents and abilities. Portfolios are a more complete indicator of a student's performance of higher-order skills than the narrow picture that is gleaned from how a student bubbles in the answers on multiple-choice standardized exams.

Performance-based assessment systems also engage students at every turn in building knowledge while reflecting on and revising their work, and the school sets milestones in order to help students stay on track and get to the next level. Teri Schrader, principal of Parker Charter Essential School, explains the ways in which her school has created a learning journey for its students that scaffolds their learning and creates a road map toward the demonstration of mastery:

> It's easy enough to give kids hard work that makes them think. Yes, they've worked hard and learned much. We can make a case for rigor, but what I think a real demonstration of mastery for a school is to demonstrate their maturity—not simply showing what a student can do on their best day after a lot of work but creating a process that has logical end points that signal a new ramping up. When I reflect on students' progress from seventh grade to graduation, I am most

proud of the fact that it's not just all of a sudden super hard, but that everything is intended to be the next logical step.

Often, exhibitions and other forms of performance-based assessments mark important milestones in the students' learning, such as the passage from one grade to another or the successful completion of high school. At other times, they are designed to create a time to pause and take stock of growth. These interim assessments are formative. They provide a concrete centerpiece for discussions during student-led conferences that involve the student's teachers and parents or other family members and that deal with assessment narratives that record and document the learning experience.

Several CES Common Principles guide school communities to rethink the roles and responsibilities of students and teachers in order to create a culture of learning that measures academic achievement through the demonstration of mastery. In a culture of learning that expects students to learn to use their mind well, the role of a teacher is not to be the deliverer of instructional services or the all-knowing sage on the stage. Rather, the teacher facilitates student learning. In the pedagogical role of coach, a teacher enables students to use their minds to make meaning as they explore and discover knowledge, individually and in groups, at a challenging yet supported pace. This culture redefines the role of students as well: they are not passively receiving information that is held exclusively by the teacher; rather, students are central to and play an active role in teaching and learning.

The student as worker is a metaphor that describes the role of the student as a creator in the classroom whose job it is to take on big ideas and "do important things." Hands-on, experiential teaching and learning approaches such as project-based learning and service learning that connect students to real-world experiences—curriculum that creates the conditions for exhibitions—are discussed in detail in Chapter Seven. These instructional approaches lend themselves to creating interdisciplinary learning opportunities that are academically rigorous, relevant, and personalized. The exhibition process provides teachers with the opportunity to co-create projects with students, tapping into students' knowledge, experience, interests, and passions and allowing students to drive their own learning with what they value. Student-generated projects allow students to integrate their life experience, questions, and interests, which become the content for the curriculum of a course or a unit of study.

The "Less is more, depth over coverage" principle states, "The school's goals should be simple: that each student master a limited number of essential skills and areas of knowledge. While these skills and areas will, to varying degrees, reflect the traditional academic disciplines, the program's design should be shaped by the intellectual and imaginative powers and competencies that the students [possess and] need, rather than by 'subjects' as conventionally defined." Moving beyond content that is a mile wide and an inch deep, CES schools prepare students to dive into areas of learning that surpass the conventional parameters, placing a high value on the notions of "less is more" and "depth over coverage." For example, through an in-depth exploration of a historic event such as the Vietnam War, students can learn essential concepts about war and peace, including propaganda as a mechanism for building social will and imperialism as the impetus for war. Through a thorough look into this event rather than a course that covers it briefly and minimally, students can learn to transpose their learning of essential concepts in the discipline of social science to other historical events. By deeply investigating a time or event in history through its people and places, students can experience multiple points of view on the ways that these events affected people like themselves.

Schools that use exhibitions employ teaching, learning, and assessment practices in classroom settings to rehearse, emphasize, and otherwise reinforce progress toward successful final exhibitions, thereby creating continuity between formative classroom assessments and high-stakes summative assessments. By emphasizing daily classroom work that connects formative assessments to final exhibitions, students and educators experience exhibitions as the culmination of an educational experience that is scaffolded from year to year, with multiple entry points for learning and a consistent quality of instruction across classrooms that is designed equitably to help all students to succeed. In these ways, exhibitions ensure continuity between classroom instruction, formative assessment methods, and high-stakes final assessments, providing a full and clear picture of the learner and her learning journey.

Providing Personalization, Support, and Structured Time for Performance-Based Assessment

In Essential schools, students are held to high standards and they are given the appropriate levels of support and resources to meet those standards. The ability and opportunity to engage in high-level intellectual explorations depend on teachers' creating the learning conditions necessary to build a knowledge and skill base so that students can meet expected standards. In order to hold students—many of whom are far behind academically when they enter our schools—to high expectations, we have to create academic safety nets, structures of support that will ensure that all students equitably receive what they need to meet the academic standards. The notion persists that project-based learning and performance-based assessment can only be implemented with students who have an advanced level of learning and that for those whose skills are not at grade level, remediation would be required before they could benefit from this kind of teaching and learning. Schools and school systems that adhere to these ideas continue to mirror the tracked systems that are prevalent in large traditional schools and perpetuate the inequities that persist in our public education system (Oakes, 1986; Oakes and Saunders, 2008).

Our experience has been that with the right kind of support, students can and do rise to the occasion of exhibitions. They revel in the experiential nature of project-based learning, and they gain the skills to become self-aware, lifelong learners and critical thinkers. One example of a student who truly rose to the occasion in presenting an exhibition of project-based learning is Jerry, a student at the High School for Recording Arts (HSRA), a CES Mentor school in St. Paul, Minnesota. The Twin Cities have a sizable Liberian population, and Jerry, a young Liberian man, came to HSRA shortly after arriving in Minnesota and after having a hard time engaging with his studies in a traditional school setting. Paula Anderson, education director at HSRA, tells the story of Jerry's first project:

> In Liberia, Jerry was one of those boys who, from the age of nine, roamed the city with other boys, armed with an AK-47 and eating out of garbage cans. He had engaged in so much violence and had become hardened by such profound trauma that coming to Minnesota and sitting in traditional classes seemed incredibly irrelevant and even silly to him. When he came to HSRA, he was a difficult student to reach, but his advisor eventually got him to work on a project about the situation in Liberia for the last decade. We were finally seeing Jerry working on something and not just roaming the halls and engaging in conflicts. Staff who were not working with him on the project were surprised to see the notable change. In fact, when Jerry took the stage,

many staff were a little anxious. We didn't know what to expect. This student had been a part of so much behavioral trouble in the school, we were all on edge when he began to speak. What followed was an unbelievably powerful, well-researched multimedia project that had us spellbound. The energy in the room was palpable, and the audience was transfixed. People's core values were in play, as Jerry's project was infused with profound questions about human nature, the politics of corruption, and the will to survive at all costs. It was no surprise that Jerry was passionate about his topic; it was his life until he immigrated to Minnesota. The content was powerfully relevant to the student; his essential questions were relevant to all. Our teachers are skilled at helping our students identify projects that are relevant to their lives and coaching them in crafting essential questions that will get them to look deeply at issues, and this often results in lasting change in the student, as well as fostering deeper thought in the school community at large.

Facilitating the kind of work that Jerry produced entails providing personalized and differentiated instruction and supports and employing explicit structures that are designed to ensure that students who need academic support do not slip through the cracks. In Jerry's case, project-based learning created the opportunity to get him hooked into his own intellectual interests. With the right topics and the right questions, students are motivated to learn what they need to know and do in order to complete the project and get to the bottom of the problem or issues at hand. Throughout the development of his project, Jerry was challenged by several academic obstacles that in a traditional classroom setting might have prevented him from moving forward, but at HSRA, a personalized learning environment, educators used the project to work on his skills. By providing learners with the tools, skills, and supports they need to succeed academically, CES schools create equitable learning circumstances so that students can achieve high academic outcomes regardless of where they have come from in their academic journey or the demographic they represent.

As they work with students, teachers uncover and understand—with the benefit and support of an equity-oriented professional learning community and in collaboration with students and their families—students' individual needs and strengths. They create personalized learning plans that prepare students to reach the academic expectations of the school and the world beyond school.

Amelia Pluto, a graduate of High Tech High, a CES Mentor School located in San Diego, tells us what this way of learning has done for her and what the role of the teacher has been in that process:

> I wouldn't have been able to grow as much as I have without the freedom to take projects as far as I can. And I think that's really great, but then, I guess, it can also be problematic. I know other students might just kind of take the easy way out or need more help to get there. So I guess that's where the teacher's job comes in, to kind of push people to do as much as they can and to help them when they don't think they can do more. This way of learning has given me the opportunity to develop my own interests, more than I would if I was sitting down just writing papers.

A culture of learning that values student assets uses those assets to create a relevant curriculum that reflects multiple perspectives and is inclusive of students' cultural and historic contributions. At El Colegio Charter School, a CES Mentor School in Minneapolis, Minnesota, teachers meet students where they are and help them to gain confidence through diverse project-based learning experiences. El Colegio co-founder and administrative director David Greenberg explains the school's process for engaging students in the exploration of new ideas:

> With many of our students, we can sit down and say, "Hey, what are you interested in? What do you like to do?" And out of that conversation, we develop learning experiences. With others, depending on their life experiences so far, they may not be ready with a list of passions and interests, so we need to help them find the sparks. Many of our students have not had the kind of living conditions that have helped them to deeply explore what excites them or what they are curious about in the world. One thing we've learned is we need to continually provide exciting, diverse, engaging learning experiences that might not immediately come from their interests, but might spark interest and then build from there.

Dedicated and structured time in the school day for students to work on building their projects is essential to maximizing the quality of the work they produce. If students are expected to demonstrate mastery through an exhibition process, there has to be time built into the schedule for the students to work on the projects and the exhibition process during the school day. This work cannot be tacked on at the end of the day. While the scheduling choices that schools make to facilitate project-based learning and demonstrations of mastery may vary from school to school, they are consistently planned to support sustained personalized learning, with time for individual coaching from teachers, mentors, and experts; time for peer feedback and revision; and time for fieldwork and research.

The quality of the work that goes into a portfolio, an exhibition, or the creation of presentations of learning will depend on the structures that are built into the school day in order for students to work with each other and get coaching and support from their teachers. CES schools use structures such as advisories to get students prepared for exhibitions. Advisors are trained to provide all students with the coaching they need to prepare, revise, present, and reflect on each exhibition in all content areas. In this way, advisories are the clearinghouses for the school's exhibition process. "Even though the expectation is to provide numerous and varied opportunities for students to engage in and practice authentic assessments, advisory—with its emphasis on personalization—became the primary place for instruction, coaching, and support towards the skills needed for our authentic assessments at Leadership High School" explains Greg Peters, former principal of Leadership High School in San Francisco. At the Met in Providence, support for exhibitions also comes from the advisor. The advisor guides students through the planning and execution of exhibitions. Advisors provide the scaffolding and structure that students need to successfully complete exhibitions three times a year, encompassing the work they have done in their internship, their academic achievements, their community service, and their personal growth.

Many schools use block scheduling to provide students with chunks of uninterrupted time in which to deeply research project topics, work collaboratively on group projects, receive intense coaching from teachers, and create multimedia presentations. The best results for exhibitions come from schools such as Empowerment College Preparatory High School that build in time for students to practice and rehearse presentations in front of community meetings, town halls, and advisory groups. For high-stakes exhibitions—exhibitions on which graduation depends—schools often offer senior institutes or senior seminar courses designed exclusively to support seniors in preparing the graduation portfolio that they will present in their final exhibition. Empowerment also offers courses that support academically driven service-learning projects that lead to exhibitions. Empowerment's former principal and co-founder Misha Lesley explains why the school designed a course—Teen Leadership—specifically to support students' work on their social action projects: "The teachers trained the students in the components and the skills they needed to create a successful project for exhibition. They worked on research skills and presentation skills. The process of developing quality projects that can be shared publicly as a way to demonstrate learning was very new to our students, so we felt it was important enough to build an actual course into our schedule that facilitated the exhibition process."

Aligning Authentic Teaching, Learning, and Assessment

Exhibitions and other performance-based assessments can transform a school by functioning as catalysts for improvement, restructuring, and school design or redesign that can result in higher intellectual quality throughout a school's program. Exhibitions can be seen as both an inquiry into students' learning and an examination of how the school has equipped each student to reach and demonstrate mastery. After nearly a decade of study of the effects of exhibitions in their early stages in CES schools, CES produced research on the power of exhibitions to illuminate a school's strengths and weaknesses that stated, in part, "By the light of its students' performances on exhibitions, the school seeks to glimpse the power and the shortcomings of its whole instructional program, and so gain the information it needs to make the right adjustments in that program or, indeed, to radically revise it" (McDonald and others, 1993, p. 3). The feedback that students receive also provides schools with the insight and opportunity to shift the instruction or instructional program to address the specific needs identified for that student.

When a school decides to create an authentic assessment process that culminates in students' demonstrating what they know and can do through portfolios and exhibitions, its educators are engaged in the work of aligning their entire educational program with a mission and a clear set of standards. The process will entail planning backward from the desired outcomes and standards and designing a focused, purposeful professional development plan that will help teachers accomplish powerful changes in teaching and learning. If an educational program is already in place, authentic assessments can help schools revisit and rethink their program.

Darling-Hammond, Ancess, and Falk (1995) note, "A new kind of assessment system requires a new kind of system to support student achievement" (p. 62). In order to address the challenges of exhibitions, both restructuring schools and new schools must plan backward from exhibitions to ensure that school culture, professional development, standards, schedules, and other structures and practices required to support them are fundamental elements of the school's design. Exhibitions and other public demonstrations of mastery connect to every intentional action in a school community, requiring educators first to develop shared expectations of acceptable and exemplary levels of accomplishment and then to refine the systems of teaching and learning geared to get each student to those levels. Performance-based assessment also allows students to demonstrate what they know and can do at any point along the continuum that runs between formative and summative assessment. At the end points of the continuum, performance-based assessments can be strictly formative, designed to provide feedback about learning and instruction. Performance-based assessments also can be summative demonstrations of student mastery at the end of a course, unit, grade, or phase of schooling as the final step in an ongoing system of performance-based formative assessment. Along the continuum, projects, in-class work, and assignments in which students are engaged form the basis for high-stakes exhibitions. Work of this sort is focused on results rather than rewards and is designed so that with proper support and scaffolding, all students can succeed (Davidson and Feldman, 2009).

In most cases, we have found that CES teachers rely on Grant Wiggins and Jay McTighe's backward planning process from the book *Understanding by Design* (Wiggins and McTighe, 2005). They use *Understanding by Design*'s guidelines and strategies to develop projects that can be used for exhibition requirements. By focusing on the end products—the projects and work that students will ultimately share in order to demonstrate mastery—educators can put in place an educational journey that will get students there. Once the educators collaboratively decide on the learning standards and graduation requirements of the school, that content knowledge, those experiences, and those skills need to be woven throughout the coursework and learning experiences that students participate in, such as internships, service-learning projects, independent projects, or group work. The teachers construct ways to spiral and scaffold knowledge and skills in every learning moment and connect those back to the academic and social objectives laid out by the school. The process often brings clarity, coherence, and structure to the educational journey crafted by the school, with built-in flexibility for personalization. Parker Charter Essential School principal Teri Schrader recollects how the school planned its gateway and exhibition processes:

> When we first started, we had to design Division 3 [eleventh and twelfth grades] up front, and the gateways that led to it, because we had twenty-four kids who had to gateway into it. The result of planning backwards is that what's relevant for the senior-year project is embedded in the seventh-grade gateway. In a thoughtful way, those expectations get positioned in seventh grade and are tended to deliberately, so when students do the seventh-grade exhibitions, you see the beginnings of what they potentially will be able to know and do in the twelfth grade, even though you'd never expect a twelve-year-old to do what an eighteen-year-old can do.

At Leadership High School, planning backward has led to the development of the following schoolwide outcomes (SWOs):

Communication: To understand and clearly and confidently express ideas, opinions, information, attitudes and feelings to and from diverse audiences, through a variety of media.

Critical Thinking: To draw conclusions, solve problems or create through analysis, reflection, interpretation, reasoning and evaluation.

Personal Responsibility: To be self-aware; to identify, access and utilize skills, knowledge and resources towards development as a life-long learner, and to be accountable to one's self.

Social Responsibility: To effectively work and lead in groups, families and communities by actively demonstrating respect and accountability to others and their differences.

At Leadership High School, as in other CES small schools, the backward planning process binds the entire staff to a set of common goals, holding them accountable for creating sturdy, consistent, equitable learning experiences for all students that fulfill these common goals across academic disciplines. In schools that have made the commitment to engage in this process, curriculum development is guided by agreed-upon graduation outcomes such as Leadership's SWOs. The process ultimately creates excellence across the board instead of the pockets of good teaching that are typical in a school at which teachers have not worked collaboratively to organize the learning process or link it back to standards.

Planning backward, CES small schools carefully develop appropriate evaluation tools that explicitly lay out the content and skill standards that a school values and expects students to master. These multifaceted measurement tools are called *rubrics.* They provide a framework for what the school sees as excellent work and present a clear path for getting there. Many CES schools have developed "habits of mind," which frame the intellectual and social expectations of the school. Science teacher Lisa Karlich explains how School of the Future uses a rubric to provide students with the fundamental structure of the exhibition process and guide them toward their best work: "Our rubric explicitly organizes the criteria by which students' exhibitions will be judged according to the Habits of Mind. This rubric is used throughout the process of the exhibition to help students check their own thinking on their project. The Habits of Mind are represented by a list of aspects of critical thinking that we focus on throughout all the courses at School of the Future." The aspects of critical thinking listed in School of the Future's Habits of Mind are using evidence, making connections, examining alternatives, seeing a problem from different points of view, understanding the significance of an issue, and communication. (Figure 8.1 shows how the School of the Future's rubric for evaluating exhibition presentations in historical research in the humanities aligns with these aspects of critical thinking. For an example of a mathematics rubric from Quest High School, see Figure 8.2. Additional rubrics, including a rubric for evaluating written humanities work that accompanies Figure 8.2, are available at the *Small Schools, Big Ideas* Web site at http://www.ceschangelab.org/.)

By naming what they ultimately want students to know and do when they graduate, educators can plan backward, working closely to design and plan curricula in all disciplines that connect back to the school's standards. This plan provides a way for educators to address the skills, knowledge, and learning experiences the school community has agreed all students should receive across all academic disciplines and levels. In this climate, performance-based assessments derive from and link back to what is actually being taught and what is being learned and practiced by the students. Whether these are formative assessments designed to enhance learning and improve instruction or summative assessments designed to measure whether a student has demonstrated mastery and is ready to move on to the next level, they attach to the learning threads that come together to create the fabric of the educational program.

Figure 8.1
Performance Exhibition Rubric for Historical Research in the Humanities, School of the Future

Rubric	POV	Evidence	Connections	Opposing Viewpoints	Significance	Communication
Mastery with Distinction (4 points)	Thesis is clear, sharp, and contentious, creatively displayed throughout the presentation, and is the overwhelming focus of the presentation.	Major arguments that strongly support the thesis are clearly displayed in outline form during the presentation, with clear citation of at least 3 supporting pieces of evidence. These arguments are creatively and compellingly presented.	Visually represents, sharply and creatively, how the topic was affected by previous events and how it has affected (and will affect) subsequent events. Demonstrates thorough and impressive understanding of the context of the topic.	Sharply and creatively responds to significant and likely challenges to thesis, major arguments, and sources during the committee questioning period, demonstrating powerful preparation.	Thoroughly demonstrates the social or global significance of the topic, through an explicit and persuasive argument supported by strong evidence. Engagingly articulates the special significance of the topic to self.	Presentation is innovative and creates an emotional impact for the committee. The presentation demonstrates serious continued thought on the topic, sustained and powerful preparation, and is worth taping and watching a second time.
Mastery (3 points)	Thesis is clear and contentious, displayed throughout the presentation, and is the primary focus of the presentation.	Major arguments that support the thesis are displayed in outline form during the presentation, with clear citation of at least 3 supporting pieces of evidence. These arguments are persuasively presented.	Visually represents, persuasively, how the topic was affected by previous events and how it has affected (and will affect) subsequent events. Demonstrates powerful understanding of the context of the topic.	Intelligently responds to significant and likely challenges to thesis, major arguments, and sources during the committee questioning period, demonstrating thoughtful preparation.	Demonstrates the social or global significance of the topic, through an explicit and clear argument supported by relevant evidence. Articulates the special significance of the topic to self.	Presentation is creative and engaging, demonstrates continued thought on the topic and thoughtful preparation.
Satisfactory (2 points)	Thesis is clear and is emphasized in the presentation.	Major arguments that support the thesis are clearly presented with citation of at least 2 supporting pieces of evidence.	Articulates how the topic was affected by previous events and how it has affected (and will affect) subsequent events. Demonstrates useful understanding of the context of the topic.	Usually responds effectively to likely challenges to thesis, major arguments, and sources during the committee questioning period, demonstrating some preparation.	Indicates the social or global significance of the topic, using some argument and evidence.	Presentation is competent and demonstrates some preparation.
Needs Revision (1 point)	The thesis is difficult to figure out.	Thesis doesn't receive much support from evidence.	The reader is left wondering why the situation ever developed, and whether it would ever affect future events.	Often unable to respond effectively to likely challenges to thesis, major arguments, and sources during the questioning period, indicating inadequate preparation.	Either fails to make an argument about why the topic is significant, or makes a poor argument unsupported by evidence.	Presentation reveals inadequate thought or preparation.

Source: School of the Future, 2005.

Figure 8.2
Standards and Scoring for Student Work in Mathematics, Quest High School

Teachers, community members, and others use this rubric to evaluate students' mathematics proficiency during exhibitions.

<u>General Rules</u>

The task is to estimate the extent to which the student's performance illustrates the kind of cognitive work indicated by each of the three standards: Mathematical Analysis, Disciplinary Concepts, and Elaborated Written Mathematical Communication. Each standard will be scored according to different rules, but the following apply to all three standards:

- ➤ Scores should be based only on evidence in the student's performance relevant to the criteria. Do not consider things such as following directions, correct spelling, neatness, etc., unless they are relevant to the criteria.
- ➤ Scores may be limited by tasks which fail to call for mathematical analysis, disciplinary conceptual understanding, or elaborated mathematical written communication, but the scores must be based only upon the work shown.
- ➤ Take into account what students can reasonably be expected to do at the grade level. However, scores should still be assigned according to criteria in the standards, not relative to other papers that have been scored.
- ➤ When it is difficult to decide between two scores, give the higher score only when a persuasive case can be made that the paper meets minimal criteria for the higher score.
- ➤ If the specific wording of the criteria is not helpful in making judgments, base the score on the general intent or spirit of the standard described in the introductory paragraphs of the standard.
- ➤ Completion of the task is not necessary to score high.

Rubric	Mathematical Analysis	Disciplinary Concepts	Elaborated Written Communication
Honors Work	Mathematical analysis was involved throughout the student's work.	The student demonstrates exemplary understanding of the mathematical concepts that are central to the task. Their application is appropriate, flawless, and elegant.	Mathematical explanations or arguments are clear, convincing, and accurate, with no significant mathematical errors.
Meets Expectations	Mathematical analysis was involved in a significant proportion of the student's work.	There is substantial evidence the student understands the mathematical concepts that are central to the task and applies these concepts to the task appropriately; however, there may be some minor flaws in their application, or details may be missing.	Mathematical explanations or arguments are present. They are reasonably clear and accurate, but less convincing.
Approaching	Mathematical analysis was involved in some portion of the student's work.	The student demonstrates some understanding of the mathematical concepts that are central to the task. Where the student uses appropriate mathematical concepts, the application is flawed or incomplete.	Mathematical explanations, arguments, or representations are present. However, they may not be finished, may omit a significant part of an argument/ explanation, or may contain significant mathematical errors. Generally complete, appropriate, and correct work or representations (e.g., a graph, equation, number sentence) should be scored a 2 if no other part of the student's work on the task warrants a higher score.
Unacceptable	Mathematical analysis constituted no part of the student's work.	The student demonstrates no or very little understanding of the mathematical concepts that are central to the task, i.e., does not go beyond mechanical application of an algorithm.	Mathematical explanations, arguments, or representations are absent or, if present, are seriously incomplete, inappropriate, or incorrect. (This may be because the task did not ask for argument or explanation, e.g., fill-in-the-blank or multiple-choice questions, or reproducing a simple definition in words or pictures.)

Source: Quest High School, 2004.

Professional Development That Supports Performance-Based Assessment

When the demonstration of mastery through performance-based assessment drives a school's design and instructional program, the school will need to develop a culture of learning among adults that mirrors the high expectations and rigorous practices that are required of students. The adults as learners are modeling the standards of high-level thinking and investigative skills that are required of students throughout their coursework and projects. Creating and sustaining a sophisticated authentic assessment system requires a well-trained and dedicated set of educators who can

- Buy into a system of teaching and learning that values inquiry and critical thinking
- Understand how to plan backward and align curriculum with standards
- Scaffold project-based learning and differentiate instruction
- Support students through a portfolio and exhibition process

The habits of learning to which the school holds students will also have to be upheld by the adults within a facilitated and safe learning experience that allows them to shift their role from traditional teacher to learning coach, as the CES Common Principle "Student-as-worker, teacher-as-coach" describes. The school will have to invest time and resources in order to implement a multifaceted professional development plan that supports the ongoing learning of all the adults in the school community.

CES small schools develop professional learning communities across schools and school districts in order to motivate and structure ongoing collaborative processes designed to refine the structures and practices that sustain a system of performance-based assessment. Because the curriculum and instructional practices undergird the learning experience for all students, it is essential that teachers work together to create a coherent educational program that moves beyond the pockets of excellent or model classrooms that exist in most traditional schools to a uniformly high quality of instruction. According to Parker principal Teri Schrader, an assessment system that culminates with the demonstration of mastery cannot exist "without a really strong professional learning community in place. Faculty in a strong professional learning community have time to talk thoughtfully and plan deliberately about program, and they can engage in a real values conversation about what good work looks like." Parker teachers have worked long and hard to arrive at criteria for excellence in order to make their agreements about what good work looks like the public standard for all students (see sidebar "Criteria for Excellence in Research at Parker Charter Essential School").

Criteria for Excellence in Research at Parker Charter Essential School

Preparation

- You brainstorm ideas and organize them visually (in lists, outlines, webs, concept maps).
- You narrow and focus your research question(s) to a manageable size.
- You identify what you already know.
- You decide what you still need to know.
- You list key words and concepts.

Search

- You identify potential search engines (library card catalog and databases; Web browsers; experts; community agencies).
- You use search engines and key words to locate a variety of sources.
- You decide which sources are relevant to your question(s).

Information Gathering

- You skim and scan to identify relevant information.
- You take accurate and sufficient notes, paraphrasing or quoting important facts and details.
- You classify, group, and label the information in your notes.
- You assess the nature and reliability of your sources (primary or secondary; fact or opinion; point of view; timeliness).
- You document your sources and compile a bibliography.

Interpretation

- You connect new information with what you know already.
- You recognize logical errors and omissions, cause and effect, and points of agreement and disagreement.
- You use the information you gathered to answer your research question(s).

Process

- You plan and manage your time effectively.
- You ask for help at appropriate points.
- You revise your question(s) as your research progresses.
- You reflect on your process and your work.

For Criteria for Excellence in other areas of academic endeavor at Parker, visit the *Small Schools, Big Ideas* Web site at http://www.ceschangelab.org/.

Source: Parker Charter Essential School, 2008a.

In CES schools, teachers routinely take opportunities at staff meetings, during team teaching, at department meetings, and in curriculum committees to review student work and calibrate their collective understanding of which examples of work reflect certain levels of achievement—for example, what meets, approaches, or exceeds the established standards for a research paper or an oral presentation. Humanities teacher Adelric McCain of Young Women's Leadership Charter School, a CES Mentor School in Chicago, recounts his experience with colleagues as they moved toward implementing a senior project:

> The humanities department was trying to make the senior project a schoolwide requirement, trying to get school staff and parents to buy in. We sat down with senior academy staff and discussed the challenges, and we told them about the mistakes we had made in the process. We put ourselves out there as a learning opportunity for the rest of the school. We had a staff meeting where we showed some of our first tapes of the graduates' presentations. We went over the assignments and the process it took to complete their projects. It was an opportunity to look at important questions about the student

performance—for example, why they freaked out at the presentations and how to support them. We peeled back all of the layers and broke down the steps and then reorganized the process to make it more suitable for student success.

The trajectory and success of students in a performance-based assessment system are directly linked to the capacity of the faculty to implement well all components of the system. To sustain the commitment to continuous improvement, the professional learning community engages in cycles of inquiry that shape and inform the educational program and the instructional approaches of the school. The bottom line is that the adults need to be able to ask hard questions and hold each other accountable for learning in ways that may be uncomfortable and demanding. Otherwise, the school risks creating an uneven and inequitable learning experience for students who are depending on well-trained, well-informed, caring adults across the board to guide them through a sophisticated journey of learning. In a system of performance-based assessment, everyone is required to demonstrate their mastery.

Community-wide Accountability for Equitable Student Outcomes

Exhibitions and other public demonstrations of learning create windows into students' learning and the educational program's ability to equitably prepare all students for graduation and subsequent success. Empowerment College Preparatory High School's founding principal, Misha Lesley, believes that schools can use the exhibition process to evaluate how effectively they are achieving their mission:

> Demonstration of mastery is an important component of our school, as it helps to actualize and measure the effectiveness of our school's mission. When we developed the mission, we looked at the needs of our community. Right now, like many other urban centers, our community is struggling with a myriad of things. We need people who are working on resolving those issues, and so our mission is to teach our students how to make a positive impact on their community. We empower our students to contribute through what we call *social action projects.* At Empowerment, the students' main exhibition of learning is focused on researching community issues and taking social actions to address those problems.

Schools use the exhibition process to provide support to the community and build relationships that can contribute to the growth of their students and the school. Public exhibitions of learning can foster community partnerships and build the community's sense of ownership and accountability. Because these forms of assessment hold students accountable to more than just their teachers, they are a powerful way to provide students with a support network that can challenge them to meet and exceed the learning standards of the school community. While the audience may differ, depending on the level of exhibition and types of performance-based assessments used, the role that community stakeholders play in this partnership of learning is potentially invaluable to the learning process of each student and the overall integrity of the school.

David Greenberg speaks about how a cultural event can serve as an opportunity for students to exhibit their work to their community and raise awareness of what students know and do. El Colegio holds a Day of the Dead evening event, which hundreds of people from the community attend. It has turned into an exhibition night at which students present their projects. Greenberg says, "We've got this built-in audience, and it is a chance for kids to show what they're doing and to share with the community what they're learning." Showcasing the students' best work during an exhibition helps the community better understand the school's learning standards. The whole process provides a forum for the community to hold the school accountable for student achievement. Used well, the community's expertise can help to lift the quality of students' work, instilling in students a sense of interdependence and support from their community.

The more we open our doors to the community, to public officials, to the business community, and to others, the more we demystify the learning and assessment process and raise awareness about performance-based assessments versus less integrated forms of assessments that do not provide a full picture of students. Linda Darling-Hammond, Charles Ducommon Professor of Education at Stanford University's School of Education, co-director of the School Redesign Network, and currently one of President Barack Obama's top education advisors, encourages educators to open their doors so that they can help open the eyes of policymakers. Darling-Hammond explains: "First of all, you're educating your local political representatives about what good education looks like, what types of assessments are supportive of good education, and what the effects are of more thoughtful assessment. That's really important because when the policy makers make these policies, they don't know what's inside the black box of testing. They really need images of what's possible and what's desirable" (Hirsch, 2007).

To support the idea of making the exhibition process more transparent for community members and policymakers, CES designated May as National Exhibition Month, and more than one hundred schools in twenty-five states participate. Schools such as Quest High School, a CES Mentor School in Humble, Texas, are opening their doors in order to reach beyond the usual school community to the press, members of the wider community, and public officials, inviting them to witness firsthand the powerful ways that students from CES schools across the country demonstrate their learning.

At Quest High School, students work closely with mentors from community-based organizations to prepare for their group senior projects. At their celebratory senior exhibitions, the mentors are present and beaming with pride as their mentees share their findings with a broad audience of community members. The community is taking responsibility for students' learning. Our schools help students make connections with experts and other caring adults who can support their learning. These methods of assessment open up real opportunities for our students to work directly with experts in the professional fields that they want to learn more about or that they have a passion for.

At the Peace Street campus of the Met, the whole educational program centers on tapping into the passions and interests of students. Kim Barsamian, a Met advisor (at the Met, advisors serve as students' academic teacher and guide as well as the center of their support network), explains: "At Peace Street, every student is involved in a long-term internship in a wide range of careers, where they work closely with experts in those areas that guide and greatly contribute to the instruction and academic support a student is receiving at the school. The mentors' involvement as an expert in the field of interest of the student is essential to their academic and social growth as learners." The opportunity for students to be immersed all day, twice weekly, in an ongoing learning experience of their choice is what drives their learning. Tapping into that well of curiosity makes it possible for students to identify real problems and learn the skills to become critical thinkers and problem solvers. Through this process, the mentors become intimately involved in the education of their mentees, taking them under their wing and becoming one more caring adult who is looking out for them and guiding them toward graduation.

Meeting and Influencing State Accountability Requirements

The prevailing national policy climate, which frequently leads schools to focus on preparing students for large-scale, externally imposed, high-stakes standardized tests that provide little or no opportunity for authentic, performance-based assessment (Nichols and Berliner, 2007), has been an impediment to the widespread use of exhibitions as classroom assessments and high-stakes culminating demonstrations of mastery. The Bush administration's central education policy, No Child Left Behind (NCLB), was touted as a silver bullet for reforming our public schools. Instead, its emphasis on results has pushed states, districts, and often schools themselves to disregard the work of creating conditions that provide a fertile environment for learning. Because "effective assessments enhance rather than interrupt student learning" (Davidson and Feldman, 2009), exhibitions and other forms of authentic assessment have the potential to improve results on state standardized tests (Wiggins, 2006). Schools that have designed their curriculum, pedagogy, schedules, professional development, and other structures and practices to support exhibitions both as daily assessment tools in classrooms and as culminating assessments are generally characterized by student-guided inquiry, sustained and deep "less is more" learning, and personalized instruction. How do such schools manage to also prepare students for the high-stakes standardized tests that many states require and that, in many cases, do not serve as authentic assessments of such pedagogy and curriculum?

The conflict is complex. Teri Schrader, Parker's principal, believes that students' preparation for Parker's school-based assessments actually prepares them well, given the knowledge and skills that the Massachusetts Comprehensive Assessment System (MCAS) demands. "I think we're fortunate," she says.

> Our MCAS scores are high, not because our students are different than those in the schools around us but because the structure of our school reflects the ways that kids learn best. Right now, we feel at peace with the tests; we can glean useful data from MCAS English language arts and math tests. But the state is phasing in MCAS science and history tests, and the data that will be gleaned will force competition between two competing philosophies. The MCAS history test assumes a chronological progression; it's not theme-based or question-driven,

and it makes interdisciplinary studies difficult. The choice is between a philosophy that educates kids deeply and helps them be scholars or a system that will help them sail through a particular test on which their diploma is based.

In Houston, Empowerment College Preparatory High School teacher April Rasmus describes the ways that Empowerment has developed to work around and with the state and district's accountability systems:

> Our exhibitions are designed to meet our habits of heart and habits of mind: communication, compassion, perspective, persistence, and coherency. Although it is a challenge to focus our teaching using performance-based assessments while the state imposes TEKS [Texas Essential Knowledge and Skills], which we have to administer, we have found thoughtful ways not to succumb to teaching to the test. We are preparing our students for college, not to pass a standardized test. We may not do well in the local benchmark exams because our scope and sequence doesn't align with the district, but in the end, when the students take the standardized test, we always meet the mark. And our scores are usually higher than our regional district and, in some cases, higher than the state average.

Performance-based assessments can be aligned to meet and exceed state learning standards, and in some places, they can take the place of high-stakes standardized exams. Several states, including Nebraska, North Carolina, and Rhode Island, include some kind of performance assessment as an integral part of their state accountability system. For example, in Rhode Island, in addition to achieving passing class grades and scores on the New England Common Assessment Program, graduating seniors must choose and pass two of three performance-based assessments: a portfolio of work selected from their four years of high school, a senior project, and a collection of end-of-course assessments that comprehensively test students' knowledge in the subjects that they have studied. Students who choose to assemble a portfolio must defend their body of work, which must include a research project that spans all four years, in front of a panel of judges. "Senior projects have included designing and implementing a poetry-writing course for adults, and building a snow machine and then using it to open a backyard sledding hill. At least half of each end-of-course comprehensive course assessment must incorporate applied-learning and performance elements, such as presenting the results of original research" (Cech, 2008).

In places where the state has been unwilling to lead or has felt pressure to conform to the status quo, the effort to move toward a more authentic accountability system has been launched by practitioners and families. The New York Performance Standards Consortium (NYPSC), a CES affiliate center, through a concerted effort by concerned parents, teachers, and students, successfully advocated for legislation that exempts its twenty-eight member schools from most of New York's state-mandated high-stakes standardized Regents tests, thus creating the conditions in the schools for a strong focus on the demonstration of mastery through portfolios and exhibitions. The NYPSC has created a system for performance assessment through exhibitions, assembling a performance review board of educators, academics, and other authorities to review student work and the processes by which it is evaluated. The NYPSC's work serves to link classroom assessment to exhibitions by creating the conditions for sustained daily focus on the knowledge and skills to be evaluated by exhibitions and by establishing the standards by which student work is evaluated, not only within a school but also among a group of schools (Davidson, 2009b).

Statewide school reform and restructuring initiatives that incorporate performance-oriented curriculum and assessment have emphasized the use of standards. These early reforms demonstrated that it is possible to create thoughtful standards and aligned, educationally productive assessments. Connecticut, Kentucky, Vermont, and Washington are examples of states that developed performance-based assessment systems based on academically rigorous standards (Darling-Hammond, 2003). Unfortunately, the federal policy climate under NCLB has not allowed for many of these states to continue to build more authentic accountability systems that stimulate creativity and intellectual growth, because they are not aligned with federal mandates. In recent years, we have seen state education commissioners abandon their posts or reduce their efforts to grant more local control over assessments to schools and districts because of the pressure to centralize control and audit performance under NCLB. Nebraska's education commissioner Doug Christensen cited these external pressures when he resigned. "For some reason, we seem to think that the only way we can get education done is by doing it outside the profession," he said, "and the assessment issue is related to that" (Abourezk, 2008).

While some states have developed thoughtful performance-based assessments that challenge students to demonstrate their thinking and learning in open-ended, extended tasks and responses, including some that are embedded in the school curriculum, they do not yet form a critical mass. "It would be useful for state consortia that had once begun to form to create more thoughtful assessments, such as one launched by the Council for Chief State School Officers, to renew their efforts to allow states to collaborate in the development of standards-based criterion-referenced assessment systems that can assess the range of abilities suggested by the standards," writes Darling-Hammond (2003).

With the support of the Ford Foundation, CES launched a national effort to focus on states' successful school-based assessment practices as a foundation for statewide systems. CES executive director Lewis Cohen says it is important for this work to develop from the ground up: "Too many times, state policies look good on paper. They are dreamed up far away from the day-to-day experience in schools. We have schools that do powerful assessments of twenty-first-century skills. The trick is to scale up state systems from what has already been proven effective in schools."

Conclusion

In schools that effectively use performance-based assessments, everyone in the school is invested in creating a cohesive educational plan with the supports and guidance in place that will allow all students to learn to use their mind well. Implementing performance-based assessment is an opportunity for a school to be clear about its own values and standards and to plan ways to reach those goals collaboratively. Everyone—educators, family members, students, and staff members—participates in ongoing conversations about what they want students to know and do when they graduate. From those agreements, the school creates tools for explicitly sharing and measuring those expectations. Public exhibitions display for examination the students' achievement, thereby holding up a mirror and reflecting back to the school its successes and failures. Through scrutiny of students' work, the school has a chance to determine where it needs to fine-tune and recalibrate its educational program and the tools it uses to set standards and measure academic growth.

The evidence of learning, growth, and mastery that students share with the community is created in partnership with their mentors through service-learning projects or internships, intentionally building a sense of mutual accountability between the school and its larger community. At the same time, such partnerships raise the community's awareness of the ways that the school is engaging young people in their learning. By being explicit about expectations, building the supports that students need to be successful, and publicly affirming and celebrating students' intellectual growth, these schools raise the bar for learning and draw on the community's will and skill in service of students.

The ways that schools engage in performance-based assessment may differ, yet the commitment from all of those schools is both huge and well worth the sometimes drastic reordering of priorities. The payoff is in the fuller picture of learners that educators obtain. While an exhibition may focus on a particular project or set of skills, it often captures a bigger picture of a student's progress in many areas of academic and personal development. Exhibitions and other forms of performance-based assessment serve as opportunities for students to integrate various aspects of their learning, helping them to make connections between academic work, real-world experiences, and personal growth. Demonstrations of mastery can be used as a yardstick to measure the growth of students over time and the value added by the educational program offered. The time and energy that schools put into public displays of mastery are validated every time a student demonstrates how well prepared she is for life after graduation and the demands of college, career, and citizenship.

Access, Opportunity, and Preparation for Postsecondary Success

> We envision students who have been historically
> disenfranchised and/or disengaged from traditional
> schools engaged in personalized, rigorous,
> meaningful learning in our schools.
>
> —Vision statement, Empowerment College Preparatory
> High School, Houston, Texas

The preceding chapters have presented the principles and practices that are essential for creating student engagement and achievement. We have looked at evidence and stories from schools designed to provide all students with the support they need to achieve at high levels and graduate ready for what comes next. This chapter looks beyond high school graduation, examining the values, habits, and practices that high schools must have in place in order to prepare students to be productive twenty-first-century citizens as well as the ways in which carefully planned preparation for postsecondary success is a vital goal of education.

According to the Bill & Melinda Gates Foundation (2008), "Today only 71 percent of American students graduate high school on time, a figure that drops to 55 percent for African-American students and 58 percent for Hispanic students. College-readiness rates are even lower. Researchers estimate that less than 25 percent of minority young people are prepared for college, at tremendous cost to themselves and to society." (See Chapter Two for additional data and analysis of the closed doors and difficult circumstances faced by many students of color and students in poverty as a result of our educational system.) Schools need to diminish the historically predictive power of demographic data by dramatically accelerating the achievement of students who, both historically and in recent times, have been inadequately served by schools. Schools and school systems need to do more than move students through their hallways and out their doors, diplomas in hand. Because higher education achievement is the best way to interrupt economic and social inequities, schools need to prepare students to attend and graduate from four-year colleges and for other options that will enrich their lives.

In the twenty-first century, a college education has become what a high school diploma was in post-Sputnik twentieth-century society: an essential key to employment and financial stability. The working lives of today's K–12 students will transpire through most of the twenty-first century. For all of them, graduating from high school is both absolutely necessary and not enough. For today's young people, a college diploma is a prerequisite for economic survival. High schools that can prepare their students not only to gain admittance to a four-year college but also to graduate from one interrupt patterns of inequity that might otherwise follow young people from their school career to and through adulthood. These patterns of inequity result in reduced lifetime earnings, decreased career choice and flexibility (Mathews, 2007), and less influence over their own children's ability to graduate from high school and college (Attewell, Lavin, Domina, and Levey, 2007).

While the decision to go on to college is a decision that belongs, ultimately, to individual young people and their families, the responsibility of preparing those young people for enrollment in four-year colleges and universities—free from the need for remediation and ready for the challenges that await—belongs to schools and the systems designed to support young people in their journeys toward adulthood. Rick Lear, director of CES affiliate center CES Northwest explains, "We use 'college ready' to suggest that the range of choices students have when they graduate from high school is critical to their futures. And the proper responsibility of schools and districts is to ensure those choices for the students they serve." Schools that have established definitions of postsecondary success and that have designed or restructured themselves accordingly expand the options of young people through

- Reworking and raising the quality of their curricula to align with higher education expectations
- Providing access to dual-enrollment, early college, or middle college experiences (hybrid secondary school–college programs that allow students to graduate with both a high school diploma and substantial college credit or an associate degree)
- Creating personalization through advisories and other structures to support higher education and career success
- Engaging families as partners
- Introducing students to the world of work and active citizenship through internships and other real-world educational opportunities
- Providing proactive support, training, and counseling to prepare students for the inevitable challenges of the postsecondary world

These practices characterize schools that have created college-going cultures and have demonstrated track records of success not only in higher education enrollment but also in higher education persistence and graduation. A college-going culture supplies the information, encouragement, examples, and support needed by students who may be the first in their family and among their friends to prepare to pursue higher education. (The "First in the Family" sidebar focuses on a set of resources designed to assist such students.) These schools have evidence—anecdotal and otherwise—of the success of their graduates as demonstrated by longitudinal (and less easily quantified) measures such as achievement in career, family and community life, and civic engagement (Davidson, 2006).

CES schools expect that every child will graduate with multiple options, including those leading to careers and postsecondary education. David T. Conley (2007) defines the qualities of a "college ready student" as "able to understand what is expected in a college course, can cope with the content knowledge that is presented, and can take away from the course the key intellectual lessons and dispositions the course was designed to convey and develop. In addition, the student is prepared to get the most out of the college experience by understanding the culture and structure of postsecondary education and the ways of knowing and intellectual norms of this academic and social environment. The student has both the mindset and disposition necessary to enable this to happen" (pp. 5–6). This means that postsecondary preparation involves more than just supporting students' intellectual growth. It includes the development of students' social capital—the ability to create, nurture, and build on social relationships and to understand the demands relevant to a variety of social situations and institutional settings.

First in the Family

First in the Family, a program produced by What Kids Can Do, offers a powerful set of resources aimed at equipping students who are the first in their family to plan to attend college with facts, support, guidance, and encouragement from their peers. First in the Family offers books and a multimedia Web site with video, tips, resources, and inspiration. The material is divided into two sections: one aimed at high school students and the other at college students. This division emphasizes the reality that getting into college, while significant, is not the same as staying in college, particularly among the students of color and students with less income who make up most of the first-generation college population. First in the Family resources are available at http://www.firstinthefamily.org/index.html.

College Preparatory Curriculum

When schools commit to supporting students through curricula that hold them all to high standards, they are putting the CES Common Principle "Goals apply to all students" in place. In full, the principle reads, "The school's goals should apply to all students, while the means to these goals will vary as those students themselves vary. School practice should be tailor-made to meet the needs of every group or class of students." The links between a challenging high school curriculum and success in institutions of higher education are well documented; research makes it clear that the strongest predictor of bachelor's degree completion is the quality of a student's high school curriculum (Bailey, Hughes, and Karp, 2002). The effect of a challenging high school curriculum on higher education persistence and graduation is particularly meaningful for students who are first in their family to attend college (Camara, 2003); first-generation college students often come from economically disadvantaged families and communities, are often students of color, and are otherwise considered to be among the groups that have been poorly served by many conventional schools and school systems.

By offering a challenging high school curriculum with appropriate support to its students, Empowerment College Preparatory High School is transforming the lives of students who historically have not been served well by schools. Empowerment opened as a new small school within the Houston Independent School District (HISD) in 2005 to serve students from anywhere in the HISD attendance zone. Part of the CES Small Schools Network as a new small school (paired in its design phase in 2004 with nearby Mentor School Quest High School and still an active reciprocal learning partner with Quest), Empowerment College Preparatory High School was founded to live out the mission of its name: to empower and prepare all of its students for acceptance into and graduation from four-year colleges and universities. Empowerment's first cohort graduated in 2009, so it is currently too early to look at results, but Empowerment's educators, students, and families feel confident that these students are on track and well prepared to succeed. The intense dedication of Empowerment's staff members to using proven practices that support their mission, and their commitment to examining those practices thoughtfully and habitually, indicate that the school community's confidence is warranted.

Traci Stewart-Jones, principal of Empowerment, explains, "Our curriculum is college prep; that's all that we focus on. Our purpose is to get kids college-ready. And we know that it's easier for kids to get into college than to stay and earn a degree, so that's part of our purpose and mission as well." Every decision that Empowerment's founders and current staff has made, from the time the school was just an idea through the phases of design, opening, and year-by-year grade additions, has focused on creating the structures and relationships that will allow Empowerment's students to be college-ready. At Empowerment, this means that all students take college-prep courses. There are no tracked classes, and the teachers make it a point to structure enough extra supports to make sure that students can handle the material.

The school's schedule and structures are deeply informed by the "less is more" principle, focusing on offering academically challenging courses at Empowerment, dual-credit courses at Houston Community College for all juniors and seniors, and an academically integrated social action project that brings students from the campus into the community and brings Houston into the students' academic life. Students have the opportunity to earn college credit through the dual-enrollment college program. Empowerment's high academic expectations for all students are made possible by its careful cultivation of relationships at all levels: between faculty and staff members, between educators and students, and among educators, students, and students' family members. "We are very deliberate why we are a small school and why our practices are what they are," says Stewart-Jones. "Everything we do is to prepare kids for college, to help them be academically ready and socio-emotionally mature enough. Everything is held to the mirror of the mission, and we are constantly looking at data." When the current senior class was getting ready to enroll in college classes as part of the dual-enrollment requirement, the staff members at Empowerment analyzed students' work. The analysis indicated that the faculty needed to increase the level of academic rigor so that all students would be ready to be admitted into community college and, upon graduation, four-year colleges. "We had to reexamine our curricular practices," recalls Stewart-Jones. The faculty analyzed the problem through their professional learning community structures. (For more on learning communities, see Chapter Five.) Using protocols that guided them to look critically at student work, at their own professional development, and at student achievement data, the Empowerment faculty members committed to the practice of biweekly formative assessment in all classes in order to have more frequently accessible data that would allow immediate pedagogical corrections and ensure that students were on track for the challenges ahead.

Stewart-Jones continues, "We communicate progress [through students' advisors] every two weeks with families so they are included in this journey. We try to make sure the students are aware of their academic standing. We don't talk about grades, but we do talk about progress and how they're meeting the objectives. Our goal is to focus less on A, B, C grades and more on persistence, commitment, and habits of mind and heart." The benefits of this approach immediately help students—and the ability of educators to support them—and have a lasting impact through college, when support structures will not be as prevalent. "At college, you get very little feedback about what you're doing, so you need to develop those habits as a part of graduating from high school," says Stewart-Jones. Carol Fran Ahmed, the mother of Empowerment senior Faruqe Ahmed, believes that the school is teaching Faruqe and his peers about the personal responsibility required for college success. "He's learned about getting his work in on time, about how to study, and about how to find information and research. If you don't research and do the work, you lose out. That's one of the things that the teachers are telling Faruqe," Carol Ahmed offers, to support her belief that her son is prepared for the academic challenges of a four-year university.

The staff members of Empowerment have recognized that a significant barrier to success in higher education is that students are not prepared for or do not understand what will be expected of them in postsecondary education: research skills, reading comprehension, high-level math skills, independent work, extensive writing, and critical thinking (Bailey, Hughes, and Karp, 2002). High schools that are designed to overcome this obstacle align their graduation requirements with college admission requirements in order to ensure that all students are eligible for college upon graduation. This backward planning approach ultimately requires systemwide realignment: planners, educators, and policymakers must also create elementary and middle schools through backward planning in order to ensure that students at all grade levels have the skills and knowledge that will put them on a path toward college.

School of the Future's six hundred sixth through twelfth graders come from across New York City, and many will be first-generation college goers. With a strong track record of college admissions for nearly all of its students, School of the Future (SOF) is developing students' capacity not just to matriculate but to succeed in higher education, restructuring the curriculum, pedagogy, and schedule during the senior year and intentionally aligning courses with college expectations so that instruction and assessments are focused on the skills and dispositions needed for college-level work.

Former principal Catherine DeLaura explained, "After the kids apply to college, we work on transitions. How are you going to register for courses? What's going to happen if you do need help with writing? What's a credit card?" In the spring, School of the Future moves its seniors to a college-like schedule, offering electives and longer, less frequent classes with intense and independent reading, writing, and other assignments designed to model college-level work. Teachers demonstrate different instructional delivery styles, including lectures. "We are engaging kids at the end of the year who would otherwise be checking out," said DeLaura. "Their last exhibition is due in March; students know they're graduating, and they tend to get lax. The students love it at first, but then they freak out, and we say to them, 'Yes, this is what it's going to be like next year. This is stress. Get it together!'" As well, along with many other exemplary CES schools, School of the Future has made the real work of preparing for and applying to college part of the curriculum, addressing the process of preparing for the transition to higher education in a weekly for-credit "college class" taken by all juniors and seniors—a clear indication that it sees higher education preparation for all students as worth significant time and resources. Many other Essential schools provide similar experiences in the form of senior seminars that support students as they prepare to finish high school and make the transition to higher education.

Schools that are aware of the cognitive strategies that college demands of students (see "Key Cognitive Strategies for College Success" sidebar) and provide a challenging college-ready curriculum accompanied by the right kinds of support create significant advantages for their students. Students are familiar with the academic life and expectations of college. Many students have earned significant college credit, which allows faster completion of an undergraduate degree, provides more flexibility in students' course of study, and mitigates the need for remediation. Students possess the skills and knowledge needed to engage in intellectual work across various disciplines and the emotional competence to resiliently and adaptably participate in the global economy of the twenty-first century.

Key Cognitive Strategies for College Success

In *Redefining College Readiness*, David T. Conley describes seven dispositions that characterize students who are ready for college success. Secondary schools can use Conley's list as a benchmark against which to compare their own statements about the qualities they expect to see in their graduates—often called *habits of mind* or *schoolwide outcomes*. Such statements from CES schools are included throughout *Small Schools, Big Ideas.*

Intellectual openness: The student possesses curiosity and a thirst for deeper understanding, questions the views of others when those views are not logically supported, accepts constructive criticism, and changes personal views if warranted by the evidence. Such openmindedness helps students understand the ways in which knowledge is constructed, broadens personal perspectives and helps students deal with the novelty and ambiguity often encountered in the study of new subjects and new materials.

Inquisitiveness: The student engages in active inquiry and dialogue about subject matter and research questions and seeks evidence to defend arguments, explanations, or lines of reasoning. The student does not simply accept as given any assertion that is presented or conclusion that is reached, but asks why things are so.

Analysis: The student identifies and evaluates data, material, and sources for quality of content, validity, credibility, and relevance. The student compares and contrasts sources and findings and generates summaries and explanations of source materials.

Reasoning, argumentation, proof: The student constructs well-reasoned arguments or proofs to explain phenomena or issues; utilizes recognized forms of reasoning to construct an argument and defend a point of view or conclusion; accepts critiques of or challenges to assertions; and addresses critiques and challenges by providing a logical explanation or refutation, or by acknowledging the accuracy of the critique or challenge.

Interpretation: The student analyzes competing and conflicting descriptions of an event or issue to determine the strengths and flaws in each description and any commonalities among or distinctions between them; synthesizes the results of an analysis of competing or conflicting descriptions of an event or issue or phenomenon into a coherent explanation; states the interpretation that is most likely correct or is most reasonable, based on the available evidence; and presents orally or in writing an extended description, summary, and evaluation of varied perspectives and conflicting points of view on a topic or issue.

Precision and accuracy: The student knows what type of precision is appropriate to the task and the subject area, is able to increase precision and accuracy through successive approximations generated from a task or process that is repeated, and uses precision appropriately to reach correct conclusions in the context of the task or subject area at hand.

Problem solving: The student develops and applies multiple strategies to solve routine problems, generate [sic] strategies to solve nonroutine problems, and applies methods of problem solving to complex problems requiring method-based problem solving. These key cognitive strategies are broadly representative of the foundational elements that underlie various "ways of knowing."

Source: Conley, 2007, pp. 13–14.

Relationships with Local and National Colleges and Universities

Empowerment's partnership program with Houston Community College is an example of the widespread and increasing practice of dual enrollment. Dual enrollment, also known as *concurrent enrollment,* allows high school students to enroll in college courses and earn college credit. Dual enrollment helps all students improve academically, particularly students of color, low-income students, and students who have exhibited low high school achievement (Hughes, 2008; Kim, 2008), increasing their likelihood of graduating from high school and successfully moving on to higher education. Support for dual enrollment is a staple of state educational policy; over forty states feature varieties of dual or concurrent enrollment practices (U.S Department of Education, Office of Vocational and Adult Education, 2005). However, despite the place of such policies on the books, few students are provided access to dual enrollment. In 2002–03, 71 percent of public high schools and 51 percent of postsecondary institutions offered programs in which high school students took college courses. However, only 5 percent of all high school students participated in such programs, and nationally, schools with the highest enrollments of students of color were least likely to offer dual-credit courses (Hughes, 2008). In order for dual enrollment to be a transformative practice, it must be available to every student, not just those who opt in or who are counseled in based on high academic achievement. Empowerment's Stewart-Jones comments, "Schools in our area have dual-credit programs, but it becomes selective. 'Good' kids go to dual-credit courses, but average kids aren't extended the opportunity, and that's when it becomes an opportunity, not an expectation."

In Empowerment's case, the school's dual-enrollment program is supported by state policy, as is the case with a variety of other Mentor Schools and new small school participants discussed in these pages, such as Oakland's ARISE High School, Albuquerque's Amy Biehl High School, the Met in Providence, Rhode Island, and more. However, dual enrollment is not the only option for high school–higher education continuity. Greenville Technical Charter High School in Greenville, South Carolina, is a CES Mentor School and is part of the Early College High School initiative, which helps schools create a remarkably supportive atmosphere for collaboration between high schools and colleges. Early College High Schools combine the final years of high school and the first years of college. Greenville Technical Charter High School was founded and is located on a community college campus. All of its students take college courses, and some of them graduate from high school with an associate degree. Staff members from both the college and the high school regularly work in partnership in a variety of ways.

Karen Kennedy, social studies teacher and early college coordinator at Greenville Technical Charter High School, describes the nature of the partnership with Greenville Technical College:

> One of the things over the last five years that's happened is that we've really started to have conversations with folks at the college on all levels, not just the upper leadership of the school but then also folks that work in the college—advisors and instructors, the department heads, and those kinds of people. Last year, we had two meetings where college instructors came over and met with high school teachers and we talked about what, as high school teachers, we could be doing to make our kids better students in college and get them ready, and they shared some things with us. Then they even asked about some things that they could maybe learn from us, and so it was real conversation. We have a monthly meeting as a part of this collaboration of a small group of college folks and high school folks. We look at lots of different issues like ways we can get kids in more college classes.

Kennedy's experience demonstrates that faculties of high schools and colleges need to have dialogue in order to align expectations so that more students graduate prepared for college, work, and life's challenges and opportunities.

Kennedy believes that the development of an ongoing professional learning community that includes educators at the high school and at the college has created organizational structures that have helped Greenville take advantage of its early college status to prepare more of its students for college success:

> For me, it's been gratifying to see. When we first came here, we didn't have that many kids taking college classes and those who did were just sort of taking classes, I guess, call it kind of willy-nilly. They just sort of picked some things out and were taking them without a clear purpose in mind. For a lot of kids, it helps to have a road map or a plan, and that's what we've started doing with the kids at the end of the freshman year. We sit down with them and help them figure out what they want to do and how we can get them into college classes.

Founded in 1987, Middle College High School, a CES Mentor School in Memphis, provides another example of concurrent high school–college enrollment. Located on Southwest Tennessee Community College's Union Avenue campus, Middle College High School graduates its students with a high school diploma and two years' worth of college credits. Principal Michelle Brantley describes the student body: "We're not acquiring the top 5 percent from middle schools throughout the city. We engage in a very intensive interview process to identify those kids for whom our mission would really ring true. Other kids look great; they have high scores. We say to those kids, 'I'm sorry, we feel like you can do well in any place.' We are for students who haven't done well in traditional settings. There's no creaming around here. We are ever mindful of support, support, support." In addition to the advantage of its small size, Middle College High School provides that support through advisories, a full-time guidance counselor and a full-time social worker, and access for students to Southwest Tennessee Community College's academic resource center.

Brantley stresses that strong relationships and good communication between Middle College High School faculty and Southwest Tennessee Community College faculty make the work possible; everyone knows the Middle College students well, and the two groups can work collaboratively to determine the best placement and means of support for students. "I think there's a strong sense of efficacy on the part of adults in terms of their belief in kids."

Not all schools in the CES Small Schools Network offer a form of concurrent college enrollment, but even those without such programs pay special attention to communication with the colleges and universities to which their students are applying. Teri Schrader, principal of Francis W. Parker Charter Essential School, a Mentor School, feels that time invested in communicating with colleges and universities to which Parker's students are applying about Parker's distinctive narrative transcripts—no GPA, no A's, B's, or C's—is well spent. "In early years, the school wisely took time to get college admission folks on board even though we only had seventh and eighth graders," Schrader says. Parker's founders invited college and university representatives to meet in order to help them understand what the school transcript would look like and how Parker could present that information without disadvantaging its students by giving colleges an excessive burden of interpretation. The three-part transcript contains an overview of Parker's academic program, counselors' recommendations about students' college readiness on behalf of Parker, and a summary of a student's ninth- through twelfth-grade progress reports and semester-end assessments. "We go through progress reports and create a story," explains Schrader. "This third part of the transcript is mostly a series of quotations lifted from progress reports." (To see a sample transcript from Parker Charter Essential School, visit the *Small Schools, Big Ideas* Web site at http://www.ceschangelab.org/.)

The outreach effort to institutions of higher education to which Parker students apply has continued. "There's a huge, wide range of colleges, and when there's a new one, our college counselor reaches out," Schrader says. "A bunch of us take phone calls from colleges that don't know us, and we take time to translate for them. While we don't have the markers that they are looking for, I think colleges have been really receptive, some early on and persistently and some realizing this is a sign of the times. With the devaluing of SATs, schools' transcripts like ours are more interesting."

As Chapter Eight describes, performance-based student assessment is a complex process that is not easily reducible to simple letter grades. Parker's experience in offering narrative transcripts that present a more holistic version of a student's academic career parallels that of many CES schools.

Communication about these detailed transcripts to college admissions officials and potential employers requires resources and time, as Schrader indicates.

Personalization Through Advisories and Other Structures

Schools that serve students who may be the first in their family to attend college (or, perhaps, to graduate from high school) must make specific, intentional efforts to create a college-going culture. This commitment manifests differently from one school to the next, depending on the structures of the school. Some schools have a dedicated college counselor; others spread the work of college counseling among all advisors; and in all cases, promotion of higher education planning and sharing information about the process are activities that demonstrate the CES Common Principle "Commitment to the entire school." Everyone on the school staff focuses on the goals related to students' postsecondary success and on the work of providing consistent, comprehensive, and personalized college counseling to support every student in navigating the college selection, application, and financial aid processes. As a result, each student receives the appropriate individual support and academic preparation needed to achieve college readiness.

For twenty years, Kizzi Elmore-Clark has taught English and related subjects at Federal Hocking High School, a CES Mentor School. Elmore-Clark has seen many groups of students through their senior year at the rural Stewart, Ohio, school, which educates 472 students in grades nine through twelve. Federal Hocking High School is the single public high school serving Stewart and neighboring towns; many of its students will be the first in their family to go on to higher education. Elmore-Clark and the rest of the Federal Hocking High School staff are committed to assuming the multiple roles of teacher, advisor, and, as Elmore-Clark says, "parent away from home" as they prepare all students academically for college, helping them develop the skills, confidence, and other resources to attend and graduate from the school of their choice. "From the time I get my advisory students as freshmen and in all of my classes, I push the idea that if you are prepared to go to college, you have options after high school. And if you don't prepare to go to college, it shuts a lot of doors," says Elmore-Clark. In order to build support and motivation among her students, Elmore-Clark convenes conversations between recent college-going graduates and current Federal Hocking High School students, starting in the ninth grade.

"Our students hear someone they know or who is like them say, 'You can do this too. It's possible.' If you grew up in a household where no one had ever been to school beyond high school—or even all the way through high school—it doesn't register that college is a possibility."

Students thrive in Essential schools because of the close relationships they develop with each other and with the adults in the school community. The personalization to which students are accustomed also influences considerations of what a good fit between the student and a higher education institution might be. Federal Hocking High School's Kizzi Elmore-Clark says,

> We try to push kids toward smaller colleges, which allows them to build relationships and go from this community to another where they can get involved. Our kids are used to instructors' knowing who they are. If there is any way we don't serve our kids well, it is that they don't really know how to function effectively as a number. Of course, that is a real positive for us. But when some students go off to Ohio State, they feel really lost. On the other hand, we've had kids go off to big schools, get involved in small communities through clubs and organizations, and thrive.

School of the Future has two counselors for its four hundred high school students. Each follows a group of students for four years, one focusing on ninth and eleventh grades, the other on tenth and twelfth, ensuring that when the time comes to start making decisions about where to apply, the counselors and students know each other well and can make appropriate choices. "It's a child-centered model," observes Catherine DeLaura. "Our school does what many middle-class families do. Kids can ask their parents, 'What do you think about this? What do you know about this topic?' But a lot of our kids don't have those resources, so we teach them how to advocate for themselves, how to find adults who will have helpful relationships with them." Kizzi Elmore-Clark reports similarities at Federal Hocking High School:

> As an advisor and in my classes, I've become a parent away from home. I'm Aunt Kizzi. I get to know my students really well. I get to know what their ability is in any given area. I get to know what they enjoy, and because I know them so well, I tend to then push them to try things that they wouldn't have thought they could do. I stay on

their butts in terms of keeping their grades up and being responsible for their own actions. Ultimately, it's that kid who feels that she or he can go to college—that's what we push for.

At Empowerment, Traci Stewart-Jones and her colleagues are applying their Mentor School's lessons about personalization to their particular situation. "We don't have a counselor because of the size of school; with the resources we have, that's not where we need staff. We do that work through advisory, relationships, and with families. Because they're teenagers, some are on the ball, and some don't even know what the ball looks like," Stewart-Jones says ruefully, clearly acknowledging that every student comes with unique assets and challenges. Empowerment advisor and science teacher April Rasmus feels that the work that she does with her twelfth-grade advisory is critical to students' prospects of college success: "Like a parent, you just want to make sure that you've provided everything, that you're ready to let them go, and that you know they have the skills that they need." And as educators at a new school that is sending its first class off to college, advisors at Empowerment are learning to determine how much support is appropriate: "With this first class, we've struggled a lot because in the beginning, they were used to being by themselves and getting a lot of attention. We supported them a lot and held their hands, and now in a lot of ways that has backfired on us." Rasmus credits ongoing conversations about advising for college preparation with teachers from Empowerment's Mentor School, Quest, as useful in helping her and other Empowerment advisors find balance. "We see where [Quest advisors] support [their students]. The kids know that the hand is there. They're not necessarily grasping it, but when they need to, they can."

Families as Informed Partners

To achieve its goals of college preparedness, enrollment, and graduation for all of its students, Empowerment's advisors work not just with individual students but with their families, demonstrating that family connections are an integral aspect of preparing students for success in postsecondary school. Among CES Small Schools Network participants, families are informed partners in the process of supporting students through school and on to college; in many schools, advisors are the main sources of information, support, and connection for family members for whom the path to higher education is somewhat or altogether unfamiliar.

Empowerment parent Carol Fran Ahmed values the relationship that she and Samantha Brooks, her son's advisor, have forged: "I have talked with [my son's] advisor about the process of applying to college. He knows what he wants in life; he knows his goals, but when they're at that age, you still have to keep on them and keep reminding them, and I have to say that his advisor, Miss Brooks, she's good. She gets him. And she gets what I need; she has talked with me about the applications to colleges, about the process." Ahmed believes that the partnership she and her son's advisor share is a result of work they put in over time. She credits the school's open-door policy, which invites family members into frequent communication, facilitated by advisors, about all aspects of students' progress, sharing a joke by her son that "It's like the school has a spell over the parents. It's that the school wants to keep the parents informed and pointing the kids in the right direction." Another mother of a senior in Samantha Brooks's advisory, Bettye Wharton-Mims, concurs, reflecting, "I have Ms. Brooks on speed dial and in e-mail; she has been my partner to get focused and stay focused on my son's education. I thought I knew the requirements for college, but there is so much more information that I've learned."

Catherine DeLaura of School of the Future suggests that college visits for family members as well as students play a crucial role in ensuring that students not only choose to go to college but choose a school that is the right fit, improving the prospect that they will persist and graduate. DeLaura recalled that Colby College in Waterville, Maine, was particularly interested in one young Latina woman from School of the Future. Colby demonstrated its commitment to the student and her non-English-speaking mother, who was concerned about her daughter leaving home, by funding the cost for the mother's visit, demonstrating to the mother that the school was safe and demonstrating to the student and her teachers, counselors, and advisor at School of the Future that Colby was a particularly good fit. DeLaura has used this strategy of making it possible for a family to visit schools in other cases, sometimes paying for the visits with funds from School of the Future. DeLaura believes that one of School of the Future's key assets in the college readiness effort is that students and their families decide higher education is important and, as a result, opt for School of the Future, which does send nearly all of its students to higher education. "Maybe I'm being naïve," says DeLaura, "but I think there are very few families that don't want to give their kids the opportunity to go to college."

Beth Balliro, a visual arts teacher and advisor at Boston Arts Academy (BAA), believes that culture differences are far more serious impediments to college persistence than academic preparedness. Boston Arts Academy is a CES Mentor School that serves 438 students in grades nine through twelve and that aims to develop artistic and academic excellence. More than half of its students will be the first in their family to attend college. Balliro and others at BAA who guide students in their college process, including student support and guidance educator Cynthia Hairston, believe that finding a good fit is crucial not just in getting students into college but in helping them stay there. Balliro says,

> Some schools have bad track records with kids of color; the kids may get in, but the schools don't advise and support them. Our students need guidance; often, they do not know what schools are right for them. They are not educated consumers and are prone to be manipulated by advertising for schools offering overpriced, non-legitimate degrees. Our families have no experience in the college world; some have paid $1,000 to attend a workshop that shares nothing useful about financial aid. These are families that are trying to do right by their kids. They are ships lost at sea, and people are out there preying on them.

Ironically, Balliro points out, her students can present themselves as tremendous assets to institutions of higher education and need to be aware of that: "One of the things we try to teach students [is] that they have to be good consumers. Though they don't see themselves this way, they are a commodity. Well-prepared urban kids of color are a hot ticket; they have clout in the higher education world, but they need to know how to use it." In Figure 9.1, Boston Arts Academy has shared its Graduation Planner, which is the road map students, advisors, teachers, family members, and counselors use to ensure that students are on track to graduation from the moment they enter the school.

At Parker Charter Essential School, principal Teri Schrader says that the staff members, especially the school's college counselor, work extensively with family members to help them understand how assessment and other practices at Parker, often markedly different from those at more conventional schools, will work in their child's favor. "Our transcript process is unfamiliar to parents; they don't always really realize that the progress reports they see are grist for the college transcript, and some of them do panic when they realize that their students aren't

Figure 9.1
Boston Arts Academy Graduation Planner

Grade 9	Grade 10	Grade 11	Grade 12
Seminar (__ Open Honors) ☐ Passed Writers Workshop/Advisory ☐ *Scored 2.5 or better on Autobiography*	**Seminar** (__ Open Honors) ☐ Passed Writers Workshop/Advisory ☐ *Passed MCAS in English/Language Arts*	**Seminar** (__ Open Honors) ☐ Passed Writers Workshop/ Advisory	**Seminar** (__ Open Honors) ☐ Passed Writers Workshop/ Advisory
Math ☐ Passed Math ☐ *Scored 65% or better on Freshman Math Assessment*	**Math** ☐ Passed Math ☐ *Passed MCAS in Math*	**Math** ☐ Passed Math	**Math** ☐ Passed Math
World Language ☐ Passed World Language ☐ *Passed Gr 8 World Language @ Latin* ☐ N/A	**World Language** ☐ Passed World Language ☐ N/A	**World Language** ☐ Passed World Language ☐ N/A	**World Language** ☐ Passed World Language ☐ N/A
Science (__ Open Honors) ☐ Passed Science 9	**Science** (__ Open Honors) ☐ Passed Science 10	**Science** (__ Open Honors) ☐ Passed Science 11	**Science** (__ Open Honors) ☐ Passed Science 12
Humanities (__ Open Honors) ☐ Passed Humanities 1	**Humanities** (__ Open Honors) ☐ Passed Humanities 2	**Humanities** (__ Open Honors) ☐ Passed Humanities 3 ☐ *Received a 3 on Hum 3 Portfolio*	**Humanities** (__ Open Honors) ☐ Passed Humanities 4
Arts Major _____ ☐ Earned a C− or better (70%)	**Arts Major** _____ ☐ Earned a C+ or better (77%) ☐ Passed Sophomore Arts Review	**Arts Major** ☐ Earned a B− or better (80%)	**Arts Major** ☐ Earned a B− or better (80%) ☐ *Received a "3" on Sr. Grant Proposal* ☐ Completed Sr. performance/ exhibition
RICO Review ☐ Completed	**RICO Review** ☐ Completed	**Junior Review** ☐ Student/Parent Night ☐ Attended PSAT Prep ☐ Took the PSAT ☐ Essay Writing Workshop ☐ BAA College Fair ☐ At least one college presentation ☐ Took SAT ☐ At least one college visit ☐ Career Exploration ☐ Senior Panel ☐ Jr. Day-Pre-College Activities	**Senior Review** ☐ Attended SAT Prep ☐ Took the SAT ☐ Completed college/career app. process ☐ Sr. Transition Workshop ☐ Jr. Step-Up/Sr. Awards ☐ Completed Sr. inspiration letter ☐ Signed-out

Note: Open Honors classes, as their name implies, are open to any student who would like to take on additional academic challenges.

going to have grades or GPAs. But like everything about the school, it works when we're building relationships. You can't just send a memo home. You can never say something just one time and have it take for good. Everything that works here is a direct result of understanding, communications, and trust. You just keep talking and proving and showing."

This ongoing communication with family members also comes into play in other circumstances, especially in communities in which many parents have not attended college themselves. Federal Hocking High School's Kizzi Elmore-Clark reflects on the intricacies of changing familial expectations about the imperative of higher education. "I never want to belittle kids because they decide not to go to college. There are wonderfully intelligent, cool people who do plenty of different sorts of jobs who haven't gone to college. But the push has to be to prepare you for options," she notes. At times, this means having discussions with families about their children's futures and helping them understand that in this century, students without a college education are at significant risk for being left behind socially and economically.

Internships and Other Real-World Educational Opportunities

This chapter has focused largely on creating secondary school environments that support all students in matriculating in and successfully graduating from four-year colleges. As well as focusing on the academic and developmental components of that work, the schools featured in this chapter also include internships, service learning, and other real-world work opportunities as essential elements of their program. As discussed in Chapter Seven, these experiences can powerfully shape young people's goals not only for college but for the rest of their lives as workers and active participants in their communities. CES co-founder Deborah Meier, former principal at CES schools Central Park East Secondary School in New York and Mission Hill School in Boston, discusses her conviction that community-based learning helps provide young people and schools with the often-missing element of connections with the adult world:

> Most of the jobs that young people tend to get on their own are in largely teenage industries, extensions of their teenage social lives. Community-based learning helps produce a more porous line between "the world" and schooling. One of the peculiar things about

the way we've organized schools is that we often place schools at a distance from adult lives, on the outskirts of suburbs instead of in town, somewhere out there surrounded by fields. This doesn't lend itself to students' seeing people working or having connections. We've built schooling so it's isolated from adult work. It wasn't so serious when many adults left school at the age of thirteen or fourteen and when their family economy was dependent on their working. But today, people are in school from four to twenty, and schools are disconnected from other adult communities. I think it can be dangerous and the idea of finding adults who are not their parents or teachers to be part of kids' lives is significantly important.

Boston Arts Academy offers a concrete example of real-life work's relevance to post-school life. BAA challenges its students to write a proficient grant proposal for an arts project as their senior capstone activity, rehearsing an activity and a set of skills that artists will need to practice and refine as their career evolves. The stakes for the grant-writing capstone project are real: 20 percent of the seniors' projects are funded. Beth Balliro says, "We are transitioning the kids from under the umbrella of the school to be out in the world. After high school, they need to know how to do real-life stuff: how to make connections, solicit letters of support, write résumés, and articulate their goals and dreams persuasively. Going through the process helps them see feasible ways to make their vision practical and related to behavior patterns they can use after high school."

Empowerment's Stewart-Jones notes that while attending a small school geared toward personalization and high academic achievement for all gives students a significant advantage, the school's small size also presents some challenges when its students vie for spots in college and university freshman classes. "We are talking about all aspects of getting access to the postsecondary experience, and for our kids, this means being able to meet admissions requirements completely and to be SAT/ACT eligible for scholarships based on academic standing. Since they won't have a typical high school experience, you have to find ways for them to shine above and beyond. Kids who attend small high schools don't necessarily have an athletic side to their experience; that's often a route to scholarships, so it really matters," acknowledges Stewart-Jones. "We do provide opportunities to lead through social action and opportunities to shine in terms of skills and leadership." As discussed in Chapter Eight, these social action experiences become the basis for Empowerment students' exhibitions of learning, on which their movement from grade to grade and, ultimately, their graduation depends. Participating in the community sparks student engagement, which creates eagerness to learn the literacy, numeracy, communication, collaboration, and other skills that students need in order to graduate prepared for higher education.

Empowerment senior Faruqe Ahmed sees connections between his social action project and his career goals. To achieve those goals, Ahmed knows that he needs to complete college. Ahmed's social action project focuses on knowing more about children's experiences in refugee camps in Darfur. In addition to research, Ahmed is interviewing refugees in the Houston area in order to comprehend their experiences. "I'm trying to get donations from people to donate crayons and coloring books that can get to them through UNICEF," Ahmed says, "to take the children's minds off the war." His interest in children's welfare was sparked by an earlier Empowerment internship in which he worked at a children's center, which, Ahmed comments, "opens your mind to what reality is and how it will be for other people to go through life." Ahmed's goal is to open hotels to provide hospitality and "to help the safety of people as well. I'm going to make programs for refugee children and cancer patients." A cancer survivor himself, Ahmed has set his sights on the University of Houston's hotel management program, from which he envisions graduating. "Once I get that diploma, I want to open hotels worldwide," he says. In Ahmed's case, participation in social action has connected with his passions and identity, fueling his desire to attend and graduate from college in order to pursue his vision.

Helping Students Deal with Impediments to Postsecondary Success

Even with many of the factors discussed in this chapter—challenging curriculum, bridges to higher education, personalized support, family inclusion, and preparation for real-world experiences—Essential school graduates will face a barrage of challenges once they are in college. Even without the challenge of inadequate academic preparation and the need for the most significant barrier to higher education success, remediation (Mehan and others, 1991), students from the schools discussed in this chapter and from similar schools face the typical trials of learning to cope on their own as well as more dire impediments such as lack of financial support and cultural barriers commonly faced by first-generation college goers.

Educators at Essential schools are acutely aware of the financial burden that students face when they opt to continue their education rather than enter the workforce full-time, join the military, or pursue other options. Boston Arts Academy's Beth Balliro reports, "Though we have a sense of which schools are generous and which aren't, kids end up over their heads. We do cultivate external relations as much as we can to create internal scholarships and take advantage of existing programs. Berklee School of Music and Massachusetts College of Arts have guaranteed us scholarships, for example." All of the schools featured in this chapter, as well as many more schools, guide students through the process of applying for loans, scholarships, and grants, working with families and higher education institutions to create the best, most sustainable situation for each student. Still, it's an increasing challenge. State and federal trends in financial aid reveal increases in loans and decreases in grants to the least financially advantaged students. Kizzi Elmore-Clark at Federal Hocking High School says, "We don't have figures on who drops out, but we know that a lot of our kids end up leaving college because they don't have financial support. Even though they're admitted to college with great full tuition packages, they can't pay for gas, their car, or books."

Education researcher Lori Chajet, a former teacher in a New York City Essential high school, argues that we need more research on the impact of CES (and like-minded) schools. "The primary goal of small, urban, progressive public schools, sending students to college, has never been fully researched," Chajet notes. Chajet's dissertation, "'But Is What We Give Them Enough?': Exploring Urban Small School Graduates' Journeys Through College" (Chajet, 2007), focuses on the journeys toward and through higher education of graduates of one CES school, in order to provide insight into two research questions: To what extent and in what ways did these students' secondary experiences at a small urban public school influence their expectations for and navigation of higher education? And how can understanding the answers to this question inform the work of both small schools and colleges? Chajet conducted ethnographic research at the high school and then did a three-part follow-up study consisting of a survey with 55 percent of three graduating high school classes, individual interviews and focus groups with more than twenty graduates, and more intensive research in which Chajet followed six students from their senior year of high school through their first three years after high school. The school, referred to pseudonymously as Bridges, educates five hundred predominantly low-income students of color in grades seven through twelve, over 90 percent of whom go on to college. They attend a broad span of higher education institutions: public and private, two-year and four-year, open-door and selective, residential and urban.

While generally they are academically prepared for college, a host of obstacles come in the way of Bridges graduates' persistence through and completion of college. Limited money for higher education was the biggest obstacle and source of anxiety for them. Among the students who stopped out of college or left it altogether, over 50 percent cited finances as a main reason. Chajet describes one student who, after two years of real success, transferred from a private college to a state university due to major yearly financial increases that made the gap between the student's resources and all available financial aid impossible to bridge. While she has maintained her record of academic success at her new school, the transfer has postponed the student's graduation by a semester; students often lose credits when they transfer.

A less-than-complete understanding of financial pressures among students' high school teachers and advisors complicates the situation. Chajet recalls,

> When I presented back at school, I heard questions from the staff about why students aren't taking out loans. Low-income students are less willing to take out loans. They are less sure that they will finish school, and they don't fully understand the process of financial aid. Taking out loans is frightening when you have no money to back you up. And they're reading the political economy pretty well: students know they can't stop, that they have to go to graduate school to get the jobs they need, and that means more loans. It can create a really daunting obstacle.

This cultural, class, and race friction between staff and students affected other aspects of the transition from high school to higher education. "When I interviewed staff members, those that were first-generation college goers and of color had a broader definition of college than those who came from middle-class backgrounds," says Chajet. "What this means for small Essential schools is that we need to try to diversify our staff, though that is not easy, given our teaching population. It is also critical to have professional development in which teachers are actively thinking through how their own experiences shape how they present information, recommendations, and advice about college."

Still, Chajet says that CES schools are doing a lot, successfully preparing students from many different backgrounds to succeed in a broad range of colleges across the country. For example, Chajet's research revealed that 82 percent of Bridges students aged twenty-two to twenty-four have some or more college, compared with 57.4 percent of adults aged twenty-five to twenty-nine nationally, according to the U.S. Census Bureau. Among black students, 84 percent of Bridges students have some or more college, compared with 44.7 percent of blacks in the general population, and among Latino students, 83 percent of Bridges students have some or more college, compared with 29.6 percent of Latinos in the general population (Chajet, 2007). "I am seeing an incredible commitment to learning among graduates and real agency around getting through obstacles. If we are able to look at them ten years out of high school, we would see even higher rates of graduation and success," Chajet says.

Traci Stewart-Jones and her colleagues at Empowerment believe that their attempt to address these barriers proactively and directly will make a difference to their students when they arrive on college and university campuses. Stewart-Jones explains,

> Personally, we all know people who were accepted into college based on high school performance, but because of lack of finances or persistence, they were not ready for the rigors of college. We try to be up front with our students. We try to demystify what it takes to stay in college. We get gripes and groans, but it's worth it. It will pay off in the end, educate them about what the expectations are, and give them the reality of it. College sounds like a dream, and for many of them it is a dream. They don't know a lot of college graduates within their circle of influence. Now, we're making that a reality for families for whom that reality didn't exist.

Conclusion

Higher education attainment is seen among a wide cross-section of American educators and families as the best way to ensure a financially sound future, and Essential schools are committed to supporting students and working with the system to change social patterns and interrupt generational inequities. The data on the improved economic conditions of college graduates are persuasive, but ultimately, for Boston Arts Academy's Beth Balliro, it's not enough: "I'm selling college to my students as economic progress: you are going to college to get a good job and have a bright future. But I do wonder about that bias. In my family, when I was in high school, I wasn't told that. I got to go there to learn." Balliro's observation provokes us to remember that all students have the right to pursue not only economic justice but the countless benefits of the life of the mind—benefits that can't be measured by job titles, bank balances, or college diplomas.

PART FOUR

Embedding Successful Change

School Culture, Practices, and Community

> A school's culture dictates, in no uncertain terms,
> "the way we do things around here."
>
> —Roland Barth (2002)

After ascending the stairway of midtown Manhattan's Julia Richman Education Complex and entering into the portion of the large building dedicated to Urban Academy Laboratory High School, visitors immediately notice that there are some things that feel decidedly un-school-like. In the expansive hallways, couches are strewn with students' personal belongings, from purses to iPods. Students constantly move in and out of the one large room that serves as the collaborative office for all of Urban Academy's staff members, including the principal, in which staff desks are piled precariously high with papers and books. Conversations with students at Urban—or at any of the schools in the CES Small Schools Network—reveal school ownership and pride. Students are articulate about why their particular school is unique and the ways in which they feel that they are a part of a strong and nurturing community.

Urban's school culture is immediately clear: we trust each other with our personal possessions (evident from valuable property left unattended) and our words (the open-door school office values the open sharing of information). Stephen Stolp (1991) offers a classic definition of school culture: "School culture

271

can be defined as the historically transmitted patterns of meaning that include the norms, values, beliefs, ceremonies, rituals, traditions, and myths understood, maybe in varying degrees, by members of the school community. This system of meaning often shapes what people think and how they act." But in circumstances in which schools are creating themselves into existence as new schools or are fundamentally transforming themselves from previously existing schools, how does this definition apply? In the transformational circumstances of the schools described by (and, we hope, inspired by) *Small Schools, Big Ideas,* members of school communities have the opportunity to consciously and thoughtfully create a school culture that supports the school's goals, mission, and habits of mind.

One of the CES Common Principles that speaks to school culture goals is "A tone of decency and trust," which states, "The tone of the school should explicitly and self-consciously stress values of unanxious expectation ('I won't threaten you but I expect much of you'), of trust (until abused) and of decency (the values of fairness, generosity and tolerance). Incentives appropriate to the school's particular students and teachers should be emphasized. Parents should be key collaborators and vital members of the school community." In CES schools, such a supportive, trusting, student-centered school culture unifies community members' experience; students and educators treat each other with respect in group work sessions to complete projects; at lunch; during community service opportunities; at community meetings; in after-school sports, arts, or other programs; and in any of the other ways that school community members interact with each other through long, productive days.

Paying special attention to building an equitable, student-centered, trusting, inquiry-driven, and academically supportive school culture is particularly essential because school culture will coalesce on its own in any event. School culture is often where issues that are not openly discussed or considered are hidden, where assumptions live, and where attitudes that work to maintain the inequities of our society remain invisible, yet entrenched. What is taught implicitly yet forcefully by school culture has been discussed by Michael Apple and others as "the hidden curriculum" (Apple, 2004), meaning that schools are constantly teaching and reinforcing attitudes and habits of mind to their community members. Every element of school experience contributes in significant ways to the conclusions that students (and the adults who work with them) come to about their abilities, the society into which they are entering, and the opportunities available to them to affect society in positive and meaningful ways.

School culture exists whether or not adults pay it any attention. Educators tend to prioritize academics above anything else that occurs in schools. If educators do not devote intentional thought, deliberation, and design to creating the qualities of community and culture of a school, a culture will form itself and it usually will not be particularly positive. Bullying, gossip, and cliques are all unintentional aspects of most schools' culture. More subtle aspects of a school's culture can also have powerfully negative effects. Without intentionally developed opportunities for student voices to be heard, some students will remain silenced. Without intentional conversations across the difference of race and class, educators and students will carry the dominant attitudes of society into school, with divisive effects on a school community. Pedro Noguera (2003b) writes, "As they get older, young people also become more aware of the politics associated with race, becoming more cognizant of racial hierarchies and prejudice, even if they cannot articulate what it all means" (p. 27). This can be particularly true in adolescence, when "the awareness of race and its implications for individual identity become more salient" (Noguera, 2003b, p. 26). Summarizing the research of Claude Steele, Noguera starkly describes the result of the hidden message of a school's culture: "In the United States we have deeply embedded stereotypes that connect racial identity to academic ability, and children become aware of these stereotypes as they grow up in the school context. Simply put, there are often strong assumptions made that if you're White you'll do better in school than if you're Black, or if you're Asian you'll do better in school than if you're Latino. These kinds of stereotypes affect both teachers' expectations of students and students' expectations of themselves" (Noguera, 2003b, p. 29).

School practices—hour-by-hour, day-by-day decisions and actions—reflect the conscious and unconscious priorities of educators and students. If our schools are to be places that achieve equitable results for students, the unconscious and unspoken rules and norms that adults or students hold and the invisible walls that are a part of every institution in our inequitable society must be surfaced and addressed. The essential question for this chapter is "What are the school practices and cultural characteristics that make a democratic and equitable school that promotes in-depth, personalized, and meaningful learning?" This chapter focuses on eight aspects of creating positive, equity-driven school culture:

- Strong relationships through advisories and other structures
- Staff members who play multiple roles

- Clear values for which the school stands
- Rituals and celebrations
- Community meetings
- Positive discipline and restorative justice practices
- Strong and positive connections with families
- Nontraditional school schedules

Strong Relationships Through Advisories and Other Structures

At the core of any school community is the series of relationships—student-to-student, student-to-adult, adult-to-adult—that shape the culture. The intentional structures and practices that CES schools use to create a positive culture have been developed to foster meaningful relationships at all levels in the service of meeting the social, emotional, and intellectual needs of all students. For adolescents in particular, finding one's place, a sense of belonging, and identity is critical, and too often in the worlds that our students live in, they seek this sense of identity and community in negative ways. Many young people turn to gangs, drugs, and sex as they seek their place and their identity. Schools that can create a strong and positive sense of identity and belonging for their students mitigate these other factors and help students feel connected to activities and people that will help move them forward in positive ways. Equally important to the quest for identity is the opportunity for young people to feel safe to be themselves, to take risks, to be seen, heard, and recognized, and to try on different ways of being as they figure out who they want to become as they reach toward adulthood. Creating the conditions that make this exploration possible is critical in our schools.

This kind of social, emotional, and physical safety is a prerequisite for learning. When students are afraid to come to school or bring fear of failure, anxiety about lack of acceptance, perceptions of racism, or fear of other inequitable treatment, learning anything will be a challenge. As Hart and Hodson (2004) describe in *The Compassionate Classroom*: "Emotional safety and the ability to learn have been correlated in contemporary education and brain research. This research has shown that the emotional center of the brain is so powerful that negative emotions such as hostility, anger, fear, and anxiety automatically 'downshift' the brain to basic, survival thinking. This can make learning very difficult, if not impossible. Under such stress, the neo-cortex or reasoning center of the brain shuts down."

Hart and Hodson go on to consider the effects on students of stress in their home and other environments outside the school: "Since many students don't experience emotional safety at home, they come to school already stressed and in a 'downshifted' state. If they have hostile, discouraging, or otherwise negative interactions with teachers, some students remain in an almost constant state of fight or flight. The brain is so thoroughly preoccupied with survival needs that these students are literally unavailable for the complex activities of the mind that learning requires." This understanding makes it clear that, especially at schools that serve students of any background for whom anxiety is likely to be a major factor at home, schools must create safety and space for students to grow, explore, and take intellectual risks so that meaningful learning experiences can occur. At the most basic level, students must come to school feeling physically safe and personally well known, well respected, trusted, and trusting.

Students are guaranteed to be able to be known well by at least one adult and by other students in advisories, which have emerged as one of the fundamentals of CES school practices. While advisories differ in format and sometimes in name from school to school, all of the Essential schools in *Small Schools, Big Ideas* (and many more CES and non-CES schools as well) have created a daily time for students to meet as a group with a staff member to focus on the bigger picture of their ongoing school experience. Advisories are a check-in time, a place to learn how to connect with others, a place for integration of one's school self into the rest of one's life, a place for school business and decisions, a place to celebrate and plan some fun, a place to integrate family into school life, a place to have hard conversations about what is happening in school and in life.

For CES Mentor School Wildwood School, advisories are an essential and practical component of the school design. Former director of communication and outreach Jeanne Fauci recalls that when Wildwood planned its high school, which opened in 2000, "advisory was a design non-negotiable. Because even in a small school, it's amazing how things slip through the cracks. It's tough work really tracking and checking in with kids and keeping up with them. But

I think having advisories is essential, because they really do provide a structure. It's a way to have operational personalization. If we're in an environment that's not caring, where there aren't those personal relationships, we're not going to stick around. And so advisory is a structure that ensures that those relationships can happen." Of course, meaningful personal relationships among students and between students and teachers happen in a wide variety of school settings, but as Fauci observes, advisories ensure equity by ascertaining that no student can slip by unnoticed. She went on to note:

> [Advisories are] a place that every student has. At its best, it ensures equity for every student, because every student has a person to connect to. Now, of course, the training and everything else is the crux of really seeing that equity. But when you think of equity in terms of a comprehensive high school or even a small high school, if you don't have advisory . . . it's the one sort of leveling place where we're saying, "Every student has the same opportunity to ___," and then you fill in the blank. Because if you want to achieve your outcomes, you have to remember that we're talking about outcomes for all kids. We're not talking about outcomes or a mission for some kids.

Much of what happens in advisories is focused and practical. Advisors often work with students' other teachers to coordinate project schedules. Advisors help students find internships for service-learning or community service requirements. Advisors coordinate family meetings at which students, their families, and their teachers can meet to discuss student progress. Advisors often serve as college counselors, a role that is explored at more length in Chapter Nine. Advisories play a powerful role in ensuring academic success; much of the power of advisories to affect student learning and achievement resides in the work of building relationships and community among participants. CES schools find advisories, coupled with inquiry and evaluation processes to determine whether a school's advisories are meeting specific goals (Makkonen, 2004), to be indispensable both for their part in the fundamental work of making sure that students are known well and as ground zero for much of the rest of the work that students need to do as they work their way through school. For more information and suggestions on advisory programs, see "Resources for Creating Strong Advisory Programs" sidebar.

Resources for Creating Strong Advisory Programs

Wildwood School's *The Advisory Toolkit,* a forty-five-minute DVD and accompanying four-hundred-page workbook that detail how to plan and implement an effective advisory program in middle schools and high schools, is distributed by Wildwood School Outreach Center. More information is available at http://www.wildwood.org/outreach/.

Educators for Social Responsibility (ESR) also provides valuable resources on advisories. Much of ESR's advisory material has been collected in Rachel A. Poliner and Carol Miller Lieber's *The Advisory Guide: Designing and Implementing Effective Advisory Programs in Secondary Schools* (Poliner and Lieber, 2004).

Looping is another way that teachers in CES schools create and maintain strong relationships with students. Looping is a practice in which educators stay with a cohort of students for several years. In some schools, it is just the advisors who follow their students for more than one year, while in others, the academic teachers stay with the students. In this way, schools can ensure that all the hard work that teachers do in getting to know both their students and their families can deepen over several years, reaping added benefits. The Met's Kim Barsamian looped with her students for all of their four years and then started again with a new ninth-grade advisory that included several younger siblings of her graduated students. She got to know practically everything about her students and developed meaningful and productive relationships with their families as well.

Staff Members Who Play Multiple Roles

Practices such as advisories influence a school's culture. In addition to strengthening relationships among students and between students and teachers, advisories affect the ways that a school chooses to allocate staff members' time and responsibilities. For example, some schools ask that all staff, from the custodian to the office manager, interact substantively with students in one way or another. In many small CES schools with limited resources, the money that traditionally would be used for a guidance counselor might support an additional teacher instead, and all teachers might be asked to double as advisors who provide the same kind of academic guidance that a counselor would.

Another CES Common Principle, summarized as "Commitment to the entire school," informs the design of many schools. The principle states, "The principal and teachers should perceive themselves as generalists first (teachers and scholars in general education) and specialists second (experts in but one particular discipline). Staff should expect multiple obligations (teacher-counselor-manager) and a sense of commitment to the entire school." The focus is on teachers being teachers of students rather than of their disciplines and asks that they approach their teaching interdisciplinarily as well as serve as advisors. For example, all teachers might teach reading and writing through their subject area or help students prepare their exhibitions in different disciplines. The school provides the sort of professional development described in Chapter Six in order to support these multiple obligations. The collective needs of the school determine the roles that individual teachers play.

Clear Values for Which the School Stands

A positive, democratic, mission-driven school culture reinforces commitments to the school. As well, it creates equity, reinforces the value of every individual in the school community, acts as a buffer and anchor during times of stormy change, and reminds the school community to seek to improve constantly during times of calm and happiness. Many school practices in Essential schools are geared to ensure that the school maintains and improves its culture of learning and sense of community. Important to that culture is commitment to the CES Common Principle called "Goals apply to all students." The full principle states, "The school's goals should apply to all students, while the means to these goals will vary as those students themselves vary. School practice should be tailor-made to meet the needs of every group or class of students." "Goals apply to all students" is inextricably connected to the "Democracy and equity" principle; all students should benefit from appropriate support and high expectations that they will graduate from high school and be successful in college and beyond. Goals apply to all students with the explicit understanding that educators must work with each student differently in order to achieve those goals. Equity does not mean that everyone gets the same. It means that everyone gets what they uniquely need.

Eagle Rock School and Professional Development Center, a CES Mentor School and CES affiliate center located in Estes Park, Colorado, is unique for many reasons, not the least of which is that it is a residential program. Most of its students did not experience success in previous schools. When they come to Eagle Rock, they find themselves in a school that invests a significant amount of time in deliberately nurturing itself as a learning community. Eagle Rock has spent a great deal of time planning and reflecting on its school practices and their effect on culture. Associate director of professional development Dan Condon comments on how the school emphasizes students as necessary partners in school governance. "We use an assets-based community development model (see sidebar) that helps us to recognize that students have as much to offer in terms of leadership and governance at Eagle Rock as our staff." Opportunities to hear students' voices, Condon says, are

> intentionally built into the governing structures of the school. We are building the students' capacity to exercise leadership for justice, so when they sit in on staff meetings and they help hire new staff, their student voice is very important. When students have the ability to really own their experience and take responsibility for their actions inside and outside of the classroom, that can make all the difference. Focusing on the gifts, talents, and assets of students at Eagle Rock allows for leveling of the playing field for our most disenfranchised students. Rather than focusing on what they don't know or aren't good at, we are able to start with what they bring to the table. And to believe that each and every student has something to offer, regardless of circumstance or ability, can really shift things.

In many schools in the CES Small Schools Network, staff members create a set of values or principles that the school is based on and to which all members of the community adhere, as discussed in Chapter Four. Providing young people with these guideposts creates a sense of belonging and accountability that minimizes disruptive behavior. In the event that students or the adults violate the agreed-upon norms, the schools have mechanisms in place to address the individual violations. At times, these values are articulated as habits of mind and heart, and the community-related norms are mostly expressed as the habits of heart. In some schools, teachers facilitate students in the development of their own norms or covenants as well.

At Humanities Preparatory Academy, a CES Mentor School in New York City, the school's Core Values inform all aspects of its program and structures. Humanities Prep's Core Values are

- Respect for humanity
- Respect for diversity
- Respect for the intellect
- Respect for the truth
- Commitment to peace
- Commitment to justice
- Commitment to democracy

Asset-Based Community Development

Dan Condon, associate director of professional development at Eagle Rock, is on the Leadership Practice faculty with Pastor Damon Lynch from Cincinnati, Ohio's New Prospect Baptist Church. (Leadership Practice is a partnership between Public Allies, Inc., and Northwestern University's Asset Based Community Building Institute.) Instead of focusing on all the reasons that have caused students to find success elusive in their previous school settings, Condon and his Eagle Rock colleagues take an asset-based community development approach, using a capacity inventory that was developed by the New Prospect Baptist Church. Rather than asking students what they did to get kicked out of school or have a strained relationship with a parent (or the dozens of other deficiencies that could be talked about), they focus on gifts, skills, and dreams, in order to have a conversation that gains strength from building on previous successes and interests in order to move students forward. These inventories have been used in classes, clubs, advisories, and within Eagle Rock residential houses to build community and to find a direction based on decency and trust.

Sample Capacity Inventory Questions

Gifts: Gifts are abilities that we are born with. We may develop them, but no one has to teach them to us.

What positive qualities do people say you have?

Who are the people in your life that you give to? How did you give to them?

When was the last time that you shared with someone else? What was it that you shared?

What do you give that makes you feel good?

Skills: Sometimes we have talents that we've acquired in everyday life, such as cooking and fixing things.

What do you enjoy doing?

If you could start a business, what would it be?

If you could learn about anything, what would it be?

What do you like to do that people would pay you to do?

Have you ever made anything? Have you ever fixed anything?

Dreams: Before we finish up our conversation, I want to take a minute and hear about your dreams—these goals you hope to accomplish.

What are your dreams?

If you could snap your fingers and be doing anything, what would it be?

Students discuss the values in advisories as well as classes, and students are celebrated for embodying the values. This articulation and constant reinforcement of the Core Values shape the school's community. The more clearly a school identifies its values and links its structures and practices to these values, the more completely they will permeate the life and culture of the school.

Rituals and Celebrations

Every school has traditions and rituals that help define the school and build community. All schools celebrate students in different ways, establishing and reinforcing messages about what is important. Often, these celebrations are limited exclusively to academic performance and athletic accomplishments. While these are obviously important, many CES schools recognize other aspects of their students' success and also seek to find ways to acknowledge the contributions of all students rather than singling out only a few. These celebrations can occur through awards ceremonies, advisories, community meetings, graduations, and exhibitions of student work.

Humanities Prep has created a way for educators and students to recognize school community members' respect for the school's Core Values. Teacher leader Maria Hantzopoulos describes the process:

> We have Core Value awards at the end of each [interim] ceremony [scheduled at regular intervals during the school year]. And then to give you a sense of how that's done, students in advisory nominate other students. They'll say, "I think Joey Smoey should get [the award for] respect for humanity, because he did this, this, and this." And you can only talk positively. We have tough guidelines. You can't trash someone. And then what we do is we collect all the names that advisories generated, and as a staff, we narrow it down. You're getting strong commitments for humanity; you're getting emerging voice. People really aspire to get those.

Humanities Prep handles such standard graduation components as valedictorian and salutatorian according to its values, inviting students with the top ten grade point averages to apply for the honors via written statements, which are evaluated on a rubric that evaluates commitment to the school's Core Values. At the Met in Providence, the notion of valedictorian is also adjusted to meet the school's values. At the Met, every graduating senior delivers a valedictory address, with testimony from advisors, mentors, friends, and family. While this practice is clearly time-intensive, it shines a spotlight on each student, demonstrating how the goals of the school truly apply to them all.

As a result of a decline in acceptances to four-year colleges and universities, Young Women's Leadership Charter School, a CES Mentor School in Chicago, developed Flower Power, a ritual to celebrate college acceptances, in which three to four times in the second half of the school year, all school activity stops and college-accepted seniors receive flowers from juniors and public accolades from the school community. Young Women's Leadership Charter School's Adelric McCain comments, "One of the explicit realities that make small schools so great is that you can create a ritual to support your students easily. It doesn't take that much to see and then socialize an issue in order to say, 'We celebrate you all.'" McCain credits Flower Power, in combination with changes in advising and college counseling, with elevating college acceptance rates. "You can talk curriculum all day," observes McCain. "How are we supporting students in other ways?"

Community Meetings

Many CES schools have community meetings that take place on a regular basis, whether daily, weekly, or monthly. These meetings are a place to connect as an entire school community, to address issues that the school is facing, to celebrate accomplishments, to appreciate the contributions of students and staff, to give everyone an opportunity to share their opinions and voice, and to build the sense of the school as a community. For example, the Met holds community meetings three times a week: on Monday and Wednesday mornings, which are called *Pick Me Ups,* and on Friday afternoons, which are called *Kick Me Outs.* Advisor Kim Barsamian explains that at the Friday Kick Me Outs, "Anyone can shout out somebody who'd done something great during the week." The rest of the time is spent with something fun, like a slide show of an advisory trip or a speaker. On one occasion, a comedy troupe that one of the students belonged to came in to perform. Barsamian states, "It's a good way to end the week. Everybody's happy, and they just lock the door, and it feels good. I think the kids like that."

In addition to fun and celebratory activities, community meetings can be a place to address serious issues such as theft or drug use, for students to apologize to the community for wrongdoing, or for students and staff members to speak to their peers about problems that are affecting them. At Eagle Rock School, schoolwide community meetings occur every weekday. According to Dan Condon, "Community meeting is a very intentional way to build our learning community." Michael Soguero, director of professional development at Eagle Rock School, extends that thinking, providing three reasons why Eagle Rock makes daily community meetings a priority: "Rituals are essential to building community; having a predictable time and place where we are assured of seeing everyone provides a daily reminder that we are a community, and if something of an urgent nature comes up, we have a place to address it. We wouldn't need to invent some special meeting" (Coalition of Essential Schools, 2007). The entire school gathers around the hearth in the school's lodge at eight in the morning. Any staff member or student can sign up to lead a ten-minute program on a topic of their choice. Community meeting is a space in which issues in the community can be discussed and processed and in which everyone can participate and practice leadership. In addition, Eagle Rock's community meeting is a place for people to grow and learn in multiple ways. In the community meeting, status differences between educators and students are intentionally minimized, allowing everyone to engage in learning. An example of how a school creates and models a learning community for youth and adults alike, Eagle Rock's community meetings are one way that that the school situates everyone in the school as a learner.

At both Humanities Preparatory Academy, a CES Mentor School, and James Baldwin High School, the new school that it created within the CES Small Schools Project, community meetings are a place to practice discourse. James Baldwin principal Elijah Hawkes explains how the Humanities Prep students who came to James Baldwin as founding students modeled their community meetings: "Town meeting, of course, is the whole-school assembly where those students can teach the other students about what it means to have a meaningful, respectful discussion as a whole school. [Former Humanities Prep students] modeled and corrected their peers, and it was very powerful to see them rise to that occasion and to see them so effectively transmit what they knew from Humanities Prep into the new school more effectively than teachers can in many ways."

Positive Discipline and Restorative Justice Practices

Student discipline is a hot topic in most schools. Unfortunately, traditional schools, mirroring our society's approach to justice in general, tend to focus on punishment rather than resolution or restoration. CES schools, which focus on students as individuals, are more concerned with helping young people learn from their mistakes, grow from challenging experiences, and, perhaps, make amends to the larger community, as opposed to the more simplistic concept of punishment. This restorative approach reflects a proactive, positive stance on supporting the values of the school community. When problems arise, as they inevitably do, the groundwork is laid for reaffirming the positive school culture that has been established rather than sorting out the "good" students from the "bad" and, ultimately, pushing students out.

The CES Common Principle "A tone of decency and trust," stated at the start of this chapter, underpins any conversation about restorative justice. The ways that a school deals with any violations of its principles and values goes hand in hand with the ways it establishes and emphasizes those principles in the first place. The more intentional the development of a positive school culture has been, the easier it is to create community norms and help students live up to those norms. One of the best examples of how a school community creates positive norms and helps students embrace them is the Fairness Committee at Humanities Prep. Teacher Maria Hantzopoulos describes it: "Fairness is a kind of more democratic way of looking at discipline in school. If someone violates a community norm, one of the core values, you can take that person to Fairness and have a more structured discussion around it." Anyone in the school community can take anyone else to Fairness Committee: a student can take a student, a teacher can take a student, a student can take a teacher, or an individual can take herself or himself. The Fairness Committee comprises a changing mix of students and teachers, some familiar with the incident at hand, some not. For example, a student who was being disruptive in class—ignoring a teacher's request by refusing to put his headphones away—was taken to Fairness Committee by the teacher for violating respect for the intellect, one of Humanities Prep's Core Values. Patrick, a Humanities Prep student, served as a student member of the Fairness Committee that handled this incident and relates what happened: "First, the Fairness Committee members asked the student to talk about why he was being disruptive in the first place. They found out that the student had had a terrible thing happen to him the night before. In the end, everyone signed a contract, and part of it was for the student to seek support from his advisor and our social worker to cope with the things going on in his life that might be throwing him off."

Writing about Fairness Committee in the journal *Rethinking Schools,* Hantzopoulos (2006) observes,

> The fairness committee models a deeper form of democracy, one that is as inclusive as possible. By allowing for the multiple perspectives of the community to be a part of the process, we dismantle hierarchical impositions of truth. Most importantly, it brings in the voices of the students, who are often marginalized from such processes. In traditional school settings, students do not necessarily have the opportunity to address concerns or issues in an organic and respectful way. This method of bringing members of the community together validates students as thinkers and decision makers, and reinforces the idea that they have a stake and voice in their communities.

As educators who are situated in structural positions of power, processes like fairness force us to take risks that challenge our positions of privilege. We have to believe that the process will yield something that is better, to put our trust in the group and respect the voices that are present at the table. Student buy-in, feedback, and action are essential in making our school move toward democracy, where people all are respected. Without ways to authentically develop this, we are just paying lip service to democratic ideals.

Not all CES schools have structures that resemble Humanities Prep's Fairness Committee, but all view discipline not as a set of rules developed by adults and imposed on young people but rather as a community-developed set of expectations and norms that values individual students and works with them as they face their challenges. Not all students make it through CES schools, even with extensive counseling and support, but many more are able to find their way than in more typically rigid and authoritative structures.

Strong and Positive Connections with Families

Particularly on the secondary level, many schools struggle to find ways to connect meaningfully with students' families. As discussed in Chapter Eight, exhibitions and performance assessments are an opportunity for CES schools to include families in meaningful ways during important moments of students' lives. During exhibitions, family members are asked to view, celebrate, and, sometimes, evaluate their children's work. Most Essential schools also take a systematic and in-depth approach to parent-teacher conferences. For example, at ARISE High School, each student meets with his or her advisor and parent or guardian for a half hour to an hour twice a year to discuss the student's progress. These student-led conferences are an opportunity for the advisor, the student, and the parent or guardian to discuss the students' strengths and weaknesses.

At ARISE, advisors make home visits to their advisees' families at the beginning of the school year. Trained in a model provided by Oakland Community Organizations, advisors use these visits to build relationships with the families outside of the confines and without the negative associations that often come with being contacted by or asked to come into schools. ARISE staff are encouraged to do the visits at the beginning of the year, before any issues come up—and even before there is any academic progress to report—so that the focus can be exclusively on building relationships with the families and hearing their hopes, fears, and expectations for their children. Advisors at ARISE stay with their students for all four years, so these relationships can continue to grow and help to support students' progress in multiple ways. When issues do come up, family members and school staff have already been talking, so there is a foundation of trust to draw on when collaborating to solve problems and help a student move forward.

Even when there is good communication between educators and students' families, sometimes students struggle with conflicting expectations from school and from their family and neighborhood. Long, demanding days at school can take students away from obligations to work or responsibilities of caring for younger siblings or older family members, a tension that many families and young people struggle with. School demands can force students to make choices between participating at school and joining in on what's happening in their neighborhood or connecting with peers who may be less invested in school and who may be a powerful distraction. As students and their families struggle with these conflicts and choices, educators need to use the strong relationships that they have built in order to support students through these conflicts. Conversation and conflict resolution in regard to these issues can happen in teacher-parent-student conferences, in one-on-one conversations, and in advisories.

Including family members in the life of a school requires educators to be aware of and responsive to issues pertaining to the family's race, ethnicity, culture, economic status, or language. In Chapter Seven, we discuss the role of culturally relevant pedagogy in personalization and enhanced learning. Culturally competent relationships with students' family members are equally important. School staff members must be able to speak families' home languages or have regular access to translators (not the students themselves) in order to communicate. School staff members need to be thoughtful about how to establish trust with family members who may be beset with anxiety about immigration status. And school staff members must be sensitive to and willing to work around families members' work schedules. Other, less practical barriers, such as distrust or misunderstanding between people of differing economic status or racial backgrounds, may be present. With strong support from school, regular outreach, and a shared mission—the success of the young people in their care—educators and family members can and regularly do surmount these challenges.

Nontraditional School Schedules

All of the building blocks of creating the kinds of schools described in this book require a different way of thinking about how time is organized. For example, for teaching that emphasizes "less is more" and depth over coverage, forty-minute periods are not enough to even get started, nor can they support authentic project-based learning. Extended blocks of instructional time, common planning time for teachers, time for advisories, time for service learning or internships, and time for community meetings are essential in order to support the interplay of strong school culture and strong academics. The block schedule from ARISE High School (shown in the sidebar) illustrates how long blocks of time can be used for deeper, longer instruction in fewer subjects per day.

CES schools toss out the traditional high school model of beginning with a huge—and hugely limiting—master schedule grid, allowing the important values of a school to guide its structures instead of letting the structures shape its program. Along with a schedule like this come limits, of course. Many CES schools offer fairly few electives, for example, in keeping with the CES Common Principle "Less is more." Longer class blocks allow instructors to bring in additional material, and personalization allows students to pursue their passions in ways that make such limits far less onerous in practice than they may seem from outside.

The commitment to grouping students heterogeneously—keeping students of different skill levels and learning abilities together in one classroom—strongly affects school scheduling (as well as other key issues, such as teacher training). Addressed in more depth in Chapter Seven, mixed-ability groups are critical to creating equitable schools, and they require extensive professional development for teachers as well as ongoing support and inquiry to help them teach with differentiation in order to address the multiple needs of a varied group of students. The commonplace practice of tracking students according to narrow perceptions of their skills and abilities has largely served to exacerbate the inequities of class and racial discrimination in schools. In tracked schools, the college-bound tracks often are mainly populated by white and affluent students, while the "general education" curricula disproportionately serve students of color and low-income students. In accordance with the CES Common Principle "Goals apply to all students," CES schools commit to preparing all of their students for college and successful lives beyond.

ARISE High School Tenth-Grade Schedule

Time	Schedule	Monday	Schedule	Tuesday	Schedule	Wednesday	Schedule	Thursday	Schedule	Friday	Time
8:45–9:40	8:45 - 10:15	Community Meeting	8:45 - 9:45	Advisory	8:45 - 9:45	Advisory	8:45 - 9:45	Advisory	8:45 - 9:45	Advisory	8:45–9:40
9:45–10:10					9:45 - 10:45	Block 1					9:45–10:10
10:15–10:25	10:15- 10:30	Advisory	9:45 - 11:40	Block 1			9:45 - 11:40	Block 1	9:45 - 11:40	Block 1	10:15–10:25
10:30–11:00	10:30 - 12:15	Block 1			10:45 - 11:45	Block 2					10:30–11:00
11:05–11:35											11:05–11:35
11:40–12:05			11:40 - 12:25	Lunch	11:45 - 12:45	Block 3	11:40 - 12:25	Lunch	11:40 - 12:25	Lunch	11:40–12:05
12:15–12:40	12:15 - 12:45	Lunch									12:15–12:40
12:45–1:10					12:45 - 1:15	Lunch					12:45–1:10
1:15–2:00	12:45 - 2:30	Block 2	12:25 - 2:20	Block 2			12:25 - 2:20	Block 2	12:25 - 2:20	Block 2	1:15–2:00
2:05–3:05											2:05–3:05
3:10–4:10	2:30 - 4:15	Block 3	2:20 - 4:15	Block 3	1:15 - 5:15	Professional Development/ Teacher Planning	2:20 - 4:15	Block 3	2:20 - 4:15	Block 3	3:10–4:10
4:15–4:35											4:15–4:35
4:35–5:15	4:15 - 5:15	Extended Day	4:15 - 5:15	Extended Day			4:15 - 5:15	Extended Day			4:35–5:15

Note: Students rotate among Spanish, Physics, and Humanities in blocks 1, 2, and 3.

Source: ARISE High School, 2009.

Conclusion

School practices and school culture are the bedrock on which a school community establishes the conditions and context for equitable student learning and achievement. While virtually anything that occurs during the school day, week, and year can be defined as a school practice, it is the intentionality of practices and how well they reflect a school's mission, vision, and values that make the difference. By employing practices such as those described in the sidebar "Essential Practices for Building a Positive School Culture," our schools can be places of safety where students of all stripes are given the space to discover who they are, take risks, and find their potential; where students are nurtured and supported in academic achievement; and where all students are learning, growing, and experiencing success, regardless of the neighborhood they live in, the color of their skin, or how much money their family members make. Our actions and decisions matter. Daily structures, practices, and decisions have the power to influence the community of a school and, ultimately, how well it will take care of and serve the children in its charge.

Essential Practices for Building a Positive School Culture

- Institute articulated and reinforced community values and norms.
- Advisories are a key structure for making sure that every student is known well by at least one adult. Make sure that advisories meet often enough and that enough time is dedicated to them (in terms of training, planning, and implementation) for them to work.
- Organize school schedules to provide significant blocks of time for classes, advisories, community meetings, and teacher planning.
- Create rituals and celebrations that recognize and acknowledge all students.

- Create a positive discipline and restorative justice system that reinforces community norms and values and emphasizes restoration and growth rather than punishment.
- Build in ways to meaningfully connect with students' families.

Strategies for Sustainability

> Go far enough, quickly enough, so you can't
> go back.
>
> —Ted Sizer

Small Schools, Big Ideas' final chapter reviews our central arguments and examples through the lens of sustainability, examining the principles and practices common to Essential schools that have experienced long-term durability and success. In these pages, we have made the case that the work of changing schools changes lives in transformative ways. As we have frequently emphasized, everyone devoted to transforming our schools—educators, district officials, policymakers, students, family members, committed citizens, elected officials—must have both the will to work hard for that transformation and the necessary skills to do that work. The skills or key areas of focus needed to build sustainability in schools that are devoted to implementing the CES Common Principles are

- Securing a commitment to CES Common Principles, mission, and vision
- Cultivating a professional learning community
- Preparing for leadership and staff transitions
- Building a sense of ownership
- Building partnerships

- Working to create supportive district and policy conditions
- Creating a power base: outreach, branding, and advocacy
- Securing funding and resources
- Participating in networks

Securing a Commitment to CES Common Principles, Mission, and Vision

It is important to remind ourselves that we do this work for our children and their future. For far too many of them, particularly children of color, that future is more likely to be behind bars than in institutions of higher learning. That bleak prospect doesn't demoralize us but instead urges us to act. In fact, we are hopeful, inspired by a stirring awakening of the forces of change. In education, this stirring has been seen in the growing resistance to No Child Left Behind, demands for adequate funding, and calls for more meaningful assessments. Real change requires our active involvement. We must all join the movement to transform schools and change lives. A relentless focus on equity and an understanding of the capacities and qualities that schools designed to effectively educate students for the twenty-first century must possess are the key elements of that transformation. A strong commitment to equity allows educators and others to develop a vision of schools and school systems that are prepared to support all learners, allowing them to emerge from schooling and into the next phase of their life knowing how to use their minds well and with the skills that twenty-first-century work, citizenship, and relationships with others demand. Without this equity stance, those who want to change schools are unfocused and so in their attempts to improve schools and school systems, they replicate the status quo through reinforcement of inequitable structures and attitudes, as discussed in Chapter Two and throughout the text. A scattershot approach to improving student outcomes all too often leads to reform fatigue, the result of schools, districts, states, and federal education policy changing direction so frequently that no restructuring effort has the opportunity to take root and produce results. Often, schools try many avenues of change at once, resulting in stagnation. Former Quest High School principal Lawrence Kohn observes, "A big mistake when doing school reform is trying too many cool things. But when you start what a lot of people describe as 'Christmas tree reform,' you really get fragmented and suffer from a sense of directionlessness and floating around." Changes, whether incremental or radical, crash over schools endlessly; the frequent response from stakeholders in the school community is to become inured to reform efforts, put their head down, and plug along until the next new thing comes along.

Transformational efforts must focus vigilantly on maintaining and evolving the core of what defines an Essential school: student-centered teaching and learning; commitment to demonstration of mastery; democratically focused, distributed leadership; and school practices and culture that support equitable, personalized, and academically rigorous schools. Sustainability requires valuing both the means (the ways that a school is run and the quality of the relationships and the actions undertaken to carry out its mission and vision) and the ends (student achievement and meaningful success). A small school's plan for sustainability means that it will be less likely to lose focus and succumb to mission drift. Those who have worked over many years in and with Essential schools observe that such schools face a real danger of getting sucked into the system of their district or otherwise straying, at first in imperceptible degrees, from their vision and mission. Dan French, executive director of the Center for Collaborative Education, a CES affiliate center charged with coordinating the Boston Pilot School Network, believes that a commitment to principles should be a non-negotiable for sustained success. Reflecting on the accomplishments of the Boston Pilot Schools over their first ten years, French comments, "One of the hallmarks of high-performing schools that are successful over time is a community united around a common vision. Once you have that common vision, then you can hire staff who all embrace the vision of the school. Being mission-driven is central to the Pilots' concept, and it needs principles that you espouse or embrace."

For long-term survival, schools need this commitment to principles such as the CES Common Principles to keep them on course. However, commitment to principle—which can be defined as will—is absolutely necessary but not enough. Schools also need the right conditions to do the hard work of advocacy and resistance in order to stick to their principles, as well as the skills to do that difficult work. Deborah Meier's analysis of the drift of Central Park East Secondary School (CPESS) powerfully illustrates the ways in which mission drift can occur even at a nationally celebrated example of a transformative small school. Meier and others founded CPESS in New York City's East Harlem neighborhood as an outgrowth of a small network of elementary schools that she had started.

Because her vision was radically at odds with the more typical large comprehensive high schools in New York in the mid-1980s, Meier cultivated relationships with city and state policymakers to obtain waivers for the number of hours a student must sit in classes as measured by Carnegie units, the basic high school graduation requirements in New York State at that time. Meier and her colleagues developed an alternative system of standards that students were required to reach that corresponded with the state's curricular requirements. This requirement of a certain level of performance—as demonstrated by exhibitions and other demonstrations of mastery—seems familiar now but at that time was radically different and profoundly transformative.

Meier achieved her goals for CPESS through a variety of factors: state waivers, strong relationships with local officials in New York City's Department of Education, a robust professional learning community among the school's educators, her own unparalleled ability to advocate for children and the sort of schooling that best supports their learning and development, and strong outside allies that included Ted Sizer, CES's founder. Sizer served as a nationally known and well-respected advocate for CPESS's mission and vision, and Meier built CPESS into powerful proof of the results that can be achieved by creating a school that lives and breathes the CES Common Principles.

Yet within ten years of its founding, CPESS drifted, losing its strong emphasis on performance-assessed multidisciplinary learning, its fierce emphasis on personalization, its fertile professional learning community, and much else that had made it effective and inspirational. CPESS still exists as a "fairly small traditional high school," according to Meier's description, but is no longer a CES member school, no longer regarded as exemplary, and no longer produces the results for students that it once did.

Meier states, "CPESS's demise was due to poor leadership plus outside pressure from the system." Many of its founders, Meier included, left CPESS, inspired by its success to found new small schools and to take on new opportunities to transform the greater educational landscape. This exodus coincided with the New York City Board of Education's push to increase the school's size from four hundred to five hundred, a move that CPESS's new leadership did not resist effectively and that increased the number of new teachers the school needed to hire. In order to cope,

CPESS made changes such as eliminating time for advisories and separating math and science instruction, which had previously been taught interdisciplinarily. "We would have survived if we had thought more carefully about the amount of teachers leaving at the same time, but we urged people to leave and embark on new ventures," reflects Meier. "We robbed Peter to pay Paul; it was an unwise decision."

At the same time, CPESS also had to contend with new demands that the school follow New York State's Regents curriculum. The school's leadership and staff were too immersed in the school's day-to-day work to fight this threat, and previously cultivated relationships with advocates and people within the system that Meier describes as "godfathers" who could have supported the school community as it stood its ground had eroded. "Some of those ties that are not institutional but personal had that risk," says Meier. "It was important to have, and we depended on them, but we had to keep making new ones." Meier reflects that this experience demonstrated that a school pushing against the system needs more than good friends in the system and informal agreements. It needs policies that will help defend it against inevitable changes in the larger educational climate. "This demonstrates how much harder it is to prevent it from happening when you have no official agreement for autonomy," says Meier. "There are a lot of advantages in making sure that you're not dependent entirely on the system that you're in."

Meier's account of CPESS's shift away from its mission and vision emphasizes the need for a school to find ways to frequently accentuate and widely distribute statements about its culture and identity. CPESS's loss of advisory time and loss of faculty meetings translated into lost opportunities for school community members to discuss and debate who they were, what they were about, and the ways they got their work done. Schools' statements of principles, purpose, and identity need to live not only inside people's minds and hearts but also externally through regular, structured discussion; leadership by example; and a school culture capable of transmitting values. With a strong commitment to principles and the necessary work of deeply understanding and developing and adapting school practices that support those principles, a school is far less likely to lose its way, its commitment to its mission and vision, and the community-developed habits and practices that made it a special place at the outset; for more on this type of commitment to principles, see the sidebar "Recommendations for Sustainability from Lehman Alternative Community School."

Recommendations for Sustainability from Lehman Alternative Community School

Dave Lehman is the founding principal of Lehman Alternative Community School (LACS) in Ithaca, New York. Lehman led LACS for thirty years, retiring in 2004 to become a coach for the National School Reform Faculty and a consultant and coach for CES small schools. LACS, named for Lehman after decades of service, is a member of the New York Performance Standards Consortium and a longtime CES affiliate that has fought the battle of sustaining itself as an Essential school. Here, Lehman shares his assessment of the key elements of developing a sustainable Essential school.

Revisiting beliefs. If we want ownership and renewal, we need to build in time to take out our belief statements, revisit them, and ask, "Is this still what we're about?" At one point, when we'd moved into our current location, students painted the school's belief statements on large four-by-eight panels and mounted them in the gym. When you come into the gym for lunch, all-school meetings, or physical activity, there are constant reminders. Two years ago, a belief statement was added about educating for sustainability as a result of a process that got parents involved. A subcommittee formed and brought suggestions to all-school meetings. The idea is not to redo the beliefs constantly; they are underlying elements that have stayed the test of time. Being willing to revisit them in a real way doesn't mean that we're suddenly dramatically going to change to a whole other radical approach to teaching, but it does mean that there is a healthy openness to revisiting.

Everyone has a voice. The goal is for everyone to have a voice, for people to feel they have a voice in their education; for teachers to have a voice in what they're teaching, what their day, week, and year look like; for students to have a voice in learning and what their time looks like. Ensuring that everyone has a voice exemplifies the power of full participation in democratic school governance; it brings in the dimension of equity and democracy described by the "Democracy and equity" Common Principle. Back in the late 1980s and early 1990s, LACS students said that the school needed a constitution. "Fine; form a committee, and write one," we said. They did so for a year and a half, meeting weekly and creating drafts. Eventually, some African American staff members said, "We have a hard time relating to the word *constitution,* so if this is something we can own and be a part of, we need to look at different wording." So the name changed to the *Decision-Making Document.* It spells out the processes by which voice is heard and decisions are made in the school. Everyone at the school signed it. Part of the document sets forth the weekly all-school meetings run by students. There are also committees that meet twice a week, such as the building and grounds committee; a recycling committee; and the LACS Café committee, a group of students working with the cook, who is an LACS alumnus, to make breakfast and lunch. Students share in the whole ownership of the school, including a student court that handles issues of a behavioral nature. Family groups, which is what we call advisories, are also a place for everyone to have a voice; they are the place to engage in personal contact and really come to know each other. Student voice is central to all other aspects of the school, including the approach to teaching and learning. When students are involved in running the school, they experience ownership and the school community experiences a sense of renewal.

Staff culture. It's vitally important to bring staff on board by finding opportunities for voices to be heard and to have real expectations for them to be thinking and engaged in conversations about how to improve our own teaching practices so that we're approaching even more effectively the work of educating all of our students for their full potential. This emphasizes the importance of having not too many new staff come in at any given time; you need a critical mass of those who carry the history and the culture forward so it keeps enveloping new staff. Once a week, LACS staff gathered in someone's home for a support meeting. There was no business; it was largely a check-in with everyone, an opportunity to consciously stop and take time to ask, "How are we doing personally?" We created different structures and mechanisms to give feedback. Sometimes we build in space for that during staff meetings or professional days, but it works better in separate space. As staff got larger, we have continued this practice. It is now once a month, and we break up into two groups that we mix up over the months.

Exhibitions. The mission of the school is to educate global citizens for the twenty-first century. This is a simple mission statement. We can all remember that and don't have to read it. It's a living mission statement at the forefront of our thinking that we have used to identify seven essential qualities of a global citizen [listed at the end of this sidebar]. These seven qualities are our graduation requirements that every student has to demonstrate. How will students demonstrate those, and how will we evaluate whether they have qualities of global citizens? What are the ways students can learn and acquire essential qualities through learning activities, classes, and internships? How can we design the school day, month, and year so those learning opportunities are there in our schedule? The answer lies in individual senior projects that are presented at graduation. Seniors also do a senior team project because we recognize that increasingly, young people as global citizens need to work with others. Seniors demonstrate their work—their mastery of the seven qualities—in their final exhibitions. Years ago, one of the senior teams I worked with (I taught one course each semester and think that every principal should teach) researched and presented about adolescent sleep patterns. They presented their rationale to the Ithaca school board to change the high school start time from eight to nine in the morning. Eventually, the board adopted their work and the district went to 9:00 A.M. start times for all secondary schools. While not all senior exhibitions have such widespread impact, all serve as the mechanism by which we can determine if students are successful in terms of the mission of the school.

Ownership. In the last week in May, we take a full week for spring trips. This began, when LACS was small, with an all-school camping trip. We wanted to engage students to connect with nature and give them the opportunity to go away from home and depend on each other. As the school grew, it was no longer feasible for an all-school camping trip, so we launched a series of spring trips, preceded by planning and fundraising. The trips were cross-country bike trips, canoe trips, hiking trips—trips with physical challenge and group challenge components. Students have gone to Canada, South America, France, and Costa Rica. They've gone to the Akwesasne Freedom School on the Mohawk Nation of Akwesasne land in upstate New York to work with students there.

Students work all year to be part of the trip groups; preparation can be a transformative experience and also a way to bring new people into the community. Every group presents skits, slide shows, PowerPoints, and so on about their trip at the end of the year at all-school meetings.

Building community by community building. In schools, the population is constantly changing. Every three to five years, you have to do something to get everybody back on board (or get them on board for the first time) that really engages people in something beyond our conversations. One way to do this is by constructing a community building. At LACS, we have done this several times, first when we moved into a wing of Ithaca's main high school. This was the opportunity to ask the students, "What would we want to have in our new facility?" Along with staff members and parents, they got involved in different ways to design this new space, move into it, and paint murals. Later, when we grew out of that wing, we moved into a closed elementary school. Again, we asked, "How do we want to redesign this space?" turning, for example, a first-grade classroom into a science room. Parents worked with a group of students one day a week and built a school store. Those projects changed our physical space. A few years later, we created an opportunity to build a yurt as a retreat center in woods outside Ithaca. This engaged all kinds of people and became the school curriculum for a week. A few years later, we built an amphitheater on the school grounds, involving all kinds of people from the community. The idea is to find some way physically to engage people with renewal.

High School Graduation Requirements for Lehman Alternative Community School Global citizens for the twenty-first century are

1. **Community participants and leaders** who work cooperatively with each other, contribute to the community, and explore career possibilities

2. **Communicators** who read, write, listen, and speak in English; listen, speak, read, and write in a language other than English; use the language of math; and use the personal computer

3. **Critical thinkers and problem solvers** who act on and reflect an anti-bias attitude, use different methods of critical thinking and problem solving, and use the processes of conflict resolution

4. **Designers, producers, and performers** who pursue concentrated study in one art area of theater, music, movement, visual arts, media, or technology

5. **Researchers with a historical and multicultural perspective** who understand U.S. history and the processes of democratic government; global studies and multiculturalism; and local, national, and global economics

6. **Contributors to sustaining the natural environment** who know the key concepts of physical, biological, and chemical components of the environment and understand their interrelatedness

7. **Healthy persons** who demonstrate physical fitness, group participation, and the meeting of personal physical challenges, and demonstrate an understanding of concepts of human sexuality and current major health issues (presently AIDS, and substance use and abuse).

Cultivating a Professional Learning Community

Sustainable small schools treat their human resources like renewable resources: they feed, nurture, nourish, and protect their staff members as well as their students. As discussed in depth in Chapter Six, schools with strong professional learning communities have been able to place many key decisions about instruction into the hands of teachers. In such schools, those educators, collaborating with students, families, and other stakeholders, make the key decisions about curriculum, assessment, school culture and practices, and other elements. This scenario, in which those responsible for enacting beliefs about how a school can help students succeed are the ones charged with developing, evaluating, and adjusting their work, differs dramatically from the more usual reform circumstances in which people with power outside a school are able to impose their ideas of how teaching and learning will unfold in that school—a scenario wearily familiar to educators everywhere, especially in urban schools serving children of color.

Former Quest High School co-founder Lawrence Kohn suggests that in addition to a community-developed, fiercely upheld mission, a school's professional learning community is the key to its continued success and fundamental ability to stay true to itself. "Research says that small schools must act like professional learning communities, collaborate, and make decisions about data. What sustains a school is sticking to a vision and not leaving anyone out," says Kohn. Schools that sustain their commitment to the CES Common Principles over time maintain a fierce dedication to their mission and vision, carefully and collaboratively considering their pedagogical and professional development approaches. This requires developing the practice of a cycle of inquiry that looks at the ways that all central design elements and structures of the school affect commitment in practice.

Professional learning communities create structures that help educators in a school community hold themselves accountable and keep themselves focused. Adelric McCain, a teacher at Chicago's Young Women's Leadership Charter School observes, "We ask our students to be rigorous, to increase what they do, and to be intentional. There needs to be alignment between what students are asked to do and what [educators] do. We are getting more deliberate about where we put our time and energy, and the girls have been able to respond positively. Many of the girls who graduated in the first couple of years felt like guinea pigs. Now they can say why we do this or that. They know why the school does certain practices. They can see value of the practices."

McCain also believes that having the time and structures in place for staff members to communicate with each other has allowed the school to take on tough issues—for example, facing the reality that many educators in the school were of different backgrounds from the students, a circumstance that was producing critical challenges to student success: "We were able to socialize an issue that a lot of people knew existed but didn't feel like they knew how to talk about. Conversations were happening in different pockets, but that doesn't help change anything. What is great about being in a small school community is that dialogue is authentic if it is supported. Our existing relationships and learning community helped us put the conversation out on the table. By socializing the problem, we're taking it on as a school. It's not left for one or two people to deal with on their own." McCain reports that having conversations about and across race and other differences focused on students, their work, and what educators could do to support them has produced tangible benefits in student achievement.

Equity-centered professional learning communities are also places of humane renewal. We cannot continue to nurture the idea that this is a thankless job. Essential schools take time to create rituals of celebration and acknowledgment. They make sure to support and acknowledge everyone's growth and contributions. This nurturing aspect is a critical part of successful learning communities. These rituals can be as small as the appreciations that many CES schools build in to the end of all of their meetings, as infrequent as an annual teacher appreciation week, or as significant as a financial bonus. In several CES schools, teachers rotate preparing lunch for each other on a weekly basis as a literal way of nurturing each other. Coming together to provide intellectual and emotional sustenance and renewal is a major goal and benefit of effective learning communities.

Preparing for Leadership and Staff Transitions

How can school communities continue to build ownership when the founders are no longer at the school? As discussed in Chapter Five, leaders who lead for equity work with their school community to distribute leadership. In Providence, Rhode Island, at the Met's Peace Street campus, principal Sonn Sam describes moving into the role of school leader, following founding principal Charlie Plant. Plant treated his role with seriousness but also as a necessarily temporary condition, perceiving at the outset that he would eventually pass leadership on to someone else. When it became clear that Sam was a likely candidate, Plant was explicit and transparent about passing on knowledge to Sam and others in the Peace Street community. Sam believes that this transmission of knowledge was crucial to his ability to take on the role: "Having leaders come from within, groomed or grown or what have you, is probably one the best scenarios that could happen. They know the culture of the school. They know the students, they know the rituals, and they know the ins and outs of the school in a way that outsiders won't be able to know or they will need to learn that along the way."

Maintaining awareness that problems will happen and that people and systems are fallible is difficult yet important. Equally crucial is the work of establishing systems and attitudes that explicitly anticipate challenges and create opportunities both to respond to them and to take advantage of positive developments. Founding Fenway High School headmaster Larry Myatt advises that in order to weather challenges and maintain internal consistency, schools should do everything they can to take away the smoke and mirrors of education and make it clear to everyone how the school runs and why decisions are being made:

> My strategy was to be as transparent as possible and encourage others to do so, too. We would always try to imagine the vision at its best and the fear fantasy at its worst. With every decision we had to make, we'd ask ourselves, "If this went well, if everything kind of materializes, how great is this going to be and where are we going to go with it?" And then ten seconds later, we'd say, "Okay, what if the absolute worst happens?" And that ended up being a really great strategy for every circumstance, with working with kids, working with teachers, and making decisions for future planning. It was part of how the leadership team grew to work in a very transparent way.

Fenway High School's current headmaster, Peggy Kemp, believes that the habits created by a long commitment to distributed leadership helped her make an effective transition into the role of school leader. When she arrived at the school, she recalls, there were three faculty members who had over twenty years of experience at Fenway. "They believed in the school and would support me and also be honest with me if they had a concern about what was happening." Kemp adds, "It meant a lot to have former Fenway headmaster Larry Myatt still in the area, available to meet with me and talk on the phone. It also mattered to be starting as a new leader in a school with such a strong culture, with parents who believed in the school. Parents had children graduate from the school; faculty members had graduated from the school; and they were loyal to the school and believed in what it had done for them. All of that was really critical."

Elijah Hawkes, former teacher at New York City's Humanities Preparatory School and current principal of James Baldwin High School, describes how Humanities Prep planned for its creation of James Baldwin, a new small school supported by the CES Small School Project that grew directly out of Humanities Prep's culture and practices:

> We envisioned that teachers and students currently working and learning at Humanities Prep would be the ones to leave and pioneer the new school. That was something that was going to be a major change for Humanities Prep, and so preparations were made so that it could be as easy a transition as possible to lose both some veteran teachers to the new school project and also some veteran students.

There were some efforts that [Humanities Prep principal] Vince [Brevetti] undertook to increase the number of teachers at the school, so that while we were planning, we could be reduced from some of our classroom teaching responsibilities, that sort of thing. There was a nice confluence of our new school initiative—the support that CES was giving to Prep as a Mentor School in the planning year—and also some leadership development programs that came up in the city at the same time, which allowed several teachers from Prep to engage in a leadership training program that allowed for some influx of some money into the school. We could be relieved from teaching. There were some operational and budgetary adjustments that were made in order to incubate the new school at Prep.

This kind of careful planning allows an existing school to recreate itself, spreading opportunities to more students, without compromising its functioning.

School cultures can be sustained rather than diminished by the process of hiring new teachers, staff members, and school leaders. Bringing new people into a school community provides an opportunity to communicate the school's values and practices. Involving students and family members along with current school staff in key roles in hiring decisions is likely to ensure that the school identifies new community members who will adapt to and thrive in the school's culture. At High Tech High, students work with staff to interview and help hire new teachers. High Tech High student Amelia Pluto liked to participate in the hiring process so she could have a say about what she expected from teachers and who got to teach at the school:

When I was a sophomore, I started interviewing teachers. It was really fun, partly because I got to get out of class, and I really changed the balance of power in the committee. I really liked being able to ask these teachers questions that I wish I could have asked teachers I've had in other schools. It was different having these teachers trying to convince you as to why they should be allowed to teach at your school. And I've met some really great teachers, and then they showed up the next year, and it was kind of like, oh, yeah. I helped make them come here.

As they mature, many Essential schools are able to hire alumni—an opportunity to provide a potent link to the school's core mission and vision. Alumni turned educators also provide that all-important match between students' backgrounds and educators' backgrounds, and their presence reinforces the school's commitment to preparing its graduates for higher education and lifetime success.

Once new staff members are hired, CES schools provide extensive orientation and opportunities for staff bonding, as well as informal and formal ways to mentor new staff. For example, Francis W. Parker Charter Essential School takes care to pair new teachers—or experienced teachers who are new to Parker—with veterans in its team-taught interdisciplinary humanities and math, science, and technology classes. A well-organized professional learning community provides new educators with an opportunity to reflect on what has happened in class and with students, allowing them to learn from and with more experienced colleagues.

Another obvious but important strategy for improving continuity is to create conditions such that staff members are less likely to leave. Dan French, executive director of the Center for Collaborative Education, notes, "Research around new teacher attrition indicates that within three to five years, 50 percent leave the profession due to lack of control and related factors. Teachers are happier when they work in environments where they have greater say about decisions and time to collaborate with colleagues."

Building a Sense of Ownership

Smart efforts to build allies and support from the outset greatly enhance a school's ability to stick to its vision. New or transforming schools need to make sure that key powerful stakeholders are committed to the school so that pressure from many sources can be brought to bear if there are threats to the essential conditions a new small school requires. When the stakeholders who are essential to developing a new or redesigned school—teachers, school leaders, community partners, students, governing board members, district administrators, and the public at large—expect a school to be a certain way and have some power in the decisions that guide its course, they are a powerful force in making sure it stays that way. Schools that accomplish this incorporate students, families, and community members into the design process and keep commitments to give those stakeholders a leading role in making decisions about the school's functioning.

In Chapter Three, we discussed the experience of Richard Alonso, superintendent of Los Angeles Unified School District 4, home of the Belmont Zone of

Choice, a newly formed constellation of schools modeled after and supported by the Boston Pilot Schools. Alonso advocates creating community buy-in and investment to buffer interruptions from administrative changes, and he has worked with the Belmont Educational Collaborative, a grassroots group that drove the creation of the Belmont Zone of Choice, as a partner. Working collaboratively with a community partner "takes longer," says Alonso. "It takes time to listen, but it creates more sustainable results."

Advisory boards and boards of directors can help schools identify and secure partnerships, connections, and resources. Boards are also a way to invite people from outside the realm of public education who may have more resources and more business and civic connections to engage with schools. Kara Bobroff is the founding principal of Native American Charter Academy (NACA) in Albuquerque, New Mexico, a new charter school with a mission to serve Native American students in grades six through twelve. NACA is a participant in the CES Small Schools Project as a new school. Bobroff and her founding colleagues built in both a governing board (the NACA Governing Council) and an advisory board (the NACA Advisors) during the school's initial planning stages, to benefit from advice and to garner significant external support. Bobroff describes the NACA Governing Council: "Each of our seven council members represents some aspect of the school's mission and vision through their role and their profession. It's a really dynamic board, and they're there to support and fulfill the vision of the school."

The NACA Advisors do not play a directing governing role, acting instead as a mechanism to bring in resources and partnerships. Bobroff explains: "There's thirty to forty people talking to you because they offer expertise in areas like curriculum, health and wellness planning, culture and language to where our teachers or myself can call upon them, ask them questions, or they come into the school. They all bring their own area of expertise, and they also embody and serve as role models for our students. We have all the major strengths that our communities draw upon to make this that much more of an enhanced experience for students." NACA Advisors are helping with the school-based health clinic, developing a service-learning program, creating a community garden, bolstering curriculum, and building a physical education and sports program.

A school's governing board is an intermediary protective organization that runs interference between the school and the district administration, representing the school with power and authority and allowing the school to focus on the day-to-day work of teaching and learning. Mike Puelle, an Albuquerque-based communications consultant, works with CES schools, including Amy Biehl High School and NACA. Puelle emphasizes the value of a strong board, saying "Get people from outside the school to help you. One of the values of a board is that you can use those people from the community to help you overcome challenges, people who trust you, whom you trust, and who want you to succeed. They are your link and bridge to the outside world."

The Boston Pilot Schools have enacted Puelle's advice; each pilot school has a board of directors that plays an active role in school governance and decision making. Peggy Kemp adds that Fenway's governing board helped maintain continuity while she made the transition into the school leader role, filling the shoes of founding headmaster Larry Myatt: "The school had a strong governance board, and it had people who had been affiliated with Fenway on that board for over a dozen years. The board brought a strong history and commitment to supporting the school, other adults outside of school walls in [the] community who understood Fenway's evolution and culture [and] were committed to making it succeed."

Building Partnerships

On any given day at NACA, there might be fifteen to twenty extra adults on campus who are not employees of the school. They are VISTA and AmeriCorps volunteers, professors from the University of New Mexico, staff from the First Nations Clinic, and student teachers. Kara Bobroff, the school's principal, credits the NACA Advisors with bringing in significant resources and partnerships that support the school's vision of blending academics with a focus on wellness and Native American culture. In addition to some of the academic support that these partnerships yield, most of the partners also help the school with its wellness and cultural goals. Coming from a wide range of professions and backgrounds, the NACA Advisors help the school tap into a range of resources that enhance the school and its programs.

Schools that are able to sustain their efforts depend on the internal resources that come from their students, staff members, and family members, and they also look beyond the school walls for supportive partnerships. Most CES schools that have been able to continue their success past the first decade have extensive partnerships with other organizations and entities within their community. As

NACA demonstrates, schools collaborate with outside partners and organizations in many ways. Partnerships might be based on academic, political, community, social, or financial connections. Partnerships can provide services for students or teachers, be a source of funding, or help leverage political support. In NACA's case, the wide range of partnerships mirrors the school's mission to serve a wide range of Native American youth. Bringing many organizations together for a single purpose evokes the school's commitment to work with young people from many different tribes and Native backgrounds.

NACA demonstrates how a school can work with multiple organizations. Bobroff describes how the school's partners were initially cultivated and became involved in the design process: "I didn't learn how to think about school differently or education differently until I got outside of the school for a pretty long period of time. In doing the work around the development of the school, I learned what's going on outside of schools, what's going on in the university setting and other settings, and what's going on in a lot of nonprofit and health care organizations that actually serve these families and students. What we learned from that made a lot more sense of how we looked at the questions we were asking ourselves in designing the school." Many of the conversations that were part of the planning phase for NACA ended up translating into the variety of partnerships that now serve the school's students.

The University of New Mexico's Tribal Service Corps is one of NACA's key partners. Ten Tribal Service Corps members work on-site at NACA, running an after-school program that supports NACA's learning philosophy and provides students with enrichment, athletics and intramural sports, tutorials, and opportunities for cultural learning. The Tribal Service Corps members are local Native American undergraduate and graduate students from the University of New Mexico who serve as positive role models for NACA students in order to help them reach their academic, physical, social, emotional, and community goals.

Working to Create Supportive District and Policy Conditions

The very notion of smallness is problematic for districts long used to striving for economies of scale. Yet smallness, though not enough, is a prerequisite condition for the personalized learning environments needed to truly prepare every student for college readiness, work, and citizenship. The ability to create innovative small schools that are flexible enough to respond to the needs of the children they serve requires transformational change at a cultural and policy level. Therefore, districts must create environments that guarantee conducive conditions through clearly articulated policies. We have described the qualities of those conditions in depth in Chapter Three and have offered examples of Essential schools that have established themselves as part of larger networks and systems that share their values and support their practices: the Boston Pilot Schools, the Belmont Zone of Choice, Big Picture Schools, and the network of the New York Performance Standards Consortium, among others.

Discussing data that indicate that small high schools that are not Boston Pilot Schools have made fewer achievement gains than Boston Pilot Schools (Center for Collaborative Education, 2007), Dan French illustrates the fundamental importance of supportive district conditions: "In Boston, the non-Pilot small high schools are hamstrung by district mandates and union constraints. We've seen grievances to the union around advisories as an additional prep, and the district refuses to help those high schools that chose humanities rather than English and history." These experiences underscore the importance of district-guaranteed autonomies and other structures and policies that will last.

NACA's relationship with the Albuquerque Public School District points to a way for charter schools to form partnerships with the districts in which they are located. NACA has a collaborative charter status, which means that the school's charter is granted by both the State of New Mexico and the Albuquerque school district. This arrangement has allowed NACA to work within the district as a charter school and as a partner to the district's efforts. NACA was the first charter school to embark on such an arrangement with the city and has paved the way for the development of other such partnerships that will allow schools to benefit from the autonomy of charter status without having to be completely isolated from the district. "We can't be a community school and not be part of an education community that's been here for a number of years and is probably going to be here for a number of years in the future," says Bobroff. "So for us as a community academy, it didn't make sense to isolate ourselves from the district, the biggest entity that is in the city. NACA can't serve all of the students, but we can do this collaboration work together to inform some practices."

Securing Funding and Resources

The Boston Arts Academy (BAA), a CES Mentor School that is part of the Boston Pilot Schools, raises millions of private dollars to support its mission of providing both an academic and an arts education to its students. Much of BAA's fundraising success is the result of the robust institutional partnerships it has fostered. The Boston Arts Academy Foundation, with a staff of five, arranges partnerships and raises more than a million dollars a year to support the school's programs. BAA's Center for the Arts in Education, which raises money and promotes the school's innovations, serves as a key liaison for nurturing these partnerships. Partners who have contributed money and other resources often become invested in the success and sustainability of the school. With all of the many issues and resource challenges that schools face, having this support network and added investment can be a significant asset.

While external funding is often key to a small school's survival, the existence of such funding opportunities makes it imperative for school communities to keep their eyes on their mission, lest the pursuit of financial support lead them astray. John McKay is principal of Skyview Academy, a new small high school that is part of the Mapleton Public Schools in Colorado. He comments:

> The wonderful thing about the Mapleton school district is that we are unique in moving to the small school initiative as a district. Our superintendent has been very clear that unless the resources meet our school's mission and vision, we won't accept them. Extra money has to support what you're doing. In a time when you have such limited funding for school budgets and when there are cuts everywhere, it seems easy to go after the money, which is out there. You can find and justify resources, but they can easily compromise your mission. We're purposeful with the work that we do in order to maintain our focus. The thing that I love about the Mapleton schools is that they're unrelenting about serving students. If I were to look for external resources, I would go speak with the superintendent and say, "This is what I am thinking about bringing in." She and her executive cabinet would ask questions and provide a filter to see if the money is aligned with our mission and the vision that we're trying to accomplish.

In the past decade, many small schools have been founded with the benefit of grants from U.S. Department of Education Smaller Learning Communities Grants, from the Bill & Melinda Gates Foundation, and other soft money sources, meaning that such funds are not built into state or municipal budgets and are necessarily of limited duration. Therefore, new small schools must have a plan for attaining financial and other resource stability when the advantages, programs, and services that result from such grants conclude. Smaller schools must do so without the economies of scale that keep larger schools afloat, and in many cases, "it generally costs more per student to run a small school than a large one, although the cost per graduate is slightly less" (Miner, 2005).

This need to find new resource streams is a complicating factor on top of an already challenging financial environment for many schools. "Everything in creating good schools is a trade-off in education," says Dan French. "We live in a society where public schools don't get enough money. But if you're vision-driven, you will be more intentional about how to use resources to attain high performance." Sonn Sam, principal of the Met's Peace Street campus, concurs, valuing the autonomy that he and the Peace Street campus's faculty have to make decisions while identifying financial planning as one of his most acute challenges: "You've got to be able to plan for the money. It's very, very important. Some of the challenges that charter schools face are exactly that. They start off very strong, but as the teachers get seasoned, they move up [the pay scale] in steps, and now they're faced with a huge dilemma. You find teachers who really love what they do, and they're there for a while. So they're faced with this very hard decision, you know?" Sam encourages what he describes as "macro-level thinking" and has challenged the staff at the Met's Peace Street campus to take a leadership role in sustaining the school financially:

> In a kind way, I hope, I say to my staff, "Listen, money is always going be an issue, no matter where you're at." I think the Met is at a point now where for the first time, after eleven years, we're starting to feel that. We were cut a half a million [dollars] last year. I'm real with my staff before anything. I try to be as honest as possible. I'll say, "It's reality. We're not protected from that." For us, sustainability means not only getting creative around still being productive as is but also being able to create initiatives to make our school better without

breaking the bank so we can plan to excel in the future. So I've asked the staff to think about an initiative that's missing in the school that they're really passionate about and to figure out how we support that, whether it's bringing someone in to help in that area or writing a grant, you know, to really support the school.

Sam's commitment to charging the Met staff members with addressing sustainability challenges is itself, of course, a sustainability strategy, given its focus on staff members as indispensable problem solvers with responsibility for the fate of the school and the resulting lessened burdens on school leadership. In this scenario, no one is protected or excused, and everyone is a leader.

Creating a Power Base: Outreach, Branding, and Advocacy

CES Mentor School Amy Biehl High School (ABHS) owes much of its existence and subsequent success to its thoughtful partnerships with a range of organizations throughout the city of Albuquerque and the State of New Mexico. These partnerships have helped to establish favorable financial conditions within the state's charter school laws, to create a community college dual-enrollment program, and to win support for the school to move to a historic downtown Albuquerque federal building (Davidson, 2005b). ABHS's move to downtown Albuquerque led to the development of downtown partners such as K&M Resources, a utility company headquartered nearby. K&M employee Larry Smith is on the ABHS board and helps to make the connections between the school and the company to provide internship and service-learning opportunities for students. K&M employees also serve as experts who sit in on exhibition assessment panels. More broadly, by fostering relationships with local businesses such as K&M Resources, ABHS is creating allies external to the school community who believe in its mission and are willing to fight for its right to exist and educate its students in uncommon ways.

Communications consultant Mike Puelle notes, "[The founders of] Amy Biehl realized that they were in the external world whether they liked it or not, so they had to be proactive with communications. People have different values and priorities. You have people who are diligent educators, who want to fulfill the CES principles and start a small school. They need to understand how they are part of a larger environment that can affect them. They need to be proactive and affect their environment."

Former ABHS director Tony Monfiletto comments that new schools have a unique communications advantage: they have a clean slate and are able to define their brand. This opportunity underscores the value of building on community participation in planning a school, as discussed in Chapter Four, by opening the school as often as possible to visitors for a wide variety of purposes, including community members' participation in evaluating students' exhibitions. Deborah Meier concurs with this open-door approach: "It's useful to have lots of visitors. It gives you advocates, makes it possible to bulwark from outside, and encourages staff and students to learn to talk about what they're doing ... and pass it on to new members of the community." As all educators and parents know, the word of mouth about a school is potent; a school's reputation can play a deciding role in its ability to attract students and teachers and can significantly affect its relationships with its district. Being able to start a communications strategy with a clean slate can have tremendous benefits for sustainability down the line.

The benefits of being open to community members, local government, organizations, businesses, and other forces outside the school extends beyond good public relations. Mike Puelle notes, "If your school is doing effective outreach in general, it's easier to make effective policy cases. The first time you talk with someone should not be when you actually want or need something from them. You should know your legislators and policymakers. If they know you're doing good work, it's much easier to make your case." The people who are served by and work in schools—students, family members, community members, and educators—need to take an active role in shaping educational policy in order to shift the policy climate to better support Essential schools. The story of parents and students who are taking up the charge to defend schools in the New York Performance Standards Consortium (shared in Chapter Five) is a powerful example of citizens who have involved themselves in decision making in order to defend schools' right to autonomy in making educational decisions.

Participating in Networks

A major theme of *Small Schools, Big Ideas* is that schools cannot work in isolation. Participation in supportive networks sustains schools for a number of reasons. The school's professional learning community can extend beyond its walls so that staff members can join with other like-minded educators. Schools can learn from each other and support each other's growth, and they can become powerful allies, helping each other deal with challenges. Due to the intense and immediate nature of schools, educators are conditioned to be in the moment. This intensity makes it essential for schools to take time for reflection and collaborative consideration of challenges, and it underscores the importance of obtaining outside perspectives through interschool Critical Friends Visits and other opportunities to step back, see more clearly what is happening in one's own school community, and benefit from challenges and new perspectives from outsiders.

Often, network support is practical and protective. The New York Performance Standards Consortium (NYPSC) is a group of twenty-eight schools that have come together to benefit from waivers granted by New York State in regard to some of the state's high-stakes Regents exams. These waivers allow NYPSC schools—which include several CES Small Schools Network participants mentioned in these pages, such as Gotham Professional Arts Academy, Humanities Preparatory Academy, James Baldwin High School, School of the Future, and Urban Academy Laboratory High School—to focus more intensively on exhibitions and other forms of performance-based assessment. The consortium also provides network support to bolster the practice of assessing students through demonstrations of mastery.

The Boston Pilot Schools are another example of a network that provides better policy conditions in order to allow CES schools and other small schools to do their work. The Boston Pilot School Network also provides networking, interschool support, and technical assistance—in this case, through the Center for Collaborative Education (CCE). CCE also administers the five-year quality review process (described in Chapter Three) that provides pilot schools with external feedback on their performance.

Both the NYPSC and CCE are CES affiliate centers. Along with twenty-four other such centers around the country, the NYPSC and CCE were developed to support Essential schools through coaching, research, and a wide range of technical assistance such as the Boston Pilot Schools' five-year quality review process. The CES SSN joined forces with this network of CES affiliate centers in order to focus specifically on its mission of creating new small schools that are committed to equitable principles and practices that lead to success for all students. Joan Ferrigno, principal of Odyssey: The Essential School in SeaTac, Washington, believes that being part of the CES SSN has been a powerful sustaining force for her school as it has gotten up and running: "I am really, really proud of being a CES school. I believe so strongly in the [CES Common]

Principles, and we've gotten so much support with the grant and the help with the conversion process. It is very grounding for us. We have people that can help us with this work who have experienced the same thing; they understand why we are not where we want to be yet. We are not the school that we hope to be yet. So the network gives a great sense of pride and a place to go for support and new learning." As Ferrigno observes, Odyssey's ability to develop as a new school within the CES network and movement improves its opportunity to become the school it wants to be, a school that will inspire transformation far beyond its walls.

Conclusion

Adelric McCain has served as a humanities teacher at Young Women's Leadership Charter School since 2002, the school's second year of operation, and has focused much of his professional inquiry on identifying ways for the school to be sustainable. McCain observes:

> Schools are transient places. Students come and go; teachers come and go. To some extent, that is the point. Because of this, sustainability has to be at the center of our conversations. It was not at first, because we believed that no one would ever leave. At first, we were all here and dedicated to creating a culture that was based on our mission and vision and values. We were spending so much time to establish ourselves that taking on another degree of conversation about sustainability was difficult. It's hard to balance creating culture and working with students while also working toward the future. Not a lot of us have practice about having that dual kind of conversation.

While schools are still in the planning stages, their founders need to develop ways to participate in that "dual kind of conversation" in order build in the ability to change while remaining committed to their core values and practices. From the start, school planners must find ways to constantly recommit to the school's equity mission through consistent cycles of inquiry and improvement, and they need to think simultaneously about the immediate short-term reality of what's next and about the school's long-term viability.

Small Schools, Big Ideas has described the principles that guide communities in creating and sustaining schools that are equitable, personalized, and academically vibrant and rigorous, as well as the practices that make commitment to those principles possible on a very practical level in the ceaselessly rapid-fire world of schools. Believing that all students can succeed means following through on achieving equity by working within a community prepared to challenge the obstacles to that belief by having hard conversations about attitudes and structures that impede students of color, in particular, from participating in a rich, personalized, and academically powerful school experience. Transformation will occur through forthrightly facing the challenges to equitable schools and school systems; securing autonomy to make decisions about educational practices and school structures; developing transformational leadership and equity-focused learning communities engaged in cycles of inquiry and action; participating in supportive networks; collaboratively developing student-centered teaching and learning that is assessed by demonstration of mastery; designing schools for access to and success in postsecondary education; and creating appropriate practices that support a school culture that nurtures and supports students, staff members, and the greater school community.

Transforming schools and school systems forces us to rethink the fundamentals of public education: relationships with students and their families, the role of educators, and the content and delivery of instruction. Given the urgency that we feel daily about the state of education, we are moving beyond quick fixes and superficial solutions that neither address systemic problems nor interrupt the status quo. The CES approach to creating new and transformed schools provides an authentic and diverse set of players—family members, community members, students, educators, district personnel, and staff members of educational support organizations—with the tools to nurture and grow schools that fit their local needs. In concert with the national learning community of the CES network, the national organization of the Coalition of Essential Schools is taking an active role in order to develop new schools, expand our regional reach, and diversify the leaders within communities and school districts in order to build a critical mass of those who are committed to restoring faith in public education. As we grow our collective practice, both our new schools and our CES Mentor Schools are engaged in a reflective process that supports their continuous improvement and provides us with a wide variety of experience and evidence. We hope that you will join us on our journey.

APPENDIX A: COALITION OF ESSENTIAL SCHOOLS COMMON PRINCIPLES

The CES Common Principles, based on decades of research and practice, are intended as a guiding philosophy rather than a replicable model for schools. This research and practice reflects the wisdom of thousands of educators who are successfully engaged in creating personalized, equitable, and academically challenging schools for all young people.

Learning to use one's mind well. The school should focus on helping young people learn to use their minds well. Schools should not be "comprehensive" if such a claim is made at the expense of the school's central intellectual purpose.

Less is more, depth over coverage. The school's goals should be simple: that each student master a limited number of essential skills and areas of knowledge. While these skills and areas will, to varying degrees, reflect the traditional academic disciplines, the program's design should be shaped by the intellectual and imaginative powers and competencies that the students need, rather than by "subjects" as conventionally defined. The aphorism "less is more" should dominate: curricular decisions should be guided by the aim of thorough student mastery and achievement rather than by an effort to merely cover content.

Goals apply to all students. The school's goals should apply to all students, while the means to these goals will vary as those students themselves vary. School practice should be tailor-made to meet the needs of every group or class of students.

Personalization. Teaching and learning should be personalized to the maximum feasible extent. Efforts should be directed toward a goal that no teacher have direct responsibility for more than eighty students in the high school and middle school and no more than twenty in the elementary school. To capitalize on this personalization, decisions about the details of the course of study, the use of students' and teachers' time and the choice of teaching materials and specific pedagogies must be unreservedly placed in the hands of the principal and staff.

Student-as-worker, teacher-as-coach. The governing practical metaphor of the school should be student-as-worker, rather than the more familiar metaphor of teacher-as-deliverer-of-instructional-services. Accordingly, a prominent pedagogy will be coaching, to provoke students to learn how to learn and thus to teach themselves.

Demonstration of mastery. Teaching and learning should be documented and assessed with tools based on student performance of real tasks. Students not yet at appropriate levels of competence should be provided intensive support and resources to assist them quickly to meet those standards. Multiple forms of evidence, ranging from ongoing observation of the learner to completion of specific projects, should be used to better understand the learner's strengths and needs, and to plan for further assistance. Students should have opportunities to exhibit their expertise before family and community. The diploma should be awarded upon a successful final demonstration of mastery for graduation—an "Exhibition." As the diploma is awarded when earned, the school's program proceeds with no strict age grading and with no system of credits earned by "time spent" in class. The emphasis is on the students' demonstration that they can do important things.

A tone of decency and trust. The tone of the school should explicitly and self-consciously stress values of unanxious expectation ("I won't threaten you but I expect much of you"), of trust (until abused), and of decency (the values of fairness, generosity, and tolerance). Incentives appropriate to the school's particular students and teachers should be emphasized. Parents should be key collaborators and vital members of the school community.

Commitment to the entire school. The principal and teachers should perceive themselves as generalists first (teachers and scholars in general education) and specialists second (experts in but one particular discipline). Staff should expect multiple obligations (teacher-counselor-manager) and a sense of commitment to the entire school.

Resources dedicated to teaching and learning. Ultimate administrative and budget targets should include student loads that promote personalization, substantial time for collective planning by teachers, competitive salaries for staff, and an ultimate per-pupil cost not to exceed that at traditional schools by more than 10 percent. To accomplish this, administrative plans may have to show the phased reduction or elimination of some services now provided students in many traditional schools.

Democracy and equity. The school should demonstrate nondiscriminatory and inclusive policies, practices, and pedagogies. It should model democratic practices that involve all who are directly affected by the school. The school should honor diversity and build on the strength of its communities, deliberately and explicitly challenging all forms of inequity.

APPENDIX B: COALITION OF ESSENTIAL SCHOOLS BENCHMARKS: PRINCIPLES IN PRACTICE

Part I: Introduction

The CES Benchmarks are designed to address the long-standing challenge of helping schools translate the Coalition of Essential Schools' guiding tenets, the CES Common Principles, into practice. Intended as a tool for teachers, schools, and support organizations that provide technical assistance and coaching, the benchmarks reflect the Coalition's principle-based approach to school reform and illustrate best practices and lessons learned in the field and from CES research and professional development. These practices have proven essential in helping schools implement strategies to increase equity and achievement for all students.

This document was created as a tool for growth and is intended to be used for self-reflection and self-assessment by individual teachers or entire schools. It is not meant to be prescriptive; rather, it outlines the best practices that reflect and support the CES Common Principles.

The benchmarks are divided into two categories: classroom practices and organizational practices. Classroom practices focus on instruction and address the question "What does a CES classroom look like?" by sharing how each practice is reflected in teacher work and student outcomes. Organizational practices are schoolwide practices that support and enable the classroom practices. Each practice is linked with the CES Common Principles most related to its implementation. In the full version of the CES Benchmarks (available online at http://www .essentialschools.org/pub/ces_docs/schools/benchmarks/benchmarksIntro.html), the highest level of implementation of the practice is described in detail, and early and developing levels are described as well. In this version, we provide a description of each benchmark, followed by the CES Benchmarks Usage Guide, which is a guide to creating a schoolwide plan based on the benchmarks.

The full online version of the benchmarks also provides a set of resources for those interested in exploring the practice more deeply, as well as assessment and reflection tools for each benchmark area.

Part II: Coalition of Essential Schools Benchmarks

Section I: Classroom Practices What does a CES classroom look like?	Section II: Organizational Practices What organizational practices support and enable the classroom?
Culturally responsive pedagogy*	Access, opportunity, and postsecondary preparation
Differentiated instruction	Family engagement and community partnerships
Essential questions	Continuous school improvement
Habits of mind and heart	Culture of fairness and trust
Interdisciplinary curriculum	Transformational leadership
Performance-based assessment	Maximizing resources for equitable outcomes
Student-centered teaching and learning	Professional learning community

*Sensitive to issues of socioeconomic status, race, gender, culture, sexual orientation, religion, ableness, age

Section I: Classroom Practices: What does a CES classroom look like?

Culturally responsive pedagogy: Culture is central to learning. It plays a role not only in communicating and receiving information but also in shaping the thinking processes of groups and individuals. A pedagogy that acknowledges, responds to, and celebrates fundamental cultures offers full, equitable access to education for students from all cultures and prepares students to live in a pluralistic society. Culturally responsive teaching is a pedagogy that recognizes the importance of including students' cultural references in all aspects of learning (Ladson-Billings, 1994).

Differentiated instruction: To differentiate instruction is to recognize students' varying background knowledge, readiness for learning, language skills, preferences in learning, and interests, and react responsively. Differentiated instruction addresses the needs of students of differing abilities and learning styles in the same class. The intent of differentiating instruction is to provide multiple access points for diverse learners to maximize growth and individual success by meeting each student where he or she is and assisting in the learning process from that point. Differentiated instruction is a series of essential strategies for working in heterogeneous classrooms and eliminating tracking.

Essential questions: Essential questions are the starting point for developing curricula. Curriculum and courses should be organized not around answers but around big ideas—questions and problems that content represents the answers to. Essential questions on every level—from the most encompassing schoolwide questions to the specific questions posed in a particular unit of a particular course—should shape the way students learn to think critically for themselves. Consequently, essential questions are related to the school's goals: that each student master a limited number of essential skills and areas of knowledge (see Habits of mind and heart).

Habits of mind and heart: The school should focus on helping young people learn to use their mind well. Habits of mind and heart are ways that a school can articulate the thinking and emotional dispositions that students need, allowing it to focus its resources. Consequently, schools should not be comprehensive if such a claim is made at the expense of the school's central intellectual purpose. Habits of mind are a set of thinking dispositions that help people develop their critical and creative thinking skills. They are the characteristics of what intelligent people do about problems whose resolution is not immediately apparent. That is, these are the mental habits that individuals can develop to render their thinking and learning more self-regulated. Habits of mind are not designed to be thinking tools; rather, they are designed to be dispositions adopted when using a thinking tool. Habits of heart are a collection of emotional dispositions designed to help people develop their social-emotional intelligence. Habits of heart help people to care for, identify with, and honor others and to respect the emotions and rights of others and how they see the world. The phrase also describes an ability, capacity, or skill to perceive, assess, and manage one's own emotions and those of other individuals and groups.

Interdisciplinary curriculum: A school's goals should be simple: that each student master a limited number of essential skills and areas of knowledge. While these skills and areas will, to varying degrees, reflect the traditional academic disciplines, the program's design should be shaped by the intellectual and imaginative powers and competencies that the students need rather than by subjects as conventionally defined. An interdisciplinary curriculum combines several school subjects into one active project or is organized to cut across subject-matter lines, bringing various aspects of the curriculum together into meaningful association. It focuses on broad areas of study because that is how children encounter subjects in the real world—combined in one activity. In an interdisciplinary curriculum, the planned learning experiences not only provide the learners with a unified view of commonly held knowledge (by presenting models, systems, and structures) but also motivate and develop learners' power to perceive new relationships and thus to create new models, systems, and structures. Interdisciplinary curriculum involves using the knowledge view and curricular approach that consciously applies methodology and language from more than one discipline to examine a central theme, issue, problem, topic, or experience.

Performance-based assessment: While any assessment system should include multiple types of assessment that are matched with the needs of teachers (to make decisions regarding instruction) and learners, demonstration of mastery on schoolwide outcomes and high-level competencies should be assessed through a performance-based system. A performance-based assessment system is an integrated approach to education that underpins the culture of a school and links a number of factors: curriculum, instruction, variety of student work over time, continual assessment, external oversight, high standards, and professional development. Using a performance-based assessment system requires that assessment not stand apart from the day-to-day work and schooling of every student; assessment must be continually incorporated into all activities. A performance-based assessment system requires students to engage in time-intensive, in-depth research projects and papers, and to engage in rigorous performance tasks that require students to think like historians, solve problems like mathematicians, conduct experiments the way scientists do, critically interpret works of literature, and speak and write clearly and expressively. As in the time-honored tradition of the Ph.D.'s dissertation defense, students in a performance-based assessment system must orally present and defend completed work to external assessors.

Student-centered teaching and learning: Student-centered teaching and learning focuses on the needs, abilities, interests, and learning styles of students and has many implications for the design of curriculum, course content, and interactivity of courses. Accordingly, a prominent pedagogical strategy will be teacher-as-coach, in order to provoke students to learn how to learn and thus to teach themselves, rather than the more traditional teacher-centered instruction with teacher-as-deliverer-of-instructional-services, which places the teacher at its center in an active role and students in a passive, receptive role. This type of pedagogy acknowledges student voice as central to the learning experience for every learner and requires students to be active, responsible participants in their own learning. To capitalize on students' capacity for active, self-directed learning, teaching and learning should be personalized to the maximum feasible extent. Decisions about the details of the course of study, the use of students' and teachers' time, and the teaching materials and specific pedagogies must be unreservedly placed in the hands of the staff and students.

Section II: Organizational Practices: What organizational practices support and enable the classroom practices?

Access, opportunity, and postsecondary preparation: Schools need to diminish the historically predictive power of demographic data on high and equitable student achievement by increasing the achievement of all groups of students and dramatically accelerating the achievement of targeted groups of students. Schools help all students set and achieve high goals and provide them with the ability to pursue postsecondary education, along with support in that effort. Schools provide information on career pathways and encourage students to become lifelong learners. Schools provide a college-prep curriculum that generates important values, the skills and knowledge to engage in intellectual work across various disciplines, the desire for and the expectation of success in high school and beyond, and the emotional competence to be resilient and adaptable in order to live and work in the global economy of the twenty-first century.

Family engagement and community partnerships: *Family engagement and community partnerships* refers to how schools develop and sustain meaningful interactive relationships with their varied communities (that is, parent, education, civic, and business groups), so that all members understand and contribute to the work of supporting children.

Continuous school improvement: *Continuous school improvement* is the process cycle of school improvement, which includes the major components of creating the vision, gathering data related to that vision, analyzing the data, planning the work of the school to align with the vision, implementing the strategies and action steps outlined in the plan, and gathering data to measure the impact of the intervention.

Culture of fairness and trust: A *culture of fairness and trust* includes explicit activities that are designed to promote and foster a safe, positive, inclusive learning community in which students are known well and their social, emotional, and intellectual needs are of primary concern.

Transformational leadership: *Transformational leadership* refers to the set of attitudes, beliefs, and practices necessary for individuals and school communities to examine the intellectual and social-emotional challenges of educational equity work, including the ability to reflect personally and professionally on one's own tacit assumptions and expectations as well as on those built into institutional culture. Leading for equity also requires shared or distributive leadership and decision making from a broad array of constituents—students, teachers, parents, administrators, and other community members—so that the people, the vision, and the work of the school are sustained and developed over time.

Maximizing resources for equitable outcomes: *Maximizing resources for equitable outcomes* refers to the school's use of its central resources—time, money, and staffing—to meet the unique needs of its students. Gaps in the funding and resources provided to schools notwithstanding, it is imperative that schools maximize their benefit from the resources they do have. Maximizing resource benefits requires that decisions be made collaboratively by those closest to the learners. *Equitable outcomes* refers to the concept that the school's goals should apply to all students, while the means to these goals will vary as those students themselves vary. All students should be prepared for both postsecondary and career pathways.

Professional learning community: *Professional learning community* describes a group of administrators and other school staff members who are united in their commitment to student learning. They share a vision, work and learn collaboratively, visit and review other classrooms, and participate in decision making. The benefits to the staff and students include reduced isolation of teachers, better informed and more committed teachers, and academic gains for students. A professional learning community is a powerful approach to staff development and a potent strategy for school change and improvement. A professional learning community provides professional development opportunities that employ best practices and allow staff members to engage as learners as well as leaders, using practices such as Critical Friends Groups. A professional learning community explicitly addresses equity in the classroom and provides collaborative planning time that focuses on instructional practice.

Part III: CES Benchmarks Usage Guide: Creating a Schoolwide Plan Based on the Benchmarks

The CES Benchmarks are designed for school staff members, school change coaches, and others involved with school redesign and transformation in order to help schools implement and integrate the CES Common Principles into effective practice. These benchmarks can be used to organize a school's improvement plan, support schools as they develop ways of assessing their reform and school improvement efforts, or guide a teacher who is seeking to improve his or her practice. In any case, the goal is to use this tool to focus reflection, to identify strengths and weaknesses, and to guide the work.

We encourage schools to examine their own operation and performance by collecting and analyzing data. A self-study driven by the overall question "How effectively are we serving our students?" provides an entry point to looking at how each aspect of a school's operation supports and improves teaching and learning.

Existing schools can use the benchmarks to find their strengths and challenges and integrate those findings into a schoolwide improvement plan. To do so, we recommend the following steps:

1. Study each of the benchmark areas and reflect on your school community's strengths and challenges.

   a. Have staff members (and students and parents) read the description of an area (or areas) and engage in a discussion of these questions: Where do we see our school reflected in this document? Where don't we see our school reflected in the document?

   b. Have staff members (and students and parents) rank the top strengths and challenges of the practices. Alternatively, have staff members (and students and parents) rate each practice as emerging, developing, or transforming.

   c. Use the assessment and reflection tools provided for each benchmark area (available at http://www.essentialschools.org/pub/ces_docs /schools/benchmarks/benchmarksIntro.html) to document and discuss current practice and choose priority areas.

   d. Individual teachers and staff can describe how close they as individuals are or the school as a whole is (whichever is more appropriate, given the practice) to each specific practice.

2. Decide which benchmark practice to focus on in order to improve your own schoolwide practices. Focus on choosing the practice that will provide the highest leverage as you endeavor to create a more equitable school.

   a. Examine the rankings, and discuss which ratings are surprising or unexpected.

   b. What is most important in terms of creating a more equitable school? Post the benchmarks around the room, and have people stand by the area they find most important or have people posts dots on the wall next to the area they think is most important. Then have each small group discuss among themselves and then share with the larger group why they believe this is the area that will provide highest leverage. As each group shares, people can ask questions. After all the groups have shared, give people a chance to change groups.

c. Have a large-group discussion that enables your school to choose two areas to work on.

d. Revisit the assessment and reflection tools provided for each benchmark area to document and discuss current practice, choose priority areas, and develop action plans.

3. Create a plan that includes the supports needed to reach the goals you have chosen.

a. Examine each area, and discuss what you need to know about this area.

b. From here, discuss what you need to know to be able to implement this area of practice. What professional development do you need? Who can you learn from inside the school? Outside the school?

4. Reexamine the impact of your work continually (see the benchmark practice "Continuous school improvement").

APPENDIX C: PROFILED SCHOOLS AND ORGANIZATIONS

Profiled Schools

Academy of Citizenship and Empowerment (new conversion school)

4424 S. 188th Street

SeaTac, WA 98188

206-433-2342

http://www.hsd401.org/ourschools/highschools/ace/

Amy Biehl High School (Mentor School)

123 4th Street

Albuquerque, NM 87102

505-299-9409

http://abhs.k12.nm.us/

ARISE High School (new school)

3301 E. 12th Street, #205

Oakland, CA 94601

510-436-5487

http://www.arisehighschool.org/

Boston Arts Academy (Mentor School)

174 Ipswich Street

Boston, MA 02215

617-635-6470

http://www.bostonartsacademy.org/Pages/index

Capital City Public Charter School (Upper School) (new small school)

3047 15th Street N.W.

Washington, DC 20009

202-387-0309

http://www.ccpcs.org/

Central Park East Secondary School

1573 Madison Avenue, Room 3

New York, NY 10029

Civitas Leadership School (new small CES school)

1200 W Colton St.

Los Angeles, California 90026

213-580-6430

Connections Public Charter School (new small school)

174 Kamehameha Avenue

Hilo, HI 96720

808-959-6037

http://www.connectionscharterschool.org/

Eagle Rock School and Professional Development Center (Mentor School)

2750 Notaiah Road

Estes Park, CO 80517-1770

970-586-0600

http://www.eaglerockschool.org/

El Colegio Charter School (Mentor School)

4137 Bloomington Avenue

Minneapolis, MN 55407

612-728-5728

http://www.el-colegio.org/index.html

Empowerment College Preparatory High School (new small school)

5655 Selinky

Houston, TX 77047

713-732-9231

http://hs.houstonisd.org/empowermenths/

Federal Hocking High School (Mentor School)

8461 State Route 144

Stewart, OH 45778

740-662-6691

http://www.federalhocking.k12.oh.us/extra/hs/index.htm

Fenway High School (Mentor School)

174 Ipswich Street

Boston, MA 02215

617-635-9911

http://www.fenwayhs.org/

Francis W. Parker Charter Essential School (Mentor School)

49 Antietam Street

Devens, MA 01434

978-772-3293

http://www.parker.org/

Gotham Professional Arts Academy (new small school)

265 Ralph Avenue, 3rd Floor

Brooklyn, NY 11233

718-455-0746

http://gothamacademy.org/

Greenville Technical Charter High School (Mentor School)

Box 5616, 506 S. Pleasantburg Drive, #119

Greenville, SC 29606

864-250-8844

http://www.gtchs.org

Harmony School (Mentor School)

909 E. 2nd Street

Bloomington, IN 47401

812-334-8349

http://www.harmonyschool.org/

High School for Recording Arts (Mentor School)

550 Vandalia Street

St. Paul, MN 55114

651-287-0890

http://www.hsra.org/

High Tech High (Mentor School)

2861 Womble Road

San Diego, CA 92106

619-243-5000

http://www.hightechhigh.org/dc/index.php

Humanities Preparatory Academy (Mentor School)

351 W. 18th Street

New York, NY 10011

212-929-4433

http://www.humanitiesprep.org/

James Baldwin High School (new small school)

351 W. 18th Street

New York, NY 10011

212-627-2812

http://schools.nyc.gov/SchoolPortals/02/M313/default.htm

June Jordan School for Equity (Mentor School)

325 LaGrande Avenue, Room 326

San Francisco, CA 94112

415-452-4922

http://www.jjse.org/

Leadership High School (Mentor School)

241 Oneida Avenue, Suite 301

San Francisco, CA 94112

415-841-8910

http://www.leadershiphigh.org/

Lehman Alternative Community School

111 Chestnut Street

Ithaca, NY 14850

607-274-2183

http://www.icsd.k12.ny.us/lacs/

Life Learning Academy (Mentor School)

651 8th Street

Treasure Island

San Francisco, CA 94130

415-397-8957

http://www.lifelearningacademysf.org/

Met Peace Street (Mentor School)

362 Dexter Street

Providence, RI 02907

401-752-3400

http://www.themetschool.org/Metcenter/home.html

Metro High School (new small school)

1929 Kenny Road

Columbus, OH 43210

614-247-2276

http://www.themetroschool.com

Middle College High School (Mentor School)

737 Union Avenue, Building E 105

Memphis, TN 38103

901-333-5360

http://www.mcsk12.net/schools/middlecollege.hs/MCHS.htm

Mission Hill School

67 Alleghany Street

Roxbury, MA 02120

617-635-6384

http://www.missionhillschool.org/

Native American Community Academy (new small school)

1100 Cardenas S.E.

Albuquerque, NM 87108

505-266-0992

http://www.nacaschool.org

Odyssey: The Essential School (new conversion school)

4424 S. 188th Street

SeaTac, WA 98188

206-433-2344

http://www.hsd401.org/ourschools/highschools/odyssey/

Quest High School (Mentor School)

18901 Timber Forest

Humble, TX 77346

281-641-7302

http://qhs.humble.k12.tx.us/

Renaissance School at Olympic (new conversion school)

4301 Sandy Porter Road, Suite D

Charlotte, NC 28273

980-343-1109

http://pages.cms.k12.nc.us/renaissanceohs/

School of Biotechnology, Health and Public Administration at Olympic (new conversion school)

4301 Sandy Porter Road, Suite E

Charlotte, NC 28273

980-343-1110

http://pages.cms.k12.nc.us/bhpeohs/

School of International Business and Communications at Olympic (new conversion school)

4301 Sandy Porter Road, Suite C

Charlotte, NC 28273

980-343-1104

http://pages.cms.k12.nc.us/ibcsohs/

School of International Studies and Global Economics at Olympic (new conversion school)

4301 Sandy Porter Road, Suite A

Charlotte, NC 28273

980-343-1113

http://pages.cms.k12.nc.us/isgeohs/

School of Math, Engineering, Technology and Science at Olympic (new conversion school)

4301 Sandy Porter Road, Suite B

Charlotte, NC 28273

980-343-1101

http://pages.cms.k12.nc.us/metsohs/

School of the Future (Mentor School)

127 E. 22nd Street

New York, NY 10010

212-475-8086

http://www.sof.edu

Skyview Academy (new small school)

9000 York Street

Thornton, CO 80229

303-853-1200

http://www.mapleton.us

South Valley Academy (Mentor School)

3426 Blake SW

Albuquerque, New Mexico 87105

505-452-3132

http://southvalleyacademy.org

Urban Academy Laboratory High School (Mentor School)

317 East 67th Street

New York, NY 10021

212-570-5284

http://www.urbanacademy.org

Wildwood School–Upper School (Mentor School)

11811 W. Olympic Boulevard

Los Angeles, CA 90064

310-478-7189

http://www.wildwood.org/

Young Women's Leadership Charter School (Mentor School)

2641 S. Calumet Avenue

Chicago, IL 60616

312-949-9400

http://www.ywlcs.org/

Profiled CES Affiliate Centers and Other Organizations

Bay Area Coalition for Equitable Schools

1720 Broadway, Fourth Floor

Oakland, CA 94612

510-208-0160

http://www.bayces.org

Belmont Zone of Choice

1055 Wilshire Boulevard

Los Angeles, CA 90017

213-241-0895

http://www.lausd.k12.ca.us/District_4/BelmontZone.htm

Big Picture Learning

325 Public Street

Providence, RI 02905

401-752-3528

http://www.bigpicture.org/

Big Picture Learning also has offices in San Diego, Australia, and the Netherlands; contact information is on their Web site.

Bill & Melinda Gates Foundation

P.O. Box 23350

Seattle, WA 98102

206-709-3100

http://www.gatesfoundation.org/

Center for Collaborative Education

1 Renaissance Park

1135 Tremont Street, Suite 490

Boston, MA 02120

617-421-0134

http://www.ccebos.org/

CES Northwest

7900 E. Green Lake Drive N., Suite 212

Seattle, WA 98103

206-812-3156

http://www.cesnorthwest.org/

Coalition of Essential Schools
1330 Broadway, Suite 600
Oakland, CA 94612
510-433-1451
http://www.essentialschools.org

Educators for Social Responsibility
23 Garden Street
Cambridge, MA 02138
617-492-1764
http://www.esrnational.org

EdVisions
501 Main Street
P.O. Box 601
Henderson, MN 56044
507-248-3738
http://www.edvisions.com/

Forum for Education and Democracy
1307 New York Avenue N.W., Suite 300
Washington, DC 20005-4701
and
P.O. Box 216
Amesville, OH 45711
http://www.forumforeducation.org/

Los Angeles Small Schools Center
2845 W. 7th Street
Los Angeles, CA 90005
310-466-0122
http://www.lasmallschoolscenter.org/

National School Reform Faculty

Harmony Education Center

P.O. Box 1787

Bloomington, IN 47402

812-330-2702

http://www.nsrfharmony.org/

New York Performance Standards Consortium

317 East 67th Street

New York, NY 10021

212-570-5394

http://performanceassessment.org/

Oakland Community Organizations

7200 Bancroft Avenue, #2 Eastmont Mall (upper level)

Oakland, CA 94605

510-639-1444

http://www.oaklandcommunity.org/

San Francisco Coalition of Essential Small Schools

300 Brannan Street, Suite 406

San Francisco, CA 94107

415-992-5007

http://www.sfcess.org

What Kids Can Do

P.O. Box 603252

Providence, RI 02906

401-247-7665

http://www.whatkidscando.org/

APPENDIX D: THE BENEFITS OF THE CES MODEL: A LOOK AT RECENT RESEARCH

CES believes that we need to use multiple measures of students' knowledge, understanding, and performance to document the impact of our efforts instead of relying on any one measure that may not adequately reflect students' true proficiencies. Key findings from three recent research studies conducted on small CES schools by CES affiliate centers in Boston, New York, and Minnesota demonstrate the impact of the CES Common Principles on students' intellectual and social growth and development. These studies' multiple measures include traditional test data, college-going rates, persistence rates, retention rates, and drop-out rates, along with measures of student engagement, student agency (whether or not a person feels motivated to obtain goals), self-esteem, problem-solving ability, and other measures of adolescent engagement and mental health.

Consistently Positive Results

Findings from *Measuring Up: Demonstrating the Effectiveness of the Coalition of Essential Schools* (Coalition of Essential Schools, 2006) demonstrate that schools that implement the CES Common Principles in small school settings improve school practice and raise student achievement by personalizing teaching and learning, emphasizing intellectual rigor, and promoting equity in achievement across student populations. Students who go to CES schools are engaged in their learning, enter college at a high rate, show growth in social-emotional skills as well as intellectual skills, and perform well on traditional measures. Highlights from the study include the following:

- Better performance by 9–26 percent on standardized test results: the nineteen Boston Pilot Schools perform better than the district averages across every indicator of student engagement and performance.

- A college-going rate 17 percent higher and a dropout rate 12 percent lower than similar NYC schools: the New York Performance Standards Consortium has developed an assessment system that leads to quality teaching and learning, enhancing rather than compromising their students' education.

- A 10 percent increase in behavioral and emotional engagement: EdVisions schools recorded significantly higher levels of autonomy, a more positive goal orientation, and higher levels of student engagement than did traditional schools. As well, their 2004–05 ACT average scores were 22.4 compared with a national average of 21.2, and the two schools that administered the SAT averaged 1300 and 1180 compared with a national average of 1072.

Boston: Students Perform Better Than District Averages on Every Measure

Progress and Promise: A Report on the Boston Pilot Schools, published in 2006 by the Center for Collaborative Education, the CES affiliate center in Boston, documents significant achievement by students who have attended the Boston Pilot Schools during a five-year period (Center for Collaborative Education, 2006b). Pilot School students performed better than the district averages across every indicator of student engagement and performance, including the Massachusetts Comprehensive Assessment System, the statewide standardized assessment. On other standard measures, Pilot School students showed better rates of attendance and fewer out-of-school suspensions, and more went on to attend university or technical college after graduation.

Why? The report emphasizes that the Boston Pilot Schools have used their autonomy to create curriculum, assessment, and school structures that support high expectations and achievement.

New York: Students Go to College at a Higher Rate

To address the question of how well small schools prepare their students for college, the New York Performance Standards Consortium is conducting a longitudinal study of the college performance of its schools' graduates, and published results appear in 2005's *College Performance Study,* which documents how the consortium's performance assessment system prepares students for college-level work and speaks to the broader issue of the efficacy of small schools (Foote, 2005). Tracking students into their third semester of college, the three-year study drew on official college transcripts for over 750 graduates. The results were impressive: not only were students who graduated from consortium schools attending competitive colleges, but they also showed higher-than-average persistence rates and earned above-average GPAs—all this despite the fact that consortium students represent a more disadvantaged population than students throughout other New York City high schools.

Why? The New York Performance Standards Consortium schools have created an assessment system that, unlike standardized tests, enhances their students' education by allowing multiple ways for students to express and exhibit learning. Consortium schools are small and are organized around a common core of principles that are intended to prepare students to use their mind well.

Minnesota: Students Show Improved Emotional Growth

EdVisions, the CES affiliate center in Minnesota, is dedicated to creating small, personalized middle schools and high schools. While EdVisions schools show exceptional growth on traditional measures, evaluating schools solely in terms of test scores does not reveal the true nature of the learning environment and how that environment contributes to adolescents' mental health and adjustment. A school that makes adequate yearly progress on standardized test scores while contributing to the frustration, apathy, loneliness, and alienation of many of its students cannot be considered a success. To measure indicators of success other than standardized test scores, EdVisions has developed the Hope Scale, a means by which schools can effectively be judged on how well they establish a culture that creates relationships, norms of behaviors, values, and obligations that lead to the development of healthy and productive adults. Hope Scale scores correlate positively with measures of optimism, self-esteem, problem-solving ability, success in college, and physical health, and they correlate negatively with measures of depression. *Less, More and Better: 2005 EdVisions 5-Year Report* indicates that EdVisions schools greatly support adolescent growth; the longer students stay in EdVisions schools, the greater the increases they demonstrate on the Hope Scale (EdVisions, 2005).

Why? EdVisions schools are committed to the values of democracy, project-based learning, and accountability. They include two very unique organizational aspects: (1) project-based learning that leads to autonomous, independent learners and (2) autonomous, democratically controlled schools.

Measuring Up: Demonstrating the Effectiveness of the Coalition of Essential Schools (Coalition of Essential Schools, 2006), along with links to the other reports cited here and additional data on student performance at Essential schools, can be found on the *Small Schools, Big Ideas* Web site, http://www.ceschangelab.org.

APPENDIX E: GLOSSARY OF USEFUL ASSESSMENT TERMS

Accountability: The demand by a community (public officials, employers, and taxpayers) for school officials to prove that money invested in education has led to measurable learning. *Accountability testing* is an attempt to sample what students have learned, how well teachers have taught, or the effectiveness of a principal's performance as an instructional leader. School budgets, personnel promotions, compensation, and awards may be affected. Most school districts make this kind of assessment public; it can affect policy and public perception of the effectiveness of taxpayer-supported schools and be the basis for comparison among schools. Accountability is often viewed as an important factor in educational reform. An assessment system connected to accountability can help identify the needs of schools so that resources can be equitably distributed. In this context, in addition to test scores, accountability assessment can include such indicators as equity, competence of teaching staff, physical infrastructure, curriculum, class size, instructional methods, the existence of tracking, the number of high-cost students, drop-out rates, and parental involvement. Test scores are a potentially important part of the accountability equation; analyzed in a disaggregated format, they can help identify instructional problems and point to potential solutions.

Assessment: In an educational context, the process of observing learning or describing, collecting, recording, scoring, or interpreting information about learning. Ideally, assessment is an episode in the learning process, part of reflection and understanding progress. Traditionally, student assessments are used to determine placement, promotion, graduation, and retention. In the context of institutional accountability, assessments are undertaken to determine the principal's performance, the effectiveness of schools, and so forth. In the context of school reform, assessment is an essential tool for evaluating the effectiveness of changes in the teaching and learning process.

Authentic assessment: Evaluation by asking for the behavior the learning is intended to produce. Authentic assessment is characterized by the process of modeling, practice, and feedback that guide students toward excellent performance, and it is designed to practice an entire concept rather then bits and pieces in preparation for eventual understanding.

Backward planning, backward design: In backward design, the teacher starts with desired classroom or graduation outcomes and then plans the curriculum based on those outcomes, choosing activities and materials that help determine student ability and foster student learning. This approach is opposed to the traditional manner in which teachers start curriculum planning by choosing activities and textbooks instead of identifying classroom learning goals and planning toward those goals.

Curriculum alignment: The degree to which an assessment program's evaluation measures match a curriculum's scope and sequence, ensuring that teachers will use successful completion of the assessment as a goal of classroom instruction.

Demonstration of mastery: A CES Common Principle that states that teaching and learning should be documented and assessed with tools based on student performance of real tasks.

Documentation: Documentation involves recording classroom observations of students and their work over time, across various modes of learning, and in coordination with colleagues.

Exhibitions: Public demonstrations of learning by students to teachers, parents, outside experts, and other community members who are interested in evaluating students' level of achievement. Exhibitions are a way that schools and their communities can assess students' mastery of both a body of knowledge and the thinking skills that are required in the real world.

Formative assessment: Observations that allow one to determine the degree to which students know or are able to do a given learning task and that identify parts of the task that the student does not know or is unable to do. Tasks or tests are developed from the curriculum or instructional materials. If properly designed, students should not be able to tell whether they are being taught or assessed. Outcomes suggest future steps for teaching and learning. Formative assessment is also described as learning-embedded assessment.

Habits of mind and heart: Habits of mind include such things as knowing where to find more information, asking original questions, reflecting on and learning from experience, understanding how to collaborate, and seeking out multiple points of view. These kinds of habits are at the heart of education but are not easily demonstrated through testing. Habits of heart are a collection of emotional dispositions designed to help people develop their social-emotional intelligence. Habits of heart help people care for, identify with, and honor others by respecting their emotions, rights, and worldview. The phrase also describes the capacity to perceive, assess, and manage one's own emotions and those of other individuals and groups.

High-stakes tests: High-stakes tests mostly or totally determine significant consequences. Tests have high stakes for students when promotion from one grade to the next or graduation depends on personal results; tests have high stakes for schools when teacher pay, funding, or control over curriculum, pedagogical style, or other factors depends on the aggregate results. In many CES schools, exhibitions and other demonstrations of mastery are high-stakes assessments. High-stakes standardized testing can corrupt the evaluation process when pressure to produce rising test scores results in teaching to the test or making tests less complex.

Metacognition: The knowledge of one's own thinking processes and strategies and the ability to consciously reflect and act on the knowledge of cognition to modify those processes and strategies.

Multiple measures: Varied ways to express and exhibit learning that support a wide range of learning styles, talents, and expression—for example, writing (literary essays, research papers, plays, poetry, lyrics); oral presentations (discussions, debates, dramatic performances, external presentations); artistic renderings (sculpture, painting, drawing, photography); and production of artifacts (three-dimensional representations, replicas, and working models).

Outcome: An operationally defined educational goal—usually a culminating activity, product, or performance that can be measured.

Performance-based assessments: Exhibitions of mastery and skill that require students to construct responses and demonstrate those responses in a variety of ways (through writing, speaking, collaboration, construction, movement, and so on). Because performance-based assessments are complex, they are scored by using rubrics that indicate levels of performance on a variety of parameters. Evaluation is narrative and not easily reduced to a number or letter grade.

Portfolio: A systematic and organized collection of a student's work that exhibits to others evidence of a student's efforts, achievements, and progress over a period of time. The student should be involved in the selection of its contents, and the collection should include information about the rubric or criteria for judging merit, as well as evidence of student self-reflection or evaluation.

Process: A method of doing something, generally involving steps or operations that are usually ordered or interdependent. Process can be evaluated as part of an assessment—for example, evaluating student performance during pre-writing exercises that lead up to the final production of an essay.

Product: The tangible and stable result of a performance or task. An assessment of student performance is based on evaluation of the product of a demonstration of learning.

Real world: Descriptive term for work that is grounded in knowledge, concepts, and perspectives of academic, professional, or applied technical disciplines. Real-world schoolwork is directed toward understanding issues, problems, or questions of significance that are usually beyond the scope of classrooms and schools.

Reliability, inter-rater reliability: Reliability describes scoring consistency from one assessment to the next. Inter-rater reliability describes scoring consistency from one scorer to the next—that is, how well all scorers understand and agree on what constitutes various levels of performance when looking at an essay, a dance, a debate, or another exhibition of skill and mastery.

Rubric: A rubric is a scoring guide that represents agreements between educators and learners about expected levels of performance and quality of work.

Senior projects: Extensive projects that are planned and carried out during the senior year of high school as the culmination of the secondary school experience. Senior projects are exhibitions that require high-level thinking skills, problem solving, and creative thinking. They are often interdisciplinary and may require extensive research.

Standards: The knowledge, skills, attitudes, and competencies to be achieved in an educational program.

Summative assessment: Evaluation at the conclusion of a unit, subject, or year's study that is designed to measure whether students have reached standards and expected learning outcomes.

Validity: Validity indicates the extent to which evaluators can make accurate judgments about what students know on the basis of their performance on an assessment. A valid assessment measures what students have been charged with knowing; an invalid assessment measures other skills and information and therefore should not be used as the basis for a judgment about students' performance.

Sources: The definitions in this glossary were derived from Baumburg, 1993; Coalition of Essential Schools, 2002; New Horizons for Learning, 1995; Pistone, 2003; Wiggins, 1989, 1998; Wolf, 1993.

REFERENCES

Abourezk, K. "Education Commissioner Christensen Resigns." [http://www.journalstar
.com/articles/2008/04/03/news/local/doc47f4f7675b644030411317.txt]. Apr. 3, 2008.

Advancement Project. "Education on Lockdown: The Schoolhouse to Jailhouse Track."
[http://www.advancementproject.org/publications/opportunity-to-learn.php]. 2005.

Alliance for Excellence in Education. "Latino Students and U.S. High Schools, Fact Sheet."
[http://www.all4ed.org/files/Latino_FactSheet.pdf]. 2009.

American Academy of Pediatrics, Committee on School Health. "Out-of-School Suspension and Expulsion." *Pediatrics,* 2003, *112*(5), 1206–1209.

American Civil Liberties Union. "Locating the School-to-Prison Pipeline." [http://www
.aclu.org/images/asset_upload_file966_35553.pdf]. 1996.

American Federation of Teachers. "Charter Schools." [http://www.aft.org/topics
/charters]. May 2008.

Amos, J. "Dropouts, Diplomas, and Dollars: U.S. High Schools and the Nation's Economy." [http://www.all4ed.org/files/Econ2008.pdf]. 2008.

Apple, M. W. *Ideology and Curriculum.* (3rd ed.) London: Routledge, 2004.

ARISE High School. "ARISE High School Tenth Grade Schedule." Oakland: ARISE High
School, 2009.

Armani, C. "SDAIE or Specifically Designed Academic Instruction in the Classroom."
[http://www.associatedcontent.com/article/970506/sdaie_or_specifically_designed_
academic.html?cat=4]. Sept. 2008.

Ascher, C. "Can Performance-Based Assessments Improve Urban Schooling?" ERIC
Digest Number 56. [http://www.ericdigests.org/pre-9218/urban.htm]. Jun. 1990.

Attewell, P., Lavin, D., Domina, T., and Levey, T. *Passing the Torch: Does Higher
Education for the Disadvantaged Pay Off Across the Generations?* New York: Russell
Sage Foundation, 2007.

Bailey, T. R., Hughes, K. L., and Karp, M. M. "What Role Can Dual Enrollment Programs
Play in Easing the Transition Between High School and Postsecondary Education?"
[http://www.ed.gov/about/offices/list/ovae/pi/hs/bailey.doc]. 2002.

Barth, R. S. "The Culture Builder." *Educational Leadership,* 2002, *59*(8), 6–11.

Baumburg, J. *Assessment: How Do We Know What They Know?* Alexandria, Va.: Association for Supervision and Curriculum Development, 1993.

Benitez, M. "Connections That Matter and Endure." [http://www.essentialschools.org/cs /resources/view/ces_res/347]. Fall 2004.

Bensman, D. *Learning to Think Well: Central Park East Secondary School Graduates Reflect on Their High School and College Experiences.* New York: National Center for Restructuring Education, Schools, and Teaching, 1995.

Bill & Melinda Gates Foundation. "The College-Ready Education Plan: Basing Action on Evidence." [http://www.gatesfoundation.org/learning/Pages/college-ready-education-plan.aspx]. 2008.

Blankstein, A. *Failure Is Not an Option: Six Principles That Guide Student Achievement in High-Performing Schools.* Thousand Oaks, Calif.: Corwin Press, 2004.

Blankstein, A. "Terms of Engagement: Where Failure Is Not an Option." In A. M. Blankstein, R. W. Cole, and P. D. Houston (eds.), *Engaging Every Learner.* Thousand Oaks, Calif.: Corwin Press, 2007.

Bloomfield, D. C. "Come Clean on Small Schools." *Education Week,* Jan. 25, 2006, *25*(20), 34–35.

Bridgeland, J. M, DiIulio, J. J., Jr., and Burke Morison, K. "The Silent Epidemic: Perspectives of High School Dropouts." [http://www.civicenterprises.net/pdfs /thesilentepidemic3–06.pdf]. Mar. 2006.

Business-Higher Education Forum. "Building a Nation of Learners." [http://www.acenet .edu/bookstore/pdf/2003_build_nation.pdf]. 2003.

Camara, W. J. "College Persistence, Graduation, and Remediation." [http://professionals .collegeboard.com/research/pdf/rn19_22643.pdf]. 2003.

Cave, J., LaMaster, C., and White, S. "Staff Development–Adult Characteristics." [http://ed.fnal.gov/lincon/staff_adult.shtml]. 2006.

Cech, S. J. "Showing What They Know." *Education Week,* June 18, 2008, pp. 25–27.

Center for Collaborative Education. "How Are Boston Pilot Schools Faring? An Analysis of Student Demographics, Engagement, and Performance." [http://www.ccebos.org /pilots.faring.2004.pdf]. 2004.

Center for Collaborative Education. *The Essential Guide to Pilot Schools: Overview.* Boston: Center for Collaborative Education, 2006a.

Center for Collaborative Education. *Progress and Promise: A Report on the Boston Pilot Schools.* Boston: Center for Collaborative Education, 2006b.

Center for Collaborative Education. "Strong Results, High Demand: A Four-Year Study of Boston's Pilot High Schools." [http://www.ccebos.org/Pilot_School _Study_11.07.pdf]. 2007.

Center for Collaborative Education. "The Boston Pilot/Horace Mann Schools Network." [http://www.ccebos.org/pilotschools/bostonpilotschools.html]. 2009.

Chajet, L. "But Is What We Give Them Enough?: Exploring Urban Small School Graduates' Journeys Through College." Doctoral dissertation, City University of New York, 2007.

Christensen, C. M., Raynor, M. E., and Anthony, S. D. "Six Keys to Creating New-Growth Businesses." *Harvard Management Update*, Jan. 2003, pp. 3–6.

Coalition of Essential Schools. "Assessment Terminology: Key Concepts for Shared Understanding." *Horace, 18*(2). [http://www.essentialschools.org/cs/resources/view /ces_res/212]. Winter 2002.

Coalition of Essential Schools. "*Horace* Talks with Eric Nadelstern: New York City's Autonomy Zone." [http://www.essentialschools.org/cs/resources/view/ces_res/375]. Summer 2005a.

Coalition of Essential Schools. "*Horace* Talks with Ted Sizer: The History, Limitations, and Possibilities of School Districts." [http://www.essentialschools.org/cs/resources /view/ces_res/369]. Summer 2005b.

Coalition of Essential Schools. *Measuring Up: Demonstrating the Effectiveness of the Coalition of Essential Schools.* Oakland, Calif.: Coalition of Essential Schools, 2006.

Coalition of Essential Schools. "Building School Community: Ask a Mentor Panel." [http://www.ceschangelab.org/cs/clpub/view/cl_askpanel/27]. 2007.

Coalition of Essential Schools. "CES School Benchmarks." [http://www.essentialschools .org/pub/ces_docs/schools/benchmarks/benchmarksIntro.html], 2008a.

Coalition of Essential Schools. "Having the Courage to Act on Your Beliefs: *Horace* Interviews Marcy Raymond and Dan Hoffman on the Founding and Influence of Metro High School." [http://www.essentialschools.org/cs/resources/view/ces_res/595]. Fall 2008b.

Conley, D. T. *Redefining College Readiness.* Eugene, Oreg.: Educational Policy Improvement Center, 2007.

Cook, A., and Tashlik, P. "Making the Pendulum Swing: Challenging Bad Education Policy in New York State." [http://www.essentialschools.org/cs/resources/view/ces_res/380]. Fall 2005.

Daniels, H., and Zemelman, S. *Subjects Matter: Every Teacher's Guide to Content-Area Reading.* Portsmouth, N.H.: Heinemann, 2004.

Darling-Hammond, L. "Standards and Assessments: Where We Are and What We Need." [http://www.tcrecord.org/Content.asp?ContentID=11109]. Feb. 2003.

Darling-Hammond, L. "Building a System of Powerful Teaching and Learning." [http:// www.nctaf.org/resources/research_and_reports/nctaf_research_reports/documents /Chapter6.LDH.pdf]. 2007a.

Darling-Hammond, L. "Evaluating No Child Left Behind." [http://www.thenation.com /doc/20070521/darling-hammond]. May 2007b.

Darling-Hammond, L., Ancess, J., and Falk, B. *Authentic Assessment in Action: Studies of Schools and Students at Work.* New York: Teachers College Press, 1995.

Davidson, J. "The Stars Aligned: A Study of System Change in Colorado's Mapleton Public Schools." [http://www.essentialschools.org/cs/resources/view/ces_res/370]. Summer 2005a.

Davidson, J. "Small School, Big Influence: Amy Biehl High School Tells Its Story." [http://www.essentialschools.org/cs/resources/view/ces_res/381]. Fall 2005b.

Davidson, J. "Longitudinal Research Indicates CES Graduate Collegiate Success." [http://www.essentialschools.org/cs/resources/view/ces_res/552]. Fall 2006.

Davidson, J. "Cycles of Inquiry and Action: CES's Ongoing Commitment." *Horace,* 2009a, *24*(4), pp. 2–5.

Davidson, J. "Exhibitions: Connecting Classroom Assessment with Culminating Demonstrations of Mastery." *Theory into Practice,* 2009b, *48*(1), 36–43.

Davidson, J., and Feldman, J. "Formative Assessment Applications of Culminating Demonstrations of Mastery." In G. Cizek and H. Andrade (eds.), *Handbook of Formative Assessment.* London: Routledge, 2009.

Davis, K. "A Girl Like Me." [http://www.mediathatmattersfest.org/6/a_girl_like_me/]. 2005.

de la Rey, C., and Duncan, N. "Racism: A Social Psychology Perspective." In R. Kopano and N. Duncan (eds.), *Social Psychology: Identities and Relationships.* Johannesburg, South Africa: Juta Academic, 2004.

Deal, T., and Peterson, K. D. *Shaping School Culture.* San Francisco: Jossey-Bass, 1999.

Delpit, L. *Other People's Children: Cultural Conflict in the Classroom.* New York: New Press, 1995.

Dewey, J. "The Need of an Industrial Education in an Industrial Democracy." In Debra Morris and Ian Shapiro (eds.), *John Dewey: The Political Writings.* Indianapolis, Ind.: Hackett Publishing, 1993.

Dillon, S. "States Obscure How Few Finish High School." [http://www.nytimes.com/2008/03/20/education/20graduation.html]. Mar. 20, 2008.

Dillon, S. "Few Specifics from Education Pick." [http://www.nytimes.com/2009/01/14/us/politics/14webduncan.html]. Jan. 13, 2009.

DuFour, R. "Schools as Learning Communities." *Educational Leadership,* 2004, *61*(8), 6–11.

Editorial Projects in Education. "Research Center: Achievement Gap." [http://www.edweek.org/rc/issues/achievement-gap]. 2004.

Editorial Projects in Education. "Diplomas Count 2008: School to College: Can State P–16 Councils Ease the Transition?" *Education Week,* 2008, *27*(40).

Education Commission of the States. *Governing America's Schools: Changing the Rules.* Denver: Education Commission of the States, 1999.

EdVisions. *Less, More and Better: 2005 EdVisions 5-Year Report.* Henderson, Minn.: EdVisions, 2005.

Eubanks, E., Parish, R., and Smith, R. D. "Changing the Discourse in Schools." In P. Hall (ed.), *Race, Ethnicity and Multiculturalism Policy and Practice.* New York: Garland, 1997.

Feldman, J., López, M. L., and Simon, K. G. *Choosing Small: The Essential Guide to Successful High School Conversion.* San Francisco: Jossey-Bass, 2006.

Figlio, D. N. "Testing, Crime and Punishment." *Journal of Public Economics,* 2006, *90*(4–5), 837–851.

Fine, M. "Not in Our Name." [http://www.rethinkingschools.org/archive/19_04/name194.shtml]. Summer 2005.

Foote, M. *College Performance Study.* New York: New York Performance Standards Consortium, 2005.

Forum for Education and Democracy. "Democracy at Risk: The Need for a New Federal Policy in Education." [http://www.forumforeducation.org/files/u1/FED_ReportRevised415.pdf]. Apr. 2008.

Fullan, M. "Changing the Terms of Teacher Learning." [http://www.michaelfullan.ca/Articles_07/07_term.pdf]. Summer 2007.

Gallagher, C. *Reclaiming Assessment: A Better Alternative to the Accountability Agenda.* Portsmouth, N.H.: Heinemann, 2007.

Gates, B. *2009 Annual Letter from Bill Gates.* [http://www.gatesfoundation.org/annual-letter/Pages/2009-bill-gates-annual-letter.aspx]. 2009.

Giné, R., and Kruse, D. "What If Less Is Just Less? The Role of Depth over Breadth in the Secondary Mathematics Curriculum." [http://www.essentialschools.org/cs/resources/view/ces_res/447]. 2006.

Greene, J. P., and Winters, M. A. "Public High School Graduation and College-Readiness Rates: 1991–2002." [http://www.gatesfoundation.org/learning/Documents/GradRatesManhattanInstitute.pdf]. Feb. 2005.

Hantzopoulos, M. "Deepening Democracy." *Rethinking Schools, 21*(1). [http://www.rethinkingschools.org/archive/21_01/demo211.shtml]. Fall 2006.

Hart, S., and Hodson, V. K. *The Compassionate Classroom: Relationship Based Teaching and Learning.* Chicago: PuddleDancer Press, 2004.

Heifetz, R. A., and Linsky, M. "When Leadership Spells Danger." *Educational Leadership,* 2004, *61*(7), 33–37.

Hirsch, L. "The Deep Irony of No Child Left Behind: Lisa Hirsch Interviews Linda Darling-Hammond." [http://www.essentialschools.org/cs/resources/view/ces_res/406]. Winter 2007.

Hord, S. "Professional Learning Communities: Communities of Continuous Inquiry and Improvement." [http://www.sedl.org/pubs/change34/]. 1997.

Hughes, K. "Dual Enrollment as a College Transition Strategy." [http://ccrc.tc.columbia.edu/Publication.asp?uid=641]. 2008.

Huseman, K., and Kohn, L. "The Power of Service Learning: One School's Quest." [http://www.essentialschools.org/cs/resources/view/ces_res/476]. Fall 2006.

Jackson, J. H. "Given Half a Chance: The Schott 50 State Report on Public Education and Black Males." [http://www.blackboysreport.org]. 2008.

Jimenez, I. "Inclusion in a Different Sense." [http://www.essentialschools.org/cs/resources/view/ces_res/462]. Nov. 2006.

Johnston, B. J., and Wetherill, K. S. "H.S.J. Special Issue Introduction: Alternative Schooling." *High School Journal,* 1998, *81*(4), 177–182.

Jones, C. P. "Going Public: Levels of Racism; A Theoretic Framework and a Gardener's Tale." *American Journal of Public Health,* 2000, *90*(8), 1212–1215.

Kim, J. "The Impact of Dual and Articulated Credit on College Readiness and Total Credit Hours in Four Selected Community Colleges: Excerpts from a Doctoral Dissertation Literature Review." [http://www.ibhe.state.il.us/DualCredit/materials/DualCreditReviewbyJKim.pdf]. 2008.

Kirsch, I., Braun, H., Yamamoto, K., and Sum, A. *America's Perfect Storm: Three Forces Changing Our Nation's Future.* Princeton, N.J.: Educational Testing Service, 2007.

Kozol, J. *Savage Inequalities: Children in America's Schools.* New York: Crown. 1991.

Ladson-Billings, G. *The Dream Keepers: Successful Teachers of African-American Children.* San Francisco: Jossey-Bass, 1994.

Laird, J., DeBell, M., and Chapman, C. *Dropout Rates in the United States: 2004.* [http://nces.ed.gov/pubs2007/2007024.pdf]. 2006.

Lambert, L. "Half of Teachers Quit in 5 Years." [http://www.washingtonpost.com/wp-dyn/content/article/2006/05/08/AR2006050801344.html]. May 9, 2006.

Lawrence, B. K., Abramson, P., Bergsagel, V., Bingler, S., Diamond, B., Greene, T., Hill, B., Howley, C., Stephen, D., and Washor, E. *Dollars and Sense II: Lessons from Good, Cost-Effective Small Schools.* Cincinnati, Ohio: Knowledge Works Foundation, 2006.

Lawrence, B. K., Bingler, S., Diamond, B., Hill, B., Hoffman, J., Howley, C., Mitchell, S., Rudolph, D., and Washor, E. *Dollars and Sense: The Cost Effectiveness of Small Schools.* Cincinnati, Ohio: Knowledge Works Foundation, 2002.

Louis, K. S., Marks, H. M., and Kruse, S. D. "Teachers' Professional Community in Restructuring Schools." *American Educational Research Journal,* 1996, *33*(4), 757–798.

Makkonen, R. "Advisory Program Research and Evaluation." [http://www.essentialschools.org/cs/resources/view/ces_res/345]. Fall 2004.

Mass Insight Education Research Institute. "The Turnaround Challenge, Executive Summary." [http://www.massinsight.org/resourcefiles/TheTurnaroundChallenge_ExecSumm.pdf]. 2007.

Mathews, J. "Multiplying Benefits of College for Everybody." [http://www.washingtonpost.com/wp-dyn/content/article/2007/05/29/AR2007052900482_pf.html]. May 29, 2007.

McDonald, J. P., Smith, S., Turner, D., Finney, M., and Barton, E. *Graduation by Exhibition: Assessing Genuine Achievement.* Alexandria, Va.: Association for Supervision and Curriculum Development, 1993.

McFeat, I. "Tackling Tracking: A Teacher Finds That Small School Reform Presents Opportunities to Teach About Tracking and Inequality." [http://www.rethinkingschools.org/archive/19_04/tack194.shtml]. Summer 2005.

Mehan, H., Datnow, A., Bratton, E., Tellez, C., Friedlaender, D., and Ngo, T. "Untracking and College Enrollment." [http://repositories.cdlib.org/crede/ncrcdsllresearch/rr04]. 1991.

Meier, D. *In Schools We Trust: Creating Communities of Learning in an Era of Testing and Standardization.* Boston: Beacon Press, 2002.

Miner, B. "The Gates Foundation and Small Schools." [http://www.rethinkingschools.org/archive/19_04/gate194.shtml]. Summer 2005.

Nathan, L. "Teachers Talking Together: The Power of Professional Community." [http://www.essentialschools.org/cs/resources/view/ces_res/492]. Spring 2008.

National School Reform Faculty. "Frequently Asked Questions." [http://www.nsrfharmony.org/faq.html]. 2003.

Nesoff, J. "The Belmont Zone of Choice: Community-Driven Action for School Change." *Horace, 23*(4). [http://www.essentialschools.org/cs/resources/view/ces_res/421]. Winter 2007.

New Horizons for Learning. "Assessment Terminology: A Glossary of Useful Terms." [http://www.newhorizons.org/strategies/assess/terminology.htm]. 1995.

New Visions for Public Schools. "Building the School of One: 2007 Annual Report." [http://www.newvisions.org/dls/AnnualReport2007.pdf]. 2007.

Newmann, F., and Associates. *Authentic Achievement: Restructuring Schools for Intellectual Quality.* San Francisco: Jossey-Bass, 1996.

Nichols, S., and Berliner, D. *Collateral Damage: How High-Stakes Testing Corrupts America's Schools.* Cambridge, Mass.: Harvard Education Press, 2007.

Noguera, P. A. *City Schools and the American Dream: Reclaiming the Promise of Public Education.* New York: Teachers College Press, 2003a.

Noguera, P. "Joaquín's Dilemma: Understanding the Link Between Racial Identity and School-Related Behaviors." In M. Sadowski (ed.), *Adolescents at School: Perspectives on Youth, Identity, and Education.* Cambridge, Mass.: Harvard Education Press, 2003b.

Nwaezeapu, N. "Why I Am a Strong Believer in My School." [http://www.essentialschools.org/cs/resources/view/ces_res/468]. Nov. 2006.

Oakes, J. *Keeping Track: How Schools Structure Inequality.* New Haven, Conn.: Yale University Press, 1986.

Oakes, J., and Saunders, M. *Beyond Tracking: Multiple Pathways to College, Career, and Civic Participation.* Cambridge, Mass.: Harvard Education Press, 2008.

Olsen, L., and Romero, A. *Meeting the Needs of English Learners in Small Schools and Learning Communities.* Oakland, Calif.: California Tomorrow, 2007.

Orfield, G. (ed.). *Dropouts in America: Confronting the Graduation Rate Crisis.* Cambridge, Mass.: Harvard Education Press, 2004.

Orfield, G., and Lee, C. *Why Segregation Matters: Poverty and Educational Inequality.* Cambridge, Mass.: The Civil Rights Project at Harvard University, 2005.

Ouchi, W. G. *Making Schools Work: A Revolutionary Plan to Get Your Children the Education They Need.* New York: Simon & Schuster, 2003.

Parker Charter Essential School. "Criteria for Excellence." [http://www.parker .org/Printed%20Resources/Criteria%20for%20Excellence%20new.pdf]. 2008a .

Parker Charter Essential School. "Curriculum and Assessment." [http://www.parker .org/CurriculumAssessment/curriculum.htm]. 2008b .

Pistone, N. *Envisioning Arts Assessment.* Washington, D.C.: Arts Education Partnership and the Council of Chief State School Officers, 2003.

Plaut, S. (ed.). *The Right to Literacy in Secondary Schools: Creating a Culture of Thinking.* New York: Teachers College Press, 2008.

Poliner, R. A., and Lieber, C. M. *The Advisory Guide: Designing and Implementing Effective Advisory Programs in Secondary Schools.* Cambridge, Mass.: Educators for Social Responsibility, 2004.

Putz, M., and Raynor, M. E. "Integral Leadership: Overcoming the Paradox of Growth." *Strategy and Leadership,* 2005, *33*(1), 46–48.

Quest High School. "Mathematics Rubric." [http://www.ceschangelab.org/cs/clpub/view /clr/633]. 2004.

Raywid, M. A., and Schmerler, G. *Not So Easy Going: The Policy Environments of Small Urban Schools and Schools Within Schools.* Washington, D.C.: ERIC Clearinghouse on Assessment and Evaluation, 2003.

Relerford, P. "Minneapolis School Enrollment Is a Glass-Half-Full Story." [http://www .startribune.com/local/29465679.html?elr=KArksUUUU]. Sept. 22, 2008.

Renchler, R. "Urban Superintendent Turnover: The Need for Stability." [http://eric .ed.gov/ERICWebPortal/custom/portlets/recordDetails/detailmini.jsp?_nfpb=true &_&ERICExtSearch_SearchValue_0=ED346546&ERICExtSearch_SearchType_0= no&accno=ED346546]. Winter 1992.

Rose, C. "A Conversation with Joel Klein, Chancellor of the New York City Department of Education." [http://www.charlierose.com/view/interview/8654]. Aug. 22, 2007.

Rose, L. C., and Gallup, A. M. "39th Annual Phi Delta Kappa/Gallup Poll of the Public's Attitudes Toward the Public Schools." *Phi Delta Kappan, 89*(1). [http://www .pdkintl.org/kappan/k_v89/k0709pol.htm]. Sept. 2007.

Rubin, J., and Mehta, S. "Fewer Students Enrolled in L.A. Unified." [http://articles .latimes.com/2007/oct/19/local/me-enroll19]. Oct. 19, 2007.

School of the Future. "Performance Exhibition Rubric for Historical Research in the Humanities." [http://www.ceschangelab.org/cs/clpub/view/clr/435]. 2005.

Singleton, G. E., and Linton, C. *Courageous Conversations About Race: A Field Guide for Achieving Equity in Schools.* Thousand Oaks, Calif.: Corwin Press, 2006.

Sizer, T. *Horace's Compromise: The Dilemma of the American High School.* Boston: Houghton Mifflin, 1984.

Smith, T. Address to the San Francisco Achievement Gap Coalition. Feb. 20, 2008.

Spellings, M. "Educating America: The Will and the Way Forward." [http://www.nasfaa .org/publications/2008/easpellings100208.html]. Oct. 2008.

Stiggins, R. "From Formative Assessment to Assessment for Learning: A Path to Success in Standards-Based Schools." *Phi Delta Kappan,* 2005, *87*(4), 324–328.

Stolp, S. "Leadership for School Culture." [http://eric.uoregon.edu/publications/digests/digest091.html]. June 1991.

Students of The Gary and Jerri-Ann Jacobs High Tech High. *The Two Sides of the Boat Channel: A Field Guide.* San Diego: High Tech High School, 2004.

Students of Leadership High School. *Talking Back: What Students Know About Teaching.* San Francisco: 826 Valencia: The Writing Center, 2003.

Swanson, C. B. "Cities in Crisis: A Special Analytic Report on High School Graduation." [http://www.americaspromise.org/uploadedFiles/AmericasPromiseAlliance/Dropout_Crisis/SWANSONCitiesInCrisis040108.pdf]. Apr. 2008.

Tatum, B. D. *Can We Talk About Race? And Other Conversations in an Era of School Resegregation.* Boston: Beacon Press, 2008.

Tomlinson, C. A. *The Differentiated Classroom: Responding to the Needs of All Learners.* Alexandria, Va.: Association for Supervision and Curriculum Development, 1999.

Tyack, D., and Cuban, L. *Tinkering Toward Utopia: A Century of Public School Reform.* Cambridge, Mass.: Harvard University Press, 1995.

U.S. Census Bureau. *U.S. Interim Projections by Age, Sex, Race, and Hispanic Origin: 2000–2050.* [http://www.census.gov/ipc/www/usinterimproj/]. 2006.

U.S. Department of Education, National Center for Education Statistics. *Qualifications of the Public School Teacher Workforce: Prevalence of Out-of-Field Teaching 1987–1988 to 1999–2000.* NCES 2002–603. Washington, D.C.: U.S. Government Printing Office, 2002.

U.S. Department of Education, National Center for Education Statistics. *The Condition of Education 2006.* NCES 2006–071. Washington, D.C.: U.S Government Printing Office, 2006.

U.S. Department of Education, Office of Vocational and Adult Education. *Update to State Dual Enrollment Policies: Addressing Access and Quality.* Washington, D.C.: U.S. Government Printing Office, 2005.

U.S. Department of Labor. "America's Dynamic Workforce." [http://digitalcommons.ilr.cornell.edu/key workplace/287]. 2006.

University Council for Educational Administration. "Implications from UCEA: The Revolving Door of the Principalship." [http://www.ucea.org/pdf/ImplicationsMar2008.pdf]. Mar. 2008.

Urban Academy. "Looking for an Argument? The Urban Academy Course in Inquiry Learning." [http://www.essentialschools.org/cs/fforum/view/ces_ff01e/159]. 2001.

Wagner, T. *The Global Achievement Gap: Why Even Our Best Schools Don't Teach the New Survival Skills Our Children Need— And What We Can Do About It.* New York: Basic Books, 2008.

Wald, J., and Losen, D. "Defining and Redirecting a School-to-Prison Pipeline." *New Directions for Youth Development,* Fall 2003, *99,* 9–15.

Warner, B., and Collins, S. "Implementing Cross-Curricular Literacy Strategies in a Democratic School." *Horace, 22*(2). [http://www.essentialschools.org/cs/resources /view/ces_res/512.html]. Fall 2006.

Washor, E., and Mojkowski, C. "What Do You Mean by Rigor?" *Educational Leadership,* Dec. 2006–Jan. 2007, *64*(4), 84–87.

Wasley, P. A., Fine, M., Gladden, M., Holland, N., King, S., Mosak, E., and Powell, A. *Small Schools, Great Strides: A Study of New Small Schools in Chicago.* New York: Bank Street College of Education, 2000.

Wiggins, G. "A True Test: Toward a More Authentic and Equitable Assessment." *Phi Delta Kappan,* May 1989, *70*(9), 703–713.

Wiggins, G. *Educative Assessment: Designing Assessments to Inform and Improve Student Performance.* San Francisco: Jossey-Bass, 1998.

Wiggins, G. "Healthier Testing Made Easy." [http://www.edutopia.org/node/1498]. Apr. 2006.

Wiggins, G. "A Conversation with Grant Wiggins: Habits of Mind." [http://www .authenticeducation.org/bigideas/article.lasso?artId=48]. Dec. 2008.

Wiggins, G., and McTighe, J. *Understanding by Design.* (Expanded 2nd ed.) Alexandria, Va.: Association for Supervision and Curriculum Development, 2005.

Wolf, D. P. "Assessment as an Episode of Learning." In R. Bennett & W. Ward (eds.), *Construction Versus Choice in Cognitive Measurement.* Hillsdale, N.J.: Erlbaum, 1993.

INDEX

A

Abourezk, K., 239

Academy of Citizenship and Empowerment (ACE), 132

Accountability: educators and, 54–59, 155–158, 234–236; for equitable student outcomes, 234–236; influencing state requirements for, 237–240

Accuracy, 251

Achievement: addressing gaps in, 26–28, 37–38; measuring with No Child Left Behind testing, 35–37; raising with educational equity, 7–8; school size and improved, 12–13; students unprepared for future, 22–23

Achievement gaps: about, 4–5; addressing, 26–28, 37–38

Administrators, 127, 129

Adult learners: developing, 151–152; knowing needs of, 153–154. *See also* Professional learning communities

Advanced Placement (AP) courses, 30–31

Advancement Project, 32

Advisory Guide, The (Poliner and Lieber), 277

Advisory programs: about advisories, 275; creating strong, 274–277, 291;

eliminating time for advisories, 297; meeting with families, 286–287; personalizing student advising, 256–258; supporting ELL students with, 196

Advisory Toolkit, The (Wildwood School), 277

Affiliate centers, 345, 346–348

African-American students: achievement gap and, 4–5; challenges in families of, 25–26; demographics increases in, 28–29; equalizing achievement for, 26–28

Ahmed, Carol Fran, 248–249, 259

Ahmed, Faruqe, 248–249, 259, 264

Alliance for Excellence in Education, 28

Alonso, Richard, 57–58, 76, 307–308

Alternative schools, 32

American Academy of Pediatrics, Committee on School Health, 32

American Civil Liberties Union, 32

American Federation of Teachers, 46

AmeriCorps volunteers, 309

Amos, J., 31

Amy Biehl High School, 46, 253, 286, 309, 314–315

Analysis, 251

Ancess, J., 217, 226

C